Path of Blood

Path of Blood

The Story of Al Qaeda's War on the House of Saud

THOMAS SMALL AND
JONATHAN HACKER

SIMON &
SCHUSTER

London · New York · Sydney · Toronto · New Delhi

A CBS COMPANY

First published in Great Britain by Simon & Schuster UK Ltd, 2014
A CBS COMPANY

1 3 5 7 9 10 8 6 4 2

Simon & Schuster UK Ltd
1st Floor
222 Gray's Inn Road
London WC1X 8HB

www.simonandschuster.co.uk

Simon & Schuster Australia, Sydney
Simon & Schuster India, New Delhi

A CIP catalogue record for this book
is available from the British Library

Hardback ISBN: 978-1-4711-3572-9
Trade paperback ISBN: 978-1-4711-3573-6
eBook ISBN: 978-1-4711-3575-0

Typeset in the UK by M Rules
Printed and bound by CPI Group (UK) Ltd, Croydon, CR0 4YY

Contents

	List of Illustrations	vii
	Introduction	xiii
	Dramatis Personae	xxi
	Map 1 Saudi Arabia	xxxii
	Map 2 Riyadh	xxxiii
	Prologue: The Head in the Freezer	1
1	Blood Moon Rising	11
2	Facing Facts	41
3	The Riyadh Compounds	71
4	A Bloody Success	91
5	The Prince's Crackdown	113
6	Salvaging a Friendship	135
7	A Ruthless New Leader	155
8	The List of Twenty-Six	185
9	Operation Volcano	205

10 Terror Strikes the Coasts 229
11 The Khobar Massacre 251
12 The Assassination Cell 269
13 The Network Splits 301
14 Stamped Out 327
Epilogue: A New Kind of Assassin 361
Glossary 381
Timeline 391
Acknowledgements 401
Notes 403
Index 431

List of Illustrations

1 Al Qaeda tapes xxxiv

2 King Fahd neighbourhood raid, 20 July 2004 1

3 Electronics training 1

4 Piecing together the evidence 1

5 Riyadh compound bombings, 12 May 2003 2

6 Crown Prince Abdullah 2

7 Yusuf al-Ayiri, killed 30 May 2003 2

8 Turki al-Dandani tracked down, 3 July 2003 3

9 Ghuday farm shootout, 28 July 2003 3

10 Jazan hospital siege, 23 September 2003 3

11 Prince Nayef 4

12 Abu Ayub 4

13 Abdullah al-Rashoud records a propaganda video 4

14 Isa al-Awshen 5

15 Cell class photo 5

16 Amr al-Shihri's funeral 5
17 Painting a truck bomb 6
18 The attack team with the Muhaya truck bombs 6
19 The Emergency Forces HQ bombers 7
20 Prince Muhammad 7
21 The Muhaya compound the morning after the bombing 7
22 Ali al-Khudayr 7
23 Campfire 8
24 Attempted rescue of Khalid al-Farraj by Abu Ayub and his men, 29 January 2004 8
25 Lorry-driving training 8
26 Children with guns 9
27 Abdulaziz al-Mudayhish before the Washm Street bombing 9
28 The 72 Heavenly Virgins 10
29 The Washm Street bombing, 21 April 2004 10
30 Crowd cheering in the aftermath of the Safa neighbourhood raid, 22 April 2004 10
31 Police questioning a young man after the Safa raid 11
32 An Al Qaeda cell at prayer 11
33 The Khobar massacre, 29 May 2004 11
34 The Soha Oasis Hotel, Khobar 12
35 Victims of the Khobar massacre in a stairwell 12
36 Kidnapping victim Paul Johnson, Riyadh, June 2004 12
37 The body of Abdulaziz al-Muqrin, 18 June 2004 12
38 The MOI headquarters attack, 29 December 2004 12
39 MOI snipers scramble to safety: the battle of Rass, 3–5 April 2005 13

40 The battle of Rass, day three 13

41 Captured AQ member Osama al-Wahaybi in a police car, 3 July 2005 14

42 The Dammam siege, 3–5 September 2005 14

43 Fahd al-Juwayr 15

44 Preparation for the Abqaiq oil refinery attack, 24 February 2006 15

45 The Munasaha programme 16

46 Abdullah al-Asiri, the would-be assassin of Prince Muhammad 16

47 Assassination attempt on Prince Muhammad, 28 August 2009 16

In memory of my friend Alexandros Petersen, 1984–2014

For Kim, and Nina, and Sam

Introduction

The Global War on Terrorism is still history in the making. Books continue to appear as journalists, analysts, and professional historians continue to grapple with the war's causes, aims, and consequences, which are ever evolving. It is a problem, however, that most books on the subject approach the conflict from the point of view of the West. The primary battlefields of the war are far from our shores, in the Middle East and the wider Muslim world. Yet most accounts have tended to obscure or de-emphasize both the contribution of other governments to the fight against Al Qaeda and the way that the war is perceived and experienced by the Middle Easterners on the front line – including the terrorists themselves. This is particularly true of the way Saudi Arabia's role in the conflict has been covered.

In May 2003, Osama bin Laden's first major regional franchise, which would go on to call itself Al Qaeda in the Arabian Peninsula (AQAP), launched a terrorist insurrection inside Saudi Arabia. Largely overshadowed by the chaos that followed the invasion of Iraq, AQAP's campaign to expel Westerners from the Kingdom, overthrow the House of Saud, and take control of the world's largest oil reserves is an essential part of the history of Al Qaeda. No campaign was more ambitious. Had AQAP succeeded, the consequences for the entire world would have been momentous. That it did not had a huge impact on Al Qaeda's future.

During the course of the government's protracted fightback, Saudi investigators inside the Ministry of Interior (better known as the MOI) amassed a huge amount of data on AQAP, based on their own intelligence gathering and interrogations of countless Al Qaeda members and terrorist suspects. Furthermore, in a series of dramatic raids on terrorist safe houses, they seized hundreds of hours of video footage shot by AQAP members themselves. Most of this footage consisted of rushes from the terrorists' film shoots which had hit the cutting-room floor as they edited their propaganda videos. Much of it, however, was uncensored 'home video' material that revealed what life was like inside a Saudi Arabian safe house, on a surveillance mission, or before a suicide attack. AQAP had never expected anyone outside their own inner circle to see it.

This book is based on that material. As much as possible, and without sacrificing objectivity, it tells the story of a little-known chapter of the war on terror from the point of view of its Middle Eastern protagonists: the Saudi Arabian security services and their mainly Saudi enemies inside Al Qaeda. From Osama bin Laden's initial inspiration to launch an insurrection inside his homeland, to AQAP's first flush of success, and all the way to the campaign's eventual demise, *Path of Blood* is, as far as this is possible, the complete story of one of Al Qaeda's most consequential regional campaigns.

The project came about as the result of negotiations between the MOI and two prominent Saudi journalists – Abdulrahman Alrashed, managing director of Al Arabiya News Channel, and Adel Alabdulkarim, a documentary film producer – for access to the MOI's archives. It took two years, but eventually the MOI agreed. They gave us a copy of all the video material to translate and study; arranged for several briefing sessions with members of the Mabahith, the Kingdom's internal security service; made their written records available to us; and set up over fifty interviews with security officers who had faced Al Qaeda on the ground. This research in hand, we got to work writing. At the same time, from the video footage we produced a documentary television series for Al Arabiya, as well as a documentary feature film for worldwide distribution.

Our aim with the book was to write a gripping narrative for the general reader. Because we have had access to the sort of detailed, inside information most other writers on the topic have not, we have been able to tell the story from multiple perspectives: Al Qaeda's top leadership in Afghanistan, Bin Laden's lieutenants in Saudi Arabia, AQAP recruits inside safe houses, the MOI's core leadership and their American counterparts, Mabahith agents engaging in tradecraft throughout the Kingdom, policemen on the ground, and ordinary Saudi civilians. We hope thereby to shed new light on two subjects which, however much they appear in the news, are remarkably little understood: Al Qaeda and Saudi Arabia.

In the popular imagination, Al Qaeda is roughly equivalent to nationalist, politically motivated terrorist groups like the IRA or the Tamil Tigers. However, whatever similarities it may share with such groups, Al Qaeda is very different: more inchoate, less disciplined, and wrapped in an impenetrable cloak of religious fundamentalism and apocalyptic utopianism. Another misconception is that it is a single, clearly defined organization with a rigid, hierarchical structure. Even in the run-up to 9/11, when Al Qaeda was more finely organized than at any other time, it was a mixed bag of characters, ambitions, strategies, and nationalities. This became even more true as global counterterrorism efforts improved after the fall of the Taliban. Al

Qaeda lost its safe haven in Afghanistan and was forced to adapt, swiftly evolving into what it is today, a potent and widespread brand which clever and/or highly motivated Islamist militants (very few militants possess both qualities equally) employ to endow their movements with greater legitimacy. The different franchises invariably take on the colour of whatever region they are in, most of which are very different from post-Soviet Afghanistan, where Al Qaeda was born. The story of AQAP's campaign in Saudi Arabia bridges the gap between these two phases of Bin Laden's movement.

A perhaps even greater misconception is that Al Qaeda fighters are like henchmen in a James Bond film, essentially faceless, cardboard cut-out villains. But in the case of AQAP's recruits, they are more often than not closer to the very human characters in the comedy film *Four Lions*, young, ignorant, and impressionable. That they are in reality very different from the image they promote of themselves as single-minded guerrilla tacticians is borne out in the video footage. It reveals their laddish banter, their fooling around when bored, and their remarkable capacity to turn even the most chilling terrorist plot into farce. Yet the threat they posed was unquestionable: they threatened the stability of their own society, killed without remorse, and even tried to acquire a nuclear bomb. To capture these nuances, we have tried as much as possible to let the terrorists speak for themselves and have kept our own analysis to a minimum. By incorporating dialogue taken directly from the video footage, as well as excerpts from the vast amount of written propaganda they produced, all of which we have trawled through and translated, we hope to offer the reader a direct, unmediated encounter with these contradictory characters.

As for Saudi Arabia, in the Western popular mind it is largely reducible to oil, a huge royal family, and a strict interpretation of Islamic law. Since the tragic events of 9/11, the Kingdom has also been associated with Islamist terror; indeed, for some the country has become essentially synonymous with Al Qaeda. But Saudi Arabia is an immense country, nearly nine times the size of the United Kingdom, and immensely complex, irreducible to any mere collection of stereotypes. A union of historically distinct provinces, as well as the focus of worldwide Muslim pilgrimage and home to millions of foreign workers, the Kingdom is much more multicultural than people realize. Westerners are quick to identify Saudi Arabia as a 'problem country', and while there are undoubtedly many aspects of the Kingdom which call out for reform, the line between what is problematic and what is simply different is a fine one, and easily blurred. Before reaching judgement, therefore, the critic must ensure that his analysis is based on an understanding of the country's cultural and political context.

As a so-called 'absolute monarchy', Saudi Arabia is conservative, authoritarian, and patriarchal. But unlike Iraq under Saddam Hussein or Ba'athist Syria, the Saudi monarchy is not a totalitarian dictatorship. Rather, its unwritten constitution is aimed at achieving balanced consensus between several different power centres, and so the king functions more like a mediator or a power broker than a dictator. Open debate is restricted and the press far from free, that is true. Nevertheless, on political, cultural, and religious questions there exists a discernible spectrum of Saudi voices – especially in private. Furthermore, genuine modernizers occupy prominent positions in the government, the media, and business. The religious establishment is certainly reactionary, but it also houses a variety of views, and although most of the culture remains well within the confines of the state-sanctioned form of Islam, called 'Wahhabism' by its critics, that too is often misunderstood and is less monolithic than is commonly thought. Finally, it is noteworthy that the people are often more conservative than the government – or rather, parts of the government, since the royal family and the bureaucratic elite represent as wide a range of views as the rest of the country.

This conservatism informed how the Kingdom experienced the twentieth century, a time of sweeping change that did not always run smoothly. Perhaps more so than any other people, Saudis have viewed change with great suspicion. For some, of course, change could not come fast enough; the majority, however, held more faithfully to the ways and beliefs of the past. Undoubtedly, in negotiating that change for its citizens, the government made some serious mistakes. Decisions taken with a view to short-term expediency ended up having unforeseen and often disastrous consequences – this book tells the story of one of them, which exploded into view at the beginning of the twenty-first century.

In truth, Saudi Arabia remains a nation in transition. Especially over the last few years, important and subtle new changes have been introduced into the country. In particular there is a new trend towards greater openness throughout the government. This shift is an indication of the country's growing sense of self-confidence, as it projects its power ever more assuredly and exerts its influence on the region and beyond. But it is also a sign of a change in leadership style. Prince Muhammad bin Nayef, currently interior minister and, during the war, head of the MOI's counterterrorism programme, is one of very few second-generation princes to preside over a government ministry. Born when the Kingdom was already on the road to modernity, and educated in the West, Prince Muhammad has spearheaded several important reforms inside the MOI. Certainly without his express approval the access which this book needed would never have been granted. That it was is perhaps a sign of things to come, as the older generation of royals irrevocably gives way to the next.

It is worth emphasizing just how open Prince Muhammad has been. The video archive, the Mabahith's intelligence briefings, and the interviews we were granted with security officers – all of this is extremely irregular, and not only for a country as reticent as Saudi Arabia. Intelligence agencies very seldom go on the record, especially to discuss their recent activities, not even agencies belonging to states with freedom of information laws. The Mabahith's openness speaks to the pride they feel in the way they successfully combated Al Qaeda. It is an important and tangible success story in a country not known for them. As incredible as it may sound, they imposed no editorial conditions upon us during the writing of it.

A brief note on language. Arabic is a notoriously difficult language to translate. As the greater portion of our research material was gathered from home video archive and interviews with ordinary Saudis, we have chosen to reflect its quality of direct, informal speech in the translations. Written Arabic, on the other hand, is very different from the spoken dialects. It is extremely formal, and so when rendering it into English we have tried to capture that formality. Also, Saudi Arabians, and especially Al Qaeda members, often pepper their speech with expressions taken from the 1400-year-old Islamic tradition, and when discussing religious topics, the speaker will often switch into a more archaic rhetorical style. Our translations have endeavoured to reflect that as well.

Because we wanted the book to be a good read, wherever appropriate we have included dialogue scenes drawn directly from the video material or from the reminiscences of interviewees. In real life, conversations meander and people often talk over each other; interviewees rely on reported speech whereas, on the page, direct speech is more dramatic; and Al Qaeda's propaganda is notoriously verbose and obscure. Crafting a coherent scene, therefore, sometimes entailed editing for clarity, while preserving the original intent of the speaker or writer. A certain amount of plausible speculation has been necessary to give incidental colour to certain scenes that would otherwise be dry, but we have kept such speculation to a minimum.

Finally, as with any foreign alphabet, the question of transliteration is thorny. Arabic's difficulty in this regard is notorious.

We wrote this book to be as accessible as possible to the ordinary reader. Therefore, instead of following the academic practice of using complex diacritical marks, we have adopted a less rigorous transliteration style, aiming to help the reader know how the words are pronounced without unduly tripping him up. The same applies to Arabic names. Whenever possible, we have used the form of transliteration preferred by the person himself. When it is not known, we have tried to render it in a straightforward way. And because Arabic names strike the non-Arab reader as exotic – which can have an unwelcome distancing effect – we include full names as infrequently as possible. New characters are introduced by their full names, but from then on are mostly referred to by their final surname (Arabs often have several). For the same reason, throughout the text we have avoided using the definite article 'al-' whenever possible.

Thomas Small and Jonathan Hacker
August 2014

Dramatis Personae

Note: The names of figures listed in the Dramatis Personae appear in bold at their first mention in the main text.

Al Qaeda Central Command

Saif al-Adel An Egyptian former Special Forces officer and explosives expert, Adel fought in Afghanistan from 1988 and took over as Al Qaeda's military chief in 2001 after the death of Muhammad Atef (aka Abu Hafs al-Masri). Adel ordered that attacks be directed against Saudi Arabia, but his detention in Iran after leaving Afghanistan limited his leadership ability, and he was replaced by KHALID SHEIKH MUHAMMAD. His current whereabouts are unknown.

Osama bin Laden (*aliases* The Sheikh, Abu Abdullah, among others) Born in Jeddah to a wealthy Yemeni family, Bin Laden fought against the Soviets in Afghanistan in the 1980s before founding Al Qaeda in 1988. Implicated in various attacks against Western targets, including the 1998

American embassy bombings and 9/11, Bin Laden fled Afghanistan in the wake of the US-led invasion in 2001 and went into hiding. He was killed in an American raid on his safe house in Abbottabad, Pakistan, on 2 May 2011.

Khalid Sheikh Muhammad (*alias* Mukhtar, 'the Chosen One') Known as KSM in security circles, Khalid Sheikh Muhammad joined the jihad in Afghanistan in the late 1980s and met Osama bin Laden for the first time in the mid-1990s. He arranged financing for the 1993 World Trade Center attack and has been identified as the chief architect of 9/11. KSM was chosen to head Al Qaeda military operations outside Afghanistan and Pakistan in late 2001, but was captured on 1 March 2003 by Pakistani and American intelligence forces and after spending several years in CIA 'black sites' was transferred to Guantánamo Bay, where, as of the time of writing, he awaits prosecution.

Al Qaeda in the Arabian Peninsula (AQAP)

Abu Ayub Born Faisal al-Dukhayyel, Abu Ayub trained at Camp Farouq in Afghanistan in early 2001. He was detained en route to Chechnya and handed over to Saudi authorities. He returned to Afghanistan in August 2001 and fought against US-led forces. A member of Abdulaziz al-Muqrin's Shura Council, Abu Ayub issued the order for his Riyadh cell to kidnap the American Paul Marshall Johnson, and filmed the hostage's interrogation and death. He was shot, along with Muqrin, by the security forces on 18 June 2004. His uncle Ahmad al-Dukhayyel and brother Bandar al-Dukhayyel were also affiliated with AQAP.

Isa al-Awshen A prominent fundraiser during the Second Chechen War, Awshen left Saudi Arabia for Afghanistan after 9/11. He never made it, however, and was detained on his return journey by the CIA, who handed him over to the Saudis. Released after a short time in prison, Awshen continued Yusuf al-Ayiri's media and propaganda work after the latter's death in mid-2003, founding and editing *Voice of Jihad* and creating propaganda videos such as *Badr of Riyadh*. Awshen died in the King Fahd neighbourhood raid in July 2004.

Yusuf al-Ayiri (*alias* Al-Battar, 'the Sabre') A veteran jihadist who fought in Afghanistan and Somalia and a prominent fundraiser for the jihad in the Balkans and Chechnya, Ayiri became a prolific writer for the jihadist cause, establishing the Centre for Islamic Studies and Research through which many of his articles were published. In July 2000, Osama bin Laden ordered Ayiri to lay the groundwork for what became AQAP. He was killed on 30 May 2003 in a shootout with security forces in the desert.

Nimr al-Baqami Baqami was involved in surveillance for the Muhaya bombing, but is best known as a member of the Jerusalem Squadron who carried out the Khobar massacre in May 2004. He was wounded when fleeing the scene and arrested. His fellow AQAP members believed him to be dead.

Turki al-Dandani (*alias* Hamza the Martyr) Dandani travelled to Afghanistan in late 2000, trained at Camp Farouq and fought against the US-led invasion. He was subsequently appointed a network commander in Khalid al-Hajj's Shura Council, heading the cell that carried out the Riyadh compound bombings in May 2003. Dandani and a group of his associates committed suicide in a mosque after a raid by the MOI on a safe house in Suwayr on 3 July 2003.

Ahmad al-Dukhayyel Uncle to Abu Ayub and Bandar al-Dukhayyel. An extremist preacher, Ahmad was, along with Abdullah al-Rashoud, present in November 2002 at the confrontation between religious students and the security forces at the General Presidency of Islamic Research and Fatwas in Riyadh. He grew close to AQAP and headed a cell in Mecca. Ahmad was killed in a raid on 28 June 2003.

Faisal al-Dukhayyel See Abu Ayub.

Ali al-Faqasi (*alias* Abu Bakr al-Azdi) After fighting in Afghanistan in the late 1990s and early 2000s, Faqasi was nominated as leader of AQAP after Abdul Rahim al-Nashiri's arrest in November 2002 but was passed over in favour of Khalid al-Hajj by Osama bin Laden. Faqasi was the leader of the Organization's Hijazi network and entered into negotiations to purchase a nuclear device from Russian arms smugglers. He escaped a raid on a safe house in Medina in late May 2003 disguised as a woman and surrendered a few weeks later on 26 June 2003.

Khalid al-Farraj Farraj was the leader of an AQAP cell operating in Riyadh. In late January 2004, his father revealed his whereabouts to the security forces and he was arrested by the Mabahith. Abu Ayub launched an attempt to free him with other members of the cell, and several security officers and Farraj's father were killed. The event led Farraj to recant, and he became a valuable source of information for the MOI. Farraj's brother, Mishaal al-Farraj, was selected as a suicide bomber for Operation Volcano and his cousin, Fahd al-Farraj, was a suicide bomber in the Washm Street bombing.

Mishaal al-Farraj Brother of Khalid al-Farraj, Mishaal was nineteen when he was chosen as a suicide bomber for Abdulaziz al-Muqrin's Operation Volcano, learning to drive a truck in preparation for the attack. Part of the team who kidnapped Paul Marshall Johnson in June 2004, Farraj was arrested in the King Fahd neighbourhood raid on 20 July 2004.

Khalid al-Hajj (*alias* Abu Hazim al-Sha'ir) Head of Al Qaeda's operations within Saudi Arabia from late 2002 to mid-2003, Hajj fought in Afghanistan in the early 1990s and became Osama bin Laden's personal bodyguard. Hajj went into hiding after the Riyadh compound bombings and died in an MOI ambush in Riyadh on 15 March 2004.

Yunus al-Hayari A Moroccan jihadist born in 1968, Hayari fought in Bosnia in the mid-1990s and, after travelling to Mecca for Hajj in February 2001, decided to stay in Saudi Arabia. He moved to Riyadh with his wife and daughter. There he met fellow countryman Karim al-Mejjati and joined AQAP. After Saud al-Qatayni's death at the battle of Rass, Hayari replaced him as AQAP leader, a position he held for only three months. Hayari was killed in a shootout with Riaydh police on 3 July 2005.

Fahd al-Juwayr A member of the extensive Farraj family, Juwayr spent a month and a half in Afghanistan. His involvement with AQAP began in 2004 when he took part in preparations for Abdulaziz al-Muqrin's Operation Volcano – in which he was recorded learning to drive a truck – and was one of the team who kidnapped Paul Marshall Johnson. The death of Saud al-Qatayni in April 2005 led Juwayr to pledge allegiance to a new leader, Yunus al-Hayari, but Hayari's death ten weeks later saw Juwayr take on the position. He led the attack on the Abqaiq oil refinery on 24 February 2006 and was killed in a raid three days later.

Karim al-Mejjati A Moroccan jihadist born to an affluent family in Casablanca in 1967, Mejjati became radicalized in the early 1990s and fought in the Bosnian jihad. Shortly before 9/11, he moved to Afghanistan with his family, and in July 2002 moved again, this time to Riyadh. Shortly afterwards he met fellow countryman Yunus al-Hayari and joined what would become AQAP. A close ally of Saud al-Qatayni, Mejjati became one of AQAP's top operatives. He was killed along with his 11-year-old son Adam in the battle of Rass on 5 April 2005.

Abdulaziz al-Muqrin (*alias* Abu Hajer) Leader of AQAP from mid-2003 until his death in June 2004. Muqrin fought in Afghanistan in the late 1980s and early 1990s, before participating in jihad in Algeria, Morocco, Bosnia, and Somalia. Imprisoned in Ethiopia and Saudi Arabia, he returned to Afghanistan in 2001 and took charge of military operations inside the Kingdom in June 2002. After KHALID AL-HAJJ went into hiding in mid-2003, Muqrin became the most prominent member of AQAP, orchestrating attacks such as the Muhaya and Washm Street bombings, as well as the Khobar massacre and the kidnapping of PAUL MARSHALL JOHNSON. He died in a confrontation with the security forces in Riyadh on 18 June 2004.

Turki al-Mutayri (*alias* Fawaz al-Nashimi) A member of ABU AYUB's cell in Riyadh, Mutayri travelled to Afghanistan six months before 9/11, where he met OSAMA BIN LADEN and fought against the US-led invasion. Mutayri met ABDULAZIZ AL-MUQRIN at Camp Farouq; the two grew close and he became Muqrin's assistant back in the Kingdom. Present at the attempt to rescue KHALID AL-FARRAJ in January 2004 and involved in preparations for Operation Volcano, Mutayri rose to notoriety when he headed the Jerusalem Squadron in the Khobar massacre of May 2004. He was killed along with Muqrin and ABU AYUB in a confrontation with the security forces on 18 June 2004.

Abdul Rahim al-Nashiri (*alias* Abu Bilal, among others) Head of Al Qaeda operations across the Arabian Peninsula from late 2001 until his arrest on 8 November 2002 by members of the CIA in the UAE. Nashiri fought in Chechnya, Tajikistan, and Afghanistan in the early 1990s and orchestrated the attacks against the USS *Cole* in October 2000 and the *Limburg* oil tanker two years later.

Sultan Bijad al-Otaybi Born in December 1976, Sultan Bijad grew up in Riyadh and became one of the most prominent 'third-generation' AQAP members, i.e. those jihadists who did not fight in the anti-Soviet jihad or the ones that followed it in the 1990s and 2000s. Originally tapped for a suicide mission, he rose through the ranks and became one of Saud al-Qatayni's deputies in Riyadh. He helped plan the bombing of the MOI headquarters in Riyadh on 29 December 2004, and was killed later that evening in the raid on the Taawun safe house.

Saleh al-Oufi Fired from his post as a prison sergeant in the late 1980s, Oufi fought in Afghanistan in the early 1990s, then in Bosnia and Chechnya. He returned to Afghanistan to fight against US-led forces in 2001. A member of Abdulaziz al-Muqrin's Shura Council, Oufi was proclaimed leader of AQAP after Muqrin's death, but his authority was limited to cells in the Hijaz. Oufi was killed in Medina by the Saudi security forces on 18 August 2005.

Sultan al-Qahtani (*alias* Zubayr al-Rimi) Qahtani travelled to Afghanistan in September 2002, having told his family that he would be going on the Hajj. He became Ali al-Faqasi's deputy in the Hijaz, and took control of the cell after Faqasi's surrender in June 2003. He was killed in a fierce firefight between militants and the security forces in an apartment block attached to a hospital in Jazan on 23 September 2003.

Saud al-Qatayni Qatayni fought in Afghanistan in the 1980s and early 1990s but did not fight against the US-led invasion in 2001. A member of Abdulaziz al-Muqrin's Shura Council from mid-2003, Qatayni led a group of cells that operated out of Najd, and became the leader of the Najd network after Muqrin's death in June 2004. Qatayni was killed in the battle of Rass between 3 and 5 April 2005.

Abdullah al-Rashoud A radical preacher from south-central Saudi Arabia, born in 1967, Rashoud joined AQAP after government clerics at the General Presidency of Scholarly Research and Fatwas in Riyadh rejected a list of nine grievances which he and eighty other opposition clerics presented to them on 2 November 2002. He became AQAP's most prominent ideologue but, feeling the pressure from the MOI, left the Kingdom and joined Al Qaeda in Iraq, where he was killed by an American air strike in June 2005.

Rakan al-Saikhan Saikhan assisted ABDUL RAHIM AL-NASHIRI in planning the attacks on the USS *Cole* in October 2000, and was put in charge of smuggling weapons and equipment into the Kingdom from Yemen. Number two in the MOI's List of Twenty-Six in December 2003, Saikhan was mortally wounded in a raid on 13 April 2004. He escaped, but his body was found buried in the desert in July of the same year.

Takfeeri Troika The sobriquet of Nasr al-Fahd, Ali al-Khudayr, and Ahmad al-Khalidi, prominent Saudi extremist clerics affiliated to Al Qaeda. Associated with the takfeerist Shuaybi school, named after the blind cleric Sheikh Hamud al-Shuaybi, all three went into hiding in early March 2003. In late May of that year they were arrested in Medina and by autumn 2003 had been persuaded to publicly recant their takfeerist beliefs.

House of Saud

Crown Prince Abdullah bin Abdulaziz, later king. Born in 1924 in Riyadh, Abdullah was the tenth of the thirty-six official sons of King Abdulaziz. KING FAHD BIN ABDULAZIZ named Abdullah crown prince in 1982 and, after the king's stroke in

1995, Abdullah became *de facto* ruler. After Fahd's death in 2005, Abdullah became king. Abdullah's relationship with his half-brother PRINCE NAYEF BIN ABDULAZIZ, the interior minister, was reportedly somewhat strained.

Prince Bandar bin Sultan Born in the Saudi city of Ta'if in 1949, Prince Bandar graduated from the British Royal Air Force College at Cranwell in 1968 and went on to be commissioned as a second lieutenant in the Saudi Air Force. He was appointed ambassador to the United States in 1983. In his twenty-two years as ambassador, Prince Bandar formed close relationships with a number of leaders, including presidents George H.W. Bush and George W. Bush.

King Fahd bin Abdulaziz Born in 1921 in Riyadh, King Fahd was the eighth son of King Abdulaziz. One of seven sons born to a princess from the Sudayri family (known as the Sudayri Seven), he was named interior minister in 1962 and succeeded to the throne in 1982. King Fahd suffered a serious stroke in 1995, and his half-brother CROWN PRINCE ABDULLAH BIN ABDULAZIZ became *de facto* ruler. He died at the age of 84 on 1 August 2005.

Prince Muhammad bin Nayef Born in Jeddah in 1959, Prince Muhammad bin Nayef is the second son of PRINCE NAYEF BIN ABDULAZIZ. Prince Muhammad completed a BA in political science in 1981 at Lewis and Clark University in Portland, Oregon, and undertook a three-year security course at the FBI in 1985. He worked in the private sector, then trained with Scotland Yard anti-terrorism units between 1992 and 1994 before working in the private sector. He became assistant interior minister for security affairs in 1999 and took charge of the Kingdom's counter-terrorism programme. Muhammad was made interior minister in 2012.

Prince Nayef bin Abdulaziz Born in 1934, Prince Nayef was the twenty-third son of King Abdulaziz and half-brother to Crown Prince Abdullah bin Abdulaziz. After serving as governor of various provinces, he became interior minister in 1975, and would serve for nearly thirty-seven years in this position. Appointed crown prince in 2011, he died in June 2012. His son Prince Muhammad bin Nayef was in charge of the Kingdom's counterterrorism campaign.

Westerners

Sir Sherard Cowper-Coles Cowper-Coles entered the British diplomatic service in 1977. He served in posts throughout the world, including Cairo and Tel Aviv, and was ambassador to Saudi Arabia from 2003 to 2006. He was later ambassador to Afghanistan.

Paul Marshall Johnson, Jr Born in New Jersey in 1955, Johnson trained as an aviation engineer in the US Air Force and, after leaving the service, went to work with AEC in Riyadh. On 12 June 2004, he was kidnapped by AQAP and held as a hostage for six days. On 18 June he was killed by his captors.

Robert Jordan A lawyer close to the Bush family, Jordan served as American ambassador to Saudi Arabia between 2001 and 2003.

James Oberwetter Previously a press secretary to then-Congressman George H.W. Bush, Oberwetter succeeded Robert Jordan as ambassador to Saudi Arabia, a post he held until 2006.

George Tenet The CIA's Director of Central Intelligence from 1997 to 2004.

Frances Townsend Townsend served in the administration of George W. Bush, first as deputy national security advisor for combating terrorism and then as homeland security advisor.

She first travelled to Saudi Arabia in August 2003 to kick-start negotiations aimed at curtailing financing for terrorist groups that originated in the Kingdom, and grew to be a close friend and colleague of Prince Muhammad bin Nayef.

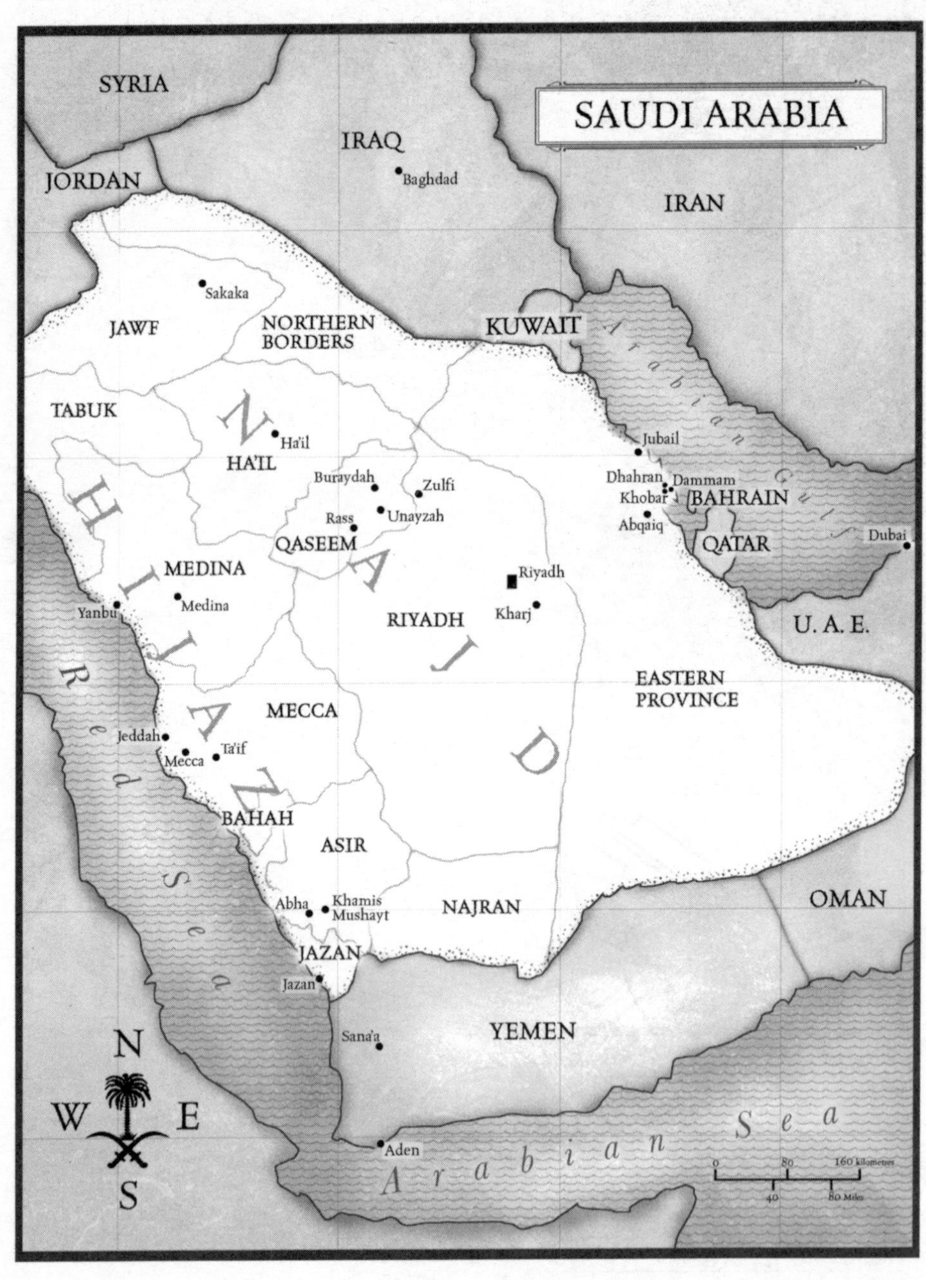

SAUDI ARABIA
SYRIA
IRAQ
Baghdad
JORDAN
IRAN
Sakaka
JAWF
NORTHERN BORDERS
KUWAIT
Arabian Gulf
TABUK
NAJD
Ha'il
HA'IL
HIJAZ
Jubail
Buraydah
Zulfi
Dhahran
Dammam
Khobar
BAHRAIN
Unayzah
Rass
Abqaiq
QASEEM
QATAR
Dubai
MEDINA
Riyadh
Medina
Yanbu
Kharj
RIYADH
U. A. E.
EASTERN PROVINCE
Red Sea
MECCA
Jeddah
Ta'if
Mecca
BAHAH
ASIR
Abha
Khamis Mushayt
NAJRAN
OMAN
JAZAN
Jazan
Sana'a
YEMEN
N
W
E
S
Aden
Arabian Sea
0 80 160 kilometres
40 80 Miles

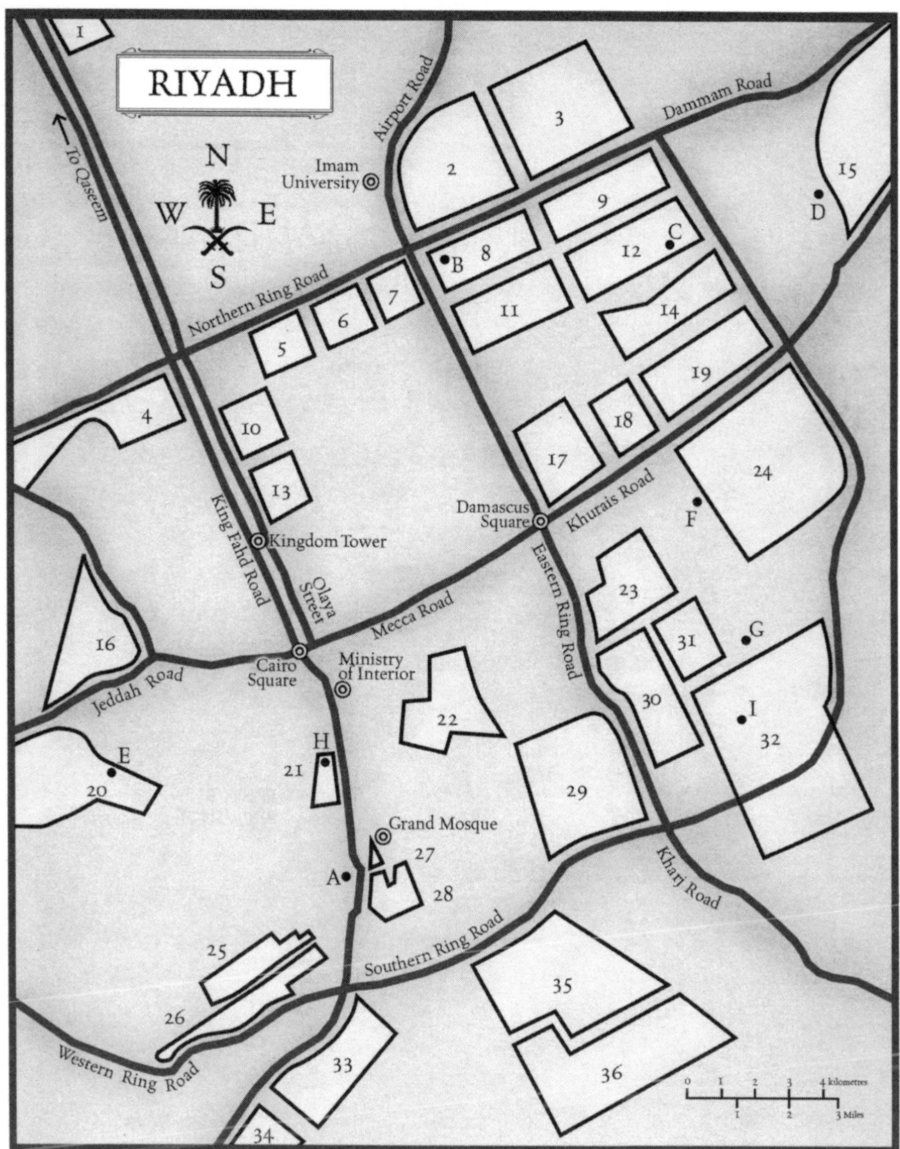

Districts

Name	Ref	Name	Ref	Name	Ref	Name	Ref
Alhambra	11	Fayha	31	Melez	22	Shifa	33
Amana	1	Granada	8	Munisiya	3	Shubra	26
Andalus	18	Izdihar	7	Nahda	19	Sulay	32
Aziziya	35	Janadriya	15	Nakheel	4	Suwaydi	25
Cordoba	2	Jazeera	30	Naseem	24	Taawun	6
Dar al-Baida	36	Khaleej	14	New Manfouha	28	Wadi Laban	20
Diplomatic Quarter	16	King Fahd	10	Rawabi	23	Washm	21
Duwayba	27	Marwa	34	Rawda	17	Wuroud	13
Faisaliya	29	Maseef	5	Seville	12	Yarmouk	9

Locations

Name	Ref
General Presidency of Research and Fatwas	A
Alhambra Oasis Village Compound	B
Dorrat al-Jadawel Compound	C
Vinnell Compound	D
Muhaya Compound	E
Hajj ambush	F
ROC Compound	G
General Directorate of Traffic	H
Emergency Forces recruitment office	I

Several hundred hours' worth of video footage shot by Al Qaeda members was seized by the Saudi government over the course of the campaign. Much of what appears in this narrative is based on those tapes.

Prologue:
The Head in the Freezer

Riyadh, Kingdom of Saudi Arabia, 20 July 2004, 11:30 p.m.

As the door of the air-conditioned armoured van slid open, the Special Forces officers inside felt a thick blast of hot air suck the cool away. The temperature wouldn't drop below 30 degrees Celsius that night. What's more, they were wearing body armour and carrying assault rifles.

The situation in Saudi Arabia's capital city had grown particularly tense over the last few weeks. A number of Westerners had been murdered while working at their desks, getting into cars, or waiting at traffic lights. One of them, Paul Marshall Johnson, had been kidnapped, and the horror of his story made headlines across the world. An American military contractor, Johnson was driving home when men in security officers' uniforms stopped him at a checkpoint and ordered him out of his car. When he complied, they rushed at him and stabbed a hypodermic needle containing a strong sedative into his arm, then bundled him into the back of their truck.

Johnson's kidnappers were members of an international terrorist organization so notorious it was referred to by the Saudi security services simply as 'the Organization'. Not long after his disappearance, video images of Johnson bound and gagged started circulating on the Internet. The Organization demanded that the Saudi authorities release Al Qaeda prisoners in exchange for the American. But the government refused to comply. Soon after the deadline, a gruesome film of his beheading was released online. His body had still not been found.

It had been fourteen months since Osama bin Laden brought the war on terror to the Kingdom, and the government's security apparatus was in full swing. Five days ago, agents had followed a van they were monitoring to a house in a residential street in north Riyadh. Intelligence analysts had determined that the van was linked to a safe house belonging to a key Al Qaeda member called Isa al-Awshen. He was on the Organization's legal committee, which released fatwas arguing that Al Qaeda's actions were in accordance with Sharia law, and was in charge of its media operation in the Kingdom, publishing videos and online books and maintaining a secure web presence. He was not known for heavy combat.

Even so, the Special Forces were called in. The security services had learnt by now that you never could be too careful. They were to take suspects alive if possible. The forward assault team checked their weapons and switched off their mobile phones. In single file, they set off silently down the street towards the house. Two armoured cars equipped with MG3 machine guns followed them at walking pace. Another team had taken up positions on the neighbouring streets, to act as a cordon in case the suspects tried to flee.

As they proceeded down the narrow street, it was difficult for the soldiers to form a clear idea of their target. A row of typical detached two-storey houses stood eerily quiet in the gloom, each house surrounded by a high perimeter wall to protect the sacred domestic space from prying eyes. Once the assault vehicles took up their positions on either side of the house, an officer raised a megaphone to his lips. 'Turn yourselves in!' His amplified voice was met with silence. 'One by one! You have five minutes to turn yourselves in!' There was no response. It was not the sort of mission they had envisioned when they signed up. In service to king and country, the soldiers were now fighting their own countrymen on their own streets.

Then, from the roof came a series of loud bangs and flashes of light. Two parked cars exploded. The officers looked up and watched as another rocket-propelled grenade (RPG) flew from the roof. It struck the neighbourhood's electricity substation and everything went dark, save the light from the flaming cars. The soldiers hesitated, shocked at their enemy's lethal professionalism. A safe house so well defended must be of vital importance to the Organization, and those inside had clearly been trained in urban warfare.

A call was raised for floodlights to be erected. Using the armoured cars for cover, the Special Forces returned fire. The external wall was soon pockmarked with bullet holes; white plaster dust merged with the black smoke from the burning cars. However, the street was too narrow, and the armoured car was too close for its gunner to get a clear shot at the roof. 'Hey, move back, move back!' an officer shouted.

'There's no room,' the gunner replied. 'Anyway, I can't see them!'

'Come down from there,' the officer ordered. As the gunner climbed down, a volley of bullets hit the vehicle and sparks flashed off the armour plating. The officer slid up inside the gun tower. He noticed that the front gate was now open. Three armed men were taking turns running out, firing a round, and running back. The officer signalled to the gunner in the other armoured car to aim for the gate. 'Cover the windows and the roof,' he called down to the men on the ground.

The two MG3s peppered the gate with bullets. Between bursts of gunfire from the Special Forces, the jihadists fired back. The soldiers started throwing grenades over the external wall into the narrow front yard; the militants tossed pipe bombs into the street. One of them ran out and began to fire just as one of his comrades' bombs blew up a civilian car parked beside him. The car exploded and the militant was engulfed by the flames. He dropped to his knees and, fearing he might be wearing a suicide belt, the snipers shot him dead. Before long, his corpse was little more than a heap of embers.

There was a lull. The Special Forces waited a few minutes, but nothing happened. Then, the electronic garage door began to inch upward. The soldiers readied their guns. Beyond the creaking door, all was darkness. Then a small saloon burst out. Its three passengers sprayed the soldiers with bullets and tossed pipe bombs out of the open windows. Shrapnel sliced through the air.

The saloon did not stand a chance against the Special Forces' firepower. Its engine exploded and the vehicle was engulfed in flame. Throwing the doors open, the passengers flung themselves to the ground. One of them, a young man with wild curly black hair who looked not yet twenty, rolled around on the ground trying to put out the flames covering his legs. The other two collapsed and lay still, bleeding and badly wounded.

Meanwhile, the sound of gunfire and the screeching of tyres could be heard from the next street. A report came in that an SUV full of gunmen had crashed through the back neighbour's garage door, and though the soldiers manning the cordon had fired on them and attempted a pursuit, the suspects had got away. The soldiers in front realized that all the carnage had been a diversion to allow an escape out the back. Terrorists had successfully employed this tactic against them several times before, but the Special Forces had since received new counterterrorism training. This sort of screw-up wasn't supposed to be happening any more.

For now, they had to make sure that the house was empty. A group of soldiers gathered together and, keeping in tight formation, made their way forward. They peered round the open gate. Motioning wordlessly to each other, they entered the outer yard and mounted the steps leading up to the front door. They nudged it open. In the torchlight, they could see a path of blood leading from the door into a larger room to the left. They followed it into the house. Inside an ordinary sitting room, a good-looking young man lay on the ground, clutching his abdomen. It was covered in blood, the bright red a striking contrast to his immaculate white Saudi *thobe*.

An officer was told to stay with the wounded man, while the rest of the team continued their sweep. No one else was on the ground floor. Along the walls lay ammunition boxes carrying Kalashnikov rounds and stacks of handmade pipe bombs, and one room had been set up as a makeshift infirmary, complete with wheeled stretcher and hospital bed. There was nothing remarkable about the kitchen; the forensics experts would give it a more thorough going-over later. Two men were assigned to clear the stairs, which were littered with pipe bombs – possibly booby-trapped.

They ascended the steps almost on tiptoe. First they explored what looked like an office of some sort – several computers, documents strewn about, video equipment – but found no one. At the other end of the corridor was a closed door. The soldier in front paused at the door and listened. He could hear muffled sounds. The soldier turned to his comrades and mouthed silently that there was at least one person in the room. They prepared to storm it.

'Do not enter!' a woman's voice called out. 'We are women!'

The soldiers relaxed, but only slightly. The Organization had proved itself quite capable of putting women into combat.

'Whose women?' the front man asked.

There was a moment's silence, then:

'I am the wife of Saleh al-Oufi. I am here with two daughters, and a baby. Please don't hurt us.'

Saleh al-Oufi was a top Al Qaeda commander and one of the Kingdom's most wanted men. 'Where is your husband?'

'I don't know. He told us to stay here, then he left.'

They had been within reach of Oufi, but he had got away. Someone would have to tell their commanding officer the bad news. That the jihadist had fled and left his wife and children behind disgusted the soldiers, but they had a more immediate problem. They wanted to question his wife, but also wanted to give her the respect she deserved as a woman.

'A special unit is on the way to take care of you,' said the officer. 'Don't worry. We will give you time to get ready.'

There was a brief pause. 'All right, we'll come out,' she said. 'But please do not hurt us. We don't know anything.' The security services had a reputation among jihadists – and among the populace at large – for brutality.

Through the door, they pushed her for more information. 'I know nothing. He and his friends, they would meet downstairs. The ground floor was for gatherings, but we never went down there. He held religious discussions and things like that. But we were always up here.'

One soldier was left to guard the door, while the rest of the team moved on to inspect the roof. The team leader radioed down. 'The area is clear and the house is safe.'

The forensics team moved in. Enlisting members of the Special Forces and the police to help them, they spread out through the building, pulling everything out of drawers, cupboards, dressers, and wardrobes, upturning sofas, slicing open mattresses and sorting everything they found into neat piles and rows. The wounded man whom the raiding party found in the sitting room had not made it. Two officers gently lifted his body and laid it out on a sofa.

Out in front, the three surviving Al Qaeda suspects were being dealt with. The officer in charge would later describe the scene. 'One of the three we captured was bleeding profusely, so we laid him on a stretcher to carry him to where the ambulances were waiting. He said, "What are you going to do with us? We don't want you here! We have come to purify the Arabian Peninsula!" It was weird, because he was in great pain, blood was pouring from him, and yet he was laughing. And he wouldn't say the name of our country, he wouldn't say "Saudi Arabia", he would only say "the Arabian Peninsula".'

A forensics cameraman was filming the other two captured militants, who had been handcuffed in an ambulance.

'So what exactly is your name?' an officer asked one of them.

'I told you, with them my name is Majed.'

'But your real name is Ahmed, huh?'

'Hamed. Hamed al-Harbi. Hamed Shadeed al-Harbi.'

'And him?' the officer asked, indicating the other one.

'That skinny guy? Yeah, I know him, but his real name, I've no idea.'

'Okay, who was with you in the house?'

'I can't remember. Um, there was Abu Mahmoud, and another guy called Faddhal, someone called Salem, someone called, oh I don't know, Tameer or maybe Tammam . . .'

The medic closed the ambulance door. The other detainee groaned. 'Give me some water! I need water!'

'I can't,' a medic replied. 'You are haemorrhaging. Giving you water now would kill you.'

The captured militant looked on the verge of fainting. With great effort, he pushed the medic away. 'We are of the people of *tawheed*, of monotheism!'

'We all are, we all are,' the medic tutted.

By now the team covering the side street had reported back. A group of seven jihadists – including Oufi – had scaled the back garden wall and, holding their neighbour at gunpoint, had taken the keys to his SUV, stormed the cordon, and got away.

A forensics expert in the garden scraped charred samples

from the burnt corpse. DNA tests would later reveal that it was the body of Isa al-Awshen, whom the soldiers had originally been sent to arrest. Meanwhile, inside the house, the sheer amount of weaponry was staggering: pistols, rifles, and Kalashnikovs, including one plated in gold. Piles of banknotes amounting to 300,000 riyals (roughly £53,000) had been laid out neatly, as had ID cards and passports featuring Oufi under several different pseudonyms. Investigators upstairs in the office sorted through the equipment. The office had been Awshen's, and it was beginning to dawn on them that they had uncovered a treasure trove of media material, including a hundred or so MiniDV tapes. One of them featured the now bullet-ridden Awshen happily recording a talk on the jihad in Chechnya.

'So, is the mic on?' he asked the cameraman.

'Yes, *inshallah*.'

Awshen sat straight. 'The truth is . . . the issue is . . . ahem . . .'

'Wait, brother,' the cameraman interrupted. 'Could you lower your headscarf? Bring the brim closer to your eyebrows.'

'Like this?'

'Yes, very fashionable, ha ha! But don't go thinking you're a Bin Laden or something.'

'So where do I look?' Awshen asked. 'Here? In this direction?'

'Just look straight in front of you. Yes, like that.'

Awshen collected himself. 'I am going to recite. It is a dialogue between a mujahid and one of his critics.' Clearing his throat, he began speaking in formal Arabic:

They asked me, why did you leave us?
I said, Because I am free,
And because I heard the lament of the free.
I heard the wailing of Muslim women
Grieving for their little ones
Ripped apart by traitors' shells.
I saw a venerable old man

With bent back, forced to raise his palms
And beg from unrighteous tyrants . . .

The poem was long. The picture it painted of Muslims was designed to inspire pity and anger. Muslims languish downtrodden, under the heel of apostate rulers in the pay of the enemy. From Kashmir to Chechnya to Palestine, Muslims are victims.

These scenes make me sad
They rouse my pride and I ask Muslims:
Where is your fervour?
For the enemy has drawn close.
Why do you not rise up to crush the attacker
And erase the humiliation in our hearts?

Then he stopped. 'Look, the issue is simple,' he continued, mimicking a liberal television preacher. 'We just have to learn to live with the Americans. God has sent them to us. After all, everything happens by divine decree, and do you dare interfere with what God has ordained? We must have an "Islam of today", a modern Islam, an Islam of tolerance and peace. And what else? Of misery! Yes, an Islam of misery!' He was not laughing. 'Enough!' He waved his arm and the video cut out.

Men began packing up the tapes as well as the other equipment and documents. This incredible intelligence haul would prove to be one of the largest of its kind anywhere: hundreds of hours of footage, many gigabytes of data, photographs, maps, and plans. Because of these discoveries, that evening's raid would become known as the raid that 'broke the back of Al Qaeda in Saudi Arabia'.[1]

There was a commotion coming from the kitchen. A group of soldiers and investigators were gathered there, craning their necks to catch a glimpse of something laid out on the counter. One of the soldiers was particularly excited.

'I'd been going through the kitchen when I felt thirsty, so I opened the fridge. Maybe there was some cold water inside, I thought. There was nothing, just some leftovers, ketchup and cola and stuff. So I opened the freezer. You never know, there might have been something there. But weirdly, all there was inside was a big box of tea. "Tea in the freezer?" I thought. "That's odd." So I took it out. It contained a bag, and when I shook the box I could tell there was something hard and round inside. I thought it might be a football. But by God, what I found when I opened the bag ... You don't expect to see such things. I mean, it's all in a day's work, but no one wants to see something like that.'

On the counter, slightly bruised and covered in frost, lay the head of Paul Marshall Johnson.

1

Blood Moon Rising

Kandahar, southern Afghanistan, four years earlier

On 16 July 2000, a lunar eclipse was seen rising over Kandahar. A reddish shadow gradually engulfed the moon, forming a circle as if of dried blood in the twilight sky. God was once again doing remarkable things in Afghanistan, and the eclipse added to the apocalyptic mood. Eclipses are sent by God, or so the Prophet Muhammad taught, to remind the faithful of the Day of Judgement.

Whereas the rest of the Muslim world languished in ignorance of the True Path, the Taliban under its leader Mullah Omar was establishing what was, in the minds of many, the only truly Islamic state on earth. Its unwritten, divinely sanctioned constitution could not be simpler. Faith in God's unity, fidelity to the Sharia, and unquestioning obedience to the Commander of the Faithful, as Mullah Omar styled himself: these were what would bring justice and order to Afghanistan after so many decades of war and unbelief.

But the Taliban had enemies. The international community, under the sway of America's godless liberalism, had denounced them and imposed economic sanctions on the country. The

Northern Alliance – a federation of opium-smuggling multi-ethnic warlords led by a hero of the anti-Soviet resistance, Ahmad Shah Massoud – stubbornly refused to submit to the Taliban's divinely sanctioned rule. The Northern Alliance controlled only fifteen per cent of the country, but they were strong and had scored some recent successes.

To support the Taliban in their ongoing struggle, hundreds of young Arab men with a thirst for jihad were flocking to training camps in the southeast. There they learned the arts of war, but more importantly, they were experiencing a Muslim fellowship they had never experienced before. Along with tens of thousands of ethnic Pashtuns from Pakistan who – with Islamabad's collusion – had also joined the fight, these Arab mujahideen felt themselves to be the holy vanguard of a sweeping resurgence. From Afghanistan they were destined to return to their own benighted lands, to fight oppression and help usher in a new Islamic Golden Age.

It was a blessed time, a recapitulation of the first years of Islam. Just as the Prophet, having been banished from his home city of Mecca, gathered his forces in Medina and emerged triumphant over his pagan enemies, so would the mujahideen emerge from their self-imposed banishment in Afghanistan and steer the Arab heartlands back to the True Path. The yoke of American and Israeli domination would be cast off and puppet governments – apostates all – would be toppled. The lions of Islam would roar and the earth would resound with the Judgement of Almighty God.

At least, that is what **Yusuf al-Ayiri** wanted his fellow Saudis back home to believe.

Ayiri was in Kandahar, it is believed, at **Osama bin Laden**'s request. The 27-year-old was well known in Saudi Arabia as a writer on jihadist themes and a talented fundraiser. Bin Laden, 'the Sheikh', had invited him to Afghanistan to interview

Mullah Omar and other leaders for a book about the Taliban. Were he to write favourably, Saudi donors might be convinced to increase their support, both for the Taliban and, by extension, for the Taliban's honoured guests, Al Qaeda.

That support had until now not been forthcoming. Many inside the Saudi clerical establishment criticized the Taliban for confusing Pashtun tribal custom with Sharia law, and censured Mullah Omar for assuming without authority the title 'Commander of the Faithful', an historic honorific of great religious significance.[1] They were now counselling would-be mujahideen to avoid the 'Afghan inferno' and not to send money Bin Laden's way. Bin Laden hoped Ayiri could help turn the situation around.

Ayiri and Bin Laden had first met about ten years before. Ayiri came from a rich and prominent Saudi family but, encouraged by his businessman father, dropped out of high school in 1989 and, at the age of just seventeen, went to Afghanistan. He trained at Camp Farouq, one of the country's most important jihadist training camps, where he caught Bin Laden's eye and was invited into his circle. Back then Al Qaeda was little more than a database of names of independent jihadists and a list of financial backers known as 'the Golden Chain'. Ayiri served as the Sheikh's bodyguard and fought in Somalia under one of his top lieutenants, but in late 1993 he decided to return to his family in Saudi Arabia. Shortly thereafter, he fell out of touch with his former employer.

From afar, Ayiri watched as the Sheikh's profile grew. Bin Laden was rumoured to be behind the bombing of the offices of the Vinnell Corporation in Riyadh in 1995 as well as an assassination attempt against Hosni Mubarak, the Egyptian president, later that same year. Then in 1998, Al Qaeda truly exploded onto the world stage. Bin Laden's operatives launched coordinated bomb attacks on the American embassies in Nairobi and Dar es Salaam, killing 212 people – including twelve Americans – and wounding over four thousand. To those Saudi Arabians who had been fed a diet of fundamentalism and anti-Americanism by the religious authorities, Bin Laden was a star. Finally, someone was hitting America where it hurt.

Meanwhile, Ayiri had turned his hand to fundraising for jihad. His family's status granted him access to the Kingdom's prominent clerics and wealthy families. But the climate for fundraising was changing. In the 1980s, raising money for the Afghan campaign against the Soviets had not only been very popular, it had official sanction and was carried out openly. But when that jihad ended, the government was landed with hundreds of trained militants full of extremist ideas, and Bin Laden's activities alerted it to how dangerous jihadist ideology had become.

This was confirmed in February 1998, when government forces discovered a terrorist cell near the Yemeni border which was planning to attack the American consulate in Jeddah with Sagger anti-tank missiles. Around eighty well-known jihadists were arrested, and pressure was put on clerics to de-emphasize jihad in their preaching.[2] From then on, fundraisers like Ayiri had to be circumspect. Their outward focus shifted to humanitarian aims such as providing food and medicine. Covertly, much of this money was still channelled to militants, including Al Qaeda.

Despite these obstacles, Ayiri had become a respected figure, adept at networking with hard-line clerics and encouraging them to speak in favour of jihad. And as the international community became more vocal in their opposition to the Taliban, Ayiri became more inclined to lend the movement his support.

That is when Bin Laden got back in touch and, shortly after, Ayiri found himself underneath a blood-red moon in Kandahar.

Ironically, the Sheikh himself was not there. The Taliban's leader Mullah Omar, a simple but uncompromising man from a peasant background, was finding his guest to be more trouble than he had anticipated.

When the Saudi billionaire's son arrived back in 1996 – stripped of most of his personal wealth and in exile from both his own homeland and from his previous base in Sudan – Mullah Omar was on the verge of consolidating his control over most of the country. Within two months, he had captured Jalalabad, where Bin Laden and his Arab supporters were staying. 'You are not just our guests and we your servants,' a Taliban government minister said to them. 'Rather, we serve the ground you walk upon.'[3] Mullah Omar supplied Bin Laden with the perfect environment for expanding Al Qaeda's operations. In exchange for this freedom, Bin Laden gave him his allegiance and backed up his claims to the title of Commander of the Faithful. He also provided him with experienced fighters and helped broker the defection of some warlords from the Northern Alliance to the Taliban.[4]

However, before long the bloom was off the rose. In 1997, Bin Laden gave an interview to CNN. 'By being loyal to the American regime,' he said, 'the Saudi regime has committed an act against Islam. Sharia law rules that this casts them outside the religious community.'[5] The royal family was outraged, and after the discovery of the Sagger missile plot the next year, they extracted a promise from Mullah Omar that he would expel Bin Laden. It was a promise he would not keep, but alienating one of the three countries in the world that had granted him formal recognition had not been pleasant.

Then in early 1998, Bin Laden issued a fatwa against the United States, his second. He was by then living outside Kandahar in an austere collection of buildings next to the airport. 'The ruling to kill Americans and their allies – civilian and military – is an individual duty for every able-bodied Muslim in any country possible,' he wrote.[6] A few months later, he made good on this by orchestrating the embassy bombings in East

Africa, which provoked the United States to respond by launching Operation Infinite Reach. Cruise missiles were fired at four Afghan training camps, including the infamous Camp Farouq.[7] Estimates differ as to how many people were killed, but the number was not great, and, because he had left one of the camps hours before, Bin Laden himself was unscathed. However, the missile strikes taught Mullah Omar that his guest could attract unwelcome attention.

American and Saudi pressure on the Taliban continued to increase. Bin Laden escaped several clumsy assassination attempts attributed to the Saudi intelligence services, and even the Taliban's staunch ally Pakistan began to wobble.[8] Then, just before Ayiri's arrival in July 2000, Mullah Omar grew worried that the Americans had discovered the location of Bin Laden's hideout outside Kandahar and, fearing another missile strike, asked Bin Laden to leave.

In a motorcade of fifty well-armoured cars, the Sheikh and a few hundred followers snaked their way northward across the Hindu Kush towards the mountainous river valleys of Bamyan Province.[9] In his remote hideout, Bin Laden returned to the ascetic life of the anti-Soviet jihad. It was how he preferred it.

Though it can never be known for certain, it is believed that Ayiri travelled on to Bamyan to meet Bin Laden.[10] On the journey he would have passed by the area's famed giant statues of the Buddha, built before Islam when Buddhism was the predominant religion in the region. They reminded him of the ever-present threat of idolatry, and he would celebrate eight months later when, to the sound of a great international outcry, they were dynamited; local Afghans reported that Bin Laden had goaded Mullah Omar into taking this action.[11] What would have seemed scarcely less scandalous to Ayiri was the fact that most residents of Bamyan were now Shi'ite Muslims, hated by hard-line Sunnis like himself.

At the camp, Ayiri embraced the Sheikh. The last time they saw each other, Bin Laden was a fugitive in Sudan. Now he was an international celebrity and the great hope of Muslims everywhere. Ayiri also met the Sheikh's top advisers. In excited whispers they spoke of a man in Yemen who was putting the finishing touches to what Bin Laden was calling the 'boats operation', a plan to attack American naval vessels off the Yemeni coast. There was something else as well, rumoured to be even bigger, called the 'planes operation'. But Ayiri must have wondered why he had been summoned.

The Sheikh explained. The vast majority of the top men surrounding the Sheikh were Egyptians; a minority were from Yemen, either native-born or, like Bin Laden himself, born in western Saudi Arabia to Yemeni families. This presented Bin Laden with a tactical problem. To galvanize support for Al Qaeda in Saudi Arabia, he would need a genuine Saudi working for him on the ground. This was especially important because he had burnt his bridges with the Kingdom's official religious establishment. 'They have aggrandized themselves with the sultan's money,' he had once written. 'The sultan's status has made them arrogant. They have been protected by his oppression and, in order to entrench the infidels in the Arabian Peninsula, they have [. . .] written fatwas permitting what God has proscribed.'[12] However, his reputation among the rank and file of Saudi Muslims was very high, and in order to get them more actively involved he would need religious sanction from well-respected clerics outside the establishment. As a proven networker among the Kingdom's dissident clerical community, Ayiri could help him get it.

Bin Laden also knew that Ayiri possessed the qualities of a senior leader and was ideally suited for what Bin Laden ultimately had in mind for Saudi Arabia. Up until now, the Kingdom had mainly been a base for fundraising and recruitment. There were jihadists already working there, as the uncovered missile plot made clear, but they were not organized. They would need to be. Because if Al Qaeda was to well and truly kick the United States out of the region, then the Peninsula's largest and most important country would have to have a fully operational Al Qaeda network of its own.

Ayiri was the man to set one up.

Around the time of Ayiri's visit to Afghanistan, an unknown Al Qaeda member writing from Saudi Arabia under the pen name Abu Hudhayfa sent Bin Laden a long letter.[13] It is an invaluable source for understanding Al Qaeda's aims inside the country at that time, and can reasonably stand in for an agenda of the points Bin Laden covered during his conversation with Ayiri. Certainly, once back in the Kingdom, Ayiri would put in place every one of the letter's recommendations.

What was Bin Laden's intention behind forming a Saudi branch of Al Qaeda? Abu Hudhayfa asks the same question. 'Is the Movement,' he writes, meaning Al Qaeda inside the Kingdom, 'a tactical transitional pressure group only, or a substitute for the present regime via a *coup d'état*?' That is, was Bin Laden seeking to reform the Saudi establishment, or did he want to overthrow it? Abu Hudhayfa makes his own preference absolutely clear. 'As for the struggle with the Saudi system, it is a war,' he writes. 'Tactical victories will be limited and ineffective if they do not lead to a decisive strategic victory by removing the system at its very roots.' Total revolution, then, is what they were after. The lure of controlling the Land of the Two Holy Mosques and the world's largest oil reserves did not need mentioning.

Abu Hudhayfa then describes what needs to happen if 'the Movement' is to succeed. First, an 'informational machine' needs to be put in place to counter the way the Movement is being portrayed by the Saudi regime and the international media. This propaganda programme must fight back by also attacking the regime's legitimacy: the House of Saud's failings need to be drummed into people's heads. Propaganda should also celebrate martyrdom operations. Those who kill themselves in the name of Islam need to become household names. The letter specifically mentions Hamas as worthy of emulation in this regard. Finally, the Movement needs a website. This is stated in no uncertain terms.

Second, the Movement requires a 'political machine' – i.e. the capability to launch military operations. The political machine should be kept separate from the informational machine, although their goals will be harmonized. The operatives should all be Saudis, both to prevent the government from characterizing the Movement as an example of foreign aggression and to get the Saudi people on side. The letter's unspoken assumption is that, while the informational machine will teach people to hate the regime, the political machine will actively recruit and train them.

After building up the Saudi people's confidence in jihad; after puffing them up with a sense of their own valour and instilling in them a hatred of the Saudi system; after launching attacks on Western targets to undermine the regime's image of invincibility, 'removing the fig leaf covering its genitals'; after extending those attacks both horizontally by covering more ground and vertically by assassinating prominent members of the establishment; after all this, what then? 'Once we have escalated the number of operations against the Crusader enemy, at a certain critical point the mujahideen commander will declare war on the whole Saudi system.' The people will then rise up and overthrow the government.

Ayiri accepted the Sheikh's commission and flew home, confident that all this would come to pass according to God's will.

In Karachi fourteen months later, **Abdul Rahim al-Nashiri** lay in bed with an acute case of tonsillitis. The ear, nose, and throat doctors of the Liaquat National Hospital did not know they were harbouring one of the world's most-wanted terrorists. On the Sheikh's orders, the 36-year-old had been planning another terrorist attack in the Arabian Peninsula. Now, recovering from surgery and unable to speak, Nashiri was alone with only his thoughts for company.

Nashiri was an operations guy; although legally a Saudi, he was in fact a Yemeni and his fierce temper was legendary. He first signed up for jihad in 1995 and had been on his way to the Tajikistan campaign when his brigade was turned away at the Afghan–Tajik border and redirected to a training camp near Khost called Jihad Wahl. There they met Bin Laden, who gave them a lecture on America's 'occupation' of the Arabian Peninsula and introduced them to Al Qaeda. 'You have a duty to expel them,' Bin Laden said. 'It is what the Prophet ordered.'[14] Most of Nashiri's fellow mujahideen disagreed with Bin Laden and left without swearing him their allegiance. Nashiri, however, stayed. He became so committed to Bin Laden's project that it was said he would happily plan a terrorist attack in Mecca were it deemed necessary; indeed, inside the holy Kaaba itself.[15]

As a first step, Nashiri was sent to Yemen to build up a network of arms smugglers. He was the one behind the thwarted Sagger missile plot in February 1998, and, impressed with his total commitment, Bin Laden put him in charge of the 'boats operation'. However, his first naval bombing attempt, against the USS *The Sullivans* in January 2000, was a dismal failure. The overloaded attack boat got stuck on a sand bank and had to be abandoned.

The screw-up so shook the Sheikh's faith in him that just before his second attempt the following October, this time against the USS *Cole* in Aden harbour, Nashiri was ordered to abort the operation and come to Afghanistan for a re-think. But he went over the Sheikh's head and told his operatives to launch anyway. Fortunately for him, the bombing scored seventeen American lives for Al Qaeda, and Nashiri became the man of the hour. To the FBI, which led the investigation into the *Cole* bombing, Nashiri was second only to Bin Laden on America's hit list.

The *Cole* attack went to Nashiri's head. Some of his Al Qaeda colleagues were annoyed that he took all the credit for its success and would not even acknowledge the two suicide bombers who had actually carried it out.[16] His ego was further inflated when Bin Laden chose to base Al Qaeda's first-ever recruitment video around the *Cole*. The video was extremely popular among young Muslims, and though it did not mention Nashiri by name, he knew his reputation had been given a big boost among the people who mattered.

Bin Laden further rewarded Nashiri by giving him an even bigger target: oil tankers in the Strait of Hormuz. Thirty-five per cent of the world's petroleum passes through that narrow stretch of water, and a successful bombing would be a bold statement. The Sheikh gave him a pile of money and sent him to Karachi to put the operation together. That's when his tonsils flared up and he was forced to go under the knife.

Nashiri stared at the ceiling and ran through his to-do list. He needed to get in touch with his operatives in the UAE who were reconnoitring the Strait and looking for a suitable fishing boat to wire up with explosives. He also needed to wrap his head around the boat registration process, to make sure that did not rouse suspicion. And there was still his honey-making business in Yemen to think about.

He did not know it yet, but Nashiri's plans were small fry compared to what was unfolding on TV screens across the world. He was but one cog in a much larger machine, and by the time the sun set on that fateful day, he would be as stunned as anyone at the enormity of the Sheikh's ambitions.

The date was 11 September 2001.

*

Nashiri cut short his recuperation and went in haste to Kabul. It was clear to everyone that America would soon invade. The Taliban had allowed Al Qaeda to operate freely on Afghan soil for five years, and though they formally condemned the 9/11 attacks, they also denied that Osama bin Laden had been behind them and refused to hand him over. 'I will not hand over a Muslim to an infidel,' Mullah Omar declared. Islamic groups across the world, including Hamas and the Muslim Brotherhood, warned the United States that attacking Afghanistan would oblige Muslims to seek revenge and urged the Muslim world to unite against 'American aggression'.[17]

Young Muslim men were already on their way to take up arms in defence of the Taliban. Most of them were Saudis like Nashiri. Bin Laden was increasingly popular amongst Saudis; an American intelligence report written just after 9/11 purportedly based on a Saudi intelligence survey claimed that 95 per cent of the population were sympathetic to Bin Laden's cause.[18] The government denied the figure was that high, but no one questioned the fact that hundreds of young Saudis were proving themselves ready and willing to fly to Bin Laden's side. They would join the several hundred others who had arrived earlier that summer. Al Qaeda's training camps were full to bursting.

When Nashiri arrived in Kabul, he found the Sheikh full of good cheer. The 9/11 attacks had been a phenomenal success and it was clear to everyone that God was on their side. The impending invasion would be a disaster for America, he thought. The 'graveyard of empires' would claim another victim, as it had claimed the Soviet Union in the 1980s and the British before that. That is what Afghanistan did; it fast-forwarded imperial decline and fall.

The Sheikh and his men were full of exultation. However, Nashiri and other prominent Al Qaeda operatives would soon realize that their confidence was misplaced. American bombs began falling on Afghanistan on 7 October and the Northern

Alliance, reinforced by US Special Forces and aerial support, was unstoppable. In a matter of weeks, Al Qaeda would be confronted with an existential crisis.

The Taliban swiftly lost ground. The northeastern city of Mazar-e-Sharif fell to the Northern Alliance on 10 November, and four days later Kabul was on the verge of succumbing.

Fleeing the capital under cover of darkness, Al Qaeda split into two equal groups. The Sheikh and his deputy Ayman al-Zawahiri headed for Jalalabad. There they would be near Tora Bora and its ferociously inaccessible network of caves, bunkers, and hidden trails, where the Soviet Union had once met its match. There were perhaps eight hundred fighters with them, but cracks in their morale were already apparent and many of them were agitating to return home.

In the second group, Nashiri followed several top commanders and eight hundred Al Qaeda fighters to Kandahar, where much of the Taliban leadership had regrouped. He had been advised by the Sheikh to leave Afghanistan and continue planning the Strait of Hormuz attack. But not far from the city, a large force of Northern Alliance fighters and US Marines were preparing to finish off the Taliban once and for all. There was no easy way out of the country.

However, they did not despair. Certainly Nashiri remained confident. During those tense few days in Kandahar, he met up with an extremely high-level Al Qaeda operative called **Khalid Sheikh Muhammad**, known in intelligence circles as KSM. Like Nashiri, KSM was an operations guy; they were doers, not thinkers.

Rotund and wildly hirsute, KSM had more than a little madness behind his eyes. An ethnic Baluch born in Pakistan and raised in Kuwait, he had gone to university in the United States but the experience did not endear him to the country and soon he was moving in jihadist circles. He arranged financing for the

1993 World Trade Center bombing and formed links to jihadists throughout South and Southeast Asia. He was initially reluctant to become a member of Al Qaeda. Not known for his piety, he had a fiercely independent streak; 'more swashbuckler than Islamist' was how one American analyst described him.[19] But by 1999 he was already working with the Sheikh on the plot that would become 9/11 – a plot which he himself had dreamed up – and finally swore him his allegiance. He was given a pseudonym: Mukhtar, 'the Chosen One'.

In their Kandahar safe house, Nashiri raised the topic of the Strait of Hormuz attack, but KSM wanted to talk about much more. Hot-headed and ambitious, KSM had been nursing a whole host of attack ideas, and was eager to reveal them to Nashiri. He wanted to bomb ships in the Strait of Gibraltar and aeroplanes at Heathrow airport; he had devised a plot to hide explosives inside video game cartridges; and he was in touch with chemical experts on an anthrax programme. Nashiri listened intently, but their conversations were cut short when, at the end of November or beginning of December, they and the other fighters in Kandahar were forced to retreat once more. This time they went to Zurmat, fifty kilometres from the Pakistani border.

Word reached them that things were not going well for the Sheikh in Tora Bora. He seemed convinced that death was imminent, and had started making arrangements to ferry his wife and children to safety. On top of that, his military chief Muhammad Atef, also known as Abu Hafs al-Masri, effectively the man who ran Al Qaeda's day-to-day operations, had been killed in a missile strike on his house in Kabul. It was a huge loss. Then on 3 December the United States began a relentless and devastating bombing campaign. For four straight days, over 700,000 pounds of explosives were dropped on the mountains. The Sheikh, certain that all was lost, ordered the Saudis who were with him to return home. 'I am sorry for getting you into this battle,' he said. 'If you are unable to resist, then you have my blessing to surrender.'[20] He handed each of them one hundred dollars and disappeared with a few bodyguards into the mountains.

Getting out of Afghanistan was at the top of Nashiri's list too. However, Al Qaeda's leadership was in total disarray and before the men in Zurmat could leave, decisions had to be taken about the future of the movement. The most senior commander there was **Saif al-Adel**. Very few men were closer to the Sheikh. A former Egyptian Special Forces officer and explosives expert, Adel was much more than a mere operative. His valour in battle was proven, and he had been working for Bin Laden as a mujahideen trainer and commander continually since 1988. As a patient, long-term tactician who never took his eye off the ultimate prize, Adel typified the qualities Bin Laden looked for in a leader. Their mutual trust was such that in July, fearing the response they might engender would be disastrous, Adel had felt free to argue against launching the 9/11 attacks.[21]

Sometime in the middle of December, Adel convened a meeting with those members of Bin Laden's council of advisers – known as a Shura Council in Arabic – who were in Zurmat. As Al Qaeda's most important operative, KSM was also invited. It is not known if Nashiri attended, but it is likely. Adel announced to the gathering that the Sheikh had asked him to take Muhammad Atef's place as military chief.[22] 'Al Qaeda can no longer afford to be overt, or to operate in the way we have been,' he told them. 'We have no choice but to spread out once again throughout the world.'[23] The fighters were to return to their home countries as best they could. For most this meant Saudi Arabia. KSM was to go to Karachi and continue developing operations targeting American interests internationally. Nashiri was to liaise with KSM there and continue with the Strait of Hormuz operation.

Adel himself would be departing soon for Riyadh.[24] He

revealed that for over a year a key operative inside the Kingdom – Yusuf al-Ayiri – had been laying the foundations of an Al Qaeda network there, the reins of which Adel would shortly take up. Adel was a cautious man and in no great rush to start blowing things up. He knew it was vital that everything be ready before the order to launch was given. Nonetheless, the time had come, he explained, to move forward with Al Qaeda's long-term aim: overthrowing the Saudi royal family.

Bearing all this in mind, Nashiri left Zurmat with a group of about fifteen fighters. The road to Karachi would not be an easy one. It swarmed with CIA agents, Pakistani intelligence, and tribal leaders in the pay of the Americans, all looking for fleeing mujahideen with prices on their heads.

As for Adel, he took the western route to Arabia – through Iran. Two years before, he had helped that country's Sunni jihadist underground set up a network of Iranian hostels to house mujahideen from Turkey, Syria, and Iraq on their way to Afghanistan.[25] Now he was fleeing in the opposite direction. He was met at the border and, after renting several flats, started making further travel arrangements.[26] He sent an operative to Riyadh with his personal effects and promised to join him there as soon as he could.

Back home in Saudi Arabia, Ayiri had been living a double life. In the eyes of the public he was the scion of a rich family, a veteran mujahid, and a pious fundraiser for jihad. He was well liked and his fervour was impressive. It was claimed that he would burst into tears at the mere mention of Muslim suffering anywhere in the world. Inside the jihadist underground, however, he was known as a brilliant ideologue and military theorist, the author of several widely read books and pamphlets, and a regular participant in online discussion forums. To this second group of admirers, he was better known by his *nom de plume*: Al-Battar, 'the Sabre'.

Upon returning from his meeting with Bin Laden the year before, the Sabre had got to work fulfilling his orders. Because he was extremely good at covering his tracks, specific information about Ayiri's activities during this period is difficult to come by. He first concentrated on getting his clerical contacts to shift their focus from Chechnya to Afghanistan, ostensibly to defend the Taliban but in fact in order to fill Bin Laden's coffers. This was necessary because most Saudi donors, and especially the wealthy ones, refused to donate to religious causes unless given assurances that they were in compliance with Sharia law. However, Ayiri's efforts were temporarily suspended in March 2001 when, driving to Mecca for a conference call he had set up between Mullah Omar and an influential sheikh, he crashed his car into a camel. Publications sympathetic to Bin Laden were discovered in the wrecked car, and as Ayiri was a known extremist, he was taken in for questioning and held in prison.[27]

It was not the first time. In June 1994, while actively raising money for the Bosnian jihad, he was rounded up with hundreds of others during a government crackdown on clerics agitating against the government, and spent a month behind bars. He was rearrested in July 1996 and held for much longer as part of another crackdown, this one following the terrorist bombing of Khobar Towers, an American army barracks in the eastern city of Dhahran, which killed nineteen Americans.

According to his Al Qaeda associates, during this second incarceration Ayiri was tortured so mercilessly by the Saudi security services that he considered confessing involvement in the bombing, despite his innocence.[28] At his own request, he was put in solitary confinement – a request he was so desperate to see granted that he went on hunger strike to ensure it. In the words of Ayiri's biographer, 'In that prison cell, he did nothing but read and memorize books. He memorized the Qur'an and the sayings of the Prophet. Once a soldier said to him, "I pity you!" "By God, it is I who pity you!" Ayiri replied. "If someone told me the day had twenty-eight hours, it would surely gladden me. I am always searching for more time!'"[29]

Upon leaving prison in June 1998, Ayiri the warrior had become Ayiri the religious scholar. He returned to his home province of Qaseem, married the sister of a well-connected extremist cleric, and launched his writing career.[30] Over the following years he produced thousands of pages of written material, and before long people were calling him 'sheikh'. He also restarted his fundraising activities, this time for the jihads in the Balkans and Chechnya, and travelled to jihad fronts in Europe and Asia. That was all before Bin Laden called and he began working full-time for Al Qaeda.

After the camel incident, he spent just under three months in prison.[31] The authorities did not know that the Sabre, whose fierce polemics against the Americans and the royal family had put him on their radar, was in fact Ayiri. Released in April 2001, he built up a team of fundraisers to take slick promotional materials to the homes of rich men and organize fundraising rallies to whip the masses into a frenzy of giving. He was also quick to see the usefulness of the Internet for getting the word out. One of Ayiri's recruits was a former Chechnya enthusiast and baby-faced PR whiz called **Isa al-Awshen**. Together they set up *Al-Nida* ('The Summons'), the closest thing Al Qaeda had to an official website. It featured publications from the Centre for Islamic Research and Study, an informal jihadist 'think tank' Ayiri had founded. His own book in praise of the 9/11 attacks appeared on the site in October 2001.

But he had been doing more than just networking with clerics, fundraising, and writing. He had also put out feelers among the Kingdom's veteran mujahideen, established a few hidden training camps in the desert, and started underground recruitment drives among known jihadist families. Some of the men he trained went to Afghanistan; some of them – like Awshen – did not. Money raised for the Taliban was also set aside; the Saudi network would need it. Finally, Ayiri had taken the first steps towards acquiring armaments and establishing weapons caches around the Kingdom.

In the weeks following 9/11, Ayiri quickly wrote a 100-page booklet entitled *The Truth of the New Crusade*, an authoritative compendium of all the religious arguments Islamists were using to justify the attacks. The book spread like wildfire throughout the jihadist community, and the Sabre's reputation received a huge boost in late October 2001 when Osama bin Laden himself praised the book in an interview with Al Jazeera, the last he would ever give.[32] 'May God bless him,' Bin Laden said of Ayiri, whom of course he did not refer to by name.

It cannot be known for certain, but it is highly likely that in late 2001, Ayiri was informed of Adel's mission. He started making sure everything was in place for his arrival.

On 19 January 2002 in the Saudi city of Buraydah, over 40,000 men from all around the Gulf were joined in prayer round the funeral bier of their spiritual and ideological leader. Sheikh Hamud al-Shuaybi had died the day before, aged 74. The others there would not have realized it, but among the sea of red-and-white headdresses was the Sabre himself. Ayiri had known Shuaybi for a long time, and had come to pay his last respects.

Ayiri's family was from Buraydah, the provincial capital of Qaseem three hundred kilometres north of Riyadh and the Kingdom's conservative heartland. Several times over the past fifty years, the people of Qaseem had clashed with the government over the introduction of technology, such as television, which was seen as a threat to its traditional way of life. Buraydah featured an important theological college, and partisans of Saudi Arabia's many clerical factions jostled for influence over the country's huge number of religious students. Shuaybi had been popular among the most radical and they had now come out in full force for his funeral.

Ayiri joined the funeral cortège as it exited the mosque and headed towards the city's graveyard. He noticed at the head of the crowd many of the dead sheikh's most prominent disciples. Blind from the age of seven, Shuaybi had been fond of receiving them inside his simple canvas tent. He eventually gained so many followers that his name was given to a whole school of hard-line teaching which openly praised 9/11 and legitimized terrorist attacks against the West.

A month before he died, Shuaybi had refused to shake a *New York Times* reporter's hand, or even to acknowledge his presence.[33] He had only agreed to give him an interview on condition that the interpreter be a Muslim. Even though the Kingdom's *de facto* ruler **Crown Prince Abdullah** had warned clerics after 9/11 to 'be cautious' and to 'weigh each word before saying it', Shuaybi was less than circumspect. 'It is the duty of every Muslim to stand up with the Afghan people and fight against America,' he said, and did not hesitate to include American civilians as targets. 'There is no difference between someone who approves of the war or supports it with money and the one who is actively fighting.' He was a little less forthright when questioned about the status of Arab governments, but anyone could read between the lines. 'I don't specify any person or group of persons. But everyone who supports America against Islam is an infidel and has strayed from the true path of Islam.' All of this would have been music to Bin Laden's ears.

It was extremely unusual for a Saudi to flout royal authority so openly. Western scholars call the Kingdom's puritanical, theologically monolithic creed 'Wahhabism', after the eighteenth-century founder of the movement. To its adherents, however, it is just Islam. Traditionally its political views boil down to a single idea: Saudis are to give their unquestioning allegiance to the ruling House of Saud. Eschewing politics, people are to focus on perfecting their personal ethics – as interpreted by the strictly conservative moral code of the country's 50,000 or so professional clerics, of course.

However, in the words of one American diplomat, a 'lonely fringe' of perhaps thirty prominent sheikhs – with Shuaybi as their figurehead – had been advocating a far more politically radical position.[34] These were the sheikhs Ayiri had begun to target, and it was in no small measure due to his lobbying that they had become more outspoken. Many of them had been imprisoned with Ayiri in 1994 after a series of illegal anti-government protests known as the Buraydah intifada. For four years, hundreds of radical sheikhs sat cheek-by-jowl in Saudi prisons. A vocal minority grew to distrust and even despise the royal family. They argued with their more moderate fellow prisoners and even began accusing some of apostasy.

This was a radical step. Someone who is quick to accuse others of apostasy is called a *takfeeri*, from an Arabic word meaning 'to charge fellow Muslims with unbelief'. Because apostasy is a heinous sin in Islam, in theory punishable by death, *takfeer* tends to result in bloodshed. Most Muslims, therefore, had grave misgivings about it. The most vocal and by far the most intelligent takfeeri among the clerics in prison was Nasr al-Fahd, and after they were all granted a royal pardon in 1998, Fahd began to organize. Two other takfeeri clerics, Ali al-Khudayr and Ahmad al-Khalidi, helped him. They were among the first to harness the Internet upon its introduction to the Kingdom in 1999. Their tendency to level charges of apostasy willy-nilly led the three of them to be known as the **Takfeeri Troika**.

The Takfeeri Troika now stood at the front of a funeral cortège that stretched for miles. By the time it reached the cemetery, people at the end were still streaming out from between the twin minarets of the mosque. Thousands of sympathizers crowded the pallbearers and the surrounding streets were jammed with cars. Other less prominent takfeeris were there too, along with thousands of moderates. Despite their disagreements, the clerical community was united in wanting to pay the great man their last respects.

After Shuaybi's body, wrapped in a simple shroud, was lowered into the grave, the assembly turned towards Mecca and prayed. Ayiri prayed with them. Perhaps his mind wandered over the crowd. Some were 'jihobbyists', as Western analysts call them, Al Qaeda sympathizers who trawled Internet forums and chat rooms sounding off on their hatred of America and Israel and dreaming of fighting for a better world. Others were pious fundamentalists who shared Bin Laden's worldview, but were unconvinced about domestic militancy.

Ayiri had them all in his sights. They were 'normal' Saudi Arabian men, not fanatical psychopaths. This suited him well, as most Al Qaeda members were pretty normal, despite what people often think. They had led sheltered lives and had learnt little about societies or religions other than their own. They were also devout and had never been encouraged to subject their faith to critical scrutiny. Ayiri would not only use their desire to escape hell and attain heaven to get them to join, he would remind them that jihad was the pinnacle of righteousness, literally 'struggling for God's sake'.[35] Most of them came from families with a history of jihad, and those familial networks would also prove helpful to Ayiri.

One thing was certain. He needed recruits.

At the end of January or beginning of February 2002, Nashiri arrived in Karachi. There he found KSM and, in hiding, perhaps 200 or 300 others. Aided by tribal sympathizers along the border, they had managed to get inside Pakistan, where members of Lashkar-e-Taiba, an Islamist group similar to Al Qaeda, smuggled them to safe houses in Karachi, Lahore, and Faisalabad. But many had not made it. The Pakistani army, at the insistence of the Americans, had apprehended hundreds of them at the border, gaunt from hunger and overcome by the bitter cold. They ended up in Guantánamo Bay.

For those who had evaded arrest, however, Karachi's teeming streets and semi-lawlessness made it an ideal place to hide until arrangements could be made to get them home. KSM found it particularly convenient, as he could take advantage of the city's relaxed banking policies to arrange financing for his ever-growing number of terrorist plans all around the world. Communication links were also good, and he was quickly able to get a media team in place, which established contact with Ayiri in Saudi Arabia.[36] Finally, in Karachi he had been able to reconnect with members of the wider jihadist underground. One such person was the London-born Pakistani terrorist Sheikh Omar, a man who had close contacts with all sort of people, including members of Pakistan's military and intelligence elite. It has also been suspected that he was a one-time MI6 agent who later went rogue. KSM teamed up with him shortly after arriving back in Karachi.

On 23 January, the South Asia Bureau Chief of the *Wall Street Journal*, an American-Israeli called Daniel Pearl, was kidnapped outside the Metropole Hotel in downtown Karachi. Sheikh Omar, who believed Pearl was a spy, had ordered the kidnapping. Using a Hotmail email address, Omar sent photos of Pearl bound and with a gun to his head to the American government, along with a number of ransom demands, including the release of all Pakistani mujahideen. The email was ignored, so nine days later Pearl was beheaded. KSM carried out the execution, which was also filmed and released online under the title *The Slaughter of the Spy-Journalist Jew Daniel Pearl*.[37]

The story made international headlines and the pressure on Karachi's jihadist community mounted even higher. On 7 February one of KSM's safe houses was raided and seventeen mujahideen were arrested, including a close associate of Nashiri who, as one of Al Qaeda's chief facilitators, had overseen the collection of more than $1 million from Saudi donors over the previous two months.[38] KSM vowed revenge and ordered two operatives to reconnoitre the American consulate in Karachi.[39] He and Nashiri brainstormed other attack ideas on American targets around the world, agreeing to work independently of each other on specific operations, such as Nashiri's in the Strait of Hormuz, in case one or the other was arrested.[40]

But the mujahideen in Karachi began to grow restless. KSM organized several training sessions for them, covering kidnapping and assassination, how to fire a pistol, and how to use a computer.[41] He told everyone to be ready to leave for home at a moment's notice, and that they should be thinking of ways to attack Western targets once they had returned. As most of them were Saudis, it was assumed that they would be answering to Saif al-Adel.

However, sometime in late February word reached KSM that Adel had not made it to Riyadh. Earlier in the month, the Iranians had bowed to American pressure and began aggressively seeking out and arresting those members of Al Qaeda who were passing through the country. Some managed to evade arrest by slipping inside Pakistan, but Adel and many others were captured. Initially it seems the Iranians treated their prisoners harshly, but they soon softened, and Adel was placed under a form of light house arrest. It is still an open question why Iran eased back. Historically Al Qaeda had considered Iran, the world's biggest Shi'ite state, one of its primary enemies, and Iran returned the sentiment. Yet most analysts believe the Iranians, in the wake of the Taliban's collapse, hoped holding Al Qaeda prisoners would deter Al Qaeda from launching attacks inside their country. Later, as the war on terror ratcheted up, they realized the usefulness of keeping a watchful eye on enemies of their enemy America.

Adel was still able to communicate with the outside world; nevertheless, his restricted circumstances presented a problem for KSM, Nashiri, and the Saudi mujahideen still in Karachi. It was decided that Adel's confinement inhibited his ability to run Al Qaeda's military affairs, and KSM claimed handwritten authorization from the Sheikh himself appointing him military chief in Adel's place. Whether that is true is unknown, but the others certainly took his word for it. He was therefore ultimately in charge of Ayiri's nascent Saudi network and set about planning how it would be organized.

He called a meeting in late February or early March. Nashiri was made head of all terrorist operations inside the Peninsula. However, because Nashiri was to focus on the Peninsula as a whole – the Strait of Hormuz was still his primary obsession – he would be spending much of his time outside the Kingdom and needed a right-hand man on the inside to keep him informed of the Organization's progress there. KSM chose **Khalid al-Hajj** for this job, another Saudi of Yemeni extraction. He was, and would remain, a little-known figure. He had recently served as one of Osama bin Laden's personal bodyguards, and was particularly close to KSM, having travelled widely throughout South and Southeast Asia networking with KSM's jihadist contacts there.

Abdulaziz al-Muqrin was selected to head up the Saudi network's military wing. An experienced jihadist – wiry, angry, and ruthless – he was thirty years old and had a lot of battlefield experience. He first travelled to Afghanistan in his late teens, where he so distinguished himself that despite his young age he was put in charge of running a training camp. He then went on to train fighters and wage jihad in Algeria, Bosnia, and Somalia. Eventually, a few days before 9/11, he went back to Afghanistan and joined Osama bin Laden there before fleeing with the others to Karachi. In time he would become Saudi Public Enemy No. 1.

KSM and Nashiri next drew up a list of mainly Saudi operatives in Pakistan at that time and assigned them each a specific task to be carried out once they were back in the Kingdom. Two were to liaise with prominent clerics and convince them to issue fatwas in support of the Organization.[42] Two were put in charge of facilitating returning fighters' re-entry into the Kingdom, one by forging passports and monitoring American most-wanted lists, and the other by going back and forth to Syria to handle mujahideen fleeing via Damascus.[43] Another was appointed to liaise between KSM and the leadership in the Peninsula, to inform Nashiri and the others of missions that KSM wanted them to carry out.[44] Others were tasked with raising money, and one was given the sensitive job of scouting potential suicide bombers among new recruits and putting them in touch with the leadership for further vetting.[45]

As for Ayiri, KSM gave instructions that he was to raise money for the global network and send it by special courier to Pakistan. It is odd that KSM did not assign him a more important role. How much KSM knew about the preparations Ayiri had already been making is not known. They are unlikely to have known each other well, as Bin Laden was wont to keep the various parts of the worldwide network separate, to protect it from infiltration. Perhaps Ayiri had signalled his displeasure that Adel had been passed over in favour of KSM, or raised doubts that the Sheikh had authorized it. Nothing can be stated with certainty. However, based on conflicts between the two which would erupt later, it is safe to speculate that he was not entirely pleased with KSM's plans for the Saudi network.

Soon after receiving their commissions, the mujahideen were given the all-clear to start returning home. Some sailed directly from Karachi. A few went to the Gulf coast of Iran and crossed over from there to the Emirates and Qatar. Others flew to Syria and Iraq and were smuggled into the Kingdom overland. By May, most of them were back. They returned to their families, kept their heads down, and tried to resume normal life.

KSM stayed in Pakistan. Nashiri and Hajj flew first to

Indonesia and Bangladesh, both of which had Al Qaeda affiliates, and then to Yemen, where they met up with Muqrin. All three then went to the UAE.[46]

The Emirates meets the Kingdom at what must be the least inviting border crossing in the world, standing on nothing but an endless expanse of sand sliced in two by a thin stretch of tarmac a thousand kilometres long. Truckers ferrying goods between the boom-towns of the Gulf make up the majority of its traffic, along with the odd carload of pleasure-seeking Saudis heading to or from Dubai. The Emirates' second city had only recently transformed itself into the region's secular Mecca, a magnet for tourists, shopping enthusiasts, and – thanks to its money-laundering expertise and propensity for turning a blind eye – international terrorists.[47]

On 12 June 2002, Nashiri stood in the queue for entry into the Saudi side, clutching a fake passport which a minor operative from Riyadh had delivered to him in Dubai a few days earlier.[48] He could not be sure his false idenitity would fool passport control; they had turned him away back in March when he tried to enter from Qatar.[49] Border security being pretty lax – since there were no computers, everything was written by hand – whether you got through or not largely depended on how fastidious the guards were feeling.[50] That day Nashiri was lucky. They waved him through without any fuss.

Nashiri climbed into a waiting car and greeted Muqrin, who had left Dubai with Hajj two days before to prepare a safe house for their leader's arrival. It was a six-hour drive to Riyadh. They had a lot of thinking to do.

The task before them was mammoth. One of its many challenges was acquiring armaments, a job they had assigned to a young jihadist called **Rakan al-Saikhan**. Twenty-three years old, he had been a close associate of Nashiri's ever since assisting in the attack on the USS *Cole*. He was an expert in explosives and constructing car bombs, and was also adept at acquiring fake identification papers. It was Saikhan who had arranged false passports for Nashiri, Muqrin, and Hajj.

Through his earlier work for Nashiri, Saikhan had links with arms smugglers in Yemen, the point of origin for much of the Kingdom's organized crime. Yemen is to Saudi Arabia as Mexico is to the United States. Its mountainous border with the Kingdom is 1500 kilometres long and very difficult to police. A glut of guns, a lack of a strong centralized authority, and rampant corruption within the military – leftovers from decades of war and instability – made Yemen a perfect hub for the underground weapons' trade. The country had five major open-air gun markets for Saikhan to choose from, the most important of which was the Souq al-Talh near the capital of Sana'a. After smuggling the weapons into the Kingdom, he would stash them around the country in underground caches and safe houses.

As they approached the capital along the Kharj Road, Nashiri and Muqrin passed the small factories and warehouses of the New Industrial Area and entered the sprawling suburbs of southern Riyadh. The vast patchwork of residential streets were home mainly to poor families living in small identikit concrete houses and apartment blocks, punctuated here and there by soaring minarets reminding the people where their primary allegiance lay. The city was still undergoing the explosive growth which had begun in the 1970s, but now most of the new builds were in the northern part of the city, where developers were avidly supplying the burgeoning middle classes with villas and shopping malls.

The capital's four million residents would have weighed on Muqrin's mind. Armaments were important, but they were not much good without soldiers to wield them. The top priority therefore was recruitment, and as head of Al Qaeda's military wing in the Kingdom, filling its training camps with warm bodies was Muqrin's responsibility. He planned to target the recently returned mujahideen first. Their younger brothers and cousins would also be a good source of recruits to tap.

The car turned left onto the Southern Ring Road. Through the early summer haze, Nashiri could just make out the newest addition to Riyadh's skyline. The Kingdom Tower was all but finished, and stood as a powerful testimony not only to the city's wealth but also to its growing ambition. Rising over 300 metres, the slender, glass-fronted building dwarfed the surrounding neighbourhood. At the thirty-fifth floor it split into two symmetrical, tapering horns, which were crowned by an illuminated sky bridge, leaving a large parabola-shaped hole through the middle.

It was not clear what the odd design was supposed to evoke, but the city's many Western expatriates joked that more than anything else the Kingdom Tower looked like a giant bottle opener. The Saudis had a joke of their own. They said the building was designed to be 9/11-proof: the gaping hole at the top was to let aeroplanes through. Whatever the symbolism, the skyscraper showed that Riyadh had arrived. The cities of the Gulf – Doha, Abu Dhabi, Dubai, Manama, and Kuwait City – may have paved the way, but Riyadh was catching up, and at the start of the twenty-first century the Saudi capital was selling itself as yet another beacon of the Peninsula's promise and prosperity.

They exited the highway and drove into a neighbourhood in the southwest called Shifa, where an operative with a fake ID card had rented a rest house for the Organization to use as a safe house. Rest houses are a peculiarly Saudi institution, spacious but humbly appointed residences with gardens where groups of young men or families gather to hang out, smoke sheesha, or play football.[51] Because rest houses are normally far from the city centre and rented for short periods, they were places where the Organization's activities were less likely to rouse suspicion.

Nashiri and Muqrin went inside, where Hajj was waiting to

greet them. A number of other high-ranking operatives were also there; it is not known if Ayiri himself was among them. They gathered in the *majlis*, a traditional sitting room with floor cushions on all four sides. Nashiri presided.

He had called them there because he brought fresh word from the Sheikh. The brothers were not to lose heart. The battle in Afghanistan had been lost but the war was far from over. The rest of the mujahideen would have to be located and reorganized. New fighters would also have to be recruited, more money raised, and additional weapons and equipment smuggled in from Yemen. For it was time to move on to the next stage of the struggle, to take the next step towards the restoration of the Caliphate and the liberation of the world's Muslims from their infidel and apostate overlords.

The time had come to bring jihad to Saudi Arabia.

2

Facing Facts

King Fahd Security College, Riyadh, 20 June 2002

Their instruments gleaming in the stadium's floodlights, the brass band marched in time to the national anthem and advanced towards the centre of the football pitch. In neat formation along the surrounding track, the college's fifty-eighth graduating class stood to attention. They wore full dress uniform, dark blue apart from white sash, belt, and spats. A feeling of excitement swept through them. In a few moments they would receive their diplomas and enter into their commissions, officers of His Majesty's internal security services.

'Long live the king! For the flag and the homeland!' The anthem reached its stirring conclusion and the graduates started to march. Each man held a rifle in his right hand; his left, clenched into a fist, swung back and forth in perfect harmony with his fellows. An ensign in front held aloft the solid-green national flag. 'There is no god but God, and Muhammad is God's Messenger' the flag proclaimed in flowing calligraphy, underlined by a single white sword. Religion backed up by the power of the state.

As the class moved around the track, family and friends looked on from the stands, all men of course. They wore the traditional white thobe and red-and-white *shemagh*, and the most important among them also had on a bisht, a light woollen over-cloak hemmed with gold silk. Many were security men themselves; a career in the security services tended to run in the family. After tonight, their sons and nephews would join one of the many forces of the Ministry of Interior, 'the MOI' to outsiders. The sporty ones would likely join a paramilitary service such as the Special Forces. The more bookish might end up as officers of the General Investigation Directorate, the Kingdom's secret police known locally as the Mabahith.

Everyone felt the joy of the occasion, yet this year a cloud hung over the proceedings. Things had not been the same since the announcement that fifteen of the nineteen suicide bombers on 9/11 had been Saudis – and not just any Saudis, but members of the mujahideen, that holy fraternity which had so heroically defended the faith in Afghanistan. Many struggled to believe that it was true.

And why was Al Qaeda directing so much public vitriol at Saudi Arabia? Saudis were on the whole faithful to the Sharia. They gave generously to charity and funded mosques and madrasas throughout the world; the royal family had managed to preserve the country's religious heritage while at the same time steering it towards prosperity. Some non-Muslims were living there, it was true, but their expertise was needed to build up the economy. And yes, America had a few military bases inside the country. But the king had agreed to them, and anyway, they were only temporary and had been sanctioned by the chief clerics. It did not make sense.

The young officers reassured themselves that Al Qaeda's rhetoric was only hot air. What was the likelihood that they would bring their warped version of jihad to the Kingdom? It was barely conceivable.

*

One man seated among the dignitaries was a little less complacent. **Prince Muhammad bin Nayef**, as assistant interior minister for security affairs, was privy to some very confidential information. And it made him uneasy.

At forty-two, the prince was one of the younger members of the House of Saud. Unlike most princes, he had a reputation for hard work and for driving his men to deliver results. Despite answering to his father **Prince Nayef bin Abdulaziz**, the then minister, those in the know were aware that Prince Muhammad was the one with a grasp of the nuts and bolts of the MOI's sprawling security apparatus. His entire education had prepared him for the job. After receiving a bachelor's degree in political science from Lewis and Clark College in Portland, Oregon, he worked in the private sector for several years, where he proved a capable manager. Then he took a three-year security course at the FBI followed by special anti-terrorism training at Scotland Yard, and joined the MOI. Initially, he was brought on board to institute badly needed administrative reforms. However, after 9/11, when he learnt how little information the Mabahith had on the fifteen Saudi suicide bombers, he realized that the agency's reforms would have to be even more radical.[1]

He sat on the dais behind his uncle, Prince Ahmed the deputy minister. Normally the minister himself would preside over the ceremony, but Prince Nayef was in Morocco recovering from knee surgery so Prince Ahmed was drafted in to take his place. The principal of the college recited an interminable speech from the podium, and Prince Muhammad allowed his mind to wander over what was really concerning him.[2]

A few weeks ago, Al Qaeda cells in Tangier, Fez, and Casablanca had been busted by Moroccan police. The operatives were Moroccan, but the three ringleaders were Saudis, and Prince Muhammad was working closely with the Moroccan authorities to get to the bottom of it. Apparently the cell had been planning to attack American and British naval vessels in the Strait of Gibraltar and were receiving orders directly from Al Qaeda leaders in Pakistan. The details of their plan – they intended to launch small dinghies loaded with explosives and ram them into ships – were uncannily reminiscent of the attack on the USS *Cole*, so once again the mastermind of that attack was at the top of everyone's wanted list, the man Al Qaeda called 'the prince of the seas', Abdul Rahim al-Nashiri.[3] Saudi intelligence had been the first to identify Nashiri as a dangerous terrorist when suspects arrested in connection with the Sagger missile plot four years before revealed under interrogation that he was their leader.[4] Now it looked like he was back in action.

That was not the worst of it, however. At the end of May, Prince Muhammad's cousin **Prince Bandar bin Sultan**, the Saudi ambassador in Washington, informed the royal court that he had received worrying news from **George Tenet**, the director of the CIA. The National Security Agency (NSA), which had been monitoring all Internet activity in the Kingdom since its introduction there in 1999, was picking up a lot of online chatter from Saudi clerics debating the legality of using weapons of mass destruction against infidels – which included, in their estimation, the royal family. This was not just a theoretical danger: it was known that Osama bin Laden had met with retired Pakistani nuclear scientists a few weeks before 9/11. The scientists later claimed they had discussed setting up a polytechnic in Kabul, but the CIA were convinced the meeting had really been about the feasibility of Al Qaeda acquiring a nuclear weapon.[5]

Even worse from Prince Muhammad's point of view, Tenet revealed that they had intercepted a communication from a middle man between Osama bin Laden and a mysterious figure in Saudi Arabia called the Sabre whose writings in support of jihad were well known but whose true identity was still undetermined. The message contained a simple order: take the plan to overthrow the government operational. 'Bad news,' Tenet told the ambassador. 'Bin Laden has changed his focus. Now it's you. It's Saudi Arabia.'[6]

That Osama bin Laden nursed a powerful hatred against the royal family was not news. He had been criticizing them for years, most recently in March in a letter published by the London-based Arabic newspaper *Al-Quds al-Arabi*. The Kingdom's rulers were traitors, he wrote, for proposing the 'Arab Peace Initiative' which called for a normalization of relations with Israel in exchange for certain concessions.[7] And Tenet's was not the first warning that the Kingdom was in Al Qaeda's sights. In February, American agents had discovered a suicide video in the rubble of a bombed house in Kabul. It featured a Saudi called Khalid al-Juhani describing his plans to martyr himself back home in the Kingdom.[8]

Prince Muhammad would later admit that many people high up in the Saudi government, including himself, were too quick to dismiss these warning signs. Their attitude was typically Saudi: God will never allow serious harm to befall us; there might be the odd problem here or there, but nothing we cannot handle. They thought the Americans were just trying to scare them into doing more to combat terrorism, also a typical Saudi response. They tended to perceive everything through the lens of political conspiracy.

Both attitudes had been on display in the months following 9/11. People had not wanted to believe that Saudis were largely behind it. It was widely rumoured that Crown Prince Abdullah – who ruled in the name of his ailing older brother **King Fahd** – privately denied that Saudis were involved. Prince Nayef was more forthright: he would go public with his accusations that 9/11 was a Zionist plot.[9] This denialism was rife throughout the Kingdom. To accept the truth would have required Saudi society to scrutinize itself rather too closely for comfort. That something had gone terribly wrong, that Saudi Arabia had given birth to an international terrorist network bent on wanton destruction – the idea was too horrible to contemplate.

Prince Muhammad stood on the dais and returned the officers' salutes as they came up to receive their diplomas. If Tenet was not bluffing, if indeed Al Qaeda cells were operational inside the country and planned to launch attacks here, then these men would be in the firing line. It was a sobering thought.

The next day, Prince Muhammad's bullet-proof car pulled into the MOI's iconic headquarters in the centre of Riyadh. A giant flying saucer covered in windows, the sinister building stood as a silent warning to anyone contemplating agitation against the state.

As the prince moved through the building's endless corridors with his various assistants, he contemplated the possible threat. Three days ago the government sent Interpol a list of the names of 214 Saudis wanted for crimes including terrorism, although these suspects – like the ones arrested in Morocco – were operating outside the Kingdom.[10] However, a few days before that, newspapers announced several arrests connected to the remains of a surface-to-air missile discovered near Prince Sultan Airbase in Kharj, a small oasis city about 75 kilometres southeast of Riyadh, from where the US Air Force had been enforcing the Iraqi no-fly zone. One of the arrested men was a Sudanese; he had been extradited to the Kingdom after Khartoum succumbed to American pressure. An Iraqi and eleven Saudis were also among the suspects. The Sudanese confessed that he had fired the missile at an American aircraft (in fact it was a Saudi AWACS plane), but it had misfired.[11]

The Kharj attack was a damp squib. The country might not be so lucky next time, and more than anyone it was up to the Mabahith to prevent any domestic threat from becoming a reality. The service had a somewhat mixed reputation. When it was established in the mid-1950s, Saudi Arabia's state apparatus was still in its infancy. The government enlisted experts from Egypt – by far the most developed and powerful Arab state at the time – to set up and even run several government departments, including the Mabahith. They adopted as their model Nasser's own secret police, which he had recently reorganized with help from the Soviet Union. This Egyptian influence remained strong even after Saudi Arabia's relations with Nasser soured, and the Mabahith became something discussed only in whispers. This was a problem.[12]

Throughout the 1990s, many jihadists published accounts of their experiences inside Mabahith prisons and described being subjected to abuse and even torture. They often emerged more radicalized than before, and nursing a powerful hatred toward the royal family. The theme is a standard one in their writings. Prince Muhammad had already advocated a new model for the Mabahith, one closer to what he experienced first-hand at the FBI and Scotland Yard.[13] But Saudi bureaucracy was infamously sclerotic and resistant to change, and anyway, he was not fully in charge. His father Prince Nayef was.

Prince Nayef – described as aloof or merely shy, depending on whom you ask, and known for his extraordinary generosity – had been the Kingdom's chief policeman for nearly thirty years.[14] He believed that a powerful clerical class backed by a strong religious police was the key to maintaining order, and so had allied himself with the Kingdom's conservatives and strengthened the powers of the Committee for the Promotion of Virtue and the Prevention of Vice, a volunteer religious police force known more widely as the Mutaween. This was more from political expediency than conviction, but his critics argued that in cultivating this conservative support base, Prince Nayef had turned a blind eye to Muslim extremism. In fact the MOI launched several crackdowns on extremist sheikhs throughout the 1990s. Nevertheless, Nayef's affiliations did have repercussions inside the royal court – which could impinge on Prince Muhammad's ability to do his job.

Prince Nayef did not always see eye to eye with his brother Abdullah, who as crown prince had been the Kingdom's *de facto* ruler since 1995, when King Fahd suffered a debilitating stroke. In fact, Nayef and Abdullah were only half-brothers, and inside the House of Saud, that distinction matters. When your father sires thirty-six sons with twenty-two different wives, as their father the Kingdom's founding monarch King Abdulaziz had, your loyalties naturally gravitate towards your mother and her children.[15]

Prince Nayef's mother was a princess from the Sudayri family who bore Abdulaziz seven sons. By all accounts a formidable woman, she cultivated a powerful sense of solidarity among them, and they became known as the Sudayri Seven. By the time of King Fahd's accession in 1982, not only had the Sudayri Seven secured the crown, but they had assumed control of the MOI, the Ministry of Defence, and the governorship of Riyadh as well.

Crown Prince Abdullah, however, did not have any full brothers, and in his eyes, the Sudayri Seven were powerful rivals. What is more, Abdullah's mother was from the Rashid family, late adopters of Wahhabism known for their moderateness in religion. The crown prince favoured a less restrictive interpretation of the faith, which pleased the moderates who comprised the bulk of his supporters, but irritated Nayef's conservative constituency.

Prince Muhammad's position in this royal conflict was often awkward. He was a devoted son, but also a moderate like Abdullah, and was aware that Nayef's cultivation of the clerics had in some ways backfired. The challenge in the months to come would be to triangulate their differences.

More pressing issues were filling the prince's in-tray. The Americans had been nipping at the Kingdom's heels. They were anxious that the government was not doing enough to counter the vast amount of money going to terrorism from inside the Kingdom – often via respected Islamic charities like the Haramain Foundation. Many Saudis, particularly those from the older generation, found it incomprehensible that their charities were linked to Al Qaeda. Delegations from Washington had paid Riyadh several visits and had left each time with promises that the government would deal with the problem. In March the Saudis had pressured the Haramain Foundation to close its branches in Somalia and Bosnia, but the Americans wanted them also to take action against the charity's Riyadh headquarters and were frustrated that no one in Saudi Arabia had yet been charged with aiding and abetting terrorists.[16] That would change on 6 September, when the government froze the assets of a founding member of Al Qaeda, Wa'el Hamza Julaidan, and designated him a supporter of terror.[17] But the Americans wanted them to close down suspect bank accounts wholesale.

Though Prince Muhammad was sympathetic, he wished the Americans would understand the difficulties involved. Technically, the MOI did not have the capability to subject bank accounts to high levels of scrutiny. Politically, the government could not be seen to be getting in the way of a Muslim's sacred duty to tithe a portion of his income to charity.[18] He also had a strategic objection.

Sir Sherard Cowper-Coles, who in time became British ambassador in Riyadh, would later agree with the prince on this. Earlier in his career Cowper-Coles had worked on combating financing of the IRA – most of which, ironically, originated in the United States. His experience taught him that it was actually better to monitor money flows to terrorists, rather than cut them off. Following the money could result in invaluable intelligence. Also, he felt it was important that, even though some donations were diverted to terrorism, most did go to legitimate causes. Turn off the tap completely, and you only played into the extremists' narrative.[19]

Yemen was also a worry. In a few weeks the prince would be

travelling to Sana'a for bilateral talks with President Saleh. Saudi agents there had spotted Nashiri walking down the street accompanied by Yemeni military officers – proving once again how useful semi-failed states were to Al Qaeda. The last thing Prince Muhammad wanted was for Bin Laden, deprived of his safe haven in Afghanistan, to set up shop just across the Saudi border.[20] The MOI had been offering substantial rewards for tip-offs about smuggling activity, which was bearing fruit.[21] But there was a long way to go. Hopefully his meeting with the president would lead to a cooperation agreement, the better to police the Arabian Peninsula.[22]

Perhaps of most pressing concern for the prince was the number of militants returning to the Peninsula. The exodus from Afghanistan had turned into a flood when, at the beginning of March, the Americans launched Operation Anaconda against the remaining 700 or so Arab fighters left in the country. Those who were not killed fled into Pakistan and joined their brothers on the long march home.

The prince did not need anyone to explain to him the importance of keeping tabs on the returning fighters. The government had not paid close enough attention to the mujahideen from the anti-Soviet jihad, with grave consequences. They would not make the same mistake twice. But at the same time, they could not lock up every mujahid. Jihad was, theoretically, a sacred duty for all able-bodied Muslims, and the mujahideen were regarded as heroes by the clerics and by the people in general. As with terrorist financing, the government feared a public backlash should it be perceived to be criminalizing a basic tenet of Islam. Instead, potential troublemakers were being questioned and followed. Of course, the systems the government had at its disposal were rudimentary; it would take some time before passport control was properly computerized.

An additional worry was the many mujahideen returning via Iran and Iraq; neither the mullahs nor Saddam Hussein were friends of the Saudi government. The Iranians were playing a particularly unsettling game. They would later hand over at least sixteen captured Al Qaeda members to the Saudi authorities, but were sheltering others such as Saif al-Adel and allowing many more to return under the government's nose.[23] Why? Did the Iranians, like the Americans, suspect that Saudi members of Al Qaeda would reorganize once they were back and start launching attacks? The possibility that this was something the Iranians were encouraging was troubling.

Nor were the Americans being as helpful as the prince would have liked. They were pressing to be given access to the detainees themselves, and to their 'pocket litter', tradecraft-speak for those items which an individual has on his person at the time of arrest: ID cards, ticket stubs, computers, and so on.[24] But in the prince's estimation, the United States was not playing fair. Names would be handed over for the Saudis to investigate, but the CIA – who simply did not trust their Saudi counterparts – habitually withheld the specific details of the intelligence they had on the men they suspected.[25]

Throughout the summer of 2002, a drip-feed of intelligence gathered from mujahideen detainees began shaking up Prince Muhammad's initial, complacent response to Tenet's warning.[26] At the end of June, one of them revealed that an Al Qaeda operative known as Abu Riha – 'Father of Perfume' – was facilitating the entry of mujahideen into the Kingdom from Iraq and telling them to prepare attacks against Western targets. The Mabahith circulated this alias around and discovered that it was linked to a 24-year-old from Buraydah called Muhammad al-Sahim. They also learned that Sahim was working for Nashiri. The Mabahith needed to find him.

Then a number of others confessed that a commander known as Hamza the Martyr had told them he would recontact them back in Saudi Arabia, with an eye towards carrying out operations there. Further investigation turned up another name, Turki al-Khalidi, about whom the Mabahith could find nothing. Eventually they realized that the commander's real name was **Turki al-Dandani**. A 30-year-old Saudi from the northern province of Jawf, Dandani had always been something of a live wire: at the age of seventeen he had been arrested and spent seven years in prison for stealing guns from a government armaments facility.[27] He finished secondary school in prison and, after getting out, enrolled in Imam University in Riyadh. Then, in 2001, he went to Afghanistan. Now it seemed he was working to establish militant cells around the capital. He too would have to be found.[28]

From what the Mabahith could tell, Dandani was somehow linked to the mysterious Sabre, about whom the Americans remained particularly agitated. So little was known about him that they focused mainly on the *Al-Nida* website, which had been posting messages from 'the Al Qaeda leadership' since early in the year.[29] Though *Al-Nida*'s ISP was in Malaysia, the Sabre was such a dominant presence on the site that it was assumed he was running it from Saudi Arabia. On 2 July the United States pressured the Malaysian government to shut it down; then on 16 July – in one of the more colourful episodes in the war on terror – a patriotic American pornographer managed to hijack *Al-Nida*'s domain name for five days, put it back on line, and gather information on those using the site. Eventually the alarm was raised. 'The infidels have taken over the site,' someone posted. 'They are tracking you. The man who is doing this is an infidel and a pornographer.' Before long the Sabre had retaken control of the site, which began operating under a different domain name.[30]

Sometime that summer, a joint US–Saudi intelligence operation thwarted an attack on the oil facility at Ra's Tanura on the Kingdom's Gulf coast. They believed Nashiri was behind it. It seems he had abandoned the sea-borne Strait of Hormuz operation – perhaps because so many men captured in Pakistan knew about it – in favour of terrestrial targets in the Gulf.[31] Officials on both sides have remained tight-lipped about this operation ever since, so the details remain obscure. According to press reports, dozens of Saudis linked to the plot were arrested, most of them employees of the state oil company Saudi Aramco, along with up to two Americans, although the American government denied that any of its nationals were involved. The episode was further proof that Al Qaeda was active on the Peninsula and was trying to hit the world where it would really hurt: Saudi oil installations.[32]

Not long after that, Prince Muhammad and the Mabahith were alerted when a group of young men in a Riyadh suburb were seen receiving weapons training at a makeshift shooting range. The man training them, a heavyset 27-year-old local boy from a well-known mujahideen family, was Faisal al-Dukhayyel – though he would go on to achieve notoriety under his Al Qaeda *nom de guerre*, **Abu Ayub**. He was known to the Mabahith. In August 2001 the Turkish authorities had arrested him en route from Afghanistan to Chechnya and informed the Saudis that they were sending him home. Upon his arrival in Riyadh, the government temporarily confiscated his passport, but as soon as he got it back he returned directly to Afghanistan. He then ended up becoming one of the jihadists whom the Iranians had freed, after holding him in prison for two months.

The Mabahith investigated the shooting range and decided not to arrest Abu Ayub but to keep him under surveillance. It is safe to say in hindsight that this was a big mistake. Abu Ayub realized the MOI was on to him and soon disappeared into the underground with his trainees. Only when it was too late did the Mabahith learn that by the end of that summer, the elusive Dandani put Abu Ayub in touch with military commander Abdulaziz al-Muqrin. Muqrin made Abu Ayub his deputy and absorbed his fledgling cell into his own rapidly expanding network.

The scorching summer drew to a close just as things started to really heat up. Throughout September 2002 it became obvious to everyone that America was planning to invade Iraq again. Since March, the US had dropped three hundred per cent more bombs on the country compared with the previous year, and seasoned observers could tell that the US Air Force was preparing the ground for all-out war by weakening Iraqi air defence systems.[33]

The Saudi government found itself once again stuck in the middle between America and its own religious establishment. It broadly shared the Bush administration's desire to get rid of Saddam Hussein – even if, behind closed doors, it questioned America's ability to deal with the consequences.[34] However, to placate the clerics, it clearly stated that the United States could not use its Saudi bases to launch an offensive against Iraq without explicit sanction by the United Nations.

The government's position did little to dampen the growing clerical unrest. The presence of five thousand American troops on Saudi soil had always been a bone of contention; the situation was further inflamed by Bin Laden's rhetoric and by the widely reported (and almost certainly inflated) figures of Iraqi dead as a result of UN sanctions. 'One million dead children' had become an oft-repeated refrain. However, to Prince Muhammad – who in the middle of October would travel to America for meetings with his counterparts there – the pros and cons of invading Iraq were secondary to the fact that any invasion would play into Al Qaeda's story that America was hell-bent on military conquest of the Middle East.

As if on cue, the number of Al Qaeda attacks in the Peninsula ticked sharply upwards, nearly all of them involving native Saudis. On 6 October the *Limburg*, a French oil tanker passing through the Gulf of Aden, was suicide-bombed by a dinghy laden with TNT, killing one crew member, wounding twelve others, and flooding the sea with 90,000 barrels of oil. International shipping in the Gulf of Aden plummeted, depriving the Yemeni government of a vital source of revenue. Everything about the attack indicated Nashiri's involvement.

Two days later, an Al Qaeda cell in Kuwait launched a suicide attack against a group of US Marines on training exercises. One was killed, another wounded. The MOI admitted the likelihood that Saudis had helped plan the attack.[35] The bombing of a Balinese nightclub on 12 October, killing 202 holidaymakers and local workers, may have occurred far from Saudi shores, but investigators soon discovered that the terrorist group that carried it out was not only affiliated to Al Qaeda but afterwards received $130,000 from Nashiri's ally KSM as a reward.[36] Compared with the carnage in Bali, the attempted hijacking on 17 October of a plane on a flight from Khartoum to the Kingdom was relatively tame. Saudi security officers on board wrestled the hijacker to the ground. But he was a Saudi, and another reminder that the country's home-grown threat was genuine.[37]

However, despite all the indisputable terrorist activity involving Saudis all around the world, the government still denied the possibility of a domestic threat. This was made clear on 29 September when a car exploded in north Riyadh, killing W. Maxmilian Graf, a German expatriate. A similar bombing in June had killed a British banker called Simon Veness, and a parcel bomb the previous May had targeted an American engineer called Michael Martin.[38] Yet a senior prince told reporters afterwards, 'There are no terrorist attacks against foreigners in our country. They are well looked after.'[39] Prince Nayef also denied it was an act of terrorism. 'I am sure most probably there are no Saudis, Muslims or Arabs involved,' he said. 'This bombing and previous ones may have happened for personal reasons and no more than that.'[40]

What the prince was referring to was ten bombings in

2000 and 2001, in connection with which a number of Westerners were arrested, including ten Britons. The Saudi government accused them of involvement in a violent turf war between rival alcohol-smuggling rings. Some of them admitted to running illegal bars, and although initially they denied having anything to do with the bombings, some eventually put their names to confessions.

However, the men later alleged that the confessions had been extracted by torture. After five were granted a royal pardon, they said they had been held in solitary confinement, granted no or only sporadic access to lawyers, and caned, beaten, and drugged.[41] Then, reaching a deal with the United States and Britain sometime in 2003, the government released the rest of the prisoners as well, almost certainly in exchange for five Guantánamo Bay detainees, although the Saudis have always denied this.[42] The accused men have since tried to raise lawsuits, both against the Saudi government and against specific individuals inside the MOI, but British and EU courts have ruled that Saudi Arabia is protected from prosecution by state immunity laws. In addition, the British Foreign Office has formally backed up the Saudi government's version of events.[43]

It is a sordid story about which very little evidence has been made public, and it may be that the truth behind these bombings will never come to light. At the time, very few people outside the Kingdom took the Saudi government's claims at face value. It seemed to these outside observers – and at least some of the bombings indicated – that expatriates were being systematically targeted by Muslim extremists.

Despite the MOI's attempts to control clerical dissent, the Kingdom's extremist clerics – a minority, but a vocal one – stepped up their criticism of the religious establishment. The tension had been growing for over a year. After 9/11, the Saudi government had begun cracking down on extremism in mosques, and two weeks after the American invasion of Afghanistan, the minister of Islamic affairs stated unequivocally that clerics did not have the right to declare jihad; that power is reserved to the ruler alone. A month later, the Grand Mufti and other senior clerics were summoned to the court and warned that extremist sermons would no longer be tolerated. Then in February 2002, the government announced that Hajj pilgrims would not be allowed to denounce the United States. Finally, on 24 October, the deputy minister announced that mosques were forbidden to disseminate extremism or recruit young men to work for Osama bin Laden.

One outspoken opposition figure was a radical preacher called **Abdullah al-Rashoud**. He taught at Riyadh's Institute for Religious Knowledge, which prepared students to pursue religious careers. For sheikhs like Rashoud, the antagonism with which they were being treated by the Ministry of Islamic Affairs simply confirmed their view that the government was horribly compromised by the Kingdom's alliance with America.

However, Rashoud was not yet entirely in the extremist camp. He wanted to give the ministry the opportunity to redeem itself in his eyes. On Saturday 2 November, shortly after afternoon prayers at the mosque next door, Rashoud led a group of about eighty young men, mainly religious students, to the severe concrete building which houses the General Presidency of Scholarly Research and Fatwas. They brought along a list of nine grievances that included Saudi Arabia's membership of the UN; 'satellite channels of mass destruction', as they called them, which spread apostasy and heresy; mujahideen prisoners in Guantánamo Bay; and the fact that the country's clerics were not condemning the government for hounding jihadist youths. Rather, they said, the government should 'shift its attention to rounding up apostates, drunkards, and secularists who rail against our religion and its people'.

According to a partial account that Rashoud recorded later,

the gathering was intended to bring together different points of view so that the rifts between the ministry and the clerics could be healed in good faith. He addressed the crowd, telling them that discipline and calm were required to ensure that their voices were heard. However, no one from the ministry came out to meet them, and before long members of the security services started to arrive. The government denies using improper force, but according to Rashoud the petitioners had to retreat back to the mosque.

They decided to return the following day. This time, security guards had been posted outside the building. Rashoud was surprised by this, because the group had shown only 'exemplary calm' the day before. Two clerics at the ministry walked past, but refused to speak with Rashoud. Eventually a soldier came out and announced that the mufti would meet with ten of them, but this was deemed unacceptable by the assembly; it was eventually agreed that fifty would be let in.

Once inside, the mufti told them they had five minutes to present their demands. When the five minutes were up, he rose and left the room, 'with a smile on his face', even though the group were still in the middle of speaking. Despite this treatment, Rashoud and the others returned to the mosque, where he delivered a brief sermon. Then, as they walked to their cars to leave, riot policemen who had assembled outside followed them in a 'frightening' manner. 'Does this not give the green light,' Rashoud asked in his audio recording, 'not only to our young men but to the community as a whole, to lose their confidence in the official sheikhs? Is this not a sign that what has been said about the sheikhs' – that they no longer truly represented the interests of the Umma – 'is completely true?'

Not long after, Rashoud went underground and became one of Al Qaeda's most prominent ideologues. He was added to the Mabahith's list of men to track down. As for the Ministry of Islamic Affairs, it continued to enforce the government's crackdown on wayward sheikhs. On 7 December the minister, Sheikh Saleh Al Ashaikh, would issue a letter prohibiting unauthorized preachers from delivering sermons at mosques. Violators would be severely punished.

Meanwhile, Prince Muhammad had been closely following the hunt for Nashiri. It was now clear to everyone that he was head of terrorist operations inside the Peninsula. Because the CIA and the FBI had established a fairly functional working relationship with the Yemeni government – and because, despite their cooperation, the Saudis were still not taking their warnings seriously – the Americans were primarily focused on the Yemeni part of Nashiri's network. The local Al Qaeda leader in Yemen was a veteran mujahid in his late forties, Abu Ali al-Harithi, who had helped plan the *Cole* bombing and was working closely with Nashiri on a number of new attacks. However, the NSA had been closely monitoring several phone numbers linked to Harithi, and on 3 November a Predator drone homed in on his mobile phone signal and fired a missile at his vehicle, killing him and five others – including one American citizen, the first to be executed by a drone.[44]

Though Nashiri's efforts in Yemen were significantly hobbled by Harithi's assassination, he was given only five days to stew over it. On 8 November, Prince Muhammad discovered to his delight that Nashiri had been arrested in Dubai and handed over to the CIA. He was carrying two false Saudi passports as well as a laptop computer and several mobile phones possibly containing terrorist contact numbers.

Given his importance to this story, Nashiri deserves to be ushered off stage in style. Unfortunately, beyond these scant details, the Emirati and American authorities remain tight-lipped about his arrest to this day. In September, a close associate of KSM, Ramzi bin al-Shibh, had been arrested in Karachi during a raid on his safe house, which threw up the identities, aliases, and phone numbers of several operatives. Maybe Nashiri was one of them. Or perhaps his arrest was part of a Swiss mobile phone tracking operation codenamed Mont Blanc, which in due course would certainly lead to several stunning arrests. Or maybe it was his inflated ego that got him in the end. Reports from the UAE revealed that he had been under surveillance for several weeks, and was seen driving expensive cars up and down Dubai.[45]

It may never be known how the Emiratis nabbed Nashiri, but he spent the next four years in CIA black sites in Jordan, Poland, and Thailand before finally ending up in Guantánamo Bay in 2006. 'Enhanced interrogation techniques', including waterboarding, eventually compelled him to confess his involvement in a number of Al Qaeda operations, including the attack on the *Cole.* But it took a long time to get him to talk. The Mabahith would have much preferred the Americans to hand Nashiri over to them. To this day, they feel he would have more willingly opened up to them, and say they would not have subjected him to the torture he suffered at the Americans' hands. As it turned out, his arrest threw up no ground-breaking information about the growing Al Qaeda network inside Saudi Arabia.[46]

The Peninsula may have lost its head of operations, but KSM and the mysterious Sabre remained threats. Also, intelligence reports from the Moroccan authorities suggested that an important operative who was with Nashiri at the time of his arrest managed to escape, someone a Guantánamo inmate described as 'even more dangerous than Nashiri' – Abdulaziz al-Muqrin.[47]

Closer to home, Prince Muhammad's men had made great strides in the search for the 'Father of Perfume', Muhammad al-Sahim. A few weeks earlier, a detainee was able to link an unknown figure called Omar to a specific mobile phone. Several other detainees then confirmed that Omar was in fact Sahim; using that mobile number, the Mabahith were able to pinpoint his location.

Late on 16 November, members of the security services surrounded a rest house in the Marwa district in southern Riyadh. Reconnaissance revealed that Sahim was indeed inside, along with fourteen others. It was Ramadan, so they would have broken their fast at sunset, and now were gathered round a young firebrand preacher called **Ahmad al-Dukhayyel**, who was delivering a lecture. Dukhayyel was known to the Mabahith; though roughly the same age as Abu Ayub, he was his uncle.

The officers had not expected the safe house to be so full, so the Special Forces were called in to provide reinforcements. However, for some reason, the officers present decided to commence the raid before the Special Forces arrived, displaying a marked lack of training and discipline in the MOI's soldiers – it would not be the last time. When they stormed the house, the ferocity of the jihadists' reaction took them by surprise. With cries of *'Allahu akbar!'*, the men inside met them with a hail of Kalashnikov fire. Luckily, no MOI officers were wounded and Sahim was caught in the returning fire, shot in the right leg. He was arrested, but all the others managed to flee, Abu Ayub among them, along with several other Al Qaeda recruits who would become infamous over the coming years.

The MOI was not able to keep a lid on the story, yet once again they chose the path of obfuscation. Prince Nayef admitted that in recent months the Mabahith had detained 100 Saudis and questioned a further 700. However, confusingly, he denied they had links to Al Qaeda. 'There are no Al Qaeda sleeper cells, and no Saudi has been arrested with links to the network,' he told the Saudi daily *Al Watan*. Sahim was in custody, but he had been wanted only for 'a security-related matter'. Nayef conceded there were veterans of the Afghan campaign inside the Kingdom, but they were all non-Saudis.[48]

Prince Nayef's denials made little sense, especially as Prince Saud al-Faisal the foreign minister had openly admitted back in

August that the government was holding Saudi Al Qaeda members in custody. The MOI's position became even less tenable when, on 28 November, *Al-Quds al-Arabi* splashed a provocative headline across its front page: 'Bin Laden says "Grab your weapon and defend your honour!"' Bin Laden warned the people of the Peninsula that 'difficult days of total war are coming,' and that America's invasion of Iraq would be only the first stage towards its complete conquest of the region. 'That being said,' he continued, 'we shall dedicate everything we have to you and to the defence of the Land of Muhammad ... Together, we shall act as one hand, until our religion has emerged jubilant and triumphant from this period of strife.'[49]

What is more, CIA director George Tenet once again approached Prince Bandar in Washington with troubling news: the nuclear threat had not gone away. A 'stream of reliable reporting', in Tenet's words, indicated that a top-level Saudi operative known to the CIA as Abu Bakr al-Azdi had entered into negotiations with illegal weapons dealers about acquiring three Russian nuclear devices – and was reporting directly to Saif al-Adel, still under house arrest in Iran. Apparently Adel had warned Azdi to be careful and had recommended that he get Pakistani nuclear scientists to inspect the devices before agreeing to buy them.

Abu Bakr al-Azdi was a known alias of a young jihadist called **Ali al-Faqasi**, who was from the city of Baha in the south-western corner of the Kingdom. Six of the 9/11 hijackers hailed from that part of the country. 'Look,' Tenet said, 'we don't know if they intend to detonate a device inside your country or just use Saudi Arabia as a transit point. But in either case, you have big trouble.'[50] Prince Bandar, initially incredulous, was soon convinced and reported back to Riyadh.

At the beginning of 2003, the MOI changed course. Out of the public eye, a joint US–Saudi counterterrorism unit was set up. Mabahith and other Saudi agents began meeting regularly with a team of their CIA counterparts based at the embassy in Riyadh. Seated opposite each other down a long table, they would cautiously pass bits of intelligence back and forth, at each side's discretion, of course. It was not always smooth sailing – both parties still complained that the other side was withholding information – but it was a big step in the right direction.[51]

The MOI began to be more open with the public as well. At the end of January they invited a five-person delegation from Human Rights Watch to inspect the country's prisons and discuss issues with Prince Nayef and the head of the Mutaween. It was the first time such an organization had been let in, and along with the government's acceptance of a petition of grievances compiled by reform-minded Saudi intellectuals, it signalled a new note of openness – perhaps in response to criticism from Islamist hardliners.[52]

They also started to concede publicly that domestic terrorism was a tangible threat. In a rare statement to the press, Prince Muhammad stated that the Kingdom had gaoled around ninety people linked to Al Qaeda. 'A number of these convicts have already completed their terms and been released,' the prince said, which would have raised a few eyebrows. Prince Nayef added that many detainees were still being held without charge while investigations into their activities continued.[53]

That year's annual pilgrimage began three days later, on 9 February, and partly due to continuing warnings from America that extremists sympathetic to Al Qaeda might use the Hajj to stage anti-American protests, security was significantly tightened. 'We will not allow any party or person to disrupt the Hajj,' Prince Nayef announced. 'Our hand is strong and decisive.'

The government was clearly serious. In Riyadh the day before, it had arrested eight Saudi jihadists in connection with a shootout with security forces on 24 January. The shootout had resulted from an arrest two days earlier of a member of a gang which the Mabahith had been tracking on suspicion of forging passports and ID cards, who were linked to suspicious individuals both inside the Kingdom and abroad. Under interrogation, the gang member had told them the gang were using a flat near highway exit 6, but that he did not know the precise location. The area around the exit had then been discreetly placed under surveillance, and before long field investigators had discovered the flat in the Maseef neighbourhood. The security services had then drawn up plans to raid it.

When the soldiers had arrived on the 24th, one of the gang members was standing outside the flat. He began to shout that the authorities had them surrounded, and fled inside. The officers smashed in the door. 'Give yourself up!' they ordered a young man standing in the corridor. To their surprise, he pulled out a pistol and a hand grenade and answered, 'If you enter this flat, I'll blow up the whole building!' The soldiers immediately withdrew. He fired at them as they went, wounding two. At the same time, a Kuwaiti stepped out of an adjacent flat and began firing as well. The officers returned fire, and the Kuwaiti fell to the ground; he would later die on the way to hospital.

The MOI was caught completely off guard. There were ten armed men in the flat. They burst out shooting. Passers-by were thrown into a panic, and the officers barely had a handle on the situation. In the chaos, all ten militants fled, stopping only to shoot a man seated in a car. They thought he was an undercover Mabahith officer. In fact he was an ordinary civilian.

Two days later the Mabahith tracked down eight of the suspects and placed them under arrest. The remaining two would also eventually be found. They all confessed to being members of a terrorist cell.[54] Prince Muhammad now knew for certain what he had long tried to ignore: Al Qaeda had established a network inside the country.

The Hajj passed without incident. Fourteen pilgrims were crushed to death during the symbolic stoning of the devil – an improvement on 2001, when a similar stampede killed thirty-five – but there was no trouble from jihadists.[55] However, as the two million pilgrims started heading home, the MOI made a couple of startling discoveries: two remote training camps for new recruits.

One of the camps, in Asfan near Jeddah, had been set up not long before by a local cell calling themselves 'the Unitarians'. The Mabahith were led to it by a number of cell recruits who under questioning had confessed they had received training from veteran mujahideen. The MOI found an incredible stash of weaponry at Asfan, including 376 submachine guns and over 23,000 bullets. An anonymous tip-off alerted the Mabahith to the second camp, in Namas in the mountains on the way to Yemen. From the food stores and other equipment hidden there, it was clearly intended to be a long-term hideout as well as a training camp.

This development further increased Prince Muhammad's fears. Not only was there an established Al Qaeda network in the country – it was growing.

On 13 February, the CIA made another breakthrough. Agents working with local police arrested five men crossing over King Fahd Bridge, which links the Kingdom to Bahrain. The NSA had picked up their chatter, and the CIA knew they were up to something. The follow-up investigation led the joint US–Saudi counterterrorism unit to a flat in Riyadh, where they confiscated a computer hard drive, which was handed over to the Americans. It contained files revealing that the Bahraini group, working closely with operatives inside the Kingdom, had the wherewithal to construct a simple chemical weapon employing an easily obtainable mixture of sodium cyanide (used in rat poison) and hydrogen – which, ominously, they intended to smuggle into America and set off inside the New York Subway system.

It was the Americans' worst nightmare. The Riyadh flat led

investigators to two others, and six Saudis were arrested. One of them was a well-known campaigner and fundraiser for jihad, who had a prison record but had not been linked to Al Qaeda. His name was Yusuf al-Ayiri. There was little hard evidence connecting any of them to the Bahrainis, yet the CIA insisted they be held. The government complied, but they also said that they would not be able to detain them indefinitely without reason. A few weeks, that was all. Yet, because the CIA still did not trust the Saudis, they refused to reveal the New York attack plans they had uncovered, and simply stalled for time.[56]

In February there was more trouble in store. Early in the month a British employee of BAE Systems in Riyadh sustained minor injuries when a carload of men fired at him. A Yemeni-born Saudi was later arrested.[57] Then, on the 20th, another BAE employee was attacked. Robert Dent, a 37-year-old father of two from Merseyside, was killed on his way home when, out of nowhere, a man shot up his car. The gunman, yet another Saudi of Yemeni origin, worked for a Toyota dealership in Riyadh and claimed that the killing was inspired by Al Qaeda.[58]

On the same day, the Mabahith received a pivotal tip-off: the location of Turki al-Dandani, the Al Qaeda commander also known as Hamza the Martyr whom they had been hunting since the summer. Officers were sent to arrest him, but he was far too well trained to give up without a fight. In the ensuing shootout, Dandani escaped, but two of his associates were arrested. Through questioning them, the Mabahith learned that Dandani's network was extensive indeed: it included cells in Riyadh, Qaseem, and the southwestern city of Khamis Mushayt, home of King Khalid Air Base, which the US Air Force had used in the Gulf War.

Finding Dandani became Prince Muhammad's top priority.

The Ministry of Islamic Affairs made good on its threat to crack down on wayward preachers. In late February, two sheikhs were arrested for defying December's strict new regime against extremist sermons in mosques.[59] Then, on 1 March, the government decided that the Takfeeri Troika, whose writings had grown increasingly toxic since the death of Shuaybi the year before, needed to be silenced. They were not believed to be formal members of Al Qaeda, but no one was under any illusions about whose interests they served. A warrant was issued for their arrest, but somehow – a tip-off from within the ministry, perhaps – they got wind of it and slipped into the underground. Three more names, then, were added to the MOI's growing list of fugitives.

Very soon thereafter, Prince Muhammad received encouraging news. Mont Blanc, the Swiss mobile phone tracking operation, had bagged its biggest quarry yet: on 1 March, the Pakistani security services working with American agents raided a safe house in Rawalpindi and came out dragging away Al Qaeda's head of worldwide operations in handcuffs. The photograph of Khalid Sheikh Muhammad being forced into a police car, lumpen and dishevelled, ricocheted around the world.[60] Like Nashiri, KSM was handed over to the CIA and disappeared into the agency's worldwide network of 'black sites'. Under torture, he confessed to a number of the charges levelled against him; however, also like Nashiri, he was essentially uncooperative. Certainly his arrest did little to prevent upcoming attacks in Madrid, London, and again in Bali – all carried out by cells with which, experts believe, KSM was well acquainted.[61]

The prince's primary concern was, of course, Saudi Arabia. Mont Blanc had thrown up several phone numbers linked to operatives inside the Kingdom, and the hope was that KSM's arrest might throw further light on the Organization's cells.[62] Perhaps with both KSM and Nashiri out of the picture, the Saudi network would fall apart – in hindsight an unlikely scenario, but the Mabahith could not be blamed for hoping.

*

Spring started with a bang – literally. On 18 March, an explosion was heard at a nondescript villa in east Riyadh. MOI officers rushed to the scene. As they gathered evidence, a portly, bespectacled lieutenant-colonel with a bushy black beard stood in the yard filming a report to a video cameraman, to pass on later to his superiors.

'In the name of God, the Merciful, the Compassionate,' he began in formal Arabic, rushing through the traditional formula. 'On this day, Thursday, the fifteenth day of the first month of the year fourteen hundred and twenty-four, an explosion was reported to the Civil Defence at precisely 12:53 p.m. The bomb squad was alerted, and officers went to a villa in the Iskan neighbourhood of the Jazeera district.' He pointed toward a black patch on the villa wall. 'This is where the explosion occurred, killing this person over here, the man under this blanket.'

Splotches of red flecked the yellow wall. The dead man had been in the middle of constructing a homemade bomb, which had accidentally gone off in his hands. 'In all likelihood the explosives were made up of materials from the local market,' the lieutenant-colonel said, indicating pieces of shrapnel scattered about. Then he beckoned to the camera. 'Come with me.'

He walked into the entrance hall. Bottles and beakers were laid out on a table. 'Here we see a number of materials – ammonium, ammonium nitrate, and sulphur – which when mixed together can make a homemade bomb. You can see here a mixing device, here is a scale to ensure the mixture contains the right amounts of the different materials, and here you see fertilizer. All in all, there is enough here for a medium-sized bomb.' He turned to a nearby huddle of officers. 'Please, guys, in God's name, give me some space!'

In the sitting room, piles of seized items littered the floor. Officers were out-shouting one another as they combed through it all. 'Come on, guys, clear out,' the lieutenant-colonel ordered. 'Just for a few seconds, that's all.' They grudgingly complied.

'Now, as you can see,' he continued, 'we have found a lot of weaponry. Bullets, machine-gun clips – in due course we will be able to give an estimate of how many rounds exactly. Beside each sofa we found a fully loaded weapon and a grenade. Like this one.' He carefully held it up. 'It's primed.'

He carried on for twenty minutes, pointing out each type of item: pistols, Kalashnikovs, mobile phones, detonators, twenty-one blocks of RDX, and so on, as well as a wad of Saudi riyals worth around £25,000. 'A complete inventory has been drawn up and a team of officers is carrying out a thorough investigation. This concludes my explanation. May God deem it pleasant to the ear.'

The man beneath the blanket was Fahd al-Saidi, who had only recently returned from Afghanistan. 'One day you will hear an explosion,' his Al Qaeda obituarist would later recall Saidi saying. 'That'll be me!'[63] Of course, he was referring to a martyrdom operation, not to being blown up as a result of his own incompetence.

Investigators wasted no time. Information from the villa led the MOI to another house in the same area, where they made several arrests. Dandani was holed up somewhere in the Seville district, a detainee told them, a neighbourhood in north Riyadh popular with Western expatriates. The Security Patrols, a branch of the MOI in charge of cordoning off and surveilling targeted areas, was sent to Seville to inspect all the cars coming in and out of the neighbourhood.

Prince Muhammad felt certain that a terrorist campaign was imminent. His fears were coming true.

The MOI was fixated on Dandani, but the Americans were still primarily interested in finding the Sabre: he was the lynch-pin, they believed, of Bin Laden's Saudi network.

Sometime in March, Saudi intelligence was contacted by their

American counterparts. An Al Qaeda informer in Karachi known as 'Ali' had told them that the Sabre had visited Pakistan in January to meet the leadership and discuss operations in the Peninsula. What was more, 'Ali' gave them a name: the Sabre was Yusuf al-Ayiri, one of the Saudis arrested in connection with the Bahraini group back in February.

This vital piece of information would have been hard for Prince Muhammad to hear. The Americans had continued to refuse the Saudi government's requests for specific information about the six detained men. So the MOI had let them go.[64]

Of course the cry immediately went out that Ayiri was to be brought back in. But it was too late. The Sabre had disappeared into the underground – with what plans in mind, Prince Muhammad still did not know for sure.

He would soon find out.

3

The Riyadh Compounds

Northeast Riyadh, a few months earlier

Not far from Imam University in northeast Riyadh lie a number of neighbourhoods bearing names that hearken back to the glories of Muslim Spain: Granada, Seville, Alhambra, and Cordoba, names that have become almost mythological symbols of cross-cultural harmony. Three men in a nondescript car drove around the area. To the casual observer there was nothing unusual about them, but they were in fact low-level members of Turki al-Dandani's cell network. Dandani had tasked them with placing the area's many Western residential compounds under surveillance.

Such compounds housed Western engineers and administrators who desired a private space where they could live in the fashion to which they were accustomed. To these three hard-line Muslims, however, they were islands of Western immorality in a sea of Sharia law, where alcohol was available to residents and their more liberal Saudi friends, and where their bikinied wives lounged around swimming pools. The presence of such people on the Arabian Peninsula, the Organization believed, was a heinous sacrilege. They needed to be expelled.

The car circled one of the compounds. The jihadist seated beside the driver filmed out the window. He focused on the compound's gates and security guards. Whenever he thought he might be seen, he nervously lowered the camera onto his lap.

'Over there,' the driver indicated. 'Look at all the soldiers. What weapons do they have, can you see? Are they paying close attention?'

'Nah, they're just standing around,' the third guy answered from the back seat.

'But what weapons have they got?'

'Just pistols.'

The car was moving too fast for the cameraman to get his shot. 'I didn't get them. Can we go back and try again?'

'Come on, you're not paying attention!'

The car turned right and zoomed down a side street skirting the western edge of the compound. As they approached the next intersection, they noticed a jeep belonging to the National Guard parked underneath a plain beige tarpaulin. The driver slowed down.

'Go forward just a bit,' said the cameraman. 'I can't catch the number plate. That's it, okay, stop.' Pedestrians passed in front of the guard post, including a young boy bouncing a ball. 'Well hello there,' the cameraman whispered.

'Zoom forward. There are too many people in front of the jeep.'

'Are they Americans?' sniggered the guy in the back.

'Some of them, yes.'

'May their numbers increase!' he replied sarcastically.

Back at the main entrance, they noticed a mosque inside. 'Hey, do you think the imam of the mosque has to stop at the checkpoint?'

'What?'

'Maybe you could pretend to be the imam, and I could be the muezzin.'

'Nah, they'd still search us.'

They drove on a bit.

'Whoa look, there's a woman inside.' Through the open gate they could see a Western woman carrying a bag of shopping. She had on a long black dress, but her blond hair was uncovered.

The idea had been Nashiri's. Before his unexpected arrest, he had planned a series of coordinated car bomb attacks at three residential compounds in Riyadh. Because of the compounds' reputation for licentiousness, he thought the operation would earn widespread support among Saudis. As Nashiri's deputy inside the Kingdom, Khalid al-Hajj was in charge of overseeing all the Organization's Saudi activities, and assigned the operation to the Dandani network, which was just one of three major networks that had grown up over the past several months. Muqrin led a Riyadh-based network with cells throughout the Kingdom, and Ali al-Faqasi, whose nuclear activities had been brought to Prince Muhammad's attention, also led a network with cells up and down the west coast.[1]

These networks were all relatively independent, both of each other and of the different layers of leadership higher up. So when Nashiri was arrested, and KSM four months later, the networks were hardly affected at all – despite what the prince, who was as yet unaware of the Organization's complexity, wanted to believe.

Then there was Ayiri. The Sabre did not lead a network of his own. Rather, he acted as the Organization's presiding organizational and ideological genius. His writings, which were still appearing at an astonishing rate, continued to inspire veterans and new recruits alike. It appears he travelled around giving lectures to the various cells, and along with Muqrin oversaw the training camps dotted around the country. And as was seen from what George Tenet would report to Prince Muhammad,

Ayiri had stayed in contact with Central Command and had even gone to Pakistan to liaise with the leadership there.

And yet, the Sabre was not happy. He was best acquainted with the lie of the land inside the Kingdom and had close links with Central Command, especially Saif al-Adel. But he had not expected KSM to emerge as the Al Qaeda leader with the most scope for manoeuvre. Nashiri and Hajj, neither of them pure-born Saudis, were imposed on the Organization, which, Ayiri felt, no one had done more than he to establish. Then, following Nashiri's arrest, KSM appointed yet another Saudi-Yemeni, a one-legged jihadist called Walid bin Attash, to take Nashiri's place as head of operations in the Peninsula. Ayiri no doubt felt he had been passed over again.

It is likely that ethnic rivalries also informed Ayiri's feelings. Al Qaeda's membership had been primarily Egyptian and Yemeni in the beginning, and they now dominated the leadership. Ayiri may have struggled with this. He hailed from the Najd, the long central desert plateau at the heart of the Kingdom, and so was of impeccable Saudi pedigree. Like many Saudis, he probably looked down on other Arabs – Yemenis in particular.[2] Lacking the oil wealth of the Gulf States, Yemenis were very poor and Yemeni immigrants did jobs ordinary Saudis were unwilling to perform. For their pains, they were regarded as socially inferior.

Sometime in late 2002 or early 2003, Ayiri called Muqrin, Faqasi, and the young arms smuggler Rakan al-Saikhan to a series of secret meetings. They were all full-blooded Saudis, and Ayiri convinced them that Hajj had to go. All they had to do was to decide who, from among themselves, was the best man to replace him. Due to his young age, Saikhan was probably never a serious candidate, but he had a lot of experience and was trustworthy. Presumably Ayiri put himself forward. Muqrin, already head of military operations in the country and with the most battlefield experience, had obvious strengths. And the 28-year-old Faqasi, though a relative newcomer to jihad, also had several points in his favour.

The conspirators weighed the pros and cons of all the options and picked Faqasi to replace Hajj. Faqasi had first left the Kingdom in 1999 bound for the Chechen campaign, but on the way he was diverted to Afghanistan and ended up at Camp Farouq.[3] He must have been a good student, for KSM considered including him in the 9/11 suicide team. Osama bin Laden nixed that idea; he thought Faqasi had greater potential as an organizer. So, before the American assault on Tora Bora, KSM sent him back to Saudi Arabia to set up ways for getting mujahideen home through Syria. He also established a sleeper cell in Medina to recruit students from the local university and was the link through which money raised by Ayiri made its way to Central Command. Despite his lack of experience on the battlefield, therefore, Faqasi had in a short time proved a capable administrator, and he was also close to Central Command.

Central Command was informed of their decision and shortly thereafter Bin Laden sent a letter through an intermediary rejecting Faqasi's appointment.[4] Instead, he made it clear that Hajj was the leader. However, he also ordered Hajj to form a Shura Council, to which all four malcontents were appointed. Turki al-Dandani – a close ally of Hajj – was also added to the council, perhaps to provide a counterweight to the gang of four who had tried to take matters into their own hands.

Bin Laden's instructions were followed and the other lieutenants accepted Hajj's leadership. However, a note of disunity had been sounded, which would reverberate ominously in the months and years to come.

Hajj had to proceed with caution. The raid on the Marwa rest house had shown that the MOI was on the case and he knew it was only a matter of time before there would be another knock on the door.

Fortunately, Hajj was under no pressure to rush. The Shura Council were agreed that they needed to keep a steady eye on their ultimate goal: to foment a popular uprising against the House of Saud. When the time was ripe, and after enough ideological grooming, the people would rise up. And when they did, the Organization would be there, armed to the teeth and numbering in the tens or even hundreds of thousands, to direct the people's rage in their own preferred direction. To carry it off, they would need more recruits, more weapons, and detailed plans of attack.

The different networks – Muqrin's, Dandani's, Faqasi's, and the rest – came up with a staggering number of attack ideas targeting Westerners and government officials. They wanted to bomb a corporate bus used by employees of Aramco; to hijack a school bus full of Western children and hold them for ransom; to bomb King Khalid Air Base in Khamis Mushayt and the American embassy in Riyadh; to attack a church in Bahrain; to send a suicide bomber to Qatar; to assassinate Prince Muhammad; and much else beside.[5] Their ideas far outstripped their capabilities, but the scale of their ambitions was a sign of their deadly seriousness.

As his acolytes inside the Kingdom put in place the pieces necessary for carrying out his aims, Osama bin Laden composed a sermon which, many believe, carried a coded message for the Saudi cell leaders. He wrote it to commemorate Eid al-Adha, the most important feast in the Islamic calendar, and on 16 February 2003, five days after the feast, Al Jazeera broadcast it to the world. The sermon came on the heels of US Secretary of State Colin Powell's appearance before the UN General Assembly, during which he presented America's case for toppling Saddam Hussein.

Bin Laden referred directly to the plan to invade Iraq, which he called the 'Bush-Blair Axis' in an allusion to the Sykes-Picot Agreement of 1916 that divided the Middle East into British and

French spheres of influence. 'The Bush-Blair Axis claims that it wants to annihilate terrorism, but it is no longer a secret – even to the masses – that it really wants to annihilate Islam. Nonetheless, in their speeches and statements, the rulers of the [Middle East] affirm their support for Bush in his "war on terror", which is in fact a war against Islam and Muslims. This is clear treachery against our faith and against the Umma.'[6] The real aim of American military aggression in the Middle East was an invasion of Saudi Arabia and the destruction of Mecca and Medina. 'Under the banner of the cross, their goal is the destruction and despoliation of the people of God's beloved prophet.'

It is doubtful that Bin Laden himself believed his inflated rhetoric, but he had taken the pulse of Muslim public opinion and knew that the proposed invasion of Iraq was deeply unpopular. Even ordinary Saudis, who had never felt any love for Saddam Hussein, were largely opposed to another American intervention, so much so that a day after the broadcast, Prince Saud al-Faisal the foreign minister publicly warned the United States against the war.[7] The growing upswell of anti-American sentiment served Bin Laden's purposes perfectly, and the rest of Central Command agreed that it would be a mistake not to take advantage of this opportunity.

And so at the beginning of his sermon – or so many intelligence analysts believe – Bin Laden selected a passage from the Qur'an which would make it clear to the cells inside the Kingdom that they should begin launching attacks as soon as possible. 'Once the Sacred Months are past,' he exclaimed, 'you may kill the idol-worshippers when you encounter them, punish them, and resist every move they make.'[8] To drive the message home, he then quoted a *hadith*, 'Expel the polytheists from the Arabian Peninsula,' explaining that the rulers of Islamic countries, including the House of Saud, were themselves little better than apostate idol-worshippers.[9]

*

Even if the sermon was not a veiled message, it is known that word reached Hajj to go ahead with the compound bombing plot. This was not, however, greeted with universal approval. Ayiri in particular was against it. He wrote letters to Saif al-Adel and KSM outlining his objections.[10] Recruitment had not been as successful as they had hoped, and they needed more time. Furthermore, Saudi donors were far from comfortable with the idea of a full-scale jihad on Saudi soil. If they recoiled too violently, money could dry up.

Adel was on Ayiri's side. In fact, from his perch in Iran, he could see that KSM's impatience to launch attacks globally threatened to further weaken the already battered movement. 'Stop rushing into action,' he upbraided KSM in a letter.[11] 'Take time to consider the succession of fatal disasters that have afflicted us over the past six months.' Bin Laden – whom Adel calls the Teacher – was to blame. 'A matter has been weighing on my mind, but I avoided mentioning it because the Teacher corresponds directly with you. I am referring to his unfortunate habit, which he refuses to give up, of simply replacing anyone who opposes him with someone who will put forward an argument in his defence. He clings to his own opinions and totally disregards everyone around him . . . He pushes you relentlessly, but unthinkingly. Has he not seen the news? Does he not comprehend what's been going on?'

Adel makes himself absolutely clear. 'We must completely halt all operations [outside Afghanistan] until we have sat down and considered the disaster we caused. The networks in East Asia, Europe, America, the Horn of Africa, Yemen, the Gulf, and Morocco have all fallen, and Pakistan is almost drowned . . . Regrettably, my brother, if you look back, you will find that you are the person solely responsible for all this. You undertook the mission, and in six months we have lost what it took six years to build . . . My beloved brother, stop all foreign operations. Stop sending people into captivity. Stop devising new plans, regardless of whether orders come from Bin Laden or not.'

KSM did not listen. Instead, he wrote to Ayiri, accusing him of negligence and of holding Bin Laden's orders in contempt. Bin Laden himself sent Hajj a direct message: launch the operation. This put Hajj in a difficult position, so he called a meeting. Dandani and Muqrin were there, and it quickly became apparent that they were at cross-purposes. As they both led Riyadh-based cells and had been entrusted with planning operations for the capital, there was already some tension between them, especially now that the security of Dandani's network had clearly been compromised. But beyond any simmering competition, Muqrin was in full agreement with Ayiri and dead set against taking any plan operational until they had better consolidated their position.

Hajj, however, inclined towards Dandani's view that the operation should go ahead and was loath to ignore Central Command. Yet he remained indecisive. He told Muqrin and Dandani that the matter was to be put on ice for two months. They should carry on recruiting, training, and planning operations, and should do their best to avoid the security services.[12]

We do not know how Central Command reacted to the Saudi network's delay. But the pressure on Hajj to launch was building. Ayiri was arrested in February in connection with the Bahraini plot, and though he was released after a few weeks, it was not a good sign. Then KSM himself was arrested on 1 March – who knew what information he would be forced to give up? Two weeks later, the accidental explosion in Jazeera blew their cover and led to more arrests. Then on 20 March the United States invaded Iraq, igniting anti-American protests across the Middle East. This was followed by the shootout in Seville and, on 29 April, another big arrest: the one-legged Attash, who had replaced Nashiri, was nabbed in Karachi.

Everything was balanced on a knife's edge. Hajj decided it was too dangerous to wait much longer. He told Dandani that the compound bombings were to go ahead. He set the date for the end of May.

Dandani's plan was to attack the three compounds simultaneously using pickup trucks wired with large fertilizer bombs. Saikhan sourced a large amount of explosive material in Yemen, stashed it in a hidden compartment inside a truck, filled the truck with fresh fish, and smuggled it into the Kingdom. At a farm in Qaseem, which Saikhan had turned into a car-bomb workshop, three trucks were wired up and driven to two safe houses in Riyadh.[13] There they were handed over to their most important elements – the would-be martyrs.

For the young men destined for martyrdom, life inside the Organization could be disorienting. They were frequently moved from safe house to safe house, often blindfolded, so they never knew where they were. They were forbidden to leave. Their food and drink were provided, and a caretaker, under whose name the house or apartment had usually been rented, would look after their basic needs. They used nicknames given them by the Organization, to ensure each other's anonymity should they be captured.

Yet despite this anonymity, they were united by bonds of camaraderie, a big attraction for young men accustomed to the ennui of Saudi life. The hint of danger surrounding Al Qaeda, of illicitness and excitement, was thrilling. Social restraints in the Kingdom's closed, conservative society limited young people's opportunities for fun and for uninhibited self-expression.

On an evening sometime in the spring of 2003, at one of Dandani's safe houses in Riyadh, a group of three young men sat in front of the camera. Cells had begun holding filming sessions to produce propaganda videos for the Internet. The leader of this threesome was Muhammad bin Shadhaf. A large man with African features, he had been a popular student at King Saud University in Riyadh. He was an active member of the university's drama department and had even performed as a stand-up comedian at university open mics. Then he had disappeared. When it emerged later what had happened to him, his former classmates were shocked. Shadhaf had never seemed a likely candidate for jihad.[14]

On the night of the filming, Shadhaf projected a sense of dignified calm. His two comrades, Muhammad al-Muqait and Ashraf al-Sayyed, were less mature. Dressed in pyjamas, they goofed around as a cameraman fiddled with the settings on the video recorder. Ashraf was a cheeky lad of about twenty. He began to sing with the melismatic stylings of a pop starlet:

> God is great! God is great!
> Oh Islam, religion of heroes,
> we all sacrifice ourselves for the Umma.
> In your service we make of our skulls
> a ladder to your glory.
> A ladder, a ladder.
> In your service we spill our blood
> For the bloodthirsty flag.
> In your service, in your service …

'… Uh … I don't know what comes next.'

'Um, Allahu akbar?' They all laughed.

'No,' Ashraf replied, and he began to mimic the Egyptian chanteuse Umm Kulthum, singing 'Aa-aa-aall myy-yy lii-ii-iife, I saa-aa-y …' and then switched to a mocking rendition of the Saudi national anthem:

> Hasten to glory and supremacy!
> Glorify the creator of the heavens
> And raise the green fluttering flag
> Bearing the emblem of light!
> Repeat: God is great! God is great! …

'Ha ha, this'll be a music video before we're done!'

Hasten to glory and supremacy!
Long live the king, for the sake of the flag!

'Yeah, right. For the sake of his stomach, more like it,' Shadhaf interjected.

'Come on, it's the anthem,' Muqait chided. 'Sing it with some enthusiasm, why don't you?'

Ashraf got up. 'I'm going, brother.'

'Where to?'

Ashraf whispered, 'To the toilet.'

'Be quick, then.'

'Yes, with all my love,' teased Ashraf.

'Ach,' called out Shadhaf. 'Have you no shame?'

Later on, the boys became more serious. Ashraf stared into the camera and began to intone solemnly, 'In the name of God ... ahem ... In the name of God, the Merciful, the Compassionate. Prayers and peace be upon the most noble of prophets and messengers, our prophet Muhammad ... ahem ... our prophet Muhammad, peace be upon him ...' He hesitated. 'My God, I feel like the whole world is watching me!' Then, in a moment of sudden inspiration, he began to recite:

I shall make them drink not water
But from the cup of death.
Our black banners are like Muhammad's banner,
Only ours return crimson!

Like so many Al Qaeda recruits, Ashraf pictured himself as a knight on horseback carrying on the martial traditions of the first generations of Muslims, who swept out of the Arabian desert and conquered much of the civilized world. His enthusiasm grew. 'My Muslim brothers everywhere and my fellow mujahideen, I dedicate these words to you, that the breasts of believers might be healed. They are written in blood, a small price to pay for the reward in store. I say this … I say this …'

Ashraf stopped. 'Um, why do I say this?'

Shadhaf waved his hands at the cameraman. 'Wait, wait. Cut!'

They had written their statements themselves. The Organization called them wills, but they were more like sermons justifying the martyr-to-be's actions. The idea was to evoke the great Muslims of old and to be an exemplar of what in Arabic is called *adab*, a cross between good manners and refined speech which is a vital aspect of Islamic piety. Sitting up straight, clothes clean and pressed, face affecting a stern and noble aspect, he would begin: 'In the name of God, the Merciful, the Compassionate,' followed by the usual blessings upon the Prophet. Then with sharp bursts of rhythmic rhyming prose, seasoned with verses from the Qur'an and excerpts from the hadith, he would describe the suffering of his fellow Muslims and call down God's judgement upon the enemies of the religion.

But the performance was often hard to maintain. The young men who joined the Organization were not, broadly speaking, at the top of the class. Tripping over unfamiliar words and straining to conjugate correctly, they came across less as modern-day Saladins than as foolish schoolboys.

Muqait took his turn in front of the camera. After several read-throughs, Shadhaf said his time was up. 'Wait,' Muqait declared. 'I've got another message, in English.' He cleared his throat. 'To everybody he watching me, I will now address the West in their own language. I speak to now, to everybody listening me in his language, I wants to send a message for him. We want from all Christian and any enemy for Muslims so … One second, ahem … We want from all Christian … Wait, where did we get to?'

'Soldiers …'

'Ah yeah, soldiers, that's good … We want from all Christian soldiers to go out from Islamic land, and stop killing Muslims and to stop killing Muslims, or we will kill them as they killing us. Islam religion is the best . . . is the best religion in the world, because I will do everything to help our Muslims . . . brothers . . . our Muslim brothers, in everywhere, even if that will take me, take my life . . .' He stopped. 'Um, it's quite bad, isn't it?'

The cell filmed their wills over and over. There was little else to do, and it was a means of reassuring themselves that what they were planning was holy.

On 6 May, Dandani was at a safe house in the Seville district, not far from the Vinnell compound, one of his targets. Inside the house was a huge stash of weaponry: nearly three hundred kilograms of explosive material, fifty-five handmade grenades, four machine guns, and over two thousand bullets. There were also travel documents, false identity papers, and nearly £19,000 in various currencies.

A newspaper report at the time stated that a 10-year-old boy named Rayan Fahd was playing in the street near the safe house when three cars pulled up beside him. The rear passenger window rolled down and a bearded man asked him for directions to a house nearby. Rayan pointed to one further down the street and the three cars pulled away.

It was about 5 p.m. A few minutes later, Rayan's mother Munira noticed her son in the street. The cars had pulled up to the house Rayan had indicated, and she watched as ten men carried large black suitcases from the house to the cars. It was odd. The man who had moved into the house a few weeks before was not known to anyone in the neighbourhood, and now this. She called out to her boy and ordered him home.[15]

Suddenly, the men scrambled back into their cars. Further down the street a group of policemen were climbing out of a van. The cars sped off, but the policemen made their way towards the safe house, their weapons drawn.

What happened next would be described at length in an Al Qaeda publication:

> They noticed some of the security forces assembling outside, so immediately Turki gave the order to retreat ... Turki and four of the brethren got into a car (it was a Honda) – it is this car that later appeared in the local papers – and drove out through the main gates. The authorities shot at them, but Turki's return fire was so heavy that those surrounding the gate ran away and the brothers fled the neighbourhood. The police pursued, keeping their distance, then a car carrying two Mabahith officers broke away from the rest, approached Turki's car, and rammed it from behind. They were trying to force Turki to pull over. But Turki turned around, fired several rounds, and killed them. Their car swerved and hit the central reservation. Turki and his companions were saved.[16]

That is the Organization's account of the event. The MOI tells a different story. The Security Patrols had been casing the neighbourhood for six weeks. Eventually they spotted Dandani's car and trailed it to the safe house, which was placed under 24-hour surveillance. Orders came in to arrest the men inside, and when MOI officers moved in, they were unexpectedly fired upon. A group of armed men fled down the street and into a car. The police followed and were able to disable the car with gunfire, so the militants got out and, forcing a man out of a passing Mercedes, drove off in it down the Eastern Ring Road. There was an opening in the chain-link fence beside the road, and they drove through it so quickly that the police cars did not have time to make the sharp turn themselves. Dandani and his men were thus able to flee unpursued into the Izdihar district, where they dumped the Mercedes and stole another car, this time a van. It was later also found abandoned.[17]

Dandani and his men had been trained to use multiple stolen

cars in escapes. By the time word had spread to keep an eye out for a specific car, that car had already been ditched for another. It ensured that the MOI was always one step behind.

After abandoning the car, Dandani and his companions disappeared into the surrounding neighbourhood on foot. They made their way to Hajj and told him what had happened. Presumably their conversation was heated; this was the third time Dandani's network had been compromised, and Hajj must have been worried that the MOI was on the verge of uncovering the compound bombings plan and shutting it down.

Two days later, a poster identifying nineteen of the Kingdom's most wanted men was published and distributed throughout the country. It was remarkably accurate: every member of the Shura Council was on the list. The Mabahith had drawn it up based mostly on evidence found at the scene of the accidental explosion in the Jazeera neighbourhood, and, in an unprecedented move, Saudi TV broadcast the names.[18] The MOI was appealing directly to Saudi citizens and to the family members of the wanted men, entreating them to ring a national security hotline or to visit their local police station, should they have any information. 'Do not give them protection or shelter,' the country was warned.[19] Mugshots of many of the wanted men were also released, though the photos were very poor in quality – in most cases the true faces behind the names of these men remained worryingly unknown.

The Organization responded to the List of Nineteen with indignation. Ayiri wrote an official response in the form of an online letter addressed to all Muslims.[20] His tone was weary. He called the charges raised against him and his brothers a 'fabrication', just another in a long list of calumnies suffered by the mujahideen. The Mabahith are only the lapdogs of the CIA, Ayiri said, and he spelt out a warning: 'Anyone thinking of handing us over to the United States or otherwise helping the United States achieve their designs on us, we will treat him as if he were an American. We shall repel this injustice and enmity by every means. Anyone who wants to be safe from us should stay clear of us.'

He ended on a personal note. 'These final words I send to my daughters, since the system of oppression and pursuit prevents me from seeing them and keeps me far from them. I have become a stranger in my own country.'

On 9 May, Dandani drove to a large safe house in the Shifa neighbourhood. It was a temporary home for those cell members whom Dandani had selected to carry out one of the three bombings. Their target was the Alhambra Oasis Village, a sprawling, leafy compound in the Granada neighbourhood, beside the highway junction where the Eastern Ring Road meets the Dammam Road. After gathering them together in the safe house's majlis, Dandani made an announcement. 'I bring you glad tidings,' he said. 'The operation will take place in seventy-two hours. Bid heaven hello for me.'

At another safe house elsewhere in the city, Rakan al-Saikhan delivered the same message to the teams that would bomb the Vinnell compound and the third target, a compound called Jadawel. Hajj had become thoroughly spooked and so had decided to move the attack forward to 12 May. Instead of using new recruits for the bombing as he had planned, he ordered Dandani to use experienced mujahideen.[21] Fourteen cell members were divided up into three teams. Muhammad bin Shadhaf, the former stand-up comic, was leader of the Alhambra team. The Vinnell team was led by Khalid al-Juhani, and the Jadawel team by Hazim al-Kashmiri.[22]

Juhani was the jihadist whose suicide video had been discovered in Kabul. He was one of the Organization's stars.[23] He had purchased the boat used in the *Cole* attack, and then worked with Nashiri on the abortive Strait of Hormuz operation.[24] But after Afghanistan, it is believed he grew depressed.

Once he had returned to Saudi Arabia, Hajj sent him to live with a Moroccan jihadist, **Karim al-Mejjati**, who was living in Riyadh with his family. Then, when the video from the Kabul house exposed Juhani's identity, he and Mejjati went into hiding.[25] Mejjati's wife was arrested and questioned about Juhani's whereabouts, and though she claimed not to know, she did say that Mejjati and Hajj had tried to find him a wife to combat his depression.[26] Perhaps, given all this, Juhani was selected to lead one of the attack teams because his usefulness to the Organization was limited. At the same time, his years of experience in Bosnia and Afghanistan made him a safe pair of hands for a difficult suicide mission.

Less is known about Kashmiri. He was the son of a retired Mabahith major-general and reveals the fact in his suicide video.[27] It is no wonder that the Organization made him such a prominent part of the attack. By recruiting the son of a high-ranking officer, they showed that even the Saudi political establishment was not immune to their call for jihad against the state and its Western allies.

In the video, Kashmiri is stern. He says in English, 'For the American soldiers, we say: you have to know that your government has become a big evil, killing innocent people, destroying homes, stealing our money, and holding our sons in gaol. We promise that you will not see from us anything else, just bombs, fire, destroying homes and cutting off your heads. Our mujahideen are coming to you very soon to let you see what you didn't see before.'

The 12th of May was a Monday. At around 10:30 p.m., five cars carrying twenty-four young men departed from the two safe houses.[28] Along with the three wired-up trucks were two support vehicles of armed men tasked with keeping the way clear for the car bombs.[29] In one of the car bombs, a jihadist lay bound and gagged; he had panicked just before they were due to set out, and his fellow cell members had been afraid to leave him behind, in case he escaped and alerted the authorities.[30] Any fraternal ties were subordinate to the mission.

The cars split up and headed towards their different targets. Shadhaf and his team were in one of the car bombs, a GMC Suburban. Their support vehicle was a Toyota saloon. 'Allahu akbar, Allahu akbar, Allahu akbar . . .' Shadhaf chanted rhythmically. The Suburban was heading for the Alhambra Oasis Village. 'O God, accept us among your martyrs.'

Muqait and Ashraf chanted in return: 'Allahu akbar, Allahu akbar, Allahu akbar . . .'

'O God, grant that we should be counted among those who punish the enemies of God . . .'

Their rhythmic chanting became more and more fervent. It was prayer, but they were also psyching themselves up for what awaited them.

'There is no god but God, I ask forgiveness from God . . . Wait, brother. Why are you . . .?'

They had turned down the wrong street.

'Reverse, reverse.' Muqait opened the rear passenger door to look behind the car. 'No, leave it, don't open it. I'm reversing.'

'Yeah, get back on the main road.'

They manoeuvred the truck back into the road. 'All right, let's begin again. In the name of God . . .'

'Allahu akbar, Allahu akbar, Allahu akbar . . .'

'Expel them, O God, expel the polytheists from the Arabian Peninsula.'

'Amen!'

'O God, expel them. Tear their bodies to shreds.'

'Amen!'

They were nearing the compound. Their Toyota support vehicle passed them and sped on ahead to the gatehouse. 'That's okay, let him pass, let him pass.'

Shadhaf slowed the car. 'This worldly life is green and beautiful,' he said, 'but what God has promised us is better and everlasting.'

'Allahu akbar!'

After a moment's silence, shots began to ring out. The Toyota had tailgated a resident's car as it passed through the barrier, and now the gunmen were shooting the gatehouse guard. They held the gate open for Shadhaf and his companions, who raced inside.

'Are you ready?' Shadhaf asked. 'We are right on the heels of the Americans and the Britons! We are getting nearer, and yet we are not afraid!' The terrorists in the back seat began shooting out the window. 'Allahu akbar! Allahu akbar!' Their enthusiasm had reached fever pitch. 'We are now inside the compound! We will bring the war to the enemies of God!'

'Allahu akbar, Allahu akbar, Allahu akbar . . .!'[31]

4

A Bloody Success

The Alhambra Oasis Village, 12 May 2003

The residents of the Alhambra Oasis Village had been settling down for the night. Many were expatriate workers, but they were not the majority. Seventy per cent of the residents were well-to-do Saudis, who had moved there to enjoy a Western lifestyle.[1]

Then the gunfire started. Residents ran for safety as two cars shot their way to the compound's community centre. Several were killed as they ran. One of the cars, a Suburban, drove into position beside the community centre's pool as the other car took cover about fifty metres away. Its passengers planned to continue killing after the explosion.

But when the bomb went off at 11:17 p.m. – in what was Saudi Arabia's first ever suicide attack – the blast was so enormous that it killed not only the suicide bombers, but the gunmen inside the Toyota as well. The supersonic shock wave cracked windows up to two miles away. The sound of gunshots and small explosions continued for some time and the surviving residents thought there were still terrorists on the loose. But the sounds were the result of 'cook-off' ammunition inside the burning Toyota.[2]

Where the Suburban had stood only moments before, there was now a smoking crater. The body of a toddler floated in the pool. Cars parked nearby had been transformed into charred wrecks and golf balls were strewn about the wreckage; the car bomb had been stuffed with them to make the explosion deadlier.[3] 'Blood is everywhere,' the local *Los Angeles Times* correspondent wrote. 'It is sprayed in great arcs across walls, it sits in dried pools along hallways and it soaks beds clear through the mattress. Here and there among the crushed chairs and shattered glass, tiny crimson footprints can be seen where bloodied children ran to escape.'[4]

Guards at the Vinnell compound heard the explosion at Alhambra and saw it flash against the night sky. They raced to their posts just as a Ford saloon carrying armed men drove up to the gatehouse followed closely by a Dodge pickup. The saloon rammed the gate but could not get through, so the attackers got out and began firing. The young guard manning the gate's machine gun did not know how to load it and was quickly shot along with the other guards.[5] The militants then entered the gatehouse and raised the security barrier.

The pickup raced deep into the compound and exploded in front of one of its large residential buildings, completely ripping off its façade. It looked like a doll's house, each small bedroom standing remarkably untouched. In several cases the beds were still neatly made. But the explosion killed seven Americans, and blood-covered survivors made their way out of the rubble to gather at the compound's pool.[6] It was a stroke of pure luck that the building had largely been empty. Most of the retired American servicemen who lived there were in the desert on training manoeuvres.[7]

Residents of the Jadawel compound were even luckier. The attack team managed to get past the first gate at the rear corner of the compound, killing a security guard, a support staffer, and a member of the Saudi Royal Air Force.[8] However, their progress was arrested outside a second gate, and they were forced to detonate there. The blast, which injured seven compound workers, killed only the bombers. The ten-foot crater was testament to the death toll they might have wrought had they been able to get closer.[9] It seems they had not properly surveilled the compound for some time, because until two months earlier the large metal gate at the service entrance was being left open between dawn and midnight.[10]

The number of those killed at the other two compounds was significant: twenty-seven innocent people lost their lives. A further 160 were wounded. Nine among the dead and more than two dozen among the wounded were Americans. The remaining casualties represented a broad cross-section of expatriate society: Egyptians, Filipinos, Jordanians, and British, and one dead each from Australia, Ireland, Lebanon, and Switzerland. In addition, seven Saudi citizens died.

The Organization's first operation inside the Kingdom was a bloody success.

When the attacks happened, **Robert Jordan**, the American ambassador, was about to turn in for the night. He had spent the day in meetings preparing for an official visit from Colin Powell, who was due to arrive in the Kingdom the following day.

The phone rang. Margaret Scobey, Jordan's deputy chief of mission, was on the line. 'The Alhambra compound has been bombed,' she told him. Not Alhambra, he thought. He had always liked that compound. Who would bomb it? It was not even remotely a military target.

He summoned his emergency response team to the embassy. Just as he was about to set off on the ten-minute drive from Quincy House, the ambassadorial residence, Scobey rang again. 'Two more compounds have been attacked, Jadawel and Vinnell.' Jordan realized he had an attack on his hands bearing the hallmarks of Al Qaeda.[11]

Jordan was livid. For months, intelligence analysts had been warning him that an attack on compounds in Riyadh was imminent. So on 29 April he had written a letter to Prince Nayef requesting more security for Western assets in the Kingdom, including housing compounds. Then on 1 May, after an American in Jubail was fired at by a Saudi gunman, forcing the embassy to issue an official warning, he wrote to the prince again.[12] Finally he wrote a third time, after the raid on Dandani's safe house in Seville. The safe house was less than a kilometre from Jadawel, and so Jordan specifically mentioned the compound as a likely target.

But his requests had received no reply. It was simply the Saudi way, he thought at first. In his words, 'You never know what they are doing until they've done it.' But when he chased it up he was given 'the inshallah thing, when they say "Yes, we're working on it," but are really just kicking the can down the road.' Now his fears had been realized.

Rushing to the embassy, Jordan rang a friend who lived at Alhambra, to make sure he was still alive. Alfie Johnson, his voice trembling, was hiding in a cupboard with his two kids. Once at the embassy, Jordan liaised with his regional security officer, the Saudi police and military, and with Washington. In the chaos, no one could be sure that there would not be more bombings. Finally, after three anxious hours, Jordan's regional security officer gave the all-clear.

At dawn, Jordan went to a hospital which was treating the victims. The emergency room was full of wounded being looked after by the mainly Western doctors and Filipina nurses. Because many were men who had left their families at home or had sent them there in the tense weeks preceding the bombings, there were relatively few family members present. But it was Jordan's responsibility to meet what family members were there, and to give them the American government's condolences.

One American woman, her young child at her side, was in a

state of shock; her Jordanian husband had died in the attack. A young American man lay in an operating theatre, covered in tubes; his head was heavily bandaged and the ambassador was told that he was brain dead. They took him off life support shortly afterwards. Another American's face had been crushed and his eye socket smashed. Jordan rang the man's family in Puerto Rico to break the news.

Once his initial anger subsided, Jordan felt disappointed. He had spent eighteen months trying to build bridges between American counterterrorism agents and their Saudi counterparts. The two sides' working relationship had improved, and after months of prodding, the Saudis had finally started doing something about terrorist financing. It was not enough, but it had been a start.

Colin Powell arrived later that morning. Directly from the airport, Jordan took him to the Vinnell compound. They were surrounded by American security and members of the press. 'This was a well-planned terrorist attack,' Powell told a reporter. 'Obviously the facility had been cased, as had the others. Very well executed. It shows the nature of the enemy we are working against.'[13] Then, as the Secretary of State and the ambassador stood looking up at the devastation, an enormous gust of wind blew so much dust, ash, and debris into the air that their nervous bodyguards grabbed them and threw them to the ground. When the wind calmed again, the two were bundled back into their car. They had an appointment with the crown prince.

They were shown into Abdullah's office. Jordan was surprised by the reception he received. 'Abdullah stood up and walked straight towards me,' Jordan recalls. 'His face looked serious, and he came right out and said, "Mr Ambassador, I owe you an apology. You asked for the additional security, and I was the one who thought you didn't need it. That was my mistake." It was clear he'd taken personal responsibility for the death of our civilians. And then he said, "We will find these criminals, and we will bring them to justice."'

Colin Powell sat down with the crown prince at a press conference. 'Let me begin today,' Powell said, 'by expressing my condolences to the families of all those who lost their lives this morning in this terrible terrorist tragedy.'[14] They both confirmed their two countries' continued commitment to close cooperation.

Because so many of the dead and wounded were Americans, the FBI immediately got involved. Under American law, the FBI has jurisdiction over any crime scene involving Americans, provided the host country agrees. Four days later, on 16 May, six FBI investigators arrived to gather evidence.[15] The Saudis had refused to let them bring their weapons with them, which had ruffled feathers. And the FBI did not trust Saudi forensics to do an adequate job. They had found them less than cooperative seven years before after the Khobar Towers bombing.[16] However, when they arrived and witnessed for themselves the sophistication of the Saudi team, as well as the equipment at their disposal for analysing DNA samples, they were satisfied, and the two teams worked together collecting evidence.[17] The Saudis were left to carry on with their investigation, free from American interference.[18]

Meanwhile, Jordan faced a grilling from the American media. In general, Americans knew little about Saudi Arabia. In their imaginations the Kingdom boiled down to sand and oil – and terrorism. Since 9/11 especially, most Americans assumed the Kingdom was crawling with terrorists. When the footage of the compound bombings reached American TV screens, voices were raised: why had security at the compounds been so lax?

So despite the crown prince's apology, Jordan felt called upon to defend himself and his government. On CBS's *The Early Show*, Jordan said, 'We contacted the Saudi government, in fact on several occasions, to request that added security be provided to all Western residential compounds and government installations in the Kingdom. But they did not, as of the time of this tragic event, provide the additional security we requested.'[19] And in an interview with *Good Morning America* on ABC, Jordan said that all non-essential American personnel should leave the Kingdom. 'We're hoping they can start leaving immediately.'[20] Jordan was not acting out of revenge. It was simply protocol. The American government was no longer sure that the Saudis could keep Americans inside the Kingdom safe.

Prince Bandar, the Saudi ambassador, tried to reassure America that Saudi Arabia repudiated the attacks absolutely. 'No words can express our feelings for the loss of innocent people who were murdered and injured,' he wrote in an official statement. 'The attack was an attack on humanity.'[21] Later, in a live television interview for NBC News, the prince was less diplomatic. 'I can assure you, when we catch those people, it's not gonna be an O.J. Simpson trial. It will be just, but it will be swift and severe. They deserve it.'[22]

The mainstream Saudi media was united in condemnation of the attacks. *Al-Riyadh* described the attackers as utterly bloodthirsty. 'The terrorists did not hesitate to delight in the sight of the blood and the body parts of the dead and wounded.'[23] The English-language daily *Arab News* was equally disgusted. 'Words are inadequate to express the shock, the revulsion, the outrage at the suicide bombings in Riyadh. Are expatriates working here an army of occupation, to be slaughtered and terrorized into leaving?'[24]

Abdullah Bajabeer in *Asharq Al-Awsat* tried to reassure. The attacks had only two possible aims: to destabilize the Kingdom, or to scare America into withdrawing its troops from the Middle East. (In a piece of morbid irony, only two weeks before, US Defense Secretary Donald Rumsfeld had announced that the United States would be withdrawing its troops from Saudi Arabia.) If the first, then the bombings were 'a national betrayal and crime against humanity', and even so, they had failed. The Kingdom's stability was assured. If the second, then they were laughably naïve. 'A few bombs and a few dead Americans won't scare the strongest country in the world. The 9/11 attacks didn't scare America into silence. Rather, they motivated it to hunt down terrorists everywhere.'[25]

Arab News argued that the bombings proved that Saudi Arabia needed to clean up its own backyard. 'For years we Saudis did not know how it felt to be victims of terrorism. That all changed on May 12th 2003 when terrorism came knocking at our own back door. We must now begin asking questions that we have shied away from in the past. We need to start examining, and taking an analytical look at, our lifestyles, our upbringing, and our tolerance of other faiths and other peoples.'[26]

The Organization added its voice to the media fray. Ayiri's online 'think tank', the Centre for Islamic Research and Studies, released a book a few weeks after the bombings. Its title is not pithy: *The Operation of 12 May: The East Riyadh Operation and Our War with the United States and its Agents*.[27] It lays out the Organization's ideology in simple terms and illustrates the psychological hallmarks of jihadist terrorists: defensiveness, paranoia, certitude, self-aggrandizement, and the subjection of everything to their own peculiar, cold logic.

The book begins with a section entitled 'The Situation in the Islamic World'. It restates the standard Islamist geopolitical narrative, which in some respects is similar to the worldview of anarcho-leftists who decry the overwhelming power of the modern nation state. The United States' position as a colonial world hyper-power, which it has enjoyed since the collapse of its erstwhile rival the Soviet Union, has few precedents. Only the mythologized figures of King Solomon and 'The Two-Horned One' (which is how Alexander the Great is referred to in the Qur'an) are described as having been similarly world-dominant. However, instead of ruling directly, America relies on local rulers to implement its policies. These rulers have subordinated the interests of their Muslim populations to the interests of an infidel power. This makes them apostates and, therefore, legitimate targets – as are all those in their service, including the military and police.

The solution, the book makes plain, is jihad. 'God has legitimized the fight against the infidels everywhere without exception. The Americans were in Riyadh, so we killed them in Riyadh. Whoever asks "Why in Riyadh?" should honestly ask himself then, "Why in Chechnya? Why in Bali? Why in Jerusalem?" . . . Removing the Americans from Saudi Arabia is a definite duty. However, removing them becomes an even greater duty when they use Saudi Arabia as a Crusader base from which to launch a third crusade against the Muslim country of Afghanistan, to kill Muslims in Iraq, and to defend Israel's security against its enemies.' Nor are Americans protected by treaties between their government and the Saudi king, because the king is an apostate.

The implications for the Saudi state were clear. For Prince Muhammad and the MOI, it was now a question of preparing themselves for battle.

The day after the bombings, Crown Prince Abdullah delivered a solemn address to the nation.

> The tragic, bloody and painful events that took place last night in the heart of our dear capital city, in which innocent citizens and foreign residents were killed and maimed, prove once again that terrorists are nothing but criminals. The whole Saudi nation stands shoulder to shoulder in condemning this heinous act. There can be no acceptance or justification of terrorism, nor any place for ideologies or beliefs which condone it. Therefore we warn anyone who would seek to justify these

crimes in the name of Islam: you shall be considered a terrorist collaborator and will share their fate.

A week later, the crown prince received George Tenet at the palace. The CIA director offered the Saudi ruler his deepest condolences, and though he must have been tempted to say, 'I told you so', he swallowed it. He was there to talk business. As he later wrote, 'I doubt if I've ever had a more direct conversation with anyone in my life.'[28]

He laid out before the crown prince everything the CIA knew. Chatter from Al Qaeda from as early as the previous autumn had been indicating that they were debating when to launch attacks in Saudi Arabia. Not if, when. The order to strike had then been given to Bin Laden's head of Saudi operations – a man the CIA knew as Abu Hazim al-Sha'ir, but whose real name was Khalid al-Hajj. And Khalid Sheikh Muhammad had confessed – probably through the ministrations of 'enhanced interrogation techniques' – that Bin Laden's first priority was to foment a Saudi revolution.

'Your Royal Highness,' Tenet said, 'your family and the end of its rule is the objective now. Al Qaeda operatives are prepared to assassinate members of the royal family and to attack key economic targets.' To prove it, Tenet revealed that an Al Qaeda affiliate in London had been overheard telling a Saudi dissident there that 'the assassination phase has already begun.'

Tenet's words had their desired effect. The crown prince was spurred into action. He gave Prince Muhammad sweeping authority to lead the fightback.

A large-scale manhunt commenced. Checkpoints were set up across the country. Even cars belonging to the royal family were searched. Security at foreign embassies was stepped up, and government spokesmen admitted that the bombings were possibly the start of an extended wave of attacks. All housing compounds as well as shopping malls and other heavily visited areas were placed under overt and covert surveillance. Police patrols combed the streets, and the intelligence services went into overdrive.[29] The information they had been collecting had proved inadequate, and they should have listened to the Americans' warnings. Such a profound failure must not happen again.

The bombings introduced a new note of anxiety and uncertainty into Saudi society, heightened by the new checkpoints and stop-and-searches. 'We need the security,' a Saudi man was quoted as admitting. 'But we are really scared now. We don't know what is going to happen next.'[30] A young man said Saudi attitudes toward Al Qaeda had radically shifted. '9/11 meant nothing in Saudi Arabia,' he admitted. 'Some didn't believe that any Saudis were involved in it, others thought it was a conspiracy or was deserved because of America's support for Israel. May 12th was our 9/11. Since then Saudis have had to recognize that Al Qaeda is not a fantasy. It is here.'[31]

There is no doubt that ordinary Saudis did not countenance the bombers' disregard for human life and property or their disruption of the peace. They found it especially disturbing that just under half of those killed were Arabs, some of them Muslims. A Saudi police officer was quoted as saying, 'They say we support terrorism. We are victims like everyone else.'[32] Abdullah al-Blehed, an aide to the governor of Riyadh whose son was one of the Saudis killed in the Alhambra bombing, told the *New York Times*, 'Those people who say they want to make jihad against the United States or Israel, what they did is pointless. Jihad is not like this.'[33]

Meanwhile at the palace, Crown Prince Abdullah began asking himself some hard questions. He knew that however much they were now lashing out at Al Qaeda, the majority of his people basically agreed with the Organization's ideological underpinnings. It was this fact above all that gave hope to his enemy.[34]

Osama bin Laden. By spilling the blood of Abdullah's foreign guests, Saudi Arabia's pre-eminent prodigal son had put the crown prince to shame. Bin Laden had been a thorn in the royal family's side for over a decade, ever since King Fahd had politely refused his offer, in the wake of Iraq's invasion of Kuwait, to deal with Saddam Hussein using mujahideen from the Afghan campaign. Bin Laden never forgave the House of Saud for passing him over in favour of American troops.[35] By 1994, he had become such an embarrassment that the king had been forced to strip him of his citizenship and persuade the fabulously wealthy Bin Laden family to cut him off financially.

Now Bin Laden was trying to turn the people against the government, and his first step was to drive a wedge between the Kingdom and America. That is why he had used so many Saudis in 9/11, Abdullah believed, and the rupture in Saudi–US relations that followed had played right into his hands. Now his fighters had come home and were using violence to push the same agenda. Abdullah doubted that the Kingdom's relationship with America would be strained to breaking point. He and President Bush had grown close during a summit at Crawford Ranch the year before, and their bond would survive the odd wobble. Rather, the question foremost in the crown prince's mind was, 'Will Al Qaeda be able to sway enough Saudis to support Bin Laden's power grab?' About that, he was less sanguine.

The Saudi structure of power is a three-sided pyramid. The king is on top, but his power is absolute only on paper. In actual fact his job is to make sure the three sides of the pyramid stay in harmony. It is a tricky balancing act; however, long practice had made the rulers of Saudi Arabia adept at it.

One side of the pyramid is made up of the rest of the royal family. They are the public face of power. By dominating the ministries, controlling the oil revenues, and presiding over polite society, the royal family's power is direct and obvious. The other two sides of the pyramid, however, are almost equally powerful. One is made up of the clerics who oversee the religious establishment, and the other is the urban bourgeoisie who run the civil service and the media and direct large swathes of the country's economy.

From the very beginning, Saudi clerics have played a crucial role in securing the royal family's legitimacy. Clerics pledge the House of Saud their loyalty, but this support is conditional. As long as the king continues to defend Wahhabism and does not encroach too much upon the clerics' right to regulate social life, religion, and the education system, then his right to rule is secure. Move the country too far in the direction of modern liberalism, however, and the clerics will withdraw their support. Saudi princes, therefore, have always had to take care to present themselves as the conservatives the clerics want them to be. This is not always easy. Many junior members of the royal family have received a Western education and are much more liberally oriented – in private at least – than the clerics.

They share this more progressive outlook with the bourgeoisie, whose support is just as crucial. Though broadly speaking very conservative, wealthy Saudis want the country to 'catch up' with the rest of the world and would be happy for religion to play a less dominant role in education and society. Around the time of the bombings, this was the class pushing for the country to make the economic and political reforms necessary for joining the World Trade Organization.[36] Should the royal family accommodate the clerics too much, the reformist voices from among the bourgeoisie would grow louder and the House of Saud's rule might be undermined.

At the base of the pyramid sits the rest of society, poor and middle-class Saudis, both Bedouin and urban. From them the royal family commands love and obedience, the clerics demand they adhere to the Wahhabi interpretation of Islam, and the bourgeoisie insist they become more open to the outside world and participate in the increasingly global economy.

There is obviously tension between these different demands, but ordinary Saudis have generally gone along with them. The royal family has earned their loyalty and even love – and the royal family's popularity cannot be denied – though some people say it has not been earned so much as bought via the state's generous welfare system, subsidies, and direct payments to citizens. The clerics are trusted because Saudis are instinctively religious and, as a rule, averse to social change – a part of their national character which had often led to bursts of reactionary populism.[37] And the bourgeoisie are welcomed because their business savvy had improved the country's material circumstances enormously.

Looking back over the previous twenty years, however, Abdullah saw that much had changed inside his country which had left the future in doubt. The middle class was shrinking. In 1980 per capita income had almost been equal to that of the United States. However, a population boom had reduced average incomes to a third of what they had been and left the country awash with unemployed young men. It was not only that decades of state largesse had made the younger generation disinclined to work, but also that the education system, which overemphasized religious instruction, had failed to give them the skills they needed to work productively. Moreover, Saudi Arabia's economy was not dynamic enough to cope with the higher population, and since the price of oil had collapsed to only nine dollars a barrel by the end of the 1990s, the state was not as able to pick up the slack.

Abdullah publicly declared in 1999 that Saudis would have to 'get used to a different way of life' after the government's budget was slashed by 16 per cent.[38] But he was not heartless. The previous December the crown prince had stunned Saudi society when he visited the poorest neighbourhoods in Riyadh and brought the press with him.[39] The government had to do something about rising poverty, and acknowledging the problem publicly was a start. It would at least help deflect attention from the country's conspicuous income inequality.

A few months before Abdullah's visit to the slums, King Fahd, despite his poor health, had raised eyebrows holidaying on the Spanish coast aboard his 234-foot yacht. He had taken fifty Mercedes and 350 attendants with him, and had had $2000 worth of flowers delivered every day.[40] Abdullah frowned on that sort of extravagance. His own holidays in Morocco were comparably modest affairs, and a few months before the bombings he informed members of the royal family – who number in the tens of thousands – that they would have to start paying their own telephone and electricity bills, as well as forking out for their own flights on the national airline.[41] It was not only that he personally disliked his family's spendthrift ways. He also knew that the gross disparity between the very rich and even the middle class in Saudi Arabia could be exploited by extremists like Al Qaeda to win support for their cause.

However, Al Qaeda did not just target the people's frustrated material ambitions. Even more than that, the group's firebrand rhetoric focused on their religious convictions. And in this area too Abdullah could see that over the past few decades problems had emerged.

Al Qaeda's takfeerism was nothing new. Wahhabism itself had started out as a takfeeri movement.[42] When the first Wahhabis began conquering the Peninsula in the eighteenth century, clerics throughout the Ottoman Empire complained that the new revivalists were accusing their fellow Arabs of not being true Muslims, and that they were using the accusation to justify killing them and appropriating their property. Indeed, one of Muhammad Ibn al-Wahhab's most enduring principles was, 'Whoever does not practise takfeer upon unbelievers, or doubts that they are unbelievers, or approves of their way of thinking, that person is himself an unbeliever.' However, over the course of the twentieth century, the state religion had grown steadily more moderate. King Abdulaziz's *realpolitik* in the 1930s and 1940s and King Faisal's pan-Islamism in the 1960s and 1970s side-lined (and in some cases liquidated) the takfeeris who still felt it their mission to purify the Umma of idol-worshippers and infidels.[43]

And yet other forms of takfeerism besides Wahhabism were on offer to Saudis. In the 1960s and 1970s, Saudi Arabia became a safe haven for takfeeri members of the Muslim Brotherhood who had been hounded out of Egypt, Syria, and Iraq by secularist nationalist dictators. This represented a change of policy. The House of Saud had previously held the Brotherhood in suspicion, but by King Faisal's reign, Arab nationalism was seen as a greater threat to the Saudi monarchy than the Brotherhood's political activism. On the principle that the enemy of my enemy is my friend, and in line with his pan-Islamic ideas, Faisal invited them in.[44]

Brotherhood members were often well educated, and because the Kingdom suffered from a dearth of teachers, the exiles – many of whom were women – filled the vacuum. Also, it was the Brotherhood which first mobilized Saudi support for jihad against the Soviets in Afghanistan.[45] Gradually, Brotherhood ideas penetrated Saudi society: re-establishing the Caliphate; the use of violence as a political means; the Islamic world as a victim of outside aggression; and the West as a corrupter of the Muslim world. As one generation gave way to the next, many new Saudi professionals – doctors, lawyers, university professors, and so on – discovered that the Brotherhood gave otherwise suspect Islamist doctrines an air of respectability.

The influence of the Muslim Brotherhood was just one cause of the conservative resurgence. The aftermath of a long siege of the Grand Mosque in Mecca in 1979 also played a role. A messianic militant called Juhayman al-Utaybi along with around 450 armed followers took over the mosque in expectation of the End Times. They held out for three weeks, but eventually the government stormed the mosque. Juhayman and his takfeeri terrorists were destroyed. But not long afterwards, a group of senior clerics handed the government a list of comprehensive social and educational reforms which were eerily similar to the ones Juhayman had demanded. Because King Fahd thought his people were largely in agreement with Juhayman's criticisms of the government, he caved in. As Robert Lacey alliterated, 'The petrodollar went pious.'[46] After two decades of rising liberalization, the clock was turned back.

Now Abdullah saw that a whole generation had grown up inside a much more reactionary system than the one their fathers had known, and the ideas that came to be associated with Al Qaeda were often no different from what was being taught in schools or preached in Friday sermons. These ideas fused puritanical Wahhabism with the political activism of the Muslim Brotherhood to create something new, what has been called takfeeri-jihadism or neo-Salafism. It was radically revolutionary, and a real threat to the Saudi royal family.

Conventional Wahhabism had always maintained that any employment of non-state violence was *fitna*, an Arabic word meaning something like 'social chaos'. To disrupt social harmony is, in the Islamic world, a great sin and a capital offence; it is to 'work corruption on the earth'.[47] Should the clerics deem the ruler's behaviour to be sinful, public criticism of him might lead to social unrest, and would be unacceptable. Criticism must be private.[48]

Al Qaeda's takfeeri-jihadist ideas were the exact opposite. They legitimized jihad even in those Muslim countries not under attack from non-Muslim armies. They encouraged individual civilians, regardless of their position in the hierarchy, to ignore the fatwas issued by the state-sponsored muftis, take the law into their own hands, and perform acts of violence against state personnel and their allies. This was fitna of the worst kind.

Abdullah knew, therefore, that although waging this war

would require the police and even the military, in the end it would be a war of ideas. To counter takfeerism, the government would have to emphasize obedience to traditional authorities and encourage an understanding of Islam more explicitly linked to ideas of moderation and tolerance. The Mutaween, whose heavy-handedness with perceived sinners was notorious, would be de-fanged, and clerics who deviated from the government's insistence on religious moderation and obedience to the state would have to be dealt with. And they were, almost immediately. On 28 May, the Ministry of Islamic Affairs announced that it had sacked 44 'incompetent' Friday preachers, 160 imams, and 149 muezzins, and had suspended a further 1,357 religious officials from their duties.[49]

Also, a public information campaign countering Al Qaeda's message would be launched. The overall message conveyed was simple: those who practise or even sympathize with violent takfeerism are outsiders who seek to advance their own agenda to the detriment of social harmony. Billboards appeared bearing slogans like 'Our religion rejects terrorism' and 'We all say no to terrorism'. The cooperation of the public with the security services was also emphasized; posters were distributed showing two clasped hands, one arm in uniform and the other wearing a thobe.

But propaganda would not be enough. If Abdullah was to prevent another generation of jihadists from growing up, the country would have to see fundamental changes. Many of these were already part of Abdullah's reforming project: the economy would have to be more open; education would have to reject obscurantism and embrace science and technology; and a society famed for being closed and intolerant would have to start respecting difference. Plans were already in place for the Kingdom's first official National Dialogue conference. The following month, representatives from all the Kingdom's Muslim communities, including Shi'ites and Sufis, gathered to discuss reform. It would be deemed so successful that in August a permanent Center for National Dialogue would be established.[50]

So the crown prince had been pondering these moves towards social progress for some time. But Al Qaeda's arrival on the scene made their implementation that much more crucial.

In the meantime, however, the crown prince looked to Prince Muhammad and the security services. They needed to find those behind the Riyadh compound bombings, Turki al-Dandani especially, and bring them to justice. At the same time, they needed to hunt down the rest of Al Qaeda's leadership, map their network of cells and sub-cells, and one by one shut them down.

Prince Muhammad had at his disposal the many departments of the MOI. But as he took stock of the MOI's capabilities, he had every reason to feel concerned.

He knew that fighting Al Qaeda would require military-grade weaponry. The Kingdom had two conventional military forces, the armed forces and the National Guard. Neither fell under the umbrella of the MOI. Both were primarily designed to protect the country from external threats, although the National Guard did help protect sensitive areas inside the Kingdom, including oil installations and some American-run facilities. The prince would need the help of these outside organizations for weapons, armour, and vehicles – including helicopters.

Directly under Prince Muhammad's control were the MOI's paramilitary and internal security forces, of which there were many: the police, the border guards, the Security Patrols, the Mujahideen (primarily a tribal police force), the Emergency Forces, the Special Forces, and others. Precise numbers are difficult to ascertain, but all of these forces put together certainly amounted to more than 150,000 men.[51]

They had serious problems. First and foremost, they had received almost no training in counterterrorism, and lacked the equipment for it. Another problem was that although they all fell under the MOI's umbrella, Prince Muhammad's forces lacked a unified chain of command. Again, on paper they all reported to Prince Nayef. But some of the forces were organized at the provincial level, and some were not. Those that were reported directly to Nayef's full brother Prince Ahmed the deputy minister, who was officially Muhammad's superior, which added another layer in the command chain. And what was even worse, coordination between the forces was not great. Only very rarely would the border guards, for example, liaise with the police or the Emergency Forces, and in the event of a major emergency, there were no systems in place to ensure a rapid, coordinated response.

Similarly unwieldy were the Kingdom's intelligence services. As is the case in most countries, there were several, and some were not under his control.

Within the Ministry of Defence, each branch of the armed forces had an intelligence agency, and they were all managed by the United Military Intelligence Command. The National Guard had its own intelligence service as well, though it was primarily aimed at counter-intelligence. There were also intelligence agencies inside the Royal Guard and the Mutaween.

Within the MOI, the border guards and the Mujahideen had their own intelligence agencies, as did the anti-drugs force and the immigration department. But the MOI's main intelligence agency was of course the Mabahith. Domestic intelligence was its remit, and it had by far the largest budget of any such service in the Middle East.[52] A special Bureau of Analysis and Studies was affiliated to it.

Finally, there was the General Intelligence Presidency. It was the CIA to the Mabahith's FBI; fully independent, it reported directly to the crown prince. In addition to gathering foreign intelligence, the GIP was also the coordinator of the Kingdom's intelligence policy and strategy generally. The other intelligence services, including the Mabahith, were in theory supposed to report to it. However, in reality by early 2003 the GIP's reputation was not what it had once been, and it would play only a very minor role in the fight against the Organization.

The proliferation of agencies inside the Kingdom is not unique. It is worth remembering that the United States has sixteen intelligence agencies. And though the Kingdom's intelligence community was not as united as it should have been, America had discovered the same thing about its own intelligence services after 9/11. They would go on to create the Director of National Intelligence to liaise with the heads of the other services and report directly to the president. Prince Muhammad knew that the Kingdom could use something similar.

Beyond the question of inter-agency coordination, however, there were two even bigger problems. First, the methods used by the Mabahith were out of date. They were not much more sophisticated than they had been back in 1995, when four terrorists bombed the offices of the Vinnell Corporation off Olaya Street in downtown Riyadh. The men, who had fought in Afghanistan, were very professional. They kept the location under surveillance for a month, sourced the explosives in Yemen, wired them up to an old pickup truck, and detonated it remotely. Five American citizens and two Indians were killed, and over sixty injured. Yet, despite the fact that all four bombers had extensive contacts throughout the global jihadist community, after being apprehended they were subjected only to a summary interrogation, and once their guilt was proven, they were executed.[53]

Prince Muhammad had no time at all for that sort of slapdash policework. What was needed now was, on the one hand, deep and structured analysis, and, on the other, closer cooperation with the international intelligence community.[54] Steps in that direction had already been taken, but the compound bombings had made the prince's reforms even more urgent.

The second problem was the Mabahith's rigid hierarchy. Everyone reported only to his immediate supervisor. That meant that those at the top came into very little direct contact with field agents and analysts at the bottom, whose reports would often reach Prince Muhammad and the other Mabahith chiefs only after having been edited or filtered by middle managers. The older generation of officers saw no problem in this. It was how things had always been done. The prince would have to change it. From now on, he would invite field agents to report to him directly. If he found discrepancies between what they had to say and the way it had been written up by their superiors, the latter would face a fierce grilling.

Prince Muhammad was facing an uphill battle. His men were under-trained, poorly coordinated, and old-fashioned. The Organization's network needed to be understood and smashed, but the MOI had only barely mapped out its operational structure. What Prince Muhammad did have was money, firepower, and some good leads. Al Qaeda would soon find out what it was like to face the wrath of the Saudi state.

5

The Prince's Crackdown

The crackdown began right away. A Kalashnikov was spotted leaning up against a wall in the Alhambra Oasis Village, and investigators determined that at least one of the attackers must have survived and fled. They combed the surrounding neighbourhoods, looking for information that would lead to his capture. Then, two days later, a member of Dandani's southern cell was arrested. The MOI would later discover that this cell had been plotting to bomb King Khalid Air Base in Khamis Mushayt. He led police to the other members of the cell, and the weapons and explosives they had stockpiled for the attack were seized.

These arrests were only the beginning. Ten days later, investigators turned up another cache of explosive material: 132 rectangular-shaped moulds stashed in two bags weighing over 280 pounds. The MOI was beginning to understand that it faced a ruthless, well-funded, and well-armed enemy with a complex network structure. It would be difficult to crack. In the MOI's favour was the Organization's lack of security discipline, and this, along with a number of intrepid field agents who agreed to pose as jihadist recruits in order to infiltrate the cells, would over time enable the MOI to gather enough intelligence to form a good idea of how Al Qaeda worked.

The main obstacle the MOI faced was that, to guarantee the safety of the network as a whole, and in keeping with classic communist/anarchist organizational theory, no one person within the Organization was privy to all the information. On paper it was a rigid hierarchy, from the leader Khalid al-Hajj to his Shura Council to the network commanders to their lieutenants to new recruits to 'civilian' affiliates. More accurately, it was like a political party, and like every political party there were frequent differences of opinion between its members and those at the top.

Hajj's relationship with the Shura Council was not authoritarian. Rather, he was first among equals, and decisions were reached through deliberation and consensus, not by mere fiat. This was reflected higher up as well, in the Saudi network's relationship with Central Command, whose orders the council treated more like strong recommendations. There was something uniquely Saudi about this; it reflected the consensual way many Saudi institutions work, including – perhaps ironically – the Saudi court. The king is at the top, but he rules in close deliberation with his ministers, who individually exercise a great deal of autonomy. How often Hajj would convene the council, and whether its meetings were held in person or conducted remotely, was not known. They were unlikely to have met regularly; gathering all the top commanders together was dangerous.

Below the level of the Shura Council were the networks, each headed by a network commander. The networks were not divvied up geographically; one commander was not given the Riyadh network and another the network in Jeddah. Instead, each commander was left to build up as comprehensive a network of cells as he was able to. Ideally all the networks would include cells throughout the Kingdom.

Each network commander worked closely with a number of trusted subordinates, with whom he would brainstorm ideas for jihadist operations to be carried out by the network, from bombings to kidnappings to assassinations. Only a small minority of these ideas ever progressed beyond the idea stage. When one did, a plan would be drawn up and the individual cells would be enlisted to play their parts in carrying it out: surveillance, acquiring the necessary equipment, and executing the operation. The people doing the grunt work were usually new recruits who existed at different degrees of remove from the higher-ups, and who had access to only the barest minimum of information about the Organization, its leaders and structure, and its plans.

Each cell had also acquired a number of safe houses. These were usually rented, either by a cell member using false identification papers, or else by an individual affiliated to the cell who would use his real name on the rental agreement but then have no further involvement with the cell's activities. All manner of residences were used, including large detached townhouses, small flats, suburban villas, desert farms, and rest houses. Top of the MOI's agenda was to locate these safe houses and, one by one, shut them down.

The west coast of the Arabian Peninsula stretching from the Sinai down to the Yemeni border is known as the Hijaz. Ali al-Faqasi, number two on the List of Nineteen, was head of a network of cells based there. He was also squarely in the MOI's sights.

The Hijaz's three major cities – Mecca, Medina, and Jeddah – were important centres for Al Qaeda. Each year the pilgrimage to Mecca attracted hundreds of thousands of Muslims from all around the world, and the city of Medina had been a centre of Islamic scholarship since the beginnings of Islam. And as a result of centuries of migration, and before the recent rise of the Emirates, Jeddah was the most cosmopolitan city in Arabia.

Faqasi's deputy was a jihadist called **Sultan al-Qahtani**. Number sixteen on the List of Nineteen, Qahtani was born in 1974 to an officer in the security services. Like Faqasi, he came from the southwest, and studied physical education at college. Two weeks before 9/11, he told his family he was going on Hajj, but in fact he travelled to Afghanistan where he joined Al Qaeda. After Tora Bora he returned via Pakistan and re-enrolled in college. Now he was helping Faqasi recruit and train university students in Medina.

But the MOI had picked up the trail of Faqasi's and Qahtani's activities and were closing in to smash their network. At 1:30 p.m. on 28 May, the Emergency Forces in Medina were ordered to go to an Internet café on Abu Bakr Street and arrest three wanted men who had been under surveillance. 'At that time, I was the commander of the forces in Medina,' Major-General Khalid al-Harbi recalls. 'We responded at once; it was our first operation against the terrorists, and though few of us had received counterterrorism training, we were excited.' The Internet café was only three kilometres away. After setting up a simple security cordon, a group of officers entered the café just as the suspects were leaving. 'We searched them, but found nothing. Then we searched their cars.' Inside one of the cars was an electricity bill for a villa on Zuhair Qabas Street in the Askan district.

At 5 p.m. a small team of men headed to that address. 'It was a villa in a residential area. We scaled the external wall and opened the gate from the inside. The terrorists must have felt confident, because the front door of the villa was open.' Two men were relaxing in the sitting room when the team burst in on them. One immediately ran for the bathroom; the other ran towards weapons which were lying nearby, but he was tackled before he could reach them. An officer kicked down the bathroom door and saw the first suspect standing over the toilet breaking up CDs and floppy disks and throwing the pieces into the bowl.

The two men were Ali al-Khudayr and Ahmad al-Khalidi, two members of the Takfeeri Troika who had been in hiding since early March. As they were hauled outside, they cursed the security men as 'infidels' and 'agents of traitors'. Major-General Harbi found the whole experience unsettling. 'It was shocking how nondescript the villa looked from the outside. You would never have thought it contained the quantities of explosives and weapons we found there. We realized that raids were no longer a question of bursting in and making arrests. Because of the weaponry at their disposal, we would need to exercise extreme caution.'

A follow-up investigation revealed the location of another villa in Medina connected to the Organization, this one in the Azhari district. So the next day, at dawn, the Emergency Forces placed the villa under surveillance. It was only two kilometres from the Mosque of the Prophet, the second holiest site in Islam.

'While we were monitoring it, one of our team noticed two women exit the villa and get into a chauffeur-driven car, which sped off. It was peculiar for anyone to leave so early in the morning on a weekend.' The car's number plate was radioed to headquarters. Then at 9:30 a.m. word came that the villa was to be raided. Once again, a man climbed over the external wall and let in the raiding team. They stormed inside and made their way to the top floor, taking five armed men completely by surprise. Before any shots were fired, they were all rounded up. 'Again, we were surprised at the number of weapons we found. The magazines had been mounted in an unusual way, like they do in Afghanistan. Clearly the men had been prepared to shoot at us.'

One of the five was Nasr al-Fahd, the missing third member of the Takfeeri Troika. 'Fahd was surprised at his arrest. He wasn't expecting us to get him so quickly.' Under questioning he told his captors that Faqasi and Qahtani had been in the villa, but escaped. They could be found at a farm outside the city.

Fahd would confirm George Tenet's report that Faqasi had begun negotiations with arms smugglers to purchase a Russian nuclear device. In fact, just a week before, Fahd had issued a long fatwa called the *Treatise on the Use of Weapons of Mass Destruction against the Infidels*. The fatwa had been requested specifically by Al Qaeda to offer ideological justification for a huge attack, possibly one employing nuclear weapons.[1]

A team rushed off to apprehend the cell leader and his deputy. 'They must have known we were close, because when we got to the farm, they weren't there, and the computers – all of which had Internet access – were smashed up.' Another team had been dispatched to follow the two women who had been seen fleeing the villa that morning. 'Their car was driving towards Mecca. After about a hundred kilometres we pulled it over.' The driver was a minor operative in Faqasi's network, and his Syrian wife sat next to him in the front. In the back, however, were two Moroccan women. One of them was Faqasi's wife, the other was Qahtani's. They were carrying cash worth £145,000.[2] The MOI took the two women into custody. They could prove to be powerful bargaining chips.[3]

The raids had been a great victory. The Takfeeri Troika had been one of Al Qaeda's most powerful propaganda tools. Now that they were out of action, the Organization had no widely respected clerics to issue fatwas on its behalf. From now on, the MOI would find controlling attitudes toward terrorist violence much easier.

The MOI was not only focusing on the Hijaz. Three days after the Medina arrests, policemen patrolling the desert roads of Ha'il province in the northwest were on high alert. They had been told to keep a lookout for any suspicious vehicles, as the Mabahith had reason to believe one or more of Al Qaeda's leadership, fleeing Riyadh and the cities of Qaseem for the less densely populated north, would be passing through the province.

Along a barren stretch of road five kilometres northeast of the small village of Taruba, a convoy of security vehicles spied a Toyota jeep. They motioned to the driver to pull over, and he complied. One of the officers approached the car and asked the two men inside, both in their mid-thirties, to show him their identity cards.

Instead, the jeep suddenly sped away. The policeman rushed back to his vehicle, and the convoy raced off in pursuit. When they caught up with the jeep, a hand grenade was lobbed at them from the passenger-side window. The blast scored a direct hit on one of the patrol cars: two policemen were killed, and two more badly wounded. The rest of the patrol continued their pursuit and, radioing back to headquarters, arranged for a roadblock to be set up ahead, which forced the jeep to stop. The two men jumped out firing, and made off into the desert on foot. The policemen followed, also on foot, and chased the suspects for ten kilometres.

Gunfire flickered back and forth. Eventually, one of the suspects was so severely wounded that he fell to the ground. His companion, seeing the futility of his position, threw his gun away and signalled his surrender. Fearing that the fallen man, who was still conscious, was wearing a suicide bomb vest, the policemen could do little else but cordon off the area and wait. Finally, just after evening prayer, he breathed his last and they were able to search the body.

He had sustained many gunshot wounds and lacerations down his right side. In several places the blood-soaked robe had dried into the torn flesh. During a thorough search of the body, they discovered a handwritten letter, stained with blood and dated to the previous December. Beneath the valediction was scrawled the name of Osama bin Laden. The dead man was someone special.

They took the body to the morgue and thoroughly searched the jeep. Evidence gathered from the car directed investigators to a safe house in Qaseem, where along with the usual store of weapons, computers, and documents, they found a library of recordings of fiery speeches. Soon the dead man's identity was confirmed beyond a shadow of a doubt. He was the infamous Sabre, Yusuf al-Ayiri himself.

It was rather whimsical of history to kill off Ayiri just as Al Qaeda's campaign was getting started. No one had done more to prepare the ground for a terrorist insurrection in Saudi Arabia. But for the MOI his death was a Pyrrhic victory. It had taken out one of the Organization's most important leaders, but could only wonder at the wealth of tantalizing information that had died along with him.

Three months later a eulogy for the fallen 'martyr' was published on the Internet. The Sabre had been humble, wise, steadfast in faith, and generous; despite coming from a prosperous family, he ate very little, to steel himself for hardship. His death came at a difficult time for the mujahideen, the eulogy explains, and 'he was hunted until his very last day, when he chose to die as a martyr of God rather than be caught by the oppressors of the Arabian Peninsula – may God punish them.'[4]

Not long after Ayiri's death, the lone terrorist survivor of the attack on the Alhambra Oasis Villa was arrested. Other apprehended suspects had revealed his whereabouts during interrogations. The Kalashnikov that investigators had found at the scene had been propped up against the wall because he had used it as a boost to climb over. The suspect, whose identity will not be made public until he stands trial, was a relatively new recruit to Al Qaeda and not high up in the hierarchy. But the information he was able to give the Mabahith helped them put together what had happened in the weeks leading up to the bombings, and on the night itself.

On 7 June the MOI formally disclosed the test results from DNA samples taken from the twelve corpses found at the sites of the compound bombings. Five of the dead had been on the List of Nineteen, so adding their deaths to Ayiri's meant that only thirteen names remained.[5] However, one man who did not feature in the DNA results was Turki al-Dandani. He was at the top of the List of Nineteen and had escaped the MOI's clutches several times. Now that the Mabahith knew for certain he was still alive, every effort was directed towards tracking him down.

Meanwhile, back in the Hijaz, investigators had been studying an English document discovered in the Medina safe house at the end of May. It was a transcription of a recording of American pilots speaking back and forth as they carried out bombing missions in Afghanistan. With it was an Arabic translation of the English bearing the name of the translator: 'Hani Mohawk'. It was an intriguing lead. One of the men arrested during the raid, who called himself Majid, confessed that Hani Mohawk was the pseudonym of a cell member whom he had trained in passport and visa forgery.[6] Hani Mohawk was also known as Reda, but that name too was a pseudonym. He had been recruited by Faqasi and Qahtani, and most interestingly, he was American. That was all Majid would tell them.[7]

Before long, they made a breakthrough. A detainee let slip that Hani Mohawk was a student at the Islamic University of Medina, so they acquired a student yearbook from the university and showed it to him. He shuffled through the rows of photos and finally stopped at a face. 'Ahmed Omar Abu Ali' was printed beside it. They had their man.

On 8 June, two unarmed plain-clothes officers were dispatched to the university. Abu Ali was taking an exam, so they waited in the corridor as a university official went to fetch him. Before long, a handsome young man in spectacles stepped out. An officer placed a hand on his shoulder. 'We have something we want to talk to you about,' he told him. They calmly escorted him to their car outside. Then they handcuffed him.

First they drove to his dorm room, searched it, and gathered his belongings. Then they took him to a prison in Medina, from which he was transferred to a facility in Riyadh a few days later. He was interrogated several times, and on 24 July the Mabahith videotaped him reading out a handwritten confession.

Abu Ali was born in Houston and grew up in Falls Church, Virginia where he went to school at the Saudi Islamic Academy. His father was employed by the Saudi embassy in Washington D.C., and his family attended a notoriously conservative mosque. Two of the 9/11 attackers had prayed there, and Anwar al-Awlaki (later an infamous leader of Al Qaeda in Yemen) was once the mosque's imam.

In the middle of 2000, Abu Ali took part in an Islamic summer study session in Medina, where he made Saudi friends and became interested in jihad. By September 2002 he had returned to Medina to start a university course in Islamic theology. A month later, a friend introduced him to Qahtani. The younger man was impressed by the veteran jihadist so they exchanged phone numbers and arranged to continue their discussions.

In January 2003, Qahtani introduced Abu Ali to Faqasi, who convinced him to join Al Qaeda properly and told him that after he finished his studies he was to return to America and await further instructions. During that initial meeting the three men also discussed a plan for Abu Ali to assassinate President Bush. They debated whether Abu Ali should try to get close enough to the president to shoot him in the street, or should use a car bomb.[8]

Over the following months, Abu Ali met several times with members of Faqasi's cell. His association deepened and he began spending periods of time at safe houses, where he was trained in using weapons and explosives, and in how to forge documents. The Organization gave him money to buy a laptop, a mobile phone, and books. At one point he decided to go to Afghanistan to join in the jihad against American forces there, but his visa application was denied. Later he was given a USB stick containing the recording of the American pilots, which he translated into Arabic for the cell.

After hearing about the raid on the Medina safe house on 27 May, Abu Ali sent Qahtani an email:

> Peace, how are you and how is your family? I hope they are good. I heard the news about the children's sickness. I wish them a speedy recovery, God willing. Anyway, please keep in touch. Greetings to the group, Hani.

Hani was one of Abu Ali's pseudonyms. The American government would later allege that the email was written according to a pre-arranged code. 'Your family' referred to the cell and 'the children's sickness' to the raids. On 6 June Qahtàni replied:

> To my brother, peace to you with God's mercy and blessings. Thank God, I am fine. I was saved from the accident by a great miracle ... I have no idea about the others. However, according to what one doctor mentioned, Adel was not with them, thank God. The important thing is to get yourself ready for the medical check-up because you may have an appointment soon. Therefore, you must keep yourself ready by refraining from eating high fat meals and otherwise.

This message was also coded. Qahtani wanted Abu Ali to know that he and Faqasi – 'Adel' – had escaped 'the accident' but that Abu Ali should take care, as he was probably at risk.[9] Two days later, Abu Ali was arrested.

The Abu Ali case was not straightforward. He was held without charge in Saudi Arabia for twenty months until the American government, responding to a lawsuit raised by his parents, asked the Saudi government to hand him over to them. As soon as he was back in the United States, Abu Ali claimed that his videotaped confession had been extracted from him through torture. Nonetheless, he was charged with receiving funds from a terrorist organization and conspiring to assassinate the president. His trial was followed closely by the American media, which tended to the view that he should be acquitted since Americans were quick to believe his accusations of torture. In the end he was found guilty, however, and sentenced to thirty years in prison. On appeal, his sentence was increased to life.

There is little doubt that Abu Ali was involved with Al Qaeda. The question is, how deeply? The Americans decided Abu Ali was so irremediably dangerous that they locked him up forever. However, it is worth bearing in mind that his assassination plans seem not to have progressed beyond the theoretical. It is possible that he was a patsy, someone pretty ineffectual whom the Organization had decided they would finger when pressed to give up one of their own. On the other hand, the CIA intercepted emails between Abu Ali and Mohammed Sadique Khan, the leader of the 7 July 2005 bombings in London.[10] Would Abu Ali have carried out something similar, had he been allowed to return home to America a free man?

The case also raised the always simmering issue of police brutality inside the Kingdom. Of course the Mabahith denied Abu Ali's accusations. And yet, at his appeal hearing the accused officers testified that they had used violence in the past during interrogations. In pursuit of terrorists, at what point does someone go from being a suspect to being potentially so dangerous that it is justified to deprive them of their rights?

In the meantime, the search continued for Abu Ali's commanders Qahtani and Faqasi.

On the night of 14 June, the MOI raided a safe house in the Khalidiya district of Mecca. Neighbours had noted that all the windows were blacked out and reported their suspicions to the authorities. 'We were informed that there were between four and six persons in the flat,' recalls Major Sultan al-Maliki, director of operations for the Mecca region. 'It was an apartment building, five storeys high, looking out onto the street on both sides.'

When Maliki's team showed up, they were shocked to discover that thirty men were inside the safe house, Saudis mainly, but also a few Chadians and Malians. They had been listening to a lecture on the legality of killing security services personnel. 'The whole event was new to us. It was the first time a group of armed militants barricaded themselves inside a building.' In several respects, the soldiers were not up to the challenge. 'One of our generals stood there pretty exposed and called out to them to turn themselves in. Then his arm suddenly jerked out and I realized he'd been injured. A few seconds later, another soldier was injured. We hadn't taken proper cover.'

Eventually the soldiers split into two groups and swept the building. When the smoke cleared on the raid, five militants had been killed and twelve arrested. 'They were young. I mean, some were so naïve they assumed they'd be sent back to their families after we arrested them.' After questioning their prisoners, investigators realized that the majority were new recruits. Several had been invited to the lecture with no knowledge of the apartment's connection to the Organization. When the MOI had arrived, guns were distributed and the young men were told to protect themselves, even though most of them had never handled a weapon. '"What brought you here?" I asked one of them, a kid who looked no older than fourteen. "They told us we were coming to Mecca for a Qur'an study class," he told me. "It was supposed to last for a week." So they lied to these young people, the leaders I mean, and in that way entrapped them in terrorism.'

Inside the flat investigators found weapons and bomb-making materials, as well as plans to attack the Ruways prison in Jeddah (where terrorist suspects were being held), to poison the water reservoirs at a foreigners' compound, and to assassinate the governor of Mecca province.[11]

Thirteen men, however, got away. They included the cell's leader Ahmad al-Dukhayyel, who had also escaped the raid on the Marwa rest house in Riyadh the previous November. This time he managed to flee out the back and climb over a wall, despite being shot in both arms.

As the month progressed, the successes of early June continued.

Ten days after the Khalidiya raid, a suspicious Land Cruiser was stopped at a security checkpoint and its three passengers were detained when weapons and ammunition were discovered inside the car. It turned out that one of the three was Muhammad al-Mubraz. Mubraz, number fifteen on the List of Nineteen, was part of Muqrin's network and commanded a cell which was planning to attack sites popular with Westerners. Shortly thereafter all eleven members of the cell were arrested and the cell itself shut down.

But there was still no sign of Dandani.

Then, on 26 June, the MOI scored an important and entirely unexpected success. Faqasi, leader of the Hijaz network, whom they had been chasing for weeks, offered to turn himself in. He made only two demands: one, that they release his wife, whom the MOI had been holding since the raid on the Medina safe house a month earlier; and two, that they not force him to appear on television. The MOI happily complied with both. Satisfied, Faqasi went to Prince Muhammad in person and handed himself over. Then the questioning began.[12]

It turned out that after fleeing the Medina safe house dressed as a woman, Faqasi had decided he had some thinking to do and went into hiding – not only from the MOI, but also from his comrades in Al Qaeda. His confidence in the Organization had been shaken after reading an article in an Islamist journal which quoted authoritative Islamic texts to

King Fahd neighbourhood raid, 20 July 2004 'From the roof came a series of loud bangs and flashes of light. Two parked cars exploded.'

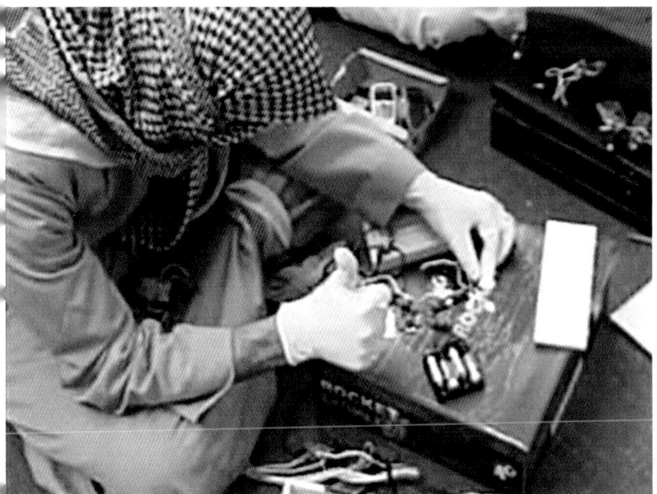

Electronics training An AQAP recruit takes a hands-on course on bomb-making.

Piecing together the evidence Investigators inspect forged number plates, blocks of RDX and ammunition seized from a safe house.

Riyadh compound bombings, 12 May 2003 'The pickup raced deep into the Vinnell compound and exploded in front of one of its large residential buildings, completely ripping off its facade.'

Crown Prince Abdullah *De facto* ruler in his brother King Fahd's name, Abdullah delivers a stern warning to the Kingdom's clerics.

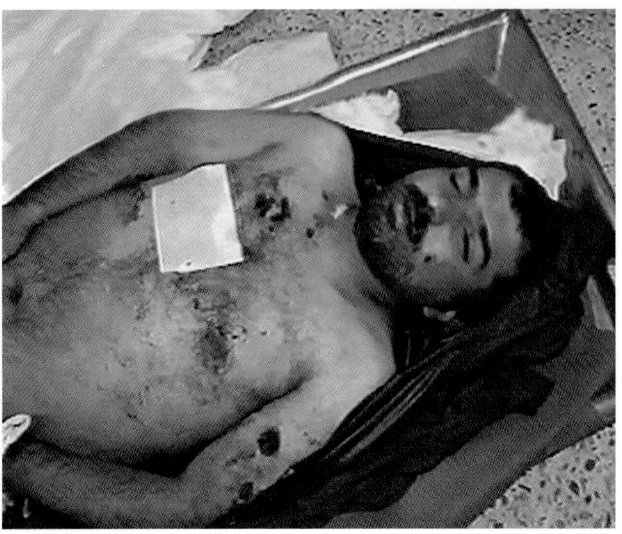

Yusuf al-Ayiri, killed 30 May 2003 'He was hunted until his very last day, when he chose to die as a martyr of God rather than be caught by the oppressors of the Arabian Peninsula.' – *Voice of Jihad*

Turki al-Dandani tracked down, 3 July 2003 'Seeing that there was no escape, Dandani and his men ran into the mosque next door and barricaded themselves inside.'

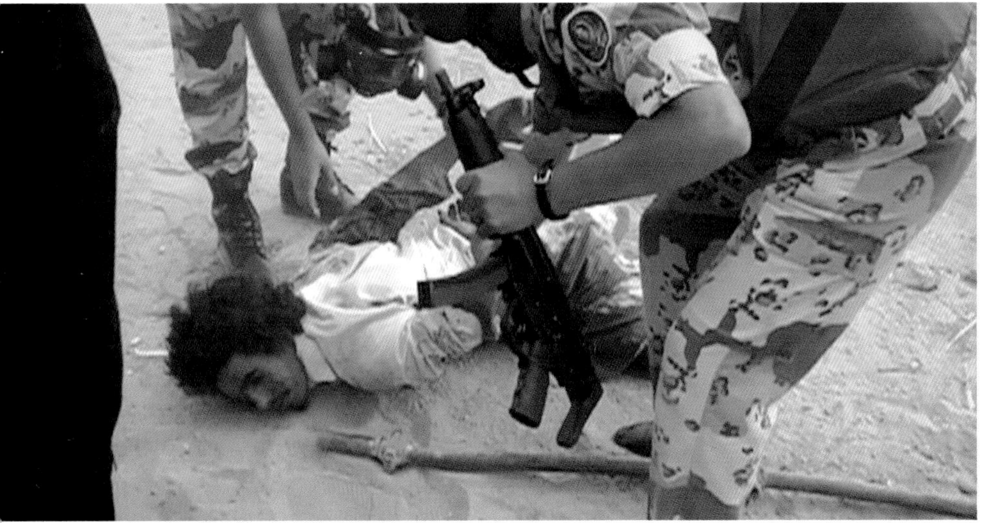

Ghuday farm shootout, 28 July 2003 'The fighting was fierce and when the smoke cleared six terrorists had been killed. Four were arrested.'

Jazan hospital siege, 23 September 2003 'Out the front, shooting had also begun. "The terrorists began firing out the windows. Heavy fire, not shot by shot."'

Prince Nayef The long-serving interior minister, at a press conference. 'The MOI is removing the Muslim militants spreading terror just as one would cut out a diseased organ.'

Abu Ayub 'The man training them, a heavyset 27-year-old local boy from a well-known mujahideen family, was Faisal al-Dukhayyel – though he would go on to achieve notoriety under his Al Qaeda *nom de guerre*, Abu Ayub.'

Abdullah al-Rashoud records a propaganda video 'Rashoud did his best pantomime villain impression into the microphone, gesticulating wildly and modulating his voice like a firebrand preacher.'

Isa al-Awshen Muqrin's media whiz kid.

Cell class photo A Riyadh cell poses for the camera in autumn 2003. Standing at the back on the far right is a hale and hearty Amr al-Shihri.

Amr al-Shihri's funeral Cell members surround Amr al-Shihri's makeshift hospital bed. 'Video footage of his funeral . . . shows how emaciated the once robust Shihri had become during his agonizing last days.'

Painting a truck bomb A cell member disguises one of the trucks for the Muhaya attack as an army vehicle. '"It looks good," the painter declares. "I don't know. Now it looks like a cow," the cameraman replies.'

The attack team with the Muhaya truck bombs The trucks are in their disguise for the 8 November 2003 attacks. Sultan Bijad, centre, holds a sign which reads 'Together in the War on the Crusaders'.

The Emergency Forces HQ bombers 'Now hit the gas and trust in God!' The suicide bombers set out to attack the Emergency Forces headquarters on 8 November 2003, the same night as the attack on the Muhaya compound.

Prince Muhammad Prince Muhammad bin Nayef, assistant interior minister for security affairs, at the scene of the Muhaya compound bombing.

The Muhaya compound the morning after the bombing 'The plateau offered a commanding view of the target . . . Muhaya was a sitting duck.'

Ali al-Khudayr 'This bloodletting must be stopped.' Extremist cleric Ali al-Khudayr, one of the Takfeeri Troika, recants on television.

Campfire 'Muqrin asked Juwayr how he was enjoying the training camp. "By God, I am pleased," he answered. "Happy and relaxed. We've eaten a lot, that's for sure!"'

Attempted rescue of Khalid al-Farraj by Abu Ayub and his men, 29 January 2004 'They found two more security officers in the sitting room and shot them both. One fell back onto the sofa and slumped there dead, covered in blood.'

Lorry-driving training Dakheel al-Ubayd prepares to bomb the Diplomatic Quarter in April 2004. 'He bounced up and down in his seat. "I've only ever driven a Toyota Camry before! Shall we try out the speed? See how fast it can go?"'

argue that military operations inside the Kingdom were totally forbidden; in the terminology of Islamic law, they were *haram*. Faqasi was afraid to confess his concerns to anyone inside the Organization. He knew how unforgiving takfeeris could be.

The article was by Safar al-Hawali, a prominent radical cleric from Jeddah. In the 1980s he had studied religion at universities in Mecca and Medina under teachers sympathetic to the Muslim Brotherhood. When Hawali graduated he incorporated his teachers' point of view into his sermons and before long was a leading figure inside a radical reform movement called the Awakening. Then, after the first Gulf War, Hawali's preaching became even fierier. He hurled thunderous diatribes against the government, whom he accused of betraying the Umma by inviting infidels into the Land of the Two Holy Mosques. He also criticized the Wahhabi establishment for neglecting the struggle against Western imperialism, which had led to so much Muslim suffering. These views inspired Osama bin Laden who drew on the writings of Hawali and others as he developed Al Qaeda's distinctive ideology.

Hawali was one of the many clerics thrown into prison in 1994. However, he surprised everyone by emerging five years later (having never been formally charged) a changed man. Though still a radical, he distanced himself from his earlier anti-government views. The fight against encroaching liberalism and Westernization could be waged better from within the establishment than from without.[13]

After reading Hawali's article, Faqasi wrote the sheikh a letter raising various points. Hawali replied and suggested they meet to discuss the issues further. Faqasi agreed. During their conversation, Faqasi came clean about his participation in Al Qaeda operations, and admitted that he had been involved in the planning stages of the Riyadh compound bombings. Hawali responded gently, objecting to the theological position which underlay Faqasi's views. In the end, the sheikh was able to convince Faqasi to turn himself in. 'Take the initiative before the initiative takes you,' he counselled. 'Better to explain your position now, before you are taken by force and no longer able to do so.'

Faqasi took the sheikh's advice and together they drove to Prince Muhammad's office in Jeddah where Faqasi handed himself over and became a ward of the state he had so vehemently hated. The MOI's policy of encouraging sheikhs – especially radical sheikhs like Hawali – to go public with their denunciations of Al Qaeda was bearing fruit. Faqasi would hand over much vital intelligence about the Organization, including its founding by Ayiri and the way the cell networks had evolved.

Faqasi's rise within the Organization had been meteoric. He had been entrusted with the mission to seek out a nuclear weapon, and, only a few months before, the top commanders in the Peninsula had asked him to lead them. Of course, Bin Laden had rejected Faqasi's promotion and told him to stick to fundraising and recruitment. Perhaps Faqasi's disappointment had played a role in his defection. Either way, bringing Faqasi in was a huge step forward for Prince Muhammad and a massive blow to the Organization. His former comrades, meanwhile, effectively erased him from their history. In all of the propaganda they went on to produce, they would never once mention his name.

Soon after that, the MOI had yet another success. One of Dandani's relatives was taken in for questioning, and he revealed to them what Dandani had been up to.[14]

On the morning of the Riyadh compound bombings, Dandani and four companions had donned black *abayas* and, posing as women, left Riyadh. His plan had been to flee the Kingdom as soon as the coast was clear. He spent four days in a safe house in Ahsa before heading to his home province of Jawf, where he moved between different hideouts until finally settling in a villa in the small town of Suwayr, 600 kilometres northwest of Riyadh.

On 3 July, just after dawn prayer, MOI soldiers began surrounding the block. The raiding team had prayed together beforehand, and morale was high. To further bolster their spirits, the officers reminded their men that the work they were doing was honourable. Lieutenant-Colonel Umar al-Adwan was one of the troops. 'I had written my will out beforehand and sealed it in an envelope. I gave it to one of the guys and told him not to open it unless I was martyred. And to be honest, I would have been proud to be martyred that day.'

The nondescript villa was owned by the imam of the neighbourhood mosque, which stood next door. The street was at the edge of town and ended at the open desert, which sloped gently upwards towards a row of rocky hills about five hundred metres away. The plan was for a 'silent raid'. It would give the troops the element of surprise. First the neighbourhood was systematically and quietly evacuated. Men on neighbouring rooftops kept a close watch on the villa to make sure that nobody inside noticed the activity on the street. An armoured car positioned itself on one of the hills and several more were stationed at either end of the street. Sniper teams were spread out strategically around the target.

Next, a group of Emergency Forces officers nimbly approached the villa's external wall with a ladder. A soldier climbed up and peered over. The courtyard was empty. He silently heaved himself over and jumped down to the ground. Checking the villa's windows, he saw no one, so he walked to the front gate and opened it for the raiding team.

Lieutenant-Colonel Adwan was part of the team. 'The building was essentially just a courtyard and a modest house,' he recalls. They began a silent sweep. 'The front door was open, a majlis lay to the left and right, and then the kitchen a bit further on. Beyond it was a sitting room, which was divided in two by a thin partition. We could hear the sound of a television on the other side of the partition. Peeking around, we saw a man seated there, watching the news. We raised our guns and burst in shouting at him to surrender. He put his hands up and we restrained him.' The man was the imam of the mosque.[15] 'He yelled loudly over and over, "I am innocent! I've not done anything!" He kept shouting this as we led him out of the house.' His shouting was louder than it should have been. The soldiers suspected he was trying to warn others inside the villa.

'We continued our sweep, moving down the corridor. At the far end there was a room with two windows, but it was completely blacked out. There were four men inside, still in their pyjamas. But the imam's shouting had worked. They had taken up positions with Kalashnikovs and pipe bombs, sort of homemade grenades.' One of them opened fire. Adwan was standing in the doorway, but remarkably the spray of bullets missed him. His comrade standing behind him was struck in the shoulder.

Gunfire erupted back and forth through the doorway. The raiding party retreated, Adwan dragging his wounded colleague away from the fighting. Then they saw a grenade bounce down the corridor. Falling to the ground, they lay flat, and luckily the shrapnel passed over them, wounding no one.

Adwan and the wounded soldier took refuge beneath the staircase. They heard the four terrorists run out of the room and up the stairs to the first floor. The soldiers knew that the villa was surrounded, so the raiding team retreated back to the street. There several squads of armed Emergency Forces officers had assembled and a surveillance helicopter circled overhead.

Meanwhile the terrorists, on reaching the first floor, leapt from a window down onto the cistern of the neighbouring mosque. Seeing that there was no escape, they jumped down, shooting in every direction, ran into the mosque and barricaded themselves inside.

A squad of men in body armour ran in loose formation

towards the mosque's external wall. One of them was hoisted up by his fellows and peered over. The cream-coloured mosque was just like thousands of other neighbourhood mosques in Saudi Arabia, an unadorned concrete box with a minaret alongside. The minaret's loudspeakers pointed in all four directions. 'Hello! Hello!' the loudspeakers blared. It was the voice of one of the men inside. He was using the microphone which the muezzin used during the call to prayer. 'You who are attacking, why persecute us for walking in the path of God? Our jihad is against the Americans! What do you want from us?'

An officer fired at one of the loudspeakers. 'Don't shoot at the mosque!' his fellow soldier shouted.

The militant went on. 'Do you not want paradise? What do you think, that this world is greater than the next world? Compared to you, we are far more faithful to God. He will punish you, you can be sure. For truly He is the most exalted!'

His words went on in a similar vein for some time. In Saudi Arabia, questioning a fellow Muslim's faith is a great provocation and the soldiers grew weary of being harangued. Several discarded their scruples and began firing at the loudspeakers. The voice went silent.

The siege lasted for several hours. From time to time, bursts of gunfire would break out between the two sides. An officer raised a megaphone to his mouth. 'This won't do at all, brothers! You can't win. I repeat, you can't win. Surrender yourselves! If you do not come out, one by one, with your hands up, you will leave us with no choice! The area is surrounded!'

There was still no answer, so the soldiers decided to use one of the armoured cars as a battering ram to punch a hole first through the surrounding wall and then into the mosque itself. Then they would throw in tear-gas grenades to force the terrorists out.

Gas masks were passed around, and the plan was put into action. The breeze-block walls were no match for the armoured car, which smashed straight through. The gas canisters were tossed inside and tear gas began to fill the air.

At the same moment, however, a sharp explosion sounded from inside the mosque. The men readied themselves for further fighting. Adwan was among the team of men who crept towards the hole in the mosque's wall. They peered through. 'Inside the mosque was a sort of haziness from the tear gas,' he remembers. 'We moved from one column to another inside the mosque, and in one of the corners there was what from a certain distance looked like a pile of clothes.' However, it wasn't simply clothes. One of them reported back to their commanding officer in the street. He ripped off his gas mask. 'It's all over.'

The four wanted men lay in a heap in the corner. Flecks of blood and pieces of flesh stained the walls on either side, and once the bomb squad had determined that none of the corpses were wearing suicide vests, the soldiers peeled the bodies out of their charred huddle. Pieces of shrapnel indicated that the four terrorists had, in the end, scrummed around hand grenades and pulled the pins.

Forensics officers went through the corpses' clothes and emptied their pockets. In one of them was an ID card. It showed a handsome face, stern and determined, wearing the red-and-white Saudi shemagh and a well-trimmed black beard.

It was the face of Turki al-Dandani.[16]

The MOI repaired the mosque wall that very day. The soldiers had not liked having to smash through it; it was precisely the sort of thing Al Qaeda could take advantage of. Some afterwards denied that it had even happened.

Along with Dandani, one of the other terrorists inside the mosque had been on the List of Nineteen. Only ten remained. The media was reporting that the leader of Al Qaeda inside the Kingdom was dead. The government was happy to give credence to that narrative. By now, however, the MOI knew that it would take far more than the death of Dandani to cripple Al Qaeda. On 18 July another huge cache of explosives was discovered in Qaseem, and three days later a series of raids in Qaseem, Riyadh, and the Eastern Province threw up sixteen suspects.

Then, on the 25th, a man was arrested in a Riyadh bookstore distributing a tract entitled *The Writings of Abu Bakr al-Siddiq on Killing Apostates*.[17] It had been written by Ahmad al-Dukhayyel, the commander who had narrowly escaped the raids on both the Marwa and Khalidiya safe houses. It turned out the man from the bookstore was one of Dukhayyel's operatives, and he told investigators that for four weeks Dukhayyel – who had been wounded – and the rest of his cell had been holed up at a safe house in Buraydah, manufacturing pipe bombs and producing the tract as well as a cassette tape called 'O People of Monotheism!'

Armed with this information, the MOI went to the safe house but found it abandoned. Following leads, they discovered that Dukhayyel had been alerted to his man's arrest and fled with some others to a remote farm called Ghuday northwest of the city. The farm was owned by the parents of a cell member. On the morning of 28 July, over one hundred security officers surrounded it.

Tall date palms stood in neat rows and small green tufts of vegetation peeked through the square sandy beds. The house and storerooms were run down. Calls to the terrorists to give themselves up were met with gunfire and pipe bombs. The fighting was fierce and when the smoke cleared six terrorists had been killed; one had been burnt beyond recognition. Two of the dead were from Chad; the other four were Saudis. Eight soldiers were wounded, and a lieutenant and a sergeant had been killed.[18]

Four Saudis who lived at the farm were arrested and charged with aiding terrorists, and one cell member who had been wounded in the fighting was captured and taken in. At the morgue he was able to identify the body of Dukhayyel, whose wounds from the Khalidiya raid had been poorly treated and were still visible.

Later that afternoon Saudi state television broadcast an official report. It listed the names of the dead and wounded on both sides, and ended sternly. 'The MOI spokesman concluded his statement by assuring terrorists that the authorities are constantly on the hunt. There is nothing to do but surrender and be judged according to God's law. Anyone who offers them accommodation, hides them, or even sympathizes with them, is advised to be mindful of the consequences.'[19]

Only nine names from the List of Nineteen remained. During a press conference, Prince Nayef remarked to reporters that the MOI was 'removing the Muslim militants spreading terror just as one would cut out a diseased organ'.[20]

6

Salvaging a Friendship

Prince Muhammad's men had had a string of successes on the ground. However, the view from higher up was not as rosy. In Washington, a political row over terrorist financing with significant implications for US–Saudi relations was about to blow up. Just as the Kingdom was entering the bloodiest counterterrorism campaign in its history, the American media was once again raising pointed questions about the Saudis' commitment to the war on terror.

The Saudi government had already taken further steps towards tackling the problem. In February its Monetary Agency had started training judges and investigators on the legal issues involved and on the methods terrorists use to launder money. Then in April, just ten days before the compound bombings, it suspended all charities' activities outside the Kingdom until mechanisms could be put in place to ensure that Saudi charitable funds were not being directed to illegal purposes. To this end, Saudi banks were instructed to stop all financial transfers by Saudi charities to foreign bank accounts.

Despite these positive developments, America believed the government had not done nearly enough. The Kingdom, on the other hand, accused American politicians of invoking the spectre of Saudi Arabia to score political points. Prince Saud al-Faisal the foreign minister said in a press conference, 'Some members of Congress refuse to believe that we are doing as much as we can to fight terrorism. We have given them the true picture of the situation, and if they still continue to persist in this belief, then it is only their opinion, not the true facts that are reflected in that.'[1]

On 26 June, the Senate held a hearing entitled 'Terrorism: Growing Wahhabi Influence in the United States'. Senator Jon Kyl of Ohio, chairman of the subcommittee on terrorism, technology, and homeland security, delivered the opening statement:

> Nearly twenty-two months have passed since the atrocity of September 11th. Since then, many questions have been asked about [Saudi Arabia's] role in that day's terrible events ... and [the role played by] its official sect, a separatist, exclusionary, and violent form of Islam known as Wahhabism. It is widely recognized that all of the nineteen suicide pilots were Wahhabi followers. In addition, fifteen of the nineteen were Saudi subjects. Journalists and experts have said that Wahhabism is the source of the overwhelming majority of terrorist atrocities in today's world. Analysing Wahhabism means identifying the extreme element that, although enjoying immense political and financial resources thanks to support by a sector of the Saudi state, seeks to globally hijack Islam, one of the world's three great Abrahamic faiths.

The Saudis would not have liked hearing 'Wahhabism' contrasted so sharply with 'Islam'. Later during the hearing, Senator Kyl questioned David Aufhauser from the Treasury Department. Aufhauser was in charge of tackling terrorist financing.

'With regard to the trail of money,' Kyl said, 'I should have asked you specifically about whether it leads in some cases to Saudi Arabia.'

'In many cases it is the epicentre,' Aufhauser replied.

'Does that trail of money also show money going to Al Qaeda?'

'Yes.'

'Is the money from Saudi Arabia a significant source of funding for terrorism generally?'

'Yes,' Aufhauser confirmed. 'Principally Al Qaeda, but many other recipients as well.'[2]

The media had used the phrase 'epicentre of terrorist financing' to describe Saudi Arabia before, but it carried an additional sting coming from a high-level member of the American government.

Things then grew heated when, on 24 July, the American government released a report on the congressional investigation into 9/11. Though the report stated categorically that there was 'no evidence that the Saudi government as an institution or senior Saudi officials individually funded [Al Qaeda],' twenty-eight of the published report's eight hundred pages had been redacted.[3] It was clear from what fell between the long lines of black marker pen that the redacted material was about Saudi Arabian support for Al Qaeda, probably financial. Congressmen, journalists, and ordinary Americans demanded to see the pages. President Bush himself refused on grounds of national security. Making the pages public 'would help the enemy,' he said.[4]

Prince Bandar, the Saudi ambassador, was one of the voices calling for the full truth to be revealed. 'Saudi Arabia has nothing to hide,' he said. 'We can deal with questions in public, but we cannot respond to blank pages.' Obscuring parts of the investigation would only encourage speculation, Bandar believed, none of which would redound to the Kingdom's credit.[5] And indeed Americans were quick to draw their own conclusions about what the redacted pages contained. 'I am convinced from having talked to knowledgeable people that this is an effort to cover up for the Saudis,' Democratic senator Chuck Schumer told reporters.[6] He then wrote a letter to Bandar calling for Prince Nayef to be replaced as interior minister. Arlen Specter, a Republican senator, said criminal sanctions against Saudi Arabia should be considered, and demanded that the Treasury Department go public with the Saudi organizations and individuals under suspicion.[7]

Newsweek reported that the redacted sections concerned 'apparent connections between high-level Saudi princes and associates of the hijackers'.[8] Robert Jordan, the American ambassador in Riyadh, grew concerned about the situation and asked to be shown the redacted pages. At first, Bush refused. As Jordan recalls, 'I had to tell them that if you really want an ambassador down here, then you'd better let me see them, or why don't you get somebody else to do this job.'

The president relented, and a CIA briefer was sent to Riyadh with the report. 'He put me in a room with the twenty-eight pages and I sat down and read them,' Jordan says. 'I was satisfied with what I saw. I think there was no cause for the kind of flap that was made over it.' He could understand why the Saudi government wanted to see the pages and why they wanted them to be made public, but he also understood the White House's position. Yet in Jordan's view, whatever allegations the twenty-eight pages contained, they were not sufficiently substantiated to justify going public with them. 'We tended to play what I call a game of connect the dots. If someone meets with A in a mosque, then A meets with B, and then B meets with C, does that mean A knew C? Probably not. But I think we went through a period of trying to connect dots that were not there.'

Saudis at the highest levels were extremely irritated. Prince Bandar and Prince Saud visited the president at the White

House. As **Frances Townsend**, Bush's deputy national security advisor for combating terrorism, recalls, 'The meeting ended very badly. The foreign minister just walked out of the Oval Office. There was a real breach in relations with Saudi Arabia, a breach which was not only unproductive, frankly it was also damaging because the United States understood it needed Saudi Arabia's cooperation to get to the problem of extremism.'

Shortly after the meeting, Townsend received a phone call. 'The president wants me to travel to Saudi Arabia. I'm told I've got to try to rebuild the counterterrorism relationship.' She had never visited the Kingdom before, so she gathered as much archive material as she could – intelligence reports from the CIA and the FBI, and protocol briefs from the State Department – and began studying.

Frances Townsend had trained as a lawyer and, before the White House, worked inside the Department of Justice and the Coast Guard, where she became an expert in international criminal law and intelligence issues. Petite but extremely confident, Townsend's personality fills a room.

Many observers questioned Bush's decision to send such a dynamic woman to the all-male world of Saudi Arabia. 'Given that there were tensions, some people thought that the Saudis would perceive it as a slight.' So Townsend went to Bush and suggested he send someone else. Bush would not hear of it. 'They're wrong,' the president said. 'The Saudis don't care if I send a man or a woman. What they care about most is that I send someone close to me who can speak on my behalf. So you're going.'

Townsend arrived in Jeddah on 5 August. She was dressed conservatively, her head uncovered. 'That was government policy. Loose clothes, but no abaya, and no hijab.' The seaside city was characteristically hot and humid. When she stepped off the plane onto the runway, her heels sank into the tarmac.

On the ride from the airport, Townsend felt the weight of the responsibility she had been given. Her task was to get the two countries' counterterrorism relationship back on track, and, from the American government's point of view, tackling terrorist financing was the top priority. 'Failure was not an option.'

Then she noticed that her security detail were fiddling with something in their pockets. Enquiring through her interpreter, she was told that they all had a string of Muslim prayer beads called a *subha,* thirty-three beads which over three circuits help the worshipper meditate upon the ninety-nine names of God. Townsend, a devout Catholic, was struck by the subha's similarity to the rosary. 'We use the rosary to meditate on the life of Jesus, and we also go around three times to complete it. I carry the rosary with me wherever I go, and at that moment I wondered if there weren't other ways we could focus on what we had in common, as opposed to our differences.'

At the Salaam Palace, the government's sprawling Jeddah headquarters on an island across from the city's glittering Alhambra Corniche, Townsend had a series of preliminary meetings with various Saudi counterparts. 'Everyone was polite, but I wouldn't call it warm. We clearly had real issues to overcome.' Eventually, just after afternoon prayer, she was shown in to see the crown prince.[9] Ambassador Jordan was there, as were the crown prince's foreign affairs adviser Adel al-Jubeir and several other high-ranking Saudi figures. The atmosphere was formal and a little tense. Abdullah was reserved, and Townsend could hear a clicking sound coming from his pocket. 'I knew what that was,' she recalls, and so she asked him to show her his prayer beads, and he did.

Then Townsend took a risk. She pulled out her rosary and presented it to the crown prince. 'You have to understand,' Townsend says, 'in the Kingdom religious objects that are not

Islamic are forbidden, not just haram but actually illegal.' Nonetheless, she explained the rosary to the crown prince, and suggested that if their two sides could only focus on the things they had in common – even simple things that were dear to them, like the subha and the rosary – then she was confident they could move forward together.

'Now, Abdullah does not often wear a broad smile,' Townsend says with a twinkle. 'But at that moment he smiled, and suddenly the tension in the room lifted. Everyone could tell that he felt comfortable with me and happy that I was willing to find that common ground.'

The way was open now for the two sides to get down to business. 'This is who you'll be working with,' Abdullah told her.

Prince Muhammad stepped forward. Townsend was a little taken aback by his cool demeanour. 'He was very official, very serious,' she recalls.

Their retinues accompanied the two of them into a long meeting room. 'I am not a politician,' the prince began. 'My interest is in the security services. You are welcome to discuss any security subject with me, but apart from that, I'm not interested.' He had not been impressed by the political furore over the twenty-eight redacted pages.

'I respected that he didn't want to get caught up in the politics of it, because frankly, neither did I,' Townsend says. 'I told Prince Muhammad that I was purely a substantive expert sent by the president to help make progress on terrorist financing.' However, it would be some time before Townsend was able to convince the prince of that. David Aufhauser's comment to the Senate back in June – that Saudi Arabia was the 'epicentre' of terrorist financing – had not been forgotten. 'I understood what Aufhauser was saying,' Townsend explains. 'But to use the words he used without stopping to consider how they would be heard in Riyadh, that was a problem. The Saudis would say to me, "When you say *Saudi Arabia finances terrorism*, the world hears that the Saudi *government* is financing terrorism. But show us a single example of government money going to Al Qaeda and we'll deal with it." And of course you couldn't.' The worst part was that the Saudis were very keen to help solve the problem. 'They were listening for acknowledgement of their help, but all they were hearing was criticism.'

Prince Muhammad then went straight to the point. The United States would have to learn that the mechanisms for combating terrorist financing inside the Kingdom were still being developed. The crown prince had ordered Prince Muhammad to lead the crackdown, but the Mabahith were not set up for that sort of thing, and it would take time before they became so. Townsend heard what he was saying. 'My response was, "You tell me what you need to build up your capabilities, and we will help you." This is where the idea arose of stationing people from the Treasury in the Riyadh embassy, both to interact with the Mabahith and to respond to the Saudi government's requests for training and assistance.'

Townsend's willingness to engage personally with Saudi society and her appreciation of the underlying cultural issues endeared her to her hosts and facilitated the renewal of cordial relations between the two countries. For she soon realized that the nub of the issue was religion. 'What we found was that the money trail led to the Kingdom's private Islamic charities, and this presented the government with a real problem.' The Saudi state sells itself as the protector of the Umma, and so they simply could not be seen to be interfering in the Muslim's obligation to donate a portion of his income to charity. 'So first and foremost we had to adopt the point of view that by policing charities we were actually protecting potential victims of crime. Because in the end, a Muslim who gives to charity with a pure heart becomes the victim of a crime if, unbeknown to them, someone else takes that money and uses it to fund terror. That approach really resonated with Prince Muhammad and the Mabahith.'

The MOI's string of early successes in the war was breathtaking and Prince Muhammad had every reason to celebrate. But his foot soldiers were overwhelmed by the sheer number of clashes they were being forced to engage in. 'We had not been trained with a view to fighting a deadly, armed underground network with branches in every city in the Kingdom,' Captain Abdul Majid bin Muammar recalls. 'We'd uncover one in Jazan one day, another in Jeddah the next, then another in Mecca, in Khobar, in villages around Qaseem and in all the neighbourhoods of Riyadh. The cells were horribly widespread, and this was more dangerous than we had ever believed possible.'[10]

The Emergency Forces in particular were feeling the strain. They had overnight become the Kingdom's anti-terror rapid-response team, but as Major-General Harbi explains, 'We were founded to tackle riots. Some officers had received counterterrorism training, but that was never really seen as one of our jobs.'[11] This lack of training was compounded by insufficient weaponry. The Emergency Forces had normally been kitted out with just standard-issue riot gear: body armour, riot shields, and batons. At the beginning of the war, they were given weapons, but at most these were submachine guns – not terribly effective against enemies armed with RPGs.[12]

The prince drafted in Special Forces trainers to advise on an intensive training programme for the Emergency Forces, which was gradually extended to the rest of the ministry's departments. The police, the Security Patrols, even the firemen and paramedics of the Civil Defence were taught how to fight the enemy, and the programme was deemed such a success that it continues to this day: all soldiers in the MOI spend one month a year renewing their counterterrorism capabilities.[13]

But first, Prince Muhammad had to ensure that his men were

free of any niggling thoughts that the terrorists were the holy warriors they claimed to be. General Mansour al-Turki, the MOI's official spokesman, explains how tricky the situation was. 'Saudi soldiers are no less sensitive to the religious dimension of life than the rest of society. This was a problem, because in Saudi Arabia when someone says, "This is haram, this is against the Sharia," people really listen, especially if he is a so-called sheikh, with a long beard and a cloak to prove it. And Al Qaeda took advantage of this. They distributed lectures and sermons through the Internet or on cassette tapes, telling the security men that killing fellow Muslims was haram. So we needed to reassure them.'

For that, they needed the help of the Ministry of Islamic Affairs. 'Look, I'm an officer. I could go and speak to the soldiers and tell them that these men are terrorists and it is your duty to fight terrorism and so on. But I'm not a religious authority. The soldiers might just think, "Oh well, he's an officer, he's pro-American," and ignore me. This is why we brought in the Grand Mufti and others from Islamic Affairs, who commanded real respect, to talk to the men.'[14]

Prince Muhammad was soon able to forge a strong sense of solidarity within the ranks. They were not only defending their homeland from terrorist insurrectionists, they were defending their faith from misguided heretics. And like the military training the men received, the MOI's monitoring of the forces' religious attitudes would long outlast the war.

In August and September, a series of poorly executed raids and shootouts shone a light on the security services' deficiencies. At around 5 p.m. on 11 August a security patrol in Riyadh's Amana district spotted a 1999 grey Volkswagen saloon which they had been on the lookout for. They approached the car, but it sped off and they chased it to a rest house. The driver, brandishing a pistol and talking excitedly into his mobile phone, jumped out and ran inside. Reinforcements were called in and police surrounded the location, but when a jeep and a pickup emerged full of armed men shooting in every direction, the security services were overwhelmed and the suspects got away. The jeep was later found abandoned by the side of the road. Inside was bomb-making equipment, including one kilogram of RDX explosive.

The rest house was thoroughly searched, and along with the usual weaponry, an ATM card was found bearing the name of Muhammad al-Mubraz, whom the Mabahith had arrested in June. Mubraz's cell had been shut down, but clearly he had been linked to a much wider network. More worryingly, there were signs that someone had been constructing a truck bomb, though the bomb itself was nowhere to be found.[15]

The following day, on 12 August, information from MOI field operatives reported that weapons had been spotted inside a broken-down 1982 Toyota pickup in the Shubra district. A security patrol was sent to inspect the truck, but it was noticed by a group of terrorists inside a nearby rest house; they fired on the officers, killing three and wounding another. Several civilians were also wounded as the terrorists fled to a row of half-constructed villas across the street. The security patrolmen shot one of the terrorists before he made it inside; he fell to the ground, wounded, and was arrested.

What happened next was a genuine embarrassment for the MOI. The Emergency Forces had been called in to provide backup, and when they began exchanging fire with the terrorists inside the villas, the gunfire caused a car to ignite. It took over an hour for firefighters to get to the scene, during which time the fire had spread to another vehicle. Furthermore, because the security cordon had not been set up properly, civilians kept wandering onto the battlefield and so the MOI was forced to arrest more men than should have been necessary. Confusion reigned.

Although one militant was killed and seven arrested, several others managed to escape from the five-hour stand-off. The whole incident revealed how easily an MOI operation could fall apart. A few weeks later Al Qaeda would publish an account of the Shubra incident from their point of view.[16] It contradicts the government's version of events in several key respects and mocks the MOI's cowardice, incompetence, and deceit.

> It was a very calm day. Five mujahideen were driving down the road in two cars. They carried their personal weapons with them, weapons which they had long loved and cherished because they were destined to be used to slaughter the Crusaders.
>
> One of the two cars broke down and they tried to fix it without success. When the mujahideen in the other car noticed that their comrades had been delayed, they rang them. 'Where are you?' they asked. 'Why are you so late?'
>
> 'The car has broken down,' the others explained. 'But we are not far from the main road.' The mujahideen, ever aware that their telephone calls were under constant surveillance, hesitated to mention the name of their exact whereabouts.
>
> However, one of the brothers shouted out, 'We are beside the Aisha bint Abu Bakr Street exit!' . . .
>
> The second carload of mujahideen arrived, and then they went to the nearest mosque to fetch some water to fill the radiator of the broken-down car; the temperature gauge was in the red. But still the car wouldn't start. The only solution was to push the car to a garage where it could be repaired. So the mujahideen began to move their belongings from the broken-down car to the other car. As they did so, a 2002 Chevy Caprice drove past, driven by a man in a track suit. He greeted us as he passed and drove on; he was on the phone.
>
> I returned the greeting but suspected his appearance and his manner. Within seconds a police car approached us and

stopped in front of our car. Seconds later another car approached us and stopped in front, with another one behind us, and yet another to the side, forming a semi-circle around our car. Instantly I prepared my weapon to fight them, knowing it would be either victory or martyrdom. We all preferred martyrdom to imprisonment in the hands of these tyrants, America's puppets.

But the commander calmed me and said, 'Wait. Let's see what they want.'

One of the officers, a sergeant, got out of his car and headed towards us. One of the brothers, Saleh al-Otaybi, got out and walked towards him, greeting him and asking what the problem was. Our initial intention was not to fight them; otherwise we would have shot them right away.

The soldiers didn't appear to want anything, they just looked at our brother Nasser who remained in the car, ready for anything, and called out to him, 'Come out! Come out! Don't be afraid!' We then noticed that the sergeant was drawing his weapon, but his hands were trembling from fear ... Finally, he raised his gun and pointed it at brother Nasser.

Commotion broke out and within seconds everybody had taken up positions. We were forced to fire several bullets at the sergeant, and he lost his life. In the meantime a soldier had got hold of Nasser and was hitting him with the back of his gun. Because Nasser had reached through the car window to grab his weapon, his head was down, so I shot at the soldier. But he kept hitting Nasser so I ran up and, shooting at him point-blank, killed him.

Two of the soldiers were now dead. Suddenly we heard a voice crying, 'Call in the troops, call in the troops!' and we noticed a soldier in one of the surrounding cars radioing for backup. We shot at that car and it stopped moving, however we don't know if we killed the driver or if he was only pretending to be dead.

Meanwhile, one of the brothers ran after another soldier who was shooting from behind as he fled. The brother scored a hit and the soldier fell down, lifted himself up, then collapsed dead.

We began our retreat ... The brothers bid farewell to their brother Nasser, who we assumed had been martyred ... We would never have left him to be taken by the tyrants if we had been in any doubt about that.

We pulled away and swiftly left the neighbourhood. All of this had occurred before the afternoon call to prayer. We went to a safe house and left again four hours later after exchanging our car for another. As we were heading towards another one of our houses, we noticed helicopters taking off from the airport and making sweeps of the area ...

Yellow cars, red cars, blue cars, black cars from the security forces, the police, the army, as well as guard dogs and flashlights were everywhere. It was almost comical! The cowards were trying to deceive the people by instilling fear in them, and to conceal their failure and defeat. They closed the entire area and even stopped people going to the mosque until the night prayer.

... Later the mujahideen sent surveillance teams who managed to survey the area where the incident took place. They saw soldiers on loudspeakers calling out to phantom fighters who were supposedly in one of the villas under construction, which those fools then began to attack. They set it on fire, destroying what remained of it, even though nobody was inside. Later they even stormed the building, which made for quite an amusing scene. They wanted to demonstrate that they were dealing with the matter.

One of the soldiers was asked how five people had managed to defeat so many soldiers equipped with modern weapons. He answered, 'It's not a matter of modern weapons ... We thought there were more of them than there actually were, and because we were worried the situation would escalate, we retreated in fear.'

Later the evil government began to deceive the people by showing them pictures of the building, claiming that their operation had been a success.

However we know the truth.

Both sides had much to gain from the way the Shubra confrontation would be remembered, and there is no way to know for sure which account is the truth, but what is beyond doubt is that the MOI had been humiliated.

Prince Muhammad had kept in close contact with the commanders during the siege, so he would have been aware of the failures on the ground. He also attended the funeral of the three 'martyred' security officers, which was held the next day.[17] Two days later a team of investigators found the vehicle the terrorists had escaped in abandoned beside a farm inside an ancient wadi. They traced its number plate to a stolen Toyota Corolla and inside found walkie-talkies, wrist watches, and computer cases modified to be used for carrying explosives.

The next four weeks saw one confrontation after another. On the 13th, a tow-truck was seized when it was spotted towing a car owned by a wanted man. While searching the car, investigators found a secret cubicle in which RPGs had been hidden. Clues from the car led police to a village in Jazan province where on the 15th they arrested twenty-one suspects, including seven wanted men. Then on the 19th, following leads from the Amana rest house, a shop on Badi al-Zaman Street in Riyadh was raided, which led investigators to yet another safe house in the Rawabi district. This was raided on 6 September and inside were found explosive compounds. Then on the 18th, a raid on a Jeddah villa turned up even more weapons.

*

On 26 August, at an official ceremony at Prince Sultan Air Base in Kharj, American officials formally returned control of those parts of the base which the US Air Force had been using since the first Gulf War back to the Saudi government. The base had been home to 60,000 American servicemen, but the Pentagon had decided it was easier to provide air support for operations in Iraq and Afghanistan from Qatar than from the Kingdom. Pundits in America wondered if the withdrawal had anything to do with Al Qaeda's campaign, but were reminded that the decision had been announced back in April, two weeks before the compound bombings.

Meanwhile, Faqasi's defection in June had meant that Qahtani, his deputy, was now in charge of his Hijaz network. Qahtani's photo had recently appeared in an FBI bulletin under his *nomme de guerre*, Zubayr al-Rimi, but the MOI had recognized him as Qahtani. His father was shown on television entreating him to give himself up, and the MOI raided a farm, thinking Qahtani was there, but he had fled. Then they received a tip-off from Jazan, a medium-sized city on the west coast, not far from the Yemeni border. At around 4 p.m. on 22 September, an informant told the local security services that a group of suspects had taken up residence in an apartment inside a housing complex for employees of King Fahd Central Hospital. One of the suspects was Qahtani.

The chief of the Emergency Forces flew immediately from Riyadh with a team of soldiers, and they liaised with their local counterparts. Captain Khalid al-Qahtani (no relation) was with them. 'We agreed that the raid would take place the next morning at eight o'clock. Most of the residents in the compound were employees of the hospital, and would be at work by then.' They decided to raid the flat from the back door. 'The hope was that, with the element of surprise, the terrorists wouldn't have time to respond and civilian injury would be avoided.

'There was an emergency exit at the back of the block of flats.

We entered and started climbing the stairs to get in position. When we were halfway up, we noticed someone peering out of the back door of the flat. He promptly slammed the door shut and locked it from inside.' The man had been washing his hands at a basin near the half-opened door and panicked when he saw the soldiers.

The slamming door alerted the rest of the cell, who grabbed their weapons. One of the cell members lost his nerve and decided to flee. Unlocking the door, he ran out just as the raiding team reached the top of the stairs. 'Another terrorist was close behind him, and came out firing. God spared the one, but in the resulting exchange of fire, the other was wounded and one of our comrades was killed immediately, may God rest his soul.' In the ensuing firefight, two other soldiers in the team of twelve were wounded, then another two. 'Only seven of us were left able-bodied, so the order came to pull back. We had taken too many losses, so we withdrew with our injured comrades, who were taken to hospital.'

Out the front, shooting had also begun. 'The terrorists began firing out the windows, heavy fire, not shot by shot. They'd fire off pretty much an entire magazine, then retreat back inside.' The usual calls went up for the militants to surrender. 'They were shouting back, "Infidels! Heretics! You should come over to us, we're the good guys!"'

The Emergency Forces chief had the idea to give them his phone number, so they could call and negotiate. But they refused. 'Then he asked us, "What do you think about going through one of their fathers, or a relative? That could put the pressure on." So we got the Mabahith to give us the number of a father of one of the suspects.' They phoned the father. 'He said, "Okay, no problem, I'll speak to my son. But I don't have his number! Try to connect me, put me through to him in any way you can, and I'll talk to him."'

Over the loudspeakers, they told the suspect inside that his father wanted to speak to him and read out the phone number. There was only silence from inside the flat for about twenty minutes, and then the captain received a call. It was the man's father. '"This son of mine!" he was shouting. "I disown him! There is no good in him!" "What happened?" I asked. He said his son had accused him of being on the side of the security men, and warned him that if he saw him, he would kill him too.'

The shooting began again, and over several hours the snipers were able to pick off three militants. The remaining two then rang the number of the chief. They wanted to turn themselves in. They were told to strip to their underwear and come out of the building slowly and with their hands in the air. 'They were no older than seventeen or maybe eighteen. Just boys, you could hear it in their voices.'[18]

By 2 p.m. the stand-off was over. Prince Muhammad flew in at four o'clock and went directly to the scene. On the stairwell lay the body of the terrorist who had been injured at the onset of hostilities. Shot in the shoulder, he had bled to death. Two other bodies lay by the window, dressed in the distinctive wrapped skirt of the people of Jazan province. One of the bodies lay face up, and the prince inspected its glassy stare. It was Sultan al-Qahtani.

There were now only eight names left on the original List of Nineteen, and when, three days later, one of the men on the list turned himself in at the Yemeni border, the number went down to seven.

However, despite having smashed many cells and taken out several leaders, the MOI could see that the Organization, much larger than they had imagined, was adapting. Orphaned cell members were being absorbed into another network about which the authorities knew little but which was consolidating its hold over the entire Organization. The wounded suspect apprehended during the botched raid in Shubra admitted during questioning that the leader of that network had been among the men who escaped the raid. Number five on the List of Nineteen, he would go on to haunt Prince Muhammad and his men and unleash a wave of terror never before dreamed of in Saudi Arabia.

That man was Abdulaziz al-Muqrin.

7

A Ruthless New Leader

Muqrin had advised Khalid al-Hajj that the Organization was not ready to launch an attack, and he had been proved correct. But the right to feel smug was no consolation. While the compound bombings were a success from one point of view, the response they engendered from the MOI was sweeping. Ayiri's death and Faqasi's defection had deprived the Organization of its top fundraisers. The smashing of Faqasi's and Dandani's networks, and Dandani's suicide inside the mosque, were all huge setbacks. Moreover, the MOI had obtained numerous leads which put many of the Organization's surviving cells at risk.

What did not help was that after the bombings it seems that Hajj went deep underground to avoid detection, so deep that he cut off all contact with his lieutenants, and to this day, little is known about his movements over the next nine months. Muqrin was now left standing alone in the rubble, pondering the best way forward.

Muqrin would later write a description of an ideal leader, and we can wonder whether it conformed to the image he had of himself: 'Among the essential requirements of leadership are inventiveness, creativity, and psychological preparedness for the worst.'[1]

Muqrin was a hard man and a straight talker. Very lean, he moved with high-strung intensity and suffered from such debilitating migraines that he was known to butt his head against the wall in despair. His religious scruples dictated he not be photographed, one of the consequences of which was that he never had an ID card. There are few known photographs of him; they reveal a very good-looking man with a stubble beard, attractive eyes, and a broad forehead.

Muqrin grew up in Suwaydi in the southern part of Riyadh. The neighbourhood underwent a population explosion in the 1970s and 1980s as working-class Saudis from the countryside settled there. Among its narrow lanes and pot-holed roads, the people of Suwaydi cultivated an intensely conservative religious outlook. Muqrin, a serious young man, was proud of his humble background. One amusement he allowed himself was football, and he played goalkeeper for his middle school team, though out of religious modesty he refused to wear shorts.[2]

He left high school without graduating, and by the age of nineteen he was married with a daughter called Hajer. He would go on to become as well known under the name Abu Hajer – 'Hajer's father' – as under his own. But something besides family life grabbed his attention. 'As everyone knows,' Muqrin would later say in an interview, 'around thirteen years ago, the only thing you'd see on television or hear about in the mosques was what was happening in Afghanistan. The government and all the preachers were supporting it. Back then jihad was acceptable. We all had family, neighbours, and friends who joined the jihad, and we would hear news of the miracles carried out by the mujahideen.'[3]

It is important to understand that stories of miracles – *karamat* in Arabic – were rife at that time. Because belief in miracles is part of Muslim culture, pious Saudis believed the stories coming out of Afghanistan. Such stories acted as a powerful motivating force for young men thinking of joining up and helped strengthen combatants' faith that God was on their side. Abdullah Azzam, the Palestinian mujahid who set up the anti-Soviet campaign, wrote a book on the subject entitled *Signs of the Most Merciful in the Afghan Jihad*. In one story, twenty-five mujahideen are facing down 120 Soviet tanks. 'Our provisions were exhausted,' the storyteller relates. 'We were convinced that we would be captured. We prayed to God and sought his protection. All of a sudden, bullets and mortar shells from all directions rained down upon the communists, and they were defeated. There had been no one but us on the battlefield. It was the work of angels.'[4] Perhaps the most widely held belief among both the mujahideen and their sympathizers in the general population was that upon the moment of their death in battle, a powerful incense-like smell would emanate from martyrs' hallowed bodies, verifying that God had granted them salvation.

Muqrin, inspired by these stories, was keen to fight. But first he faced an obstacle. The Saudi clerics had not made fighting in the Afghan jihad an obligation for each individual Muslim. Participating in other ways, such as by donating money, was perfectly acceptable, but in order to fight, a devout Muslim was duty-bound to ask his parents' permission. 'I tried to convince them to let me go, but they refused. Then I found a sheikh to give me a fatwa obliging me to *train* for jihad, and therefore I no longer needed my parents' permission.'

This anecdote reveals a lot about Muqrin's attitude towards the clerics. It also reveals how easily casuistry can slip into Islamic law, allowing a jurist to derive whatever ruling he wants: fighting requires parental permission, but *preparing* to fight does not.

Many Saudis travelled to Afghanistan at this time and the Soviet jihad took on a mythological dimension. However, the reality was less glorious. When Soviet troops entered the country in December 1979, the Umma did not immediately rise up and come to Afghanistan's aid, despite what Saudi veterans of the Afghan jihad would go on to believe. Saudis in particular did not start arriving in numbers until 1985, nearly six years later, and very few of them became battle-hardened. Most of them stayed only two or three months, usually during their summer holidays, did a bit of training at the camps, and went home. Studies have shown that between fifty and three hundred Saudis died in the campaign against the Soviets. Estimates of the number of Saudis who visited the training camps, however, run from between 12,000 and 20,000. Most of these were looking for a bit of adventure, a dose of *baraka*, and a large helping of self-esteem.

Muqrin states that he arrived 'around thirteen years ago'; that would have been in late 1989 or early 1990. The Soviets had finished their withdrawal from Afghanistan the previous February. So when Muqrin and the others of his generation showed up, the fight was not against the Russians, but against the communist government in Kabul which the Russians left behind. Muqrin had in fact got himself involved in an Afghan civil war.

The camp he went to was called Jihad Wahl. It was not far from the city of Khost near the Pakistani border. 'I spent a long time there and became knowledgeable in many fields. We sons of the Arabian Peninsula are not used to military exercises and discipline, although God sends his mercy to some.' Muqrin was a good student and stood out from the others. 'I was asked to stay and learn more, in order to become a trainer myself one day and to help others – particularly those inside the Land of the Two Holy Mosques.' He did become an effective trainer of new arrivals. However, despite lacking parental permission to fight, he was soon on the battlefield.

His first experience of actual fighting taught him an important lesson. 'It was in an area called Jawar not far from the training camp. One of the brothers saw some soldiers, so our leader Abu Ata divided us into groups. I was in his group.' The mujahideen launched a surprise attack, but the soldiers responded with heavy gunfire. 'I was sitting in the hills composing myself, praying to God and asking Him to make us steadfast and to accept me if I was killed. I was extremely afraid but – praise be to God – that fear soon dissipated when I heard the brothers shout "Allahu akbar!" After that experience I saw that things are actually very simple: if God decrees that you be killed or captured or injured, then that is your destiny and no amount of precaution can save you from what has been predetermined.'

It is not known for certain how long Muqrin stayed in Afghanistan, but he probably returned to Riyadh after the fall of Kabul to mujahideen forces in April 1992. In the two years or so since his departure, the wife he had abandoned had divorced him and taken his daughter to live with her family. It does not seem to have fazed him. 'I worked in trade, buying and selling,' he recalled bluntly. 'I took care of myself.' He was a great believer in self-reliance. 'People today imagine that without government jobs they won't be able to provide for themselves. This is a malicious lie which the treacherous and apostate government has put into the people's minds, that without government aid they would not be able to eat or drink. I have looked after myself, praise God.'

Muqrin's 'laissez-faire' beliefs manifested themselves in a simple stall in front of the Sheraton Hotel, out of which he sold dates. One day, however, functionaries from the local government tried to shut down his stall. Reportedly he fought back, attacking them with an iron bar before driving off in his car. The experience will not have made him feel any friendlier towards the Saudi state.

Soon, the call of jihad was too powerful to resist, and over the next few years he saw action in every major jihadist front except Chechnya. He worked as a gun smuggler in Algeria, bringing European firearms into the country via Morocco. His cell there was uncovered and all the members were captured or killed – but he escaped. Then in Bosnia he trained mujahideen in the fight against the Serbs. During this time he befriended a Saudi-Yemeni jihadist called Nasser al-Bahri who would go on to become better known as Abu Jandal, 'the powerful killer'. Hearing of Ethiopian attacks on Somalia, the two of them travelled together to the Horn of Africa, after a short stopover in the Kingdom and in Yemen.

Muqrin believed that the 'Crusader State of Ethiopia' was trying to force Christianity on the Somalis. 'I personally saw the churches in this area, despite the fact that one hundred per cent of the Somali people are Muslims.' One evening he and Abu Jandal sat discussing the future, and when Abu Jandal suggested he wanted to return home to settle down and start a family, Muqrin was shocked. 'You're crazy! Leave behind the afterlife and the Heavenly Virgins and jihad and martyrdom? To get married?' Of course, Muqrin had once been a married man, and had abandoned his wife.

Abu Jandal grew suspicious of the Somalian mujahideen; they were only in it for the money, he thought, so he left Somalia and went to Afghanistan. There he would join Al Qaeda and go on to become one of Bin Laden's bodyguards. Muqrin stayed behind, however, and his further adventures in Somalia soon landed him in prison. He was deported back to the Kingdom and given a four-year sentence, but was granted early release in August 2001 for good behaviour.[5] 'A month later, God allowed me to go back to Afghanistan, and once again I trained with the brothers. Then we took part in the recent fight against the Americans.' It was during this period that Muqrin met Bin Laden and joined Al Qaeda.[6] 'My relationship with the Sheikh is like that between a father and a son. I had the honour of sitting with him and pledging him my love and allegiance as the leader of the path of jihad.'

Muqrin had thus been fully immersed in the world of jihad for over a decade. His whole worldview was coloured by the ideology of war against the infidel. 'My goal is to raise the flag of Islamic monotheism and to expel God's two enemies – the Crusaders and the Jews – from the Land of the Two Holy Mosques. Muslim lands will be liberated and things will go back to how they were. I pray God grants us long lives, that we might enrage our enemies and plunge our swords into them until every last one of them either enters the religion of God – or is killed.'

With these thoughts in mind, and with Hajj in hiding, Muqrin decided to take responsibility for the Organization onto his own shoulders. How the shift in power from Hajj to Muqrin happened is not clear, but it seems that over the following months Hajj was slowly marginalized. He confined himself to his safe house in Shifa, where he remained leader in principle and maintained his links with Central Command. Muqrin absorbed the surviving jihadists from the other networks into his own, and over time became the *de facto* head of the Organization. (There is some suggestion that Bin Laden later confirmed Muqrin's leadership, but that is not known for sure.) With the exception of the odd independent sub-cell here and there, Muqrin's was the only network left.

In his typically decisive and self-assured way, Muqrin gathered the remaining lieutenants around himself and began re-building the Organization. He first needed to appoint new men to replace Ayiri, Faqasi, and Dandani on the Shura Council; arms smuggler Rakan al-Saikhan was still a member, as was Hajj, if only nominally. Muqrin selected three men who had already served him faithfully as sub-commanders: his deputy Abu Ayub; a veteran mujahid called **Saud al-Qatayni**, who was both a writer and an expert bomb-maker; and a very experienced jihadist and former Saudi prison guard called **Saleh al-Oufi**. They reported to him directly, and Muqrin unified all the cells he could under his own centralized command.

*

The Shura Council could see that the summer had been a disaster. Muqrin needed to pick up the pieces and put things back on a firm footing, and in order to do that he would need to cultivate intense objectivity and take a long, hard look at every aspect of the Organization.

His short-term problem was avoiding the MOI. This he did very well. In the long term, his biggest obstacle was the Organization's dire lack of recruitment. The Shura Council had hoped that the Riyadh compound bombings would act as a bugle call to Saudi youth, yet the thousands of fighters they had dreamt of had not materialized.

Exact figures are difficult to estimate, but it is clear that the number of active members in the whole network at the beginning of summer 2003 – and by active members is meant, essentially, someone who had sworn their allegiance to a cell commander and carried a weapon – was probably no more than 250.[7] And though there were many, many more Saudis affiliated in some way to the Organization – not full members but supporters able to be trusted with small tasks such as buying cars or renting flats – they were not fighting fit and would be of little use in pitched battles with the MOI.

There are two principal reasons why recruitment was and would remain so sluggish. First, the vast majority of clerics denounced Al Qaeda's activities, and that carried weight with the populace. 'It is important,' Muqrin would write, 'to attract clerics and to keep them safe. The role they play in recruiting the young and in raising money is very important. This is on top of the social influence they wield, and their role in rousing the people.'[8] Those clerics who supported them – most prominently the Takfeeri Troika – had been quickly side-lined. The Organization had thereby lost an important source of its legitimacy, and in the absence of an authoritative voice to counter the condemnations coming from the government-sponsored clerics, the population tended to step into line with the official rulings.

The second factor in the lack of recruitment was Iraq. In the run-up to the American invasion, Al Qaeda had believed that the whole region would rise up against the 'Crusader invader' and its 'puppet government' inside Saudi Arabia. Instead, the Iraq invasion had created a noticeable split in the Saudi jihadist community, and almost immediately after the compound bombings in May, online discussion forums became verbal battlefields. Most of the contributors condemned the bombings, not because they were immoral, but because they distracted attention from Iraq.[9] Month after month, hundreds of Saudis flocked to the jihad in Iraq, and each one who did was a potential recruit lost to Al Qaeda in Saudi Arabia.[10]

The popularity of the Iraqi jihad exposed the most important factor in the Organization's lack of recruitment. Its jihadist project inside the Kingdom was simply too radical, even for committed jihadists, the vast majority of whom interpret jihad as essentially defensive, to be invoked only when a clear case could be made that a part of the Umma was under attack. The mere presence of American troops on Saudi soil and the government's friendly relations with the United States were not tantamount to invasion, and certainly did not represent sufficient threat to justify killing innocent civilians.

Besides the difficulties in recruitment, Muqrin also had financial problems. 'Allow me to stress,' he would write, 'any jihadist movement anywhere in the world has a nervous system, a musculature, and a skeleton. An experienced leadership and its cadres are the muscles. Armed mujahideen are the bones. But the nervous system of jihad, that's money ... Urban operations especially require a great deal of money, because the cost of living is higher in the cities than in the mountains. Indeed, cities burn up money.'[11] But his access to money had become worryingly restricted.

Ayiri, with his connections to wealthy donors, was a sore loss. On top of that, the arrest of the Takfeeri Troika affected fundraising in the same way it affected recruitment: donors relied on fatwas and clerical guidance. The government crackdown contributed as well; a new law forbidding the distribution of charity boxes in mosques and other public spaces was a blow – though it would take some time for the law to be implemented fully.[12] Finally, the Iraqi jihad was considered far more worthy of charity than the questionable jihad in Saudi Arabia. Muqrin urgently needed money.

It was vitally important that Muqrin take an objective view of the situation and regroup. But he was primarily a man of action. He possessed martial cockiness and was a true believer, qualities better suited to the clash of battle than the war room. He exemplified George Santayana's aphorism, 'Fanaticism consists of redoubling your effort when you have forgotten your aim.'

Muqrin believed that flamboyant violence and spectacular acts of violence would, on their own, bear fruit. 'Attacks inside cities,' Muqrin wrote, 'are considered "diplomatic-military", the sort of diplomacy that is written in blood, embellished with corpses, and perfumed with gunpowder.'[13] Big attacks at the onset of a guerrilla campaign would convey a message to the people. 'The mujahideen use military attacks to shatter the regime's prestige and to make it clear to the Umma that the regime is not able to stop the attacks, which will encourage the people to oppose the enemy ... The targets should be Jewish and Christian. This will embarrass the state in the people's eyes and make it clear to all that the regime collaborates [with the infidel].'[14]

In pursuit of this strategy, Muqrin brought about the Organization's total destruction. Along the way, however, many people would die.

Muqrin's plan was similar to Dandani's, but with an additional twist. This time, in addition to a residential compound, the Organization would simultaneously attack the security services.

At his disposal were cells all over the Kingdom, but particularly in Riyadh. They were organized according to principles which Muqrin had picked up over the years and which he was in the process of writing down. 'Operations within a city require small independent units. The people in the unit, who should number no more than four, should be residents of the city, for then they will understand the way it works and know the layout of its streets ... Without question, [they] must be able to move around the city easily and in secret, because the city – home of wealthy, powerful people and symbol of the state's prestige – is full of spying eyes.'[15]

In fact most of the operatives in Muqrin's Riyadh cells – which would be by far the most active of all the cells in the network – had either been born in the capital or had studied there.[16] Not that his men were particularly well educated. About half of them had not progressed beyond middle school. Many had dropped out of high school. There were very few university graduates among them. There is less information available about the sorts of careers they had pursued, if any, before joining the Organization, but from what is known, a large proportion of them had worked in the religious sector, mainly as imams. There was also a smattering of former teachers, policemen, and soldiers. It is possible and even likely, however, that the majority had been unemployed.

Muqrin knew as he geared up for the next big bomb attack that his cells would be sorely tested. He put his deputy Abu Ayub in charge of reconnoitring possible residential compounds. Abu Ayub selected a team of three cell members and sent them to investigate a number of compounds across the city. They were to consider the location, the number of entrances and exits, and the security in place. While they were busy doing that, Qatayni prepared the explosive material at a farm in Qaseem. He had sourced a set of industrial scales and a large grinder, and used them to transform the ammonium nitrate, fertilizer, and coal he had obtained into the raw ingredients of a truck bomb. Two tons of explosives were stored in hundreds of cartons normally used for shipping dates, and sometime in July Qatayni quietly handed the cartons over to Abu Ayub at a souq in Riyadh, who in turn distributed them to the Riyadh safe houses.

In addition to the safe house in the Shifa district where Hajj was holed up, the network had three primary safe houses in Riyadh, one in Amana, one in Shubra, and one in Rawabi. All three were raided in August and September, and the raids were a series of close calls for Muqrin. He must have worried that the MOI had uncovered his bomb-making plans, but he calmly arranged for the network to acquire three new safe houses to replace the ones he had lost. He entrusted this task to a handsome young recruit who was to become one of Muqrin's closest team members, Ibrahim al-Durayhim. On 24 September, Durayhim rented a rest house in the Dar al-Baida district, and the two truck bombs they had in storage were moved there. Another rest house, this one in the Munisiya district, was also rented in Durayhim's name. This is where the majority of Qatayni's date cartons were stored. A further safe house was established in the Suwaydi district.

Muqrin's government target was the headquarters of the Emergency Forces, the MOI's armed rapid-response unit. His residential target was a compound called Muhaya. It lay west of the city centre just south of the Diplomatic Quarter. He would later describe it as a 'den of spies'.[17] Its geographical position made it ideal. Situated within a well-watered spur of Wadi Hanifa, an ancient 120km-long valley that traverses western Riyadh, the compound's front gates were just opposite a steep hillside which fifty metres up rounded sharply into a flat plateau. The plateau offered a commanding view of the target. The compound's tidy streets and modest condominiums, nestled amongst thick clusters of palm trees, lay stretched out like a map. The high ground not only allowed for extensive surveillance, but more importantly it would enable a backup team to provide covering fire. Muhaya was a sitting duck.

That was the plan. One assault team was to bomb the Emergency Forces building in the city centre, and the other team was to attack Muhaya. From the hillside above the compound, a jihadist was to launch a surprise RPG attack on the gatehouse, then an assault vehicle down below would clear the way for the truck bomb, which would drive deep into the compound and detonate.

Muqrin faced continual harassment from the authorities. On 8 October, the farm in Qaseem was raided, although luckily by then Qatayni had finished mixing and transporting the explosive material. One officer died in the raid, and three suspects escaped in a pickup. There were further raids in Riyadh on the 12th and the 20th, and on the 19th Muqrin's Dammam cell was shut down, including its desert training camp. Yet despite all this police activity, Muqrin held back. He had another iron in the fire, another jihadist project that was as close to his heart as military operations. Until this new project was up and running, the Organization's attacks would never have the impact he needed.

Muqrin was as aware as Prince Muhammad that the real war was over hearts and minds. The Organization's media apparatus had been established previously by Ayiri, but for the most part, apart from some audio recordings, the material available on the *Al-Nida* website was limited to pamphlets, sermons, and books. Before he died, Ayiri had planned to take things further. Muqrin decided the time had come to do so.

He was more than ably assisted in this by Ayiri's assistant, Isa al-Awshen. Awshen would become very important to Muqrin. His family were deeply immersed in jihad; two younger brothers had died fighting alongside the Taliban before 9/11, a cousin had died even earlier in the first Afghan jihad, and another cousin eventually became an inmate at Guantánamo Bay.[18] According to his Al Qaeda obituary, Awshen was born in Riyadh in 1976 and attended Imam University there. After graduating, he spent two years working both in the higher court and in the Riyadh magistrates' court before starting a course in higher legal studies. But he became an ardent fundraiser for the Chechen jihad, then in full swing, and sometime in late 2000 attracted the attention of Ayiri, who recruited him to Al Qaeda.

After 9/11 Awshen left the Kingdom to fight in Afghanistan – it is possible Ayiri encouraged it, as he believed in the importance of gaining fighting experience – but something got in the way and he never made it. En route back home through Syria, he was detained by the CIA – or the 'Christian secret police', in the words of his obituarist – who handed him over to the Saudi authorities. The Mabahith banged him up in Ha'ir prison, their maximum-security detention centre, but he did not stay there long. Like several other detained mujahideen, he was soon released – and returned to Ayiri's growing media outfit.[19]

According to the Saudi media, Awshen was married to the daughter of a senior Saudi cleric, which meant he was well connected. He also became involved in recruitment. In a letter that circulated around Saudi summer camps, Awshen tried to convince the young campers to leave their bunk beds and join Al Qaeda.[20] But his primary work was as a webmaster, editor, and writer, and he worked extremely hard. Under his pseudonym Muhammad al-Salim he wrote and published a book which quickly became popular with online jihadists, *Thirty-Nine Ways to Serve and Participate in Jihad*. Included in his list are 'wholeheartedly ask God for martyrdom', 'look after a wounded or captured warrior's family', 'publicly shame hypocrites and apostates', and 'keep mum about the mujahideen and make sure their secrets do not fall into government hands'.[21]

Awshen was Ayiri's natural heir, and he was ably assisted by a range of writers and editors. In addition to his deputy Mujab al-Dosary, there was the preacher Abdullah al-Rashoud, who had led the clerical protest outside the General Presidency; a former imam called Faris al-Zahrani; Abdulaziz al-Anzi, a computer expert; Abdul Majid al-Manie, a Sharia scholar with military training who was better known by his nickname Abu Hassan; and several others. None of them had had distinguished careers before joining Al Qaeda. Several had been fired from the Ministry of Islamic Affairs for incompetence. But what they lacked in polish they made up for in commitment. Some joined the underground and were integrated into the cell structure. Others continued to live ordinary lives, working secretly for the Organization on the side, well off the MOI's radar.

Muqrin ordered Awshen's media team to move forward with Ayiri's plans for a glossy Internet publication. It was to be a full-colour periodical, and though they were not yet able to produce something completely professional-looking, nevertheless their new magazine would represent a dramatic leap forward in Al Qaeda's print propaganda. It was to include ideological material as well as martyr biographies, poems, interviews with prominent jihadists, question-and-answer sections, and vivid descriptions of attacks and operations from the point of view of the men on the ground. Muqrin and Awshen called the magazine *Voice of Jihad*, and it took the global jihadist community by storm.[22]

The first issue was released in the first week of October. 'A fortnightly magazine covering jihad and the mujahideen in the Arabian Peninsula' was written above and below the title, and its featured contents were splashed across the violet-pink cover: 'First, some doctrine to rouse the believers, and then . . . an interview with one of the wanted men from the List of Nineteen!' It also promised readers a eulogy for the 'martyred' Ayiri. The author of the issue's brief opening editorial (anonymous but probably written by Muqrin) painted a picture of hardship and disappointment. 'In a time infused with hypocrites and hypocrisy, when deserters are many and trustworthy advisers are few, the mujahideen have become strangers to their families and their loved ones, to their relations and their friends. You find only a few charitable people willing to lend a helping hand, and it is only by God's grace that supporters on the road are found at all.' But do not despair! '*Voice of Jihad* has arrived to bring relief to the mujahid, to lighten his path and guide him along the way.'

Muqrin was not targeting the masses. He was appealing directly to the mujahideen and their sympathizers. His audience already hated the House of Saud, a hatred stoked still further by excerpts from a *New Yorker* article which Awshen included in the first issue. The article quoted National Security Agency accounts of its wiretapping programme of senior Saudi royals. 'In the intercepts, princes talk openly about creaming off state coffers, and even argue about what is an acceptable percentage to take.'[23] This sort of stuff was music to Al Qaeda's ears. The translation embellished the original, and of course Awshen omitted accusations that Saudis were refusing to help the CIA and the FBI track down information about the 9/11 bombers. But it is an early example of what Al Qaeda would become very good at: taking the words of American pundits and employing them against their enemy.

Six issues of *Voice of Jihad* were published over the following three months, at which point the Organization's media wing released a sister periodical covering military matters. *Camp of the Sabre* was named in Ayiri's memory.[24] 'Many of Islam's young people today do not know how to carry weapons, let alone use them,' explained the inaugural editorial. 'For this reason, your mujahideen brethren on the Arabian Peninsula have decided to publish this magazine.' An article on the Kalashnikov outlined its technical specifications and different models and included instructions on how to load, fire, and clean it. A selection of fitness programmes was also featured, including dieting advice and an ideal two-week jogging regime: 'make sure your route avoids automobile exhaust and areas of industrial air pollution,' the writer advised. The rest of the issue was devoted to an article on guerrilla warfare written by Muqrin, a poem praising wanted men, and a number of sermons – including one by Saif al-Adel, still under house arrest in Iran.

Voice of Jihad and *Camp of the Sabre* were both big hits. Put together, they constituted a full-service guide to every aspect of the jihadist 'lifestyle'. Online message boards were full of praise. 'A veritable encyclopedia of the finest articles ever written on jihad,' raved one anonymous poster.[25] But pleased though he surely was by his readers' enthusiasm, Muqrin also wanted to realize Ayiri's ambitions for jihadist videos, and on 15 October, Awshen & Co.'s first video production appeared.

And Incite the Believers featured a simple set mocked up to resemble a talk-radio studio and starred Muqrin's in-house ideologue, the anti-establishment agitator Abdullah al-Rashoud. Rashoud did his best pantomime villain impression into the microphone, gesticulating wildly and modulating his voice like a firebrand preacher. At one point he offered to answer questions from 'listeners', just as any radio shock jock would. On cue, an arm appeared and handed him a slip of paper. Rashoud unfolded it with a flourish. 'A brother has written to us,' he read. '"I'm wanted by the Mabahith for taking part in the Afghan jihad. My question is, is it permissible to hand myself in?"' Rashoud smiled and leaned in towards his audience. 'This question is most timely,' he answered. 'My noble brethren, listen to me! Muslim brothers everywhere, attend to my words! I refer our fugitive brother to the words of a jihadist scholar of great renown: "I would rather die than live in disgrace."'

Three days after *And Incite the Believers* appeared online, Muqrin's media team released *Wills of the Heroes* as well, a long-awaited commemoration of the Riyadh compound bombings.[26] This forty-five-minute film was much more exciting; it included not only the wills of the attackers but a live recording of their assault on Alhambra. However, to commemorate the upcoming attacks on the Emergency Forces building and on Muhaya, Muqrin wanted something even more impressive.

Preparations for the attacks continued throughout the month of October. Muqrin selected the assault teams and picked out the four members who would be inside the truck bombs when they went off: **Sultan Bijad al-Otaybi** and Musaed al-Subaei would target the Emergency Forces building, and Nasser al-Sayyari and Ali al-Muabbadi would target Muhaya. Only Muabbadi was an experienced jihadist; he had fought in Bosnia and Afghanistan, knew Bin Laden, and in the late 1990s worked with Nashiri and Saikhan smuggling weapons from Yemen, for which crimes he spent time in prison. The others, by contrast, were relatively recent recruits, all in their early twenties.

Muqrin's conception for the video commemorating the upcoming bombings was ambitious. He arranged several filming sessions at safe houses around Riyadh. Cell members dressed all in black and wearing black balaclavas were filmed performing indoor guerrilla manoeuvres: sweeping an apartment, bursting in on targets, practising hand-to-hand combat. Training sessions were also filmed. A group of young jihadists – again, all in black, faces hidden – sat listening as an anonymous veteran used a whiteboard to instruct them on how to operate an RPG. Nine RPGs were lined up against the wall beside him.

Then, over an afternoon, a cameraman filmed a large group of cell members as they painted two truck bombs to look exactly like security services vehicles. They were at the Dar al-Baida safe house, and perhaps to hide the sound of the spray guns from the ears of prying neighbours, five of them played a game of football in the yard. A cream-coloured Chevy Sierra pickup was parked in the villa's drive; a Toyota Landcruiser was in the back garden. Jihadist slogans had been scrawled on the Chevy in black marker pen: 'Death to America and to the Hypocrites!', 'Expel the polytheists from the Arabian Peninsula!', and 'I bring you slaughter!'.

Subaei sat cross-legged on the raised truck bed and calmly sipped from a glass. He held a Kalashnikov in his lap. 'This is the best cup of tea I've ever had,' he said. 'I wish I had filmed my will from up here. It would have looked really cool.'

Inside the garage, cell members sat on the posterboard-strewn floor and cut out stencils of Saudi government crests which would be paint-gunned onto the trucks. The crests featured rather elaborate calligraphy, and one guy practised writing it out. 'Principality of Riyadh', he penned with a flourish. 'Where are the two swords and the palm tree?' he joked, referring to the two most prominent elements on the royal crest. Rifling through the pages of poster paper, he found what he was looking for and pieced all the items together. 'Film it, film it,' he told the cameraman.

'Hey, play fair!' one of the football players out in the yard shouted.

'Shoot! Shoot!' another cried out. A kick, and the ball flew out of sight.

'Oh come on!' They went scrambling for the ball. 'Where is it? Have you seen it?' one of them panted, directing his question at a group of cell members huddled around the Chevy.

They ignored him. One of them held up a spray gun and began applying a first coat of light-brown paint to the truck. The graffiti which had earlier been scrawled all over it were not easily covered over. One referred to Prince Nayef and was particularly offensive. It read, 'A gift to the Minister of Thievery!', but instead of using Nayef's real surname, they gave him one that rhymed with it, Nayef bin Abdulingliz, 'the son of England's slave'. Nayef's father King Abdulaziz had been, in the mind of jihadists, simply a pawn in the British Empire's imperial war games.

'It hasn't been fully painted over, you can still read it. Give it some more!' the cameraman shouted above the din of the gun.

When they finished, they switched to black paint and began spraying on the distinctive camouflage blotches typical of Saudi army vehicles. 'It looks good,' the painter declared.

'I don't know. Now it looks like a cow,' the cameraman replied, only half-joking.

'Oh shit, look at the drips.' Thin black streaks were running down the side of the truck.

'We haven't got the balance right. You need more air.'

'Yeah, more air.'

The disguise was not convincing enough, so they decided to begin again. Out in the yard, where the boys were still kicking around a ball, they re-mixed the paint. One of the football players wandered over. 'What's in there?' he asked, indicating the paint can.

'It's a very dangerous explosive mixture,' the man drily replied.

'Hey, fatty, don't scare them like that,' the other painter chided. 'They'll believe you.'

The paint mixed and loaded, they returned to the truck. The spraying operation was much more successful this time. 'Good job, Sadeeq!' an onlooker cried out. Immigrant labourers are referred to as Sadeeq by the Saudis. The cell members were bemused at how much hard work they were doing. Ordinarily they would not be caught dead painting a car.

The guy manning the spray gun decided to play along. Adopting an exaggerated South Asian accent, he said, 'Hey boss, I'm working as fast as I can,' and everyone burst into laughter. Then they gathered around and watched as the stencil with the Saudi army crest was attached to the driver's side door and carefully painted on.

Meanwhile in the back garden, another team had completed the transformation of the Landcruiser into an Emergency Forces vehicle. Both trucks were then lined up side by side for a photo shoot with the men who would be driving them to martyrdom.

The Landcruiser's windscreen bore a sign reading 'The Turki al-Dandani Brigade'; the one on the Chevy read 'The Yusuf al-Ayiri Brigade'. Sultan Bijad stood between the two vehicles holding a sign which declared with a flourish, 'Together in the War on the Crusaders!' A paper number plate bearing the number 314 had been taped to the Landcruiser.

'This number, 314,' Sultan Bijad explained, 'symbolizes the number of companions who along with the Prophet – peace be upon him – fought in the great battle of Badr, which took place in the month of Ramadan, the month we are now in . . .'

'Hey, brother, don't go on and on,' someone called out, and they all laughed.

Later that night the cell members changed into white thobes and assembled in the villa's majlis for a further filming session. Unusually, Muqrin and several top commanders were there. Seated on the floor, everyone present held a Kalashnikov and one or two wore RPGs slung across their backs. Apart from the four soon-to-be martyrs, everyone's face was covered. Abdullah al-Rashoud the firebrand preacher entered, sat down, and delivered his usual diatribe. Then he invited a young child called Osama, no more than eight years old, to stand before the mujahideen and chant.

'Will you repeat verse by verse, or shall I do it alone?' Osama asked.

'Without repetition,' Rashoud instructed.

Osama's voice was sweet.

> The blood of martyrdom flows in my veins
> Oh! What is sweeter than death in the gardens of faith?
> My longing for the eternal paradise of Eden spurs me on.

There was no applause, but as Osama returned to his place on the floor he was greeted by soft exclamations of approval from the audience. 'Oh wow!' 'Incredible.' 'What a sweet face.'

The night wore on. They chanted several poems all together, call-and-response style, each man taking his turn to lead the group. The poems praised past mujahideen leaders in Afghanistan and serenaded the four sacrificial victims, who were soon to meet God like a bride meeting her bridegroom.

God, wed the martyr and may the wedding befit him
Wed the martyr in his second house in paradise
Wed the martyr in his garment of bloody wounds
His forehead is scented, don't wipe the dust away from it

Between each verse the group, now standing, replied rhythmically 'Allah, Allah!' and swayed gently from side to side.

I want martyrdom in a bright burial ground
And afterwards, the Heavenly Virgins in paradise
In paradise with my bountiful Lord
Today I do not want this world
I want martyrdom in a bright burial ground

On and on the chanting went, but despite the fervency of the lyrics, the mood was rather sombre. The four uncovered faces were thoughtful, pensive, even anxious.

Later, the suicide bombers sat in a row and gave interviews to the camera.

'Brother Hassan,' the cameraman asked Sultan Bijad, known as Hassan by the cell members. 'It has been said by the media that the compound bombings in May only killed nine Americans. How many American victims do you estimate there were?'

Sultan Bijad adopted an objective air. 'The corrupt media wants to make it seem like only a few Americans died, in order to encourage people to hate the mujahideen. But those three locations were chosen carefully. The Vinnell Corporation is a branch of the American intelligence corps, and the Seville compound was actually a settlement for Christians and Jews, and it was owned by the American Department of Defense. As for the Alhambra compound, well, that was actually a big church where they worship a god other than Allah. The American media initially reported that ninety Americans were killed. That is the truer number, but then they conspired to make the number appear lower.'

Sultan Bijad was a good talker. 'I want to talk about an experience I had, oh, about five years ago. The Saudi government – those slaves of America – are always saying that their doors are wide open, that if you ever need anything, then they would be glad to receive you. So some brothers and I decided to go talk to them about how they were not fulfilling their obligations to God. We only wanted to advise them, to fulfil our own obligations by offering them our advice. Nothing radical, nothing any good Muslim wouldn't agree with. So we went to Jeddah and sought an audience with the crown prince and his advisers.

'When we arrived, they rejected our application and sent us to someone else, someone minor whom I had not heard of. We waited and waited and eventually he asked us, "What do you want?" Of course we didn't tell him that we wanted to see the crown prince to give him religious advice. No. Instead one of the brothers said, "We are poor, we need land, we need money." It was a good ruse because when he heard that, he thought he had made a mistake. You see, they had actually known why we were really there, and that's why they hadn't let us in.

'So after a while two of us were allowed in to see him. We were four, but they only let two of us in, again after waiting a long, long time. The two went in and spoke to the crown prince. They brought up certain points and pointed out a few transgressions. And he had to agree with them, even his stupidest adviser agreed. They had no choice, it was obvious. But as is their habit they only said, "Inshallah, all will be well," and sent us on our way. And of course they did nothing. In the five years since, their transgressions have only increased.'

Sultan Bijad related several other similar anecdotes in which the mujahideen try to engage productively with the royal family and the religious establishment but are rebuffed. The cameraman then turned to Sayyari. 'Brother, perhaps you would like to say something to Crown Prince Abdullah?'

Sayyari was very soft-spoken. 'I have nothing to say to him, other than: repent, turn back to your God and return to Islam. Give up your allegiance to infidels, shun secularists, and stop ruling the country according to un-Islamic precepts. Abandon all this, for if you do not, we will come with our swords and bring you death.'

Muqrin had decided that the operation would be launched on 12 November, which was the seventeenth day of Ramadan, the 1422nd anniversary of the battle of Badr – the battle that turned the tide of the Prophet's war with the polytheists of Mecca. On 1 November, a house in the Aziziya district was raided, and Muqrin knew the MOI would have found empty cans of paint along with the stencils which his men had stashed there after their painting session in Dar al-Baida. Yet despite the MOI nipping at his heels, Muqrin maintained remarkable composure.

The pressure then began to increase. On 3 November his cell in Mecca was uncovered thanks to an anonymous tip-off, and its safe house in the Sharaye district was raided. It was no ordinary raid; the MOI brought armoured cars and used search helicopters to shut down the whole neighbourhood. Five of Muqrin's men were arrested, but even so, the raid was an example of the officers' poor training. The massive security coverage should have prevented anyone getting through the cordon, yet two carloads got away: a pickup truck carrying two militants and a

Toyota Camry carrying three with a further man in the open boot providing cover with an RPG.

The Camry was pursued, one cell member was killed, and the others were arrested. As for the pickup truck, it was chased to a mountainous area between Mecca and Ta'if. In the darkness before dawn, the two fugitives abandoned the vehicle next to a goatherd's shack and ran up into the hills.[27] As the sun rose on the steep rocky hillside, they could see more and more security men gathering until a veritable army of police stood spread out across the plain below. Two helicopters circled. Officers in groups of six or seven spread out and began snaking their way up the slope, clambering over boulders and ducking to avoid the thorns of the acacia trees. Seeing the writing on the wall, the two cell members detonated their suicide belts. The soldiers collected the scattered body parts and carried them down the hill.

Two days later in Riyadh, two men affiliated with Muqrin's cell there were spotted at a garage attempting to buy a specific kind of sheet metal used to line the beds of truck bombs. They were arrested, though not before one of them threw a grenade which he had hidden in his pocket. It never went off.

Those arrests led to two more, and Muqrin began to get worried. He stayed holed up in his safe house in the Suwaydi district; instead of going to his operatives, they came to him. Visitors to the villa would not ring the front bell. Instead, they would park two houses down and ring the villa using their mobile phones. Then someone would open the door for them and they would slip inside. What Muqrin did not know was that this odd behaviour attracted the attention of the neighbours. They reported it to the authorities, who placed the villa under surveillance.

At dawn on 6 November, six days before the operation was due to launch, Muqrin was horrified to find the villa surrounded by a detachment of Emergency Forces and a team from the Security Patrols. They demanded that those inside give themselves up. Muqrin had five men with him, all well armed. He and four others put on army fatigues and climbed into their car, which was parked in the driveway behind the villa's perimeter wall. The remaining cell member, Abdullilah al-Otaybi, was ordered to strap on a suicide vest and clear a way for them to escape.

It was a death sentence, but Otaybi did as he was told. Running out into the street with his Kalashnikov, he pelted the surrounding soldiers with gunfire. This drew their attention just long enough for the car carrying Muqrin and the others to ram through the driveway's aluminium gate and speed away. Otaybi was cut down by the soldiers' return of fire. Muqrin and his men managed to wound eight soldiers in their flight, but their exhilaration was tempered when a cell member called Amr al-Shihri was shot. He was alive, but the wound was bad.

A queue of vehicles forced them to stop at one of the regular checkpoints that had proliferated around the city in recent months. They got out of the car, and Muqrin and another man forced a random citizen out of his vehicle and sped away. The other three car-jacked a silver Mazda and made their getaway in that, though a few minutes later they switched cars again. They drove up to two civilians and informed them that they were requisitioning their vehicle. They ordered them out and forced them to help them move Shihri, who was bleeding profusely. As the two men watched their car drive off, the car-jackers called out, 'We are your mujahideen brethren! Imagine the reward in store for you, for helping us today!'[28]

Muqrin had come extremely close to being killed, or worse – captured. Too close. He could not afford to wait until the anniversary of the battle of Badr on the 12th. The attack needed to be launched immediately.

Abu Ayub was in direct charge of the operation. He organized two attack teams. Each team comprised three cars: a truck bomb and two support vehicles.

At the last minute, Muqrin changed his mind about who the

suicide bombers should be for the attack on the Emergency Forces. We do not know why, but Sultan Bijad and Subaei were replaced by two others who remain unknown. And the plan was no longer to use the disguised Chevy Sierra, but a white Datsun which had also been wired up. Muqrin's group always had several truck bombs stashed away, and at the last minute he decided it would be better if the truck bomb did not look like a military vehicle. Maybe he thought the MOI would be especially on the lookout for such a vehicle after discovering the stencils in the Aziziya house. Whatever the reason, it was a white Datsun that headed towards the Emergency Forces building.

Its two support vehicles, a Ford saloon and a Jeep Cherokee, left from a separate location. The plan was for the three cars to rendezvous at an empty lot off the Jeddah Road. The man in the passenger seat of the jeep filmed the journey to the rendezvous point.

'We're gonna get there ahead of time, we're not running late at all,' the driver said. They were cruising down the highway, the saloon up ahead.

'Shall I film them?' the cameraman asked, referring to the guys in the Ford. 'Overtake, overtake!'

The jeep zoomed forward and passed the saloon, whose passengers noticed the camera. They gave the cameraman a thumbs-up.

'Did you get them?' the driver asked.

'Yeah, I filmed them.'

He lowered the camcorder onto his lap and silence descended. The dashboard clock read 11:13 p.m. 'Allahu akbar, Allahu akbar. There is no god but God,' the driver chanted softly.

The cameraman's mobile phone rang. 'Hello? *Salaam alaykum*. Hello? ... No, you've got the wrong number.' He hung up. It had not been a wrong number; it was code, in case the authorities were listening in. 'He's looking for you, Abdul Rahman.'

'Who was it? I can't ring him back, my phone is locked and I don't have the password.'

The driver slowed down. 'Traffic light cameras, gotta be careful,' he said.

They sat in silence. Then the driver asked, 'Hey, guys, did you do the evening prayer?'

'Yeah, we did.'

'Individually, or all together?'

'Individually.'

When they arrived at the empty lot, the driver suggested they get ready to film the Datsun when it arrived. 'Film the overpass, there. We'll see them pass by.'

The man called Abdul Rahman continued to fret about his mobile phone. He did not have the code to unlock it. 'Well, who set the phone up?' someone asked him.

'The other guys. They'll be here in a minute.'

After ninety seconds or so, the Datsun pulled up. 'Film, film!' the driver inside the jeep ordered. Then he leaned out the window and shouted at the two suicide bombers. 'Hey, sheikh! Listen, what's your unlock code?'

'2049.'

'2049, right,' he confirmed.

'Hey, you behind the wheel!' the cameraman called out to one of the bombers. 'Show us your face!' The bomber resisted. He did not want to be filmed. 'Come on, show us your face!' He finally relented, and when he leaned forward, the group inside the jeep burst into praise for the martyrs-to-be.

'Now hit the gas and trust in God!' The Datsun sped away. The men inside the jeep continued to holler. 'God grant you every success! May your mission be successful, brothers! Allahu akbar!'

'Do I have to film the others?' the cameraman asked, referring to the Ford which had not yet arrived.

'No,' the driver said. 'Let's go, I still need to do evening prayers.'

Abdul Rahman typed in 2049 on his mobile phone and called someone, probably Abu Ayub, to let him know that the Datsun was on its way to its appointed target.

At the safe house in Dar al-Baida, the Muhaya bombing team had been getting ready to leave. Abu Ayub was climbing into a Nissan Pathfinder. He and one other were in charge of driving to the top of the cliff opposite the compound's front gates, from which they would fire an RPG at the guardhouse to start the attack. Then a Nissan Maxima carrying three cell members with assault rifles and grenades was going to ram the gate and kill the security guards. Once the way was clear, the Landcruiser disguised as an Emergency Forces vehicle would drive into the compound and Sayyari and Muabbadi would martyr themselves.

Just before setting out, they had had one last informal shooting session with Sayyari. He had shaved off his moustache for the special occasion, in imitation of the Prophet.

'What's the reason for your new look, sheikh?' the cameraman asked.

'Well, um . . .' Sayyari smiled. 'We have a matter to settle with, um, with the Christians.'

'Ooo, a battle!'

'Well, let's just say we're bringing them a present.'

'Oh yeah? How big is this present?'

Sayyari's innocent-looking face gazed suggestively into the camera. 'About half a ton.'

8

The List of Twenty-Six

The vast majority of Muhaya residents were Muslims, despite what Al Qaeda may have believed. They had broken their Ramadan fast at around 5 p.m. After eating a date or two, as tradition dictated, and quenching their day-long thirst, the men had gone to mosque for the sunset prayer and then had gathered with their families for a generous *iftar* meal. Happily fed, the men had then returned to mosque for evening prayer at 7:15, and the more pious among them stayed on for *taraweeh*, a special night session of further prayers and Qur'anic recitation. The rest had returned home, or called on friends, with whom they intended to continue celebrating long into the night.

At precisely 11:50 p.m., the sound of a small explosion pierced the convivial atmosphere. Someone had fired an RPG from the steep hillside opposite and the gatehouse had been hit. Then, a few seconds later, a Nissan Maxima drove up and rammed the gates. Two militants got out and shot the guards, tossing grenades into the burning gatehouse for good measure. Once the way was clear, a Landcruiser painted to look like an Emergency Forces vehicle drove ninety-one metres into the compound and detonated.

The massive explosion could be heard for miles around. Soldiers from the nearest Emergency Forces building were immediately dispatched to the blast site. They would later find out that, as they drove off, they had passed another truck bomb parked outside the building and that they had been its target. However, the suicide bombers, who had arrived as planned, had then panicked and failed to detonate. When they saw the soldiers speed away from the building, they realized that the Muhaya bomb must have already gone off, and seeing as the building was now empty, they aborted the mission and drove back to their safe house.

At Muhaya, the traffic police and the Security Patrols secured the perimeter, in case there were attackers still inside or more on the way.[1] Inside the compound, large floodlights illuminated the clouds of concrete dust that hung in the air. The hum of generators was deafening. Smoke poured out of the Landcruiser's smouldering chassis, and hundreds of soldiers, paramedics, and rescuers thronged among the palm trees and the rubble. The buildings around the crater had been almost completely demolished. Top floors had collapsed, crushing the floors below, and rescuers were busy claiming bodies from the devastation. In the chaos and confusion, forensics teams were struggling to label the corpses. Many of the victims were children.

A boy of seven or eight lay on a stretcher. He was wearing only pyjama bottoms, and though he had been killed in the blast, mercifully his body bore only signs of bruising and superficial lacerations.

'Anyone know his name?' someone called out.

'Just write "Lebanese boy" for now,' replied another, as he placed a number 4 on the boy's chest from a pile of numbered cards.

'Wait, if he's the fourth, then who is the third?' the first man asked. 'I mean, there are two children over there . . .'

'Yeah, and this is the fourth. There's a woman, over there. She's the third.'

'Ah, the woman, right. Do you have her name yet?'

'Maya Sharbil something . . .'

The forensic officer politely but firmly turned towards a cameraman. 'I beg your pardon, move back a little.' Cameras were recording everything. 'Now, what was her name?'

'Maya Sharbil al-Mizhri.'

'Bring me a pen, to write her name.'

The cameraman approached the body labelled number 1.

'Just write "female child" on her,' an examining officer said.

Someone called out, 'Wait, hasn't anyone found out her name yet?'

'No, not yet.' The cameraman moved closer to the dead girl. A towel was draped over her face. 'You can lift the towel if you need to film it, but there's no face.' The cameraman's assistant lifted the towel. 'God give you strength,' the forensic officer muttered.

Further away, a man in a bloodied thobe was being interviewed by investigators. 'I only saw one guy, but there were two cars. One exploded, and one drove off.'

'One drove off?'

'Yeah, I mean, had that car stayed inside, it would have been destroyed too.'

A call went out. 'We've got sandals!' A group of workmen were clambering over a mesh of iron poles, electrical wiring, and cement pieces. 'There's someone trapped inside. Fetch a torch!'

The cameramen raced to the scene. One of them asked, 'Alive or dead?' They crowded in on the rescuers, who were using crowbars to lever away bits of masonry. 'Listen, will you move out of the way?' one of them spoke sharply into the camera. 'Take a step back, please!'

Two small legs clad in turquoise pyjama bottoms protruded

out from underneath a huge slab of concrete. A rescuer heaved his crowbar with all his might. 'I'm weakening it, I'm weakening it.'

'Crowbar! Another crowbar!' someone cried. A second one was set to work against the slab.

'Okay, I see a belly,' a paramedic said. He had positioned himself below the trapped legs. They could see that the body belonged to yet another little girl. The top of her nappy was sticking out above her pyjamas. 'Careful, just a little bit more.' The slab gave way another inch and the paramedic was able to slide underneath enough to release the body. A stretcher was waiting. 'Quickly, quickly,' the paramedic motioned, and two of his colleagues assisted him in gently lifting the limp body onto it, which was then raised above the fray.

'Is she dead?' someone called from the back. No answer was given, or needed.

The MOI was quick to take advantage of their enemy's error. The compound was home mainly to Muslim Arabs, some even Saudis. The footage from the MOI's in-house camera teams was collated, edited, and distributed to the media. TV crews were sent to the hospitals that had received the wounded to interview victims and their doctors. One of them, a young Lebanese woman, was in shock. Small flecks of blood lined her face from the glass that had struck her, and gauze patched one of her eyes.

'There were foreigners, but three-quarters of them were Lebanese. I don't know the reason for this attack, as there were no foreigners ...' – she meant Westerners – '... living in that part of the compound.'

'And what sort of businesses were present in the compound?'

'Seventy-five per cent of them were Arab companies. There were Lebanese, Syrians, Palestinians. There were some Indians, and some Westerners, but very few.'

'Did they all work for one particular company?'

'No, no, all kinds of companies.'

'Thank you, we hope you get better soon.'

Another interviewer pulled aside a young medic. 'Dr Fahd, we have been told that there are many children among the patients.'

'Yes,' the doctor replied. 'More than five of the wounded here are children – that's approximately twenty-five per cent of all the injured.'

On Saudi state television, the newsreader soberly delivered a summary of the dead and wounded. 'The Muhaya compound in Wadi Laban in west Riyadh has been assaulted by armed men and a car loaded with explosives. People of different nationalities have been killed, primarily Arab nationals.' He then announced that eleven people had been killed. The following day that number would rise to seventeen: seven Lebanese, four Egyptians, a Saudi, and a Sudanese, along with four others whose nationalities were not made public. A hundred and twenty-two people had been injured. The newsreader signed off. 'The Ministry of Interior is saying that it has begun an investigation and will issue an official communiqué soon, and asks that God grant them every success.'

Shortly after, Prince Nayef held a press conference. 'I cannot stress this enough,' the 70-year-old interior minister said. 'No mercy or leniency will be shown to anyone who even contemplates perpetrating such acts. We will catch them, by God, however long it takes. Among the sons of our nation, at the forefront in the fight are the security forces. They shall work unceasingly until we are all completely confident that our country has rid itself of every devil and sick evil-doer, and rooted out every traitor to God's religion and to the nation.' The message was much the same as the crown prince's after the Riyadh compound bombings. However, its characterization of the security services as heroes of a united nation was a new note. And it foreshadowed a very real shift in the public's perception of the conflict, a shift largely precipitated by Muhaya. Certainly, the public had condemned the Riyadh compound bombings as criminal and unacceptable. Following Muhaya, however, their antipathy to Al Qaeda became outspoken, even passionate.

A week after the bombing, Ali al-Khudayr, one of the Takfeeri Troika, was persuaded to publicly recant his previous jihadist positions. 'This bloodletting must be stopped,' he said. The following month, Ahmad al-Khalidi and Nasr al-Fahd also publicly recanted, and all three sheikhs appeared in a TV programme on national television. 'It is now clear,' Khalidi said, 'that without a doubt, some of the fatwas we issued ... were false.' About their fatwa legitimizing the killing of members of the Saudi security services, Fahd was unequivocal. 'The soldier is a Muslim, and he remains a Muslim as long as he bears witness that "there is no god but God".' Khudayr agreed, and went on to address the question of foreigners. 'As for those with whom we have entered into a treaty of protection ...' – i.e. non-Muslims inside the Kingdom – '... the texts are clear that an attack upon them is forbidden.'

In the same programme, a panel of Islamic legal specialists addressed at some length the particularly thorny issue of takfeer. One of the panellists, Professor Kamal Habib, said, 'Some of our younger clerics have taken up the topic of takfeer, saying that he who does not declare an infidel to be an infidel is himself an infidel. They even started branding our elites as apostate.' The professor made it clear that such an approach is unlawful. 'Just like a ruling on murder, a ruling on takfeer must be brought before a judge, a specialist in Sharia law backed up by the state.' The three former takfeeris echoed the professor's judgement.

That the programme and the rest of the government's counterterrorism media campaign had the desired effect of shifting some extremist Saudis away from takfeerism and towards moderation in religion is amply demonstrated by Al Qaeda's reaction. The fourth issue of *Voice of Jihad*, which came out two weeks after the Muhaya bombing, included an impassioned screed condemning the government's propaganda campaign which followed it.

> They began to tell the people that the explosions ... caused very little damage and that no more than ten people had been killed ... What's more, they announced that most of the victims were women and children, as if that military base, the Muhaya compound, was nothing but a refuge for widows and orphans ... [These announcements] served one purpose only: to confirm that the residents were Muslim Arabs and that there was only a very small number of Westerners ... But since when does the ex-pat Arab community live in such extraordinary luxury? It is known that these places cost 300,000 riyals [£47,000] per annum! Which Arabs are these that are protected by the government's soldiers and tanks ...? If these were Muslims and Arabs, what happened to the hundreds who were injured or killed, and why have we not seen any footage of them or their families? They interviewed only three or four people on television ... If the mujahideen wanted to target Arabs or Muslims as they are trying to claim, why wouldn't they have chosen the thousands of places in the Peninsula that are congested with Arabs and Muslims, which have no security or tanks to protect them? ... They continue to spread their lies and deception, but I can assure you that their media use the policy of 'lie, then lie some more, until the people believe you'.

But the people did believe what the government told them. As a result, ordinary Saudis began playing an increasingly significant role in the fight against terrorism. Acting as a government informant had had a stigma attached to it. Now the hotlines which had been set up early in the campaign for people to phone in suspicious activity began to be used more frequently. Prince Muhammad would go on to say that more than anything else, the greater willingness on the part of the public to help the security services in the fight was the single most important factor in the government's continuing success.

In the aftermath of the Muhaya bombing, the MOI further ratcheted up security. There were more checkpoints, more metal detectors, and more patrols, especially in Riyadh. On 13 November a patrol surveying rest houses in the Dar al-Baida district noticed a parked car with its door standing open. The officers got out and peered through the windows. Noticing a box of ammunition, they raised the alarm and the rest house was raided. It was the safe house that Abu Ayub's attack team had used in the run-up to the bombing. No one was inside, and along with the usual assortment of weaponry, two computer disks were found containing information on planned bombings and – ominously – targeted assassinations.

That raid led to another, six days later, on the rest house in the Munisiya district. Again the rest house was empty, and there was not much weaponry inside, but even so it contained evidence indicating that it was an important Al Qaeda safe house. There was a machine for forging ID cards, electrical tools, a video camera, and documents and newspaper clippings related to the Organization's activities. They would later discover that the attack team targeting the Emergency Forces building had been based there.

On the 26th, the patrols saw some real action. They spotted a car bearing a suspicious number plate, and when they signalled to the driver to pull over, he opened fire on them and sped away. They pursued him to a rest house in the Sulay district. He ran inside to join a colleague, and a shootout ensued between them and the soldiers. The two suspects then got into another car and sped away, one of them behind the wheel and the other inside the open boot carrying an RPG. They managed to break through the security barrier, but the patrolmen were on their heels and during the pursuit the terrorist in the boot was shot dead before he had a chance to fire a rocket. The driver ended up stopping the car in an unpaved lot. He got out and ran into a nearby rest house. The soldiers followed him but luckily kept their distance: he suddenly exploded. He had been wearing a bomb vest. Evidence from the raid led to an arrest the following day and to the seizure of a SAM 7 surface-to-air missile and other weapons, as well as plans and surveillance footage of the Seder residential compound in Riyadh.

Despite the MOI's successes, the situation remained tense and the Kingdom's reputation as a safe place to live and work was deteriorating. The American government was informed about the surveillance footage, and at the beginning of December the State Department warned its nationals of the possibility of a further attack. At the same time, the Foreign Office warned Britons to avoid all but essential travel to Saudi Arabia.[2]

On 4 December a new chapter in the war began. Abdulaziz al-Huwayrini, a major-general in the Mabahith and the Kingdom's foremost expert on Al Qaeda and Islamist terrorism, was wounded in an attack in Riyadh, along with his brother, an officer in the Air Force. There had been attacks on security men in the past, but no one so senior. More would follow.

Two days later the MOI released a new most-wanted list containing twenty-six names: seven from the original list who were still at large and nineteen new ones. On 8 December the list officially shed its first name. Ibrahim al-Rayyes, a veteran jihadist who had helped organize the Muhaya bombing, was killed in a shootout at a petrol station in the Suwaydi district. A civilian tip-off had led police to his location. On 20 December number twelve on the list, Mansour Faqih, turned himself in. Twenty-four from the List of Twenty-Six remained at large.

At the end of December, another high-level Mabahith officer was targeted. On the morning of the 29th, Major Ibrahim al-Dhaali, a notorious interrogator, got into his Lexus and was about to turn the ignition when the smell of something burning rose up from underneath his seat. Reacting quickly, he threw the door open and hurled himself onto the ground outside. Moments later, his car exploded. Luckily he escaped with only minor injuries. Video footage discovered the following year showed masked Al Qaeda members building the bomb, transporting it to Dhaali's flat, putting it in place beneath the driver's seat, and videotaping the explosion from a car across the street.

Following the assassination attempts on the three officers, press releases appeared on the Internet from an organization calling itself the Haramain Brigades taking responsibility for the attacks. The MOI suspected this was merely a front, a fake organization concocted to shift the focus of blame away from Al Qaeda after any attack deemed particularly heinous by the general population. Detainees would later confirm this suspicion.[3] They would also reveal that Muqrin had established a cell overseen by Abu Ayub specifically for assassinations.

The pressure on the MOI was beginning to show. Major-General Saud al-Halal was in charge of the Riyadh Security Patrols and remembers the mood of the time. 'I was personally targeted, I was one of the names on Al Qaeda's assassination list. It didn't worry me much. But I knew it would be difficult for my family, so I kept it from them, even from my mother. She'd see a report on the news and ask, "You weren't involved in that, were you?" and I'd say "No, they sent my colleagues," but of course I had been there.

'Actually the worst thing was witnessing the death of fellow soldiers. The Security Patrols were often tasked with carrying away the dead and wounded. I remember once a colleague and I were transporting a dead patrolman off the field, when his mobile phone rang. It was his wife checking up on him. That sort of situation is just tragic, and though you try not to let it upset you, when you get home the truth you hold inside begins to hurt. It begins to hurt a lot.'

On 19 January 2004, police in the Naseem district in east-central Riyadh came under fire when they tried to inspect a suspect vehicle's number plate. 'A person accompanying the driver opened fire at the police patrol,' the city's chief of police said in a statement. 'The driver and his companion later stopped in a crowded area, hijacked the car of a citizen at gunpoint, and fled.' They had used a civilian as a human shield during the shootout.[4]

Not long afterwards, a father contacted the authorities about the whereabouts of his son, **Khalid al-Farraj**, who was wanted by the MOI. Farraj, they would discover, was closely connected to Abu Ayub's assassination cell. A logistics guy, Farraj was in charge of the cell's day-to-day operations.

Farraj was placed under surveillance. On 29 January two agents followed him to a plumbers' merchant store he owned.[5] He entered the shop, leaving his wife in the car. The Mabahith followed him inside and placed him under arrest. They escorted him to their car and drove to his house in Fayha. On the way they passed a jeep coming in the opposite direction. It slowed down suspiciously, and the Mabahith officers asked Farraj if he recognized it. He said he didn't, and they drove on. When they reached his house, five more MOI agents were waiting, along with Farraj's father. They began to search the place.

Two agents went upstairs with Farraj. 'I was on the second floor when the gunshots began,' Farraj later recounted on television. In fact he had recognized the guys in the Jeep; they were Abu Ayub's men. Though she was never charged with a crime, Mabahith agents allege that Farraj's wife had phoned his colleagues from the car in front of the shop after watching the security men lead her husband away. (Why they did not arrest her along with Farraj is a telling comment on gender relations inside the Kingdom.) Farraj expected his fellow Al Qaeda members to stage a rescue. 'But I never expected it to happen the way it did.'[6]

Abu Ayub and five others from the assassination squad drove up to the house. Muqrin was with them. They leapt out of their car, guns blazing. Farraj's father was standing outside the front gate with two security men; all three were instantly killed. One of the squad ran up to a parked police car and pumped two bullets into the policeman in the driver's seat. Two gunmen then stood guard as Abu Ayub and two others headed for the house.

Farraj was upstairs with the two officers, who were searching his bedroom. Upon hearing the shooting, the officers slammed the bedroom door. As one of them shoved a large wardrobe in front of it, the other pushed Farraj against the wall, drew his pistol and pointed it at him: stay quiet, or else.

Meanwhile, Abu Ayub and his two men had killed the officer stationed in the front garden and entered the house. They found two more in the sitting room and shot them both. One fell back onto the sofa and slumped there dead, covered in blood. The other fell face down onto the floor. Abu Ayub ran upstairs but was unable to get inside the barricaded bedroom. Knowing they did not have time to spare, he signalled a withdrawal and they all made their way back to the car. As they drove off, they fired a few shots at a soldier on the roof of Farraj's house, though he escaped without injury.

Farraj and his captors heard the attackers' car speed away. 'One of the intelligence officers with me walked over to the window and peered down at the ugly scene below,' Farraj said. They then made their way downstairs. 'It was a real shock, I mean a huge shock. I never imagined I would find a pool of blood in my own home. On our way out of the house, I saw bodies in the living room. There was blood everywhere.' The security men managed to hurry Farraj outside and into a police car without him noticing his own father lying among the corpses. 'Later I found out that my father had also been killed, may God rest his soul. At first I refused to believe that the ones who had killed him were from the cell. I just couldn't believe it.' In the interrogations of Farraj that followed, the MOI emphasized Muqrin's culpability in his father's death. Farraj grew to despise Muqrin, and became one of the MOI's most important informants. 'We had worked alongside each other. I had helped him in his work. After everything we had been through together, this is how he repaid me, by killing my father.'[7]

A television report prepared by the MOI described the gruesome details. The killing of a father struck a chord in a society so mindful of the respect due to parents. 'Hamoud bin Juwayr al-Farraj, the suspect's father, was the model of a caring and loyal citizen,' the report said. 'He died instantly, may God have mercy on him, along with six members of the security forces. Orders have been given to pay them the respect they are due, including the civilian Hamoud al-Farraj. We ask God to accept them among His martyrs.'[8]

Investigations led the MOI to three further safe houses in the area. They seized even more weapons and explosives, as well as a wired-up pickup, and made seven further arrests.

One of the safe houses contained a makeshift infirmary complete with hospital bed and medical supplies.[9] The MOI learnt that it was where Amr al-Shihri had been taken after the raid on Muqrin's safe house in Suwaydi the previous November; the network had not risked taking him to hospital. One of the walls was covered with egg cartons to muffle his screams as, slowly and painfully, he died.

Video footage of his funeral, which was discovered later, shows how emaciated the once robust Shihri had become during his agonizing last days. His body is wrapped in a white sheet, and his gaunt face and bulging glassy eyes still bear the marks of his agony. Armed, masked Al Qaeda members stand in rows on either side of the bed. Network preacher Abdullah al-Rashoud stands above the corpse and delivers another thunderous sermon. 'The desire of those who kill in the name of God – their most beautiful, most fervent desire! – is to meet the Almighty, having been granted such an honourable fate as this,' he says, indicating the shrouded Shihri laid out before him. His sermon over, he instructs the jihadists either side of him to honour their fallen brother. One by one they bend over and kiss Shihri's cold forehead.

Footage of a video will that Shihri had filmed the previous summer would also be discovered. In it he quotes a companion of the Prophet Muhammad, and prays that the words would one day apply to him: 'Oh how I wish I could fight and die in the path of God, and then be revived and be killed again, and then revived and killed again!'

Twenty-three names were now left on the MOI's wanted list.

Mabahith headquarters were in an ugly and cramped concrete building in the busy Ulaysha neighbourhood, just south of the city centre. Next to it lay the women's campus of King Saud University. The proximity of young women and the density of the surrounding neighbourhood may have been reasons why the Organization had not targeted the building.

Traffic in and out of the area was horrible. Agents habitually complained about the length of their commutes, although by that point in the war, many felt lucky to be able to go home at all. It had become common for the most hard-pressed and dedicated analysts to work through the night, snatching sleep whenever possible by stretching out on the floor beside their desks.

Saudi civilians were dialling the agency's emergency hotline more and more. Most of the time, it was for reasons of genuine suspicion. But there were also a lot of frustrating false alarms to wade through. People would ring up absolutely certain they had passed someone from a wanted list in the street – someone who had been killed months before. There were more egregious abuses as well, such as when people would ring up to denounce neighbours with whom they had been arguing. Some of these less serious tip-offs gave rise to unexpected but welcome moments of levity. A wife rang up one day, convinced her husband was running a terrorist cell from their house. Or so she claimed. In fact, when investigators went round, they soon realized that her husband had been hosting a number of male visitors who, in the eyes of his wife, had rather overstayed their welcome. She thought that by denouncing them to the Mabahith, she might get rid of them.

Dealing with genuine suspects was also a strain, though it was also sometimes amusing. Interrogators soon realized that their prisoners had been taught to lie about the dissolute lives they led. Debauched weekends in Dubai or Bahrain were a particularly common story. It was a losing strategy, however. The interrogators were themselves far too familiar with those places for the lie to hold water. 'Oh, so you had a night out on the town in Bahrain, did you?' they would ask. 'How much did you drink? On which street did you find your prostitute? How much did you pay for her?' The suspect, who was in fact almost always extremely naïve about such things, would invariably bungle his answer.

On 8 February the Mabahith noticed a flurry of excitement on jihadist websites. An uploaded video file called *Badr of Riyadh* celebrating the Muhaya bombing was being downloaded by jihadists around the world. It was the Organization's follow-up to *Wills of the Heroes*, but it was a much more sophisticated production. The footage which had been filmed back in October of cell members manufacturing grenades, constructing and camouflaging the two truck bombs, and feting the martyrs at the Dar al-Baida safe house had been slyly edited together with their suicide wills and Western media footage in such a way as to make the Organization appear professional, meticulous, and utterly serious. The football, the crude jokes, and the screw-ups had been left on the cutting-room floor. There was of course no mention of the abortive attack on the Emergency Forces building.

From the Mabahith's point of view, what was most disturbing about the video was the footage of the GMC Sierra. It was clearly there in several shots, but it had not been used in Muhaya. Where was it, and what did the Organization intend to do with it? On 13 February the MOI warned residents of Riyadh that another truck bomb attack could be imminent. The following day they offered a reward of $1 million for information leading to the recovery of a GMC Sierra loaded with explosives. On 16 February, British Airways, citing 'security reasons', cancelled its London flight to Riyadh.[10]

Khalid al-Hajj was still nominally the leader of Al Qaeda's operations on the Arabian Peninsula, and though it is now known that Muqrin was effectively in charge, in March 2004 that was not yet clear to the Mabahith. They had been hunting Hajj for nearly a year and hoped to take him alive. His close links to Central Command could yield valuable intelligence. Then, in a major breakthrough, interrogations revealed the location of Khalid al-Hajj's safe house in the Shifa district.

They placed the flat under surveillance. Hajj hardly left, but he was regularly visited by a man unknown to the MOI who drove a new Nissan SUV with unfamiliar plates. Upon investigation, the MOI discovered the man was Ibrahim al-Muzayni. He seemed to be Hajj's personal aide, but was otherwise unknown to them.

On occasion Hajj and Muzayni were seen leaving the safe house in the SUV. Undercover officers followed them, charted the routes they took, and started making plans.[11] The MOI opted not to raid the Shifa flat because experience had proved that raids often escalated to extreme violence and collateral damage. So they decided to ambush Hajj during one of his perambulations around Riyadh. But as his movements to and from the flat were not regular, the ambush was difficult to plan.

Then a tip-off came in from a currency trader. Hajj had contacted him to change a large amount of Euro notes into Saudi riyals. The exchange was scheduled for 15 March, giving the MOI the window of opportunity they had been waiting for.

They would ambush him as he drove home. It would be difficult. Broad daylight and roads packed with civilian cars posed two major challenges. Communications were set up off the normal security channels, just in case Hajj or other Al Qaeda members were monitoring them. Hajj's mobile phone was tapped; headquarters would be listening in on whatever calls he made during the expedition. Major-General Abdulrahman al-Maqbal was an officer in the traffic police at the time. 'The most important element for the success of this operation was the sharing of information between the services quickly and accurately: the vehicle, who was driving, the weapons they had, and so on. All of this information would aid the agents on the ground.'[12]

It was a Monday afternoon. Hajj and Muzayni, in white thobes and sunglasses, left the flat in Shifa and made their way to the location for the money exchange. Hajj was driving, and a number of undercover cars followed him. The exchange took place, and then the two targets got back into their car and drove north on King Fahd Road.

About ten kilometres away was the busy highway junction known as Cairo Square. Maqbal, monitoring Hajj's movements on the ground, kept in constant communication with headquarters. 'It would have been easy to close off the east–west Mecca Road and trap him in Cairo Square,' Maqbal explains. Easy, that is, except for all the traffic. 'Our first responsibility was to ensure the safety of the civilians on the road. A criminal like Hajj would not have hesitated to do anything. He might have killed someone, hijacked a car, or taken someone hostage for a last stand.'

Headquarters looked to Maqbal to advise them. 'The commanding officer kept asking, "Should we shut down Cairo Square, or not?"' But the traffic was just too intense and Hajj was left to continue on his way. He passed the MOI headquarters, slipped onto the interchange at Cairo Square, and headed east on the Mecca Road.

The Security Patrols, meanwhile, prepared an ambush inside the National Guard underpass about six kilometres down the road. 'Trap him in the underpass and he'd have nowhere to go, neither backwards or forwards, left or right,' Major-General Halal explains. 'Also, it had high, thick walls on either side. Any stray bullets would hit the walls and not fly into the surrounding neighbourhood.' They were good to go, but suddenly Hajj's car lurched across several lanes to a feeder road which avoided the underpass. He must have sensed something was up, which surprised Halal. They had given him a wide berth – even undercover police cars had been ordered not to get too close.

Hajj kept driving eastwards. He crossed over the spaghetti junction above Damascus Square where the Mecca Road becomes Khurais Road. After another five kilometres, he finally turned off the main road and began heading south into the neighbourhood of West Naseem. This was worrying, as the area was full of car showrooms and workshops, and that day it was bustling.

However, the MOI were convinced it could be their last chance to get Hajj. Police rushed to cut him off. They sped northwards up Abdulrahman ibn Awf Street and set up a cordon on all three sides of the intersection with Ahmed ibn Hanbal Street. The streetlights were switched to red, and all civilian traffic was kept away.

Hajj pulled in to the intersection and stopped. There was no escape. 'We let him sit there for a few minutes,' Halal says. 'We wanted him to have some time to consider surrender. If he chose otherwise, we were ready to engage him.'

He chose otherwise. Hajj drew a pistol from his thobe pocket and began firing out the window. Muzayni just sat there, too stunned to react. Bullets shattered a furniture shop's plate-glass display window and civilian onlookers started fleeing in panic, but luckily no one was hit. Hajj then leaned over to retrieve a machine gun from the back seat. It was the last move he would ever make.

The order was given and, from all four sides, Hajj was engulfed in a maelstrom of gunfire.

9

Operation Volcano

Khalid al-Hajj was dead, along with whatever influence he had continued to wield inside the Organization, and another name was struck from the List of Twenty-Six. Two days later Muqrin, now formally leader, gave the Organization a new name: Al Qaeda on the Arabian Peninsula, AQAP for short.[1] AQAP was the first Al Qaeda franchise to adopt such a name, a move later emulated by other franchises around the region: Al Qaeda in the Islamic Maghreb (i.e. Morocco), Al Qaeda in Mesopotamia (i.e. Iraq), and so on. In an online statement Muqrin vowed revenge. 'The mujahideen will teach the enemies of God, the mercenaries of the Saudi intelligence service, a lesson they will never forget,' he wrote.

The lesson Muqrin had in mind was an operation so bold in design and so destructive as to make headlines around the world and give AQAP the upper hand in the war. He called it Operation Volcano.

Several considerations underlay Muqrin's thinking. Muhaya had been a public-relations disaster. It was necessary that all attacks attributed to AQAP stay on message: the enemy are the Crusaders in our midst, not our fellow Muslims. Secondly and more importantly, the Organization's campaign thus far had failed to carry off something iconic on a par with 9/11. As Muqrin explained in issue after issue of *Camp of the Sabre*, he believed that such attacks would have a unique ability to rally Muslims' anger at the West and to motivate them to rise up and throw off Western dominance. The sight of Muslims dancing in the streets on 9/11, cheering as the Twin Towers came crashing down, would have informed that belief. But nothing Al Qaeda had done since had elicited a similarly enthusiastic response. It is debatable whether any attack inside the Kingdom could ever garner such acclaim. Saudis were uncomfortable with the very idea of a guerrilla campaign inside their own country. That uncomfortable truth does not seem to have entered into Muqrin's calculations.

At the end of February he called a meeting of his top lieutenants and they hashed out the plan. Like most big Al Qaeda attacks, Operation Volcano was to involve multiple simultaneous bombings. The first target was the ROC compound, situated off the Eastern Ring Road between the Sulay and Fayha districts. It was owned by the Vinnell Corporation and was where its expatriate workers had been re-housed after the attack on their compound the previous May. Vinnell was still a byword for the American military's influence inside the Kingdom, and so an attack on the ROC would likely avoid the sort of outrage that followed Muhaya.

But this was only small potatoes. The main course was something much more audacious. Muqrin planned to hijack three gas tankers, wire them up, and drive them across town and into the heart of the Diplomatic Quarter. The bombs would be enormous, the death toll would include a healthy number of foreigners, and the blasts would devastate what was – officially at least – foreign soil.

The two targets were on opposite sides of the city. This would divide the MOI's attention and weaken their response. The first explosion would attract the security services in its direction and smooth the way for the second, much bigger explosion.

The first task was to scope out both targets thoroughly. Abu Ayub was assigned the ROC compound; in fact he was already familiar with it, as the ROC had been one of the compounds under consideration as an alternative for the Muhaya attack. As before, the neighbourhood was covertly videotaped from a moving car. Abu Ayub's surveillance operation was more thorough than before. The Organization was learning.

It was a hazy day. Islamic chanting wafted gently from the cassette player. Abu Ayub manned the camera. 'There's a checkpoint up ahead,' he told the driver. 'But it'll be okay, keep driving.' That part of Sulay was basically one big building site. Compounds and the odd solitary villa were surrounded by empty lots. 'Right, let's go straight down the main street and then turn around and take the next street.'

'Will there be a checkpoint there too?'

'No, I don't think so.'

They neared the compound. There were roadblocks, but they stuck to side streets and managed to avoid them. As they pulled into a long, wide road, the large compound emerged into view. They turned right and headed away from it. Abu Ayub filmed out the back window.

'Slow down. Go straight, right to the end of the street.' Abu Ayub zoomed in. The compound's walls were high and surmounted by barbed wire; in front of the wall, placed a metre apart, were concrete Jersey barriers. There were several guard towers, erected after the earlier Riyadh compound bombings. The Vinnell Corporation had upped its security measures considerably.

When the surveillance vehicle reached the end of the street, it rounded the block and approached the southern side of the compound. They made a pass and filmed that stretch of wall close up. A car ahead of them entered through the gates. 'See that saloon going inside? Who do you suppose they are?' They drove on. At an intersection, a white four-door drove past. 'And who's this?' Abu Ayub asked.

'Don't know,' the driver replied. 'But you can just feel that it's a foreigner, can't you? Shall we go?'

'Wait a minute.' Abu Ayub continued to film the white car driving away. It veered to the left and stopped beside another car at the side of the road. A red-and-white pickup was also heading in that direction. 'Are they foreigners? Or Mabahith?' Abu Ayub said to himself. A large bundle of steel girders attached to a tall crane hovered over the cars in the distance. The white car turned into the compound. 'They are definitely foreigners.'

'Yeah, they are the Vinnell lot for sure.'

Abu Ayub may have been concerned about the tight security, because he returned for another day's filming. This time he brought Muqrin along. 'They are installing security improvements now,' he explained. 'The compound's exit is over there. See the concrete blocks and the barbed wire?'

'Yes, I see,' Muqrin replied. 'And over there is the entrance?'

'Yes, the entrance for the whole compound.'

'The only entrance? And it has only one gate?'

'Yes, just one for going in, and one for going out.'

'Interesting. Faisal, turn left here and pull into the rest house opposite the entrance. We can film it from there.' Muqrin was cranky. 'Slow down, slow down!' he ordered, and then said to himself, 'I say slow down and the idiot carries on.'

The car stopped outside the rest house but too far forward. 'Why have you stopped here?' Muqrin complained. 'I can't see anything from here. How am I supposed to film?'

They circled again. Passing a mosque, Muqrin pointed out the minaret and said he had considered climbing up it and filming the compound from above. (In fact, other footage suggests that he would go on to do just that.) They argued about how best to use the car's odometer to measure the distances between the entrances and exits, to calculate how long it would take to drive between them. They passed a tall security tower and Muqrin asked, 'Is there a marksman up there?'

'Yes, one,' Abu Ayub replied.

They spent some time surveilling a bridge over the road not far from one of the compound's gates. It seems they considered firing an RPG from it at the start of the attack, much as they had done at Muhaya.

'Drive on,' Muqrin ordered. 'I'm done.'

As for surveillance on the Diplomatic Quarter, Muqrin decided to oversee it himself. He personally undertook another filming mission but grew increasingly concerned that one of the security men would notice the camera. So he came up with a different plan.

A small camera was attached to the front of an SUV, hidden behind the grille, and a member of Muqrin's surveillance team returned to the quarter to film the interior. The camera glided among the cars and checkpoints like a predatory animal. The driver had to make two trips; on the first one he was so nervous that he drove too fast for the footage to be of much use. The second try was more successful.

Muqrin decided to assign an assault team of three vehicles to each target to pave the way for the bombs. He directed cell members to steal six government vehicles.[2] Three were hidden at a rest house in Suwaydi which acted as Muqrin's temporary headquarters. The other three were handed over to Abu Ayub for the ROC compound attack. He stashed them close by at a safe house in Fayha, along with the GMC Sierra that had been wired up back in October.

The caretaker of the Fayha safe house was Khalid al-Subayt, who lived there with his wife and children along with a collection of cell members, some of whom had also brought their families with them. Subayt was a veteran jihadist who had fought the Russians in Afghanistan, Turkmenistan, and Chechnya, and who more recently had been helping Awshen's media team distribute to sympathizers videotapes of *Badr of Riyadh* and hard copies of *Voice of Jihad*.

Life inside the safe house appears to have been rather jolly. They did a lot of filming, both formally and informally. One day the adults dressed up two toddlers who lived there in military fatigues and made them perform for the camera. The boys were wearing balaclavas and practised drawing toy pistols from holsters strapped to their thighs. The assembly laughed and cheered as the boys lunged at the camera with their weapons.

'No no, extend your arm fully in front of you when you fire,' Subayt instructed the taller of the two boys. He gave it another go. 'That's better! What a man!'

The kid soldiers went through a series of military exercises: crouching and firing, doing offensive somersaults, and firing while lying on their sides. 'They're getting the hang of it!' someone chipped in. Afterward, the adults cajoled the boys into doing press-ups and sit-ups. Subayt laughed, 'They're better than the brothers!'

Among the cell members living there were Abdulaziz al-Mudayhish, aged thirty-three, and the 20-year-old Fahd al-Farraj. They had been selected to be the suicide bombers in the ROC compound attack. Fahd – a cousin of the captured Khalid al-Farraj – was overweight and wore extravagant sideburns. He did not command a fierce intelligence. 'The best thing about dying in a car bomb,' he told his cell mates over dinner, 'is that the martyr feels nothing. He just goes up, like this, poof!'

Mudayhish sat sprawled out slovenly on the floor cleaning his teeth with a traditional Muslim toothpick called a *miswak*. He was seldom seen without one in his mouth. He was one of the older cell members, but even so, his baby-face was still not able to grow a proper beard and he had a teenage twinkle in his eye and a teenager's vanity. What he lacked in intelligence he made up for in charm.

All these qualities were on display the day he gave a filmed interview to an unknown cameraman called Mubarak. Mudayhish, in a dark-brown thobe, reclined on the floor like a grandee, his left arm propped up against a cushion, his left leg tucked underneath his right knee. His head was bare; he had draped his plain white shemagh over his shoulders. Behind him propped up against the wall were a loaded RPG launcher and a rocket, and beside them lay an ornate copy of the Qur'an. Around the walls of the room sat other cell members, their shemaghs wrapped around their faces, revealing only menacing eyes.

The room was full of chatter and Mudayhish revelled in the attention he was getting. Mubarak – a serious, thoughtful voice – called them to order.

'Quiet, brothers,' he said.

'Calm down,' Mudayhish echoed. He chewed a date noisily. 'Don't start filming yet. I want a coffee.' Mudayhish looked around at the others in the room. 'I'm not going to have to answer him and him and him, am I?'

'No no, it's just you and me.'

'That's good.' Mudayhish smacked his lips at the camera and smiled.

'Brother Ali,' Mubarak began, using Mudayhish's cell nickname. The others settled down. 'You will soon defeat and humiliate the infidel in a big operation which will shock the whole planet. Why are you doing this?'

Mudayhish cleared his throat. His answers had all been prepared in advance. 'In the name of God, the Merciful, the Compassionate,' he began, scratching his upper lip. A hand passed him a cup of coffee and, stifling a laugh, he took a sip. 'First of all . . .' he said, and then paused as another cell member walked through the frame holding a Kalashnikov. 'What I'm doing is in answer to God's call,' he continued, and then quoted the Qur'an.[3] '"O believers, what is the matter with you, that when you are told to go forth in the way of Allah, you adhere to earthly things? … The delight of worldly life is but little compared to life in the hereafter …" Please guys, don't make me laugh!' he implored, smiling.

'Just look at the camera,' Mubarak calmly instructed. 'And don't recite as if you're reading off a piece of paper. Just act normal, be comfortable.'

'Okay,' Mudayhish said. 'Let's go again, from the beginning … Wait a minute!' He turned to his right. 'Do I have to beg you for a refill?' They started laughing again, and Mudayhish handed his cup over.

'Settle down, brothers.' Mubarak asked his next question as if today was the day of the attack. 'Brother Ali, in only a few moments' time, God willing, you will head out to obliterate the castles of the infidel …' He paused. A coffee cup was held out for Mudayhish.

'Hold on,' Mudayhish said. 'There are twenty clean coffee cups there, and he's giving me back the dirty one!' They all burst out laughing.

Mubarak grew impatient as Mudayhish continued to clown around. 'Brother, cut it out,' he ordered. 'Concentrate.'

Mudayhish calmed down and the question was asked again. He flubbed the quotation of the Qur'an and quickly ran through his lines a few times under his breath. 'You don't have to recite the whole verse,' they suggested. 'Just the beginning.' Mudayhish signalled he was ready, but this time Mubarak flubbed the question. 'I'm finally serious, and now you start making mistakes!' Mudayhish teased.

'Given that the Arabian Peninsula is home to many sacred sites,' Mubarak continued, 'why have you chosen to carry out jihad here?'

'Didn't I answer this question already? Like I said, because of the infidels here and so on.'

'No, that was the answer to the other question, the one about fanaticism.'

'What question do you want me to answer, then?' Mudayhish's cheerful disposition was beginning to crack.

It went on and on. Mudayhish grew tired. He was tense and confused. 'Continue, continue!' Mubarak ordered.

'Can't you see, I'm falling apart here! And please, I'm asking you, make the questions clearer.'

'In a few moments' time you shall climb into your car . . .'

'Look, he's gone back to that again! Why do you keep saying it like that, so drawn out?'

'What am I supposed to say? "A bit later you'll pop into your car . . .?"'

'Well, at the very least instead of "in a few moments' time" you could just say "today".'

Mubarak began yet again. 'In a few moments' time you will climb into the saddle of your horse . . .'

This got them going again. 'Now my car is a horse!' Mudayhish laughed. 'Listen, guys, I'm telling you, any little thing can completely distract me . . .'

'If you please, brother Ali . . .' Mubarak implored.

Mudayhish did not want to play along. 'Look at this idiot messing around,' he said, indicating one of the brothers. 'And you, where do you think you're going?' he asked one who was leaving the room.

'I've got lessons,' came the reply.

'Oh lessons, well, take your head to class and leave your body here, I'll teach it a thing or two.' Mudayhish began to stand up.

'Sit down!' Mubarak said. 'Where are you going? We've still got questions to ask.'

'No please, my brother. Turn it off, enough . . . It's just not coming, I can't get it out!'

'Listen, just look in the camera . . .'

'Ugh, that damn camera . . .' Mudayhish said.

'Brother, I'm gonna slap you, now look into my eyes, look at me and talk. Talk!'

That day's filming was a write-off. A few days later, Mudayhish sat down again in front of a camera, but this time it was a much more sombre affair. He wore a conventional white thobe and red headscarf, and looked worn down and dejected. Speaking in a mumble, he simply read a pre-prepared text from off a sheet of paper. It was a far cry from the heroic image Mubarak had tried to coerce out of him.

But then, heroism was not Muqrin's main criterion when nominating suicide bombers from among AQAP's lower ranks. A far more practical consideration was paramount: that whoever was chosen would not back out at the last minute, which for understandable reasons was always a very real possibility. That was one reason for filming the videos in the first place. Once a martyr had set out his firm intention on video, it was much harder to renege without losing face.

The truth is, AQAP's members were not all filled with an overwhelming desire to martyr themselves. Motivated by a fiery sense of injustice and filled with depression and despair, suicide bombers in places like Palestine, Iraq, or Chechnya might feel they have no choice but to strap on a bomb vest. AQAP's martyrs were different. Inarticulate and oftentimes clueless about the cause they were fighting for, they parroted propagandistic clichés about the persecution of Muslims, but had never experienced it themselves. Indeed, in Saudi Arabia there is, officially at least, no religious freedom for anyone *except* Muslims. What is more, most of them were middle class and had grown up in relatively comfortable homes. Had they wanted, they could have lived fulfilled, productive lives.

Instead, their lives were hijacked by an ideology which taught them to believe that a literal, physical heaven waited for them on the other side, as real as stepping off an aeroplane in a foreign country. Obviously such a belief runs counter to a person's natural instinct for self-preservation, which explains the on-again off-again conviction of someone like Mudayhish. Nevertheless, the promise of an eternity of bliss with seventy-two Heavenly Virgins (known as *houris* in Arabic) was a powerful pull. And so, however much they may have convinced themselves that their motives were self-sacrificial, under the surface lurked self-interest.

Manipulating all these confused feelings and ideas from behind the scenes were men like Muqrin. He chose his bombers carefully. To make sure they stayed the course, he would often select the most childlike, naïve personalities, boy-men eager to please their leader and afraid to let down their fellow cell members. An absence of critical thinking was essential – and, luckily, in abundance – as was a certain narcissism. The ideal bomber enjoyed the camera's attentive gaze, was easily puffed up with a sense of his own importance, and liked to imagine himself driving courageously to meet his destiny.

Muqrin's plan to use gas tankers required trained truck drivers. So he set up a day of driving practice and selected four operatives to be trained: **Fahd al-Juwayr**, **Mishaal al-Farraj**, Dakheel al-Ubayd, and Muhammad al-Ghaith. All four were recent recruits and would go on to play, in their own ways, important roles inside the Organization. Ghaith, who was from a rich family, had recently sold his Lexus and, with the money, bought a bulldozer for Muqrin. The leader intended to use it in the attack.

Awshen or someone from his media team accompanied the four trainees and filmed them from inside the cab of the large truck that had been acquired for the day. Muqrin had ordered Awshen to document every stage of the preparations for Operation Volcano. He was certain the video celebrating the attack would be an even bigger hit than *Badr of Riyadh*.

At thirty-two, Juwayr – yet another member of the extensive

Farraj family – was relatively old. He had the first go and sat relaxed behind the wheel. From the wide grin on his face it is clear he was having fun. Awshen upbraided him for smiling; he was supposed to look serious.

Mishaal went next. The 19-year-old was Khalid al-Farraj's full brother. According to MOI investigators, the Organization had told Mishaal that the security services were responsible for the death of his father, and held out the promise that by joining them he could get his revenge. He was a short kid and had difficulty reaching the pedals. Also, the filming made him self-conscious; he kept adjusting his shemagh so as to look his best. 'Can you hear all right with it wrapped around your head so tightly?' Awshen asked.

'No, not really,' Mishaal admitted. 'Should I take it off?'

'No no, just style it differently.' Mishaal took one corner of the red-and-white headdress and flipped it over his head, exposing his right ear. 'Ah, now we can see your features, my boy.' Mishaal stifled an embarrassed smile; his buck teeth accentuated his boyish looks. He reached up and pulled the cord for the truck's horn. It was very loud, and Mishaal laughed.

Ubayd had a scraggly beard and a big toothy grin. He bounced up and down in his seat. 'I've only ever driven a Toyota Camry before!' he said. 'Shall we try out the speed? See how fast it can go?'

The sun was now setting. Awshen set up a few establishing shots to complete the picture. He filmed them climbing in and out of the truck from different angles, and sitting proudly in the driver's seat. Ubayd beamed and gave the camera a thumbs-up. Juwayr was asked how he felt.

'How do I feel? I feel an incredible desire for God. I pray for the humiliation of His enemies, and for His religion to conquer.'

Muqrin was refining his plan. He scouted out potential carjacking locations along the Dammam–Riyadh road, and selected a weighing station for tankers on their way to the capital from the oil refineries of the Eastern Province. Muqrin and his team planned to install themselves at the station, wait for a tanker to pull up, and, without anyone noticing, kidnap the driver. After injecting him with a sedative, they would tie him up and stash him in one of the half-built houses at a nearby construction site. Then a bomb specialist would attach an explosive device to the tank and a suicide bomber would drive off in it. This would be repeated twice; three tankers were to be used.

It was a bold plan. Perhaps too bold. Muqrin was keen on it because, were he to pull it off, the resulting explosions would be spectacular. However, he had a backup plan in place. He had ordered Saud al-Qatayni to prepare six ordinary truck bombs at his new manufactory in Buraydah. It would be good to have them on hand in case the tankers proved too difficult to carjack.

A media man was sent to Buraydah to film the bomb-makers. Their workshop was a farm outbuilding. A group of three young men in balaclavas shovelled coal into the mouth of an industrial grinder and collected the resulting coal dust in buckets. The room, the grinder, and their bodies were covered in the black dust. They used their fingers to write 'Jihad!', 'Victory and glory are ours!' and 'Death to tyrants!' in the dust on the grinder.

Another group of cell members in an adjoining room mixed the coal dust with fertilizer and iron filings in a long trough. They then tipped the mixture into the bed of a pickup truck and smoothed it out with a trowel.

Fertilizer bombs are extremely stable. They need another explosion to set them off. In yet another room, three cell members sat cross-legged on the floor stuffing yellow RDX explosive into detonating cords made out of strips of thin plastic tubing. Once prepared, they took the cords into the main manufactory where they laid them crosswise over the half-filled truck bed and attached them to a trigger device in the cab. The cords were then covered by another layer of fertilizer mixture, which a young man in wellington boots packed down tightly by using his feet to roll a heavy gas cannister back and forth on top of it.

'Should I bring one more cannister?' someone called out.

'No, one is enough,' the man in boots replied.

Muqrin gathered the Diplomatic Quarter squad at the rest house in Suwaydi and split them into four groups: three assault teams armed with rifles and RPGs, and a suicide crew. He then described the plan.

Assault team no. 1 would set things off by firing directly upon the first security checkpoint on Abdullah al-Sahmi Street between the Jeddah Road and the Egyptian embassy. Team no. 2 was to get out of their car (all but the driver) and position themselves behind the trees near the second checkpoint, which they were to attack as soon as they heard the first team open fire. Team no. 3 was assigned the third checkpoint on the other side of the street. After seeing off the security men stationed at the checkpoints, all three groups were to clear the street to allow the tankers free passage. Muqrin had not yet determined which three of the four driving trainees would drive the tankers, but once they were safely through, the assault teams were to withdraw, dump their vehicles, and rendezvous with getaway drivers using CB radios. They were also given mobiles, just in case.

On the same day, Abu Ayub gathered his men in Fayha and laid out the attack plan for the ROC compound. He too split them up into three assault teams to assist Mudayhish and Fahd al-Farraj, the suicide bombers. Assault team no. 1 would raid the front gates and fire RPGs at the northern and southern guard towers. This was the cue for assault team no. 2 to attack the security guards on the southern side of the compound and secure that location. Assault team no. 3 would take out the guardhouse from the northwest. The entire perimeter thus secure, one of their team was to drive the bulldozer Ghaith had purchased up to the gates and use it to remove the barriers, allowing the truck bomb through. Then all three assault teams were to withdraw.

Sometime in late March, Muqrin and Abu Ayub drove up to a remote training camp with a group of about twenty cell members. They spent the weekend there, not only to refresh their skills, but also to shoot footage for upcoming propaganda videos. A three-camera film crew shot everything. The men jogged among the dunes chanting marching songs with jihadist slogans and, as a team-building exercise, held a particularly joyous wheelbarrow race. They erected a barbed-wire boot-camp obstacle course, makeshift rooms out of plywood to practise indoor attacks, and a track with roadside targets for lessons in drive-by shootings. In a tent they practised cleaning their weapons, and a rusty old truck was used for explosives and ambush training. After evening prayer a shooting range was set up and Abu Ayub instructed them in long-range firing using pistols and assault rifles.

Night fell on a long day. The 'soldiers' stood in four neat rows, their guns held at attention. Two pickup trucks were parked behind them, headlights on; the men's silhouettes cast long shadows into the desert beyond. Abu Ayub stood to the side, acting every inch the drill sergeant.

'Camp of the Sabre!' he cried. 'Atten-shun!'

They stood up straight, puffed out their chests, and shouted something back. 'No no, that won't do, brothers! Louder!'

A masked figure in army fatigues, probably Muqrin, circled the men. He led them in call-and-response.

'Jihad!'

'Power!'

'Glory!'

That evening, there was a violent thunderstorm. Rivulets of rainwater swirled round their encampment, and they splashed in the puddles and whooped and hollered in childlike glee. After a meal of rice and lamb, they sat around the campfire. To shield themselves from the chill desert wind, they had erected tall cloth windbreaks on two sides. They chanted jihadist hymns and feted Juwayr, Ubayd, and Ghaith, the suicide bombers selected for the Diplomatic Quarter bombings, who sat together with their faces uncovered. They held Kalashnikovs in their laps.

The assembled men sang so heartily that their words rang out clear:

> Perform your long-awaited strike!
>   Strike, strike, strike!
> Kill as many infidels as you like!
>   Strike, strike, strike!
> And for our compatriots make gravestones ...
>   Stones, stones, stones!
> For the defeated armies of the infidel!
>   Destroy! Destroy!
>   Make no compromise!
> We salute the glorious ones who struck Manhattan!
>   Destroy, destroy!
>   Make no compromise!

'Stand up and get in line,' ordered Muqrin. The whole group stood up and, holding their weapons, sang an improvised song whose refrain was 'Woe upon you, House of Saud!' This went on for almost an hour.

It started to drizzle. Someone placed a tea kettle on the fire, and glass teacups were passed around. They discussed what to recite next. 'Let it be something to do with God's religion,' someone suggested. 'And begin with a blessing. Anything that doesn't begin by mentioning God's name bears only rotten fruit.' This elicited sounds of approval from some, but others, notably Ubayd, laughed loudly.

'What about the Holy Qur'an?' someone called out. He began to recite.

By the brightness of morning
And by the still darkness of the night
Your Lord has not forsaken you
Nor has He grown displeased.
The Hereafter is better for you than this first life.
Your Lord will give and you shall be content.
Did He not find you an orphan and protect you?
Did He not find you lost and guide you?
Did He not find you poor and make you rich?
Therefore oppress not the orphan,
Nor the beggar drive away,
But proclaim your Lord's generosity.[4]

Ghaith held his glass of tea to his lips and stared pensively into the fire, a flicker of fear in his eyes. Juwayr was philosophical, and Ubayd's expression was uncharacteristically blank. It was a rare moment of candour – and in typical Saudi fashion, as soon as they realized they were being watched, their faces reverted to smiling, childlike contentedness.

The recitation ended. Muqrin asked Juwayr how he was enjoying the training camp. 'By God, I am pleased,' he answered. 'Happy and relaxed. We've eaten a lot, that's for sure!'

The men laughed in agreement.

'And you, Rakan?' Rakan was Ubayd's cell nickname. He smiled and said hoarsely, 'My voice is wrecked! I can't talk!' There were more laughs.

Ghaith was asked in turn. There was no longer any sign of the worry he had betrayed a few minutes before. 'I am happy,' he said.

'Eh?' Muqrin asked.

Ghaith raised his voice. 'I am happy, praise God. Inshallah the operation will be successful.'

'And the rain today? Did it annoy you?'

'No, on the contrary, the weather has been very nice.'

'Yeah, but tell us what you felt when you heard the thunder!'

They all laughed.

'The jihadist youth, they're fed up,' Juwayr said. 'They're called indiscriminate and reckless, but no, they don't take a step without first studying it thoroughly, without knowing first what its results are likely to be.'

'Things will get harder for the renegades,' Ghaith ventured, referring to the House of Saud and the security services, 'unless they stop what they are doing and return to their religion.'

Juwayr agreed. 'As for confrontations with the security services, they push us to do it. They are the aggressors, they kill our leaders and our members ... So if a soldier's standing in front of an American building, or hunting down a brother who has killed an American, well ... Whatever happens, happens.'

The day arrived, probably sometime in the first week of April. Muqrin was at the petrol station on the Dammam–Riyadh highway with his three chosen martyrs, Ubayd, Juwayr, and Ghaith's replacement, Mishaal (why Muqrin changed his mind about Ghaith is unknown). The six attack teams were in position awaiting Muqrin's order to commence the operation. Everything was in place.[5]

Then, in a moment of rare hesitation, Muqrin stood everyone down. Why he did so is not clear. Most likely the decision followed a shootout between two cell members and the MOI on 5 April. One cell member died, and the other was arrested after barricading himself inside a nearby house for seven hours.[6] He was well acquainted with the Operation Volcano plans, and Muqrin may have been afraid that he had blabbed. Or perhaps, standing at the petrol station, Muqrin realized just how difficult the plan would be to pull off. Kidnapping the three truck drivers, wiring the tankers to explode, and driving them through the centre of town – all in the plain light of day – would have caused even the boldest man to waver.

Not that he cancelled the operation. He merely postponed it and put his backup plan into place. Instead of tankers, they would use Qatayni's truck bombs.

However, more trouble was to come. A captured cell member had indeed revealed the location of the Fayha safe house to his interrogators. On 13 April it was raided while a group of cell members were reviewing the surveillance footage of the Diplomatic Quarter. The house's caretaker Khalid al-Subayt – the one who had given the cell's toddlers toy guns and encouraged them to play soldiers – was driving through the neighbourhood with fellow cell member Muhammad al-Farraj (another Farraj!) when they saw the police and Emergency Forces arrive. What happened next would be eulogized in *Voice of Jihad*:

> They immediately returned to the house to warn their brethren, but when they drove up to the front gate they were fired upon. Khalid, who was driving, was wounded and his body slumped onto Dhafir al-Ajami [Muhammad's cell nickname] beside him. Khalid recited 'There is no god but God' and gave up his spirit. Dhafir then engaged the enemy, killing Ghadir al-Qahtani [a private in the Emergency Forces who would later be given a prominent funeral attended by Prince Muhammad and other members of the royal family]. He got out of the car and, taking two hand grenades, threw one to the left and the other to the right. The tyrants' soldiers turned and fled. The bullets which wounded Khalid had also punctured the car's fuel tank. It ignited along with our companion Khalid, whom God has gathered into the company of martyrs who perished by fire in the path of God.[7]

Subayt's dramatic death was the diversion the rest of the cell needed to escape. Mudayhish, who had so struggled during his video interview, fled in the wired-up GMC Sierra with his fellow suicide bomber Fahd al-Farraj. In a moment of panic or misdirected heroism, they headed towards the ROC compound. Their intention was to do what they could to penetrate the compound and detonate. However, they either came to their senses or, what is likelier, Abu Ayub called them and told them they would never get past the compound's defences. Better to save themselves for another mission, another day. So they abandoned the truck bomb at the side of the road and ran away. Abu Ayub picked them up and took them to another safe house. (The bomb was discovered by police three days later.)

As he fled the Fayha house, Rakan al-Saikhan – a member of the Shura Council from the very beginning and AQAP's most experienced expert in sourcing explosive material – was mortally wounded along with another cell member. They managed to get away, but suffered the same slow death as had befallen Amr al-Shihri the previous autumn. Their deaths brought the MOI's most-wanted list down to twenty-one.

The MOI's interference with Muqrin's plans did not stop there. By sheer chance, 13 April was also the day Qatayni chose to bring the six truck bombs he had prepared for the postponed attack on the Diplomatic Quarter to Riyadh. Seven other cell members went with him.[8] The plan was to take three truck bombs first and return later for the other three. Everyone was armed. They set out in a group. One support vehicle travelled in front of the motorcade, the other one was at the rear. Before long, however, they spied a security checkpoint and decided to split into two groups.

On their way south, two of the truck bombs stopped at a petrol station to fill up.[9] While they were there, a security patrol passed by. When it returned to make a second pass, the drivers panicked and fired upon it, killing two patrolmen. Their support vehicle did not wait around; it fled immediately to Riyadh so they decided to abandon the bombs and hijack a civilian's car.

On their way south they passed another security patrol and fired upon it as well, killing another two patrolmen. Then, at a checkpoint, they got out of their car, threatened the policemen with their weapons, and forced an Indian man in another car to drive them on. Before they reached the capital, yet another security patrol fell foul of their gunfire; one patrolman died and another was injured. What happened to the Indian man is not known.

Qatayni, who had taken the third truck bomb, was also forced to abandon it after driving off road and getting stuck in the sand. He returned to Riyadh in his support vehicle. Once in the capital, he met up with Muqrin, who cannot have been happy. Four truck bombs lost and one safe house raided: Operation Volcano would have to be permanently shut down. He ordered Qatayni to return to Qaseem immediately and to bring at least one of the remaining three truck bombs to Riyadh. Qatayni managed to pull that off, and delivered the bomb to Muqrin, who stashed it at a safe house in the Janadriya district. Qatayni then returned a second time with two helpers to fetch the remaining two truck bombs. However, the sheer volume of Security Patrols once again compelled them to abandon the bombs by the side of the road.

Muqrin had been comprehensively humiliated by the MOI. His dreams for an attack to rival 9/11 were shattered. Newspaper headlines trumpeted the truck bomb seizures and the Saudi media was full of stirring eulogies for the fallen patrolmen. The American embassy upped its threat warning for the Kingdom and urged even diplomats and their families to evacuate because of 'credible and specific' intelligence indicating imminent terrorist attacks against Western targets. Security at residential compounds was made even tighter. Riyadh was on lockdown.

But Muqrin was not one to roll over and play dead. He had

one truck bomb in reserve, and he ordered the Qaseem cell to make him two more, so its technicians went to work on a white pickup and a green SUV. They were filmed by Awshen's media team in such a way as to throw down the gauntlet before Prince Muhammad. Against the SUV's rear bumper, they propped up newspaper clippings reporting the seizure. On the dusty tailgate they wrote, 'For every two trucks you seize, we'll make two more.'

Muqrin chose his target: it would be the instrument of his humiliation, the headquarters of the Emergency Forces in Washm Street in the Nasiriya district – right in the centre of town. He had tried and failed to bomb it back in November. He would not fail again.

The attack was to take place on 21 April. It would be simple: just the suicide vehicle, no support vehicles were necessary. As before, Mudayhish and Fahd al-Farraj were the chosen martyrs. The night before the operation, they sat in the cab of the truck bomb and described the machinery that would usher them into paradise.

'That is the bomb there,' Mudayhish said, indicating the truck bed. It contained 1200 kilos of mixed ammonium nitrate. 'God willing, it will explode in the place He sees fit and avoid our Muslim brothers.' He was not referring to the soldiers of the Emergency Forces. By this point the Organization's takfeerism had rendered all Saudi security men infidels in their eyes.

'This collection of detonator wires is connected to the bomb. And these are two detonation switches.'

'The second one is a backup,' Fahd explained.

The camera panned down to Fahd's feet. A large battery lay beneath the glove box. 'This ignites the charge,' Mudayhish said. 'And here is the backup charge. It is connected to the truck's own battery.'

On the dashboard sat the CB radio. 'This is the brothers' radio,' the cameraman said.

'And these are tissues,' Fahd added, pointing to a box beside the radio handset. They laughed.

'Tissues?' the cameraman giggled. 'What brand?'

They mocked up a fake number plate in paper and attached it to the front bumper. The licence was HWR 072, which in Arabic can be read as '72 Heavenly Virgins'. Mudayhish leaned down and gave it a big kiss. Then he jumped onto the bonnet and, with the hood ornament between his thighs, bounced up and down excitedly.

Mudayhish removed the paper number plate and covered his eyes with '72 Heavenly Virgins'. Fahd began flipping the truck's headlights on and off and Mudayhish stretched his arms out toward the camera. He moved forward slowly, eerily, completely overwhelmed by the glorious destiny that was about to overwhelm him.

10

Terror Strikes the Coasts

Just after 2 p.m. on 21 April 2004, a white pickup truck tried to storm the gates of the Emergency Forces headquarters, but was foiled by security. So it drove fifty metres along the perimeter wall and detonated on the street. The blast left behind a crater five metres wide and one metre deep. The explosion resulted in only minor damage to the attackers' primary target but it totally demolished the eastern side of a building used by the General Directorate of Traffic – essentially the traffic police. Sixty cars parked nearby were destroyed, and numerous homes were wrecked. Inside a flat opposite, 11-year-old Wijdan al-Kunaydri was crushed when a large concrete block fell on her in full view of her little brother. She was one of five killed that day, including a colonel in the Department for Public Security, and its financial director. A further 148 were injured, many of them civilians, and within the week one more would die from his wounds. All the casualties were Muslims, and Wijdan became the atrocity's poster child.[1]

It was the largest-ever attack against a Saudi government building. The Arab press reported that the attack represented a shift in AQAP's strategy. 'This latest terrorist attack comes as a huge shock to Saudis,' wrote *Asharq Al-Awsat*. 'It is a milestone. The terrorists have taken the war to a new level. They are now against not just the state itself, but all Saudi society.'[2] Prince Nayef visited the wounded at King Faisal Hospital and told reporters that 'by targeting the security services, these terrorist cells have declared their moral bankruptcy. We remain determined in our pursuit of them.' In what can only be a reference to the recently foiled Operation Volcano, the prince was keen to point out that, despite the tragedy of the Washm Street bombing, 'we have in recent days prevented a number of operations the like of which exceeds anything you can imagine.'

Ironically, a three-day conference at Imam University on the connection between terrorism and Islam had held its closing session that morning. The conference for religious scholars set as its primary goal 'uncovering the roots of terrorism, violence, and extremism' which 'are the result of deviant ideas which Muslim scholars over many centuries have warned against'. They also hoped to 'make plain the moderateness of Islam and the idea of justice that lies behind its teachings, which reject violence and call for dialogue, persuasion, and argument'. These were the talking points which the crown prince had established a year before when he first formulated the government's ideological response to the terrorist threat. Following the Washm Street bombing, these ideas would be further popularized. Another child had died, and the 'heroic' security services – portrayed by the state media as devoted and God-fearing fathers, sons, and citizens – were being slaughtered by an increasingly brutal enemy who sought to overturn the basis of Saudi society: stability.

Not that AQAP was taking responsibility for the attack. Once again they rolled out the fake Haramain Brigades to shoulder the blame. Muqrin released an audio recording on the Internet – parts of which were broadcast on Al Jazeera – denying any involvement; however he also warned Americans that they would be targeted wherever they were and advised Saudi citizens to stay away from places where Americans congregated.[3]

The funeral for those killed in the bombing was an elaborate affair. Broadcast on state TV, it was held at Imam Turki bin Abdullah Grand Mosque in the centre of the city. Prince Muhammad prayed alongside his men and hundreds of ordinary citizens, row upon row of whom lined up in front of the fallen, their corpses laid out on simple wooden biers and shrouded in plain brown winding-sheets. The small body of Wijdan stood out among the bodies of the fully grown men. After the prayers ended, the biers were born aloft and carried to the hearses which transported them to a large cemetery outside the city. The burials were marked by the austerity typical of Saudi religious sensibilities.[4]

Onlookers contemplated the scene. Some covered their faces with grief; others stared stoically at the newly filled-in graves. 'Look at the consequences of what those men have done,' one of them said. 'Four men buried in a single day. Where is Islam in this?'

The evening after the Washm Street bombing, the MOI raided another one of Muqrin's safe houses in Suwaydi following unspecified leads. No one was there, but the raid was not a failure. Inside the flat they uncovered a huge amount of video material. They would later confirm that the safe house had been used by Isa al-Awshen as a media centre. The tapes included behind-the-scenes archive footage of the Riyadh compound bombings, Muhaya, and the foiled Operation Volcano, as well as numerous video wills and candid material shot by bored cell members.

It would be the largest seizure of such material over the course of the war.[5]

While the government had been engaging AQAP militarily, it was also making strides in the fight to shut off terrorist financing.

Frances Townsend and Prince Muhammad had met twice more since her initial visit in August the previous year, and despite the odd political hiccup in Washington, she had been able to facilitate a productive partnership between the Saudi ministries and their counterparts in America, especially the Treasury Department. On 28 February a royal decree was announced establishing the Saudi National Commission for Relief and Charity Work Abroad, a government watchdog to ensure that citizens' charitable contributions went to humanitarian causes and not to terrorists. Such a commission had been high on Townsend's list of priorities, and it had been carefully designed so as not to stand between a Muslim and his obligation to give *zakat*.[6]

US–Saudi relations were on the mend. So much so that in March, State Department counterterrorism coordinator J. Cofer Black testified before Congress that Saudi Arabia was a key ally in the war on terror. 'Their performance has not been flawless,' he said, 'and they have a large task before them. But we see clear evidence of the seriousness of purpose and the commitment of the leadership of the Kingdom to this fight.' Treasury Department representative Juan C. Zarate echoed Black's conclusions: 'The targeting actions and systemic reforms undertaken by the Kingdom of Saudi Arabia clearly demonstrate its commitment to working with us and the international community to combat the global threat of terrorist financing.'[7] This was clear progress from David Aufhauser's expression of frustration a year before, when he called the Kingdom 'the epicentre of terrorist finance'.

However, there was another challenge to tackle. The CIA were having a hard time coping with the way the Mabahith did things. 'The problem was partly cultural,' Townsend explains. 'We sorely underestimated the challenges presented by our cultural differences. Saudis are by their nature very reserved, and Mabahith investigators held their cards very close to the chest. It wasn't that they were unwilling to cooperate. They had been trained to listen to questions from the CIA and others, to receive them politely, but not to reveal anything without going through the chain of command. And they didn't have a mechanism to do that quickly.

'So imagine, a CIA agent comes in with some questions – and he'll have learned from bitter experience that it's best to write them down and get them translated beforehand. He hands them to his Saudi counterpart, who thanks him politely and says he'll get back to him. The Mabahith agent then has to send the questions up and down an incredibly complicated bureaucratic system in order to get permission to answer. Now, if you're the CIA officer, once you've finally got your answer, you immediately have follow-up questions, to which the Saudi officer would say, "Absolutely, please write them down," and the whole process would start again.

'That's a very slow bureaucratic process. No one on either side was acting in bad faith; it was simply the way the system had been set up. And in a post-9/11 environment, where cases are moving quickly, minute by minute, day by day, by the time the CIA would get their answers, three weeks might have passed and something might have blown up by then. So American officers, under tremendous pressure, start burying their Saudi counterparts. They're bringing three dozen requests, each with follow-up questions already written down, and the Saudis are overwhelmed. Again, it wasn't that they were unwilling to answer them. The system they were working within didn't work.

'It's one of the reasons I was going to Riyadh so often. I told Prince Muhammad, "Look, you guys have your system, we have ours, fine. But we have to reduce the timeline, because one day you're going to need something from us quickly and you're not going to want us to answer questions the way you do." And so pretty quickly we agreed that what we needed was a real task force, a place where the CIA and the Mabahith could sit together, where there would be computer terminals with access to all the info, where they could trust each other enough to pass a question officer-to-officer. And it worked really well. The greatest indication of that was the jealousy that arose among American agencies. The FBI, the Treasury Department ... Everybody wanted a seat at that table.'

Riyadh and the Najd had been the primary focus of AQAP's activities for several months, but the Mabahith's officers in the rest of the Kingdom were not sitting idle. A series of shootings had revealed that there was a new cell in the Hijaz, replacing the two that had been shut down the year before. On 5 April a policeman was shot dead at point-blank range as he questioned a suspect outside a shop. Then on the 9th another policeman was killed by a gunman in a car he had pulled over to inspect. The security services in Jeddah were on high alert.

On 21 April – the same day as the Washm Street bombing – the Jeddah bureau received a call from Riyadh. The Mabahith there had intercepted a suspicious mobile phone call indicating that an AQAP operative from the capital would soon be travelling to the Hijaz to meet local cell members. The identity of the caller was known to the authorities, and so Mabahith agents were planted at every security checkpoint along the road to Jeddah. They spotted him at a checkpoint north of the city and followed him to Palestine Street in the centre of town. He parked his car outside a block of flats and went inside. An MOI team rented a flat in the building opposite, and set up a round-the-clock surveillance operation. His phone was tapped.

They did not have to wait long. The following morning, on the 22nd, a phone call revealed that their suspect and someone in the flat with him would be meeting Organization members later that day at a nearby roundabout. As arranged, the two suspects set off from the flat on foot. Mabahith agents followed. It soon became clear, however, that the suspects were aware they were being trailed; they kept looking over their shoulders and grew agitated. Afraid the suspects would do something rash, the trailing officers placed them under arrest. It was a smart move: one of them was carrying a small bomb.

Under questioning, the man from Riyadh confessed everything. He was on his way to meet Talal al-Anbari, number twenty on the List of Twenty-Six and head of Muqrin's Jeddah cell. Anbari was fully Saudi, but his pronounced African features had inspired his fellow cell mates to nickname him *al-Khaal* – 'the Slave'. Anbari had been a member of the Sharaye cell, the man explained; during the raid on the cell the previous November, he had been wounded in the leg. Even so, Anbari had managed to flee and, after joining Muqrin in Riyadh, he had participated in the Muhaya bombing. At the end of February, however, Muqrin decided he wanted to re-establish operations in the Hijaz so he sent 'the Slave' to Jeddah along with seven other Riyadh operatives. He gave him three instructions. First, acquire a number of safe houses. Then recruit new members through existing family contacts and among trustworthy jihadist sympathizers. Finally, plan and carry out bombing operations inside American residential compounds.[8]

Anbari's contact in Jeddah was an operative called Abdulmajid al-Talhi. Talhi had rented a villa in expectation of Anbari's arrival, but Anbari followed orders and immediately instructed Talhi to start looking for another one. That he did, and in early March Anbari moved into a flat in the Quraysh district. But Talhi was a live wire. It was he who killed the two policemen at the beginning of April. Anbari knew the MOI would be looking for him, so he found yet another flat, this one in the Safa neighbourhood. Leaving two men to look after the Quraysh flat, Anbari and his cell moved to Safa.

This much the Mabahith were able to learn from the suspect from Riyadh. However, he did not know the Safa flat's address. The man arrested with him – who was very young – had once been taken there, but he had been blindfolded during the journey and did not know the exact location. With little else to work with, the officers went to Safa with the young suspect and walked him up and down the neighbourhood's streets, in the hope that something – a door, a car, anything – would jog his memory. It worked. He recognized the door to the apartment building, and verified that the ground-floor flat was Anbari's.

The Emergency Forces were immediately called in. Captain Sirhan al-Ghamdi was among them. 'The flat had two entrances, one from the building's central corridor and one directly from the main street. Intelligence had confirmed that there were three men inside.' When the team arrived, they crossed the security cordon and took up defensive positions outside the entrances. 'We began our usual appeals for them to surrender. Their response, however, came as a surprise.' The men inside the flat opened fire. 'They began shooting through the door which led directly onto the street.' The officer at the door ducked down quickly enough for the bullets to miss him, and he crawled to safety. 'The gunfire was extraordinarily heavy. After the first burst, the situation began to . . . well, it began to get a bit out of control.'

The Emergency Forces returned fire, and their assault blew the front door open. The men inside lobbed pipe bombs through the doorway, which the officers easily avoided. From the terrorists' point of view, the layout of the flat and the street put them at a disadvantage. The front door was completely exposed.

The gunfire died down. 'After the door was secured,' Ghamdi continues, 'we threw tear gas canisters into the apartment to force the three guys out.' Within minutes, all three ran out onto the pavement. 'One of them came out wearing a suicide belt. The other two were trying to give him enough cover to get close to us before detonating.' The officers shot them down before they had made it two metres from the door. Blood trickled across the pavement tiles towards the gutter. The one with the suicide belt lay sprawled on his back, his spectacles still snug on his face.

However, there was further action to come. Investigators had set up large ventilators inside the flat to rid it of the lingering tear gas. They were uncovering a huge amount of weapons and explosives, when suddenly the security cordon was fired upon by two unknown assailants. The attackers fled on foot into the neighbourhood, hijacked a civilian's car, and drove off. Policemen followed. During the pursuit, gunfire was exchanged, until finally the two men were cornered. One of them was shot and the other detonated his suicide belt. But it misfired and only ripped up his insides.

Back at the flat, hundreds of locals congregated behind the police tape. 'That was the most extraordinary thing about that night, from my point of view,' Ghamdi remembers. 'Even now it stands out in my memory. We had relaxed the security cordon, because the job was done and the three guys were dead. And then people began to gather. Saudis yes, and Pakistanis, people from all the different communities in that area. But they were all cheering. "Long live the Emergency Forces! Long live the Umma!" they cried. They were whistling too, and hanging out of windows. There was a tremendous excitement in the air.' Nearby, a half-built three-storey building was full of onlookers cheering along. One young man climbed on top of a police car and goaded the people on. 'There was a lot of noise. It was indescribable; a feeling of elation, of achievement. But really, I haven't got the words to describe it.'[9]

Later that evening, the bodies were brought to the morgue. A young man, whose name is unknown but who was affiliated to the cell, was summoned to identify the bodies. He stared at them with little emotion; it is likely he was feeling the shock of the cell's sudden collapse.

'Who is this?' the officer in charge asked him. They were standing over the corpse of the man whose suicide belt had failed to detonate properly. He was black.

'Talal al-Anbari,' the young man mumbled.

'What? Speak up, boy,' the officer replied sternly.

'Talal al-Anbari.'

'How do you know it's him?'

'Abu Muhsin introduced me to him . . .'

'Huh? No, I don't care how you met him. How do you know it is him lying there?'

'That scar, there on his leg,' he said, and pointed. There on the inside of the dead man's left leg was a large white scar.

Sixteen men remained on the List of Twenty-Six.

James Oberwetter had taken over from Robert Jordan as American ambassador back in December. Like Jordan, Oberwetter was a Dallas man and a long-time associate of the Bush family. He had been the elder Bush's congressional press secretary, and then worked in a series of governmental roles. He had become vice president of a Dallas-based oil company when Bush *fils* designated him to be his representative to the Saudi court.

'It was an "interesting" time to become ambassador,' Oberwetter recalls. 'I arrived in Riyadh in February and by April had made the decision to evacuate all American dependants and non-essential personnel from the embassy.' It was not an easy decision. 'But you have to take account of the facts. More terrorist events had happened in the few months prior than had happened in the decade before 2003. It did not make our Saudi hosts happy that we decided to evacuate. But looking back at what was about to happen, I think it's clear we made the right decision. It had become an act of courage just to go to the grocery store or take a trip into the desert. Even the compounds didn't feel safe any more.'

In the last week of April 2004, Oberwetter travelled to Dhahran on the east coast to attend a meeting of prominent American expats, who were very concerned. 'I warned them to be on the lookout. It wasn't a question of if, it was a question of when. Of course, I didn't know then that when they struck it would be on the west coast.'

On May Day, Oberwetter received a call from the consulate in Jeddah. 'The Consul-General said there was a situation in Yanbu, north of Jeddah, and that, well, that it was pretty awful. A number of terrorist guys dressed in military uniforms were scattered around the city shooting up the grounds of foreign companies. To put it mildly, they did a lot of damage.'

Yanbu is an ancient city. Situated on the Red Sea coast about three hundred kilometres north of Jeddah, for millennia it had been a small trading town, an important stop on the incense and spice route from Yemen to the Mediterranean. In 1975, however, the Saudi government decided that Yanbu was ripe for modernization. They made it the centre of the Kingdom's shift from simply pumping oil to refining it. In 2004 there were nearly 200,000 residents, many if not most of them workers from abroad.

Oberwetter immediately went there. 'There were awful scenes of, well, of death and destruction, and that's really as much as I want to say about it.'

The attack had started that morning. At around seven o'clock four attackers wearing khaki National Guard uniforms invaded the local headquarters of ABB Lummus, a Swiss engineering multinational. Three of the gunmen were Lummus employees and so had badges granting them access. They let the fourth one in through an emergency exit. Non-Muslims were singled out for execution. Afterwards, they tied one of the victims to the back of their truck – whether he was still alive or already dead is not known – and dragged him around town for several miles. They tossed a pipe bomb into the grounds of an international school, shot up a McDonald's, and when police engaged them outside a Holiday Inn, they stole a couple of cars and fled into a nearby residential complex. Gunfire from police then caused one of the cars to catch fire; the two men inside were burnt alive. The other car was eventually stopped by policemen, who killed one of the terrorists and injured another. He later died in hospital.

Six people had been killed, all from the English-speaking world apart from one Saudi policeman. Twenty-five had been injured. Investigators discovered that the attackers were two sets of brothers from the Ansari family. The elder pair of brothers were the uncles of the younger pair. One of the uncles, whose name was Mustafa, had had a long career in Al Qaeda. In the 1990s he spent some time in Britain, where he worked for Khalid al-Fawwaz at Bin Laden's London media bureau, which was called the Advice and Reform Committee. Later he was imprisoned in Yemen, but had escaped and sneaked into the Kingdom.

The MOI immediately raided the Ansari brothers' homes and rounded up possible collaborators. Eleven men were later charged with terrorist crimes and stood trial. It was, incidentally, the first trial in Saudi Arabian history covered openly by the media.

The fallout from Yanbu was significant. The price of oil went up, but that was only temporary. What was worse, the international coverage further damaged the Kingdom's reputation. 'ABB Lummus basically decided to evacuate,' Oberwetter says. 'The company clean upped and left because the memories of that day were so bad.'

Two weeks later Muqrin took to the Internet and claimed responsibility for the massacre. But the MOI believes that the Ansari cell operated independently of AQAP.

In a press conference the day after the massacre, Crown Prince Abdullah made a statement which quickly spread to newsrooms across the world. 'Zionism is behind it. It has become clear now. It has become clear to us. I don't say, I mean . . . It is not 100 per cent, but 95 per cent certain that Zionist hands are behind what happened.'[10] Prince Saud al-Faisal the foreign minister did not make things any better when he was asked to clarify Abdullah's remarks three days later. 'It is no secret,' he said, 'that extremist Zionist elements are waging a fierce campaign against Saudi Arabia, levelling false accusations and fabricated slanders at the Kingdom. The desperate attempt by the terrorist group to undermine security, stability, and national unity serves the interests of these Zionist elements.'[11] It was a clumsy attempt to ameliorate what the crown prince had said, and only served to fan the flames of the controversy.

Seasoned observers were dumbfounded. For over a year Al Qaeda had been running rampant throughout the Kingdom, and yet the government was rolling out the same old bogey-man which had played scapegoat for the Saudis – and many other Arab governments – so many times before, most sensationally after 9/11. To the West – which of course condemned the statements – it appeared that the royal family had learnt nothing.

Ambassador Oberwetter met Prince Saud to express his concern, and an official later described the meeting as 'not particularly constructive'.[12] Senator John Kerry, then Democratic front-runner in the presidential primaries, described the crown prince's remarks as 'outrageous' and 'anti-Semitic'. There was a further battle of words when Saudi princess Fahda bint Saud stepped in attacking the crown prince's detractors. Making a distinction between anti-Semitism and pro-Palestinian anti-Zionism, she wrote in *Arab News* that this was 'a smear campaign to pressure this country into abandoning its commitment towards the Palestinians.'[13] The princess's article will not have placated the Kingdom's critics. And it did not address the original problem: the crown prince's bizarre comments.

Whatever lay behind them – a desire to obfuscate the extent to which his country was overrun with terrorists, an unwillingness to accept the truth of the situation, or just plain old anti-Israel paranoia – the remarks were a backward step in the government's campaign to rehabilitate the Kingdom's image. After all the progress it had made over terrorist financing, once again the country was being vilified by American Congressmen.

That the government's response to the Yanbu massacre was confused was pointed out by AQAP itself on the news pages of *Camp of the Sabre*:

> It has become obvious from the blessed Yanbu operation that the Saudi regime is floundering ... Officials of the failing regime gave discrepant reports of the event. Abdullah blamed the Zionists, Nayef blamed Al Qaeda, and the MOI's press release blamed opposition leaders abroad. Their most absurd blunder in all this was when the interior minister told a Yemeni newspaper that these ridiculous reports contained no contradictions! Perhaps the operation's scale and its intense effect have made them lose their minds.[14]

As the controversy raged, the MOI kept up the chase. On 20 May officers raided the rest house in Qaseem where the Operation Volcano truck bombs had been manufactured. The raid had been a month in the making. On the day before the Washm Street bombing, a pickup truck had randomly fired at a group of policemen in Buraydah and fled. A suspect was brought it and he revealed that he did not know exactly where the pickup and its occupants were, because when he visited their rest house he had been blindfolded, but he was able to specify the general area. The Mabahith launched a massive secret surveillance operation, discreetly investigating every rest house inside the area the suspect had indicated. Three weeks later, an investigator was searching an empty rest house when, peering through a pair of locked garage doors, he spied the pickup's number plate. The rest house was placed under surveillance.

Four days later, on the 20th, five known terrorists arrived and the raid swiftly commenced. Two Emergency Forces officers were injured during the raid, and four of the five terrorists were killed. One of them was Talhi, the cop-killer who had caused so much trouble for Anbari in Jeddah. Apparently he had fled the Hijaz after the Safa raid and had sought refuge in Qaseem.

It was a minor victory. Little did the MOI know that just over a week later AQAP would launch a counterattack taking the war to a new level of depravity and viciousness.

Until now the elite Special Forces had played only a minor role. They specialized in offensive operations, and thus far the MOI had largely been reactive. A member of the Security Patrols, or perhaps an ordinary policeman, would be fired upon at a checkpoint or at a suspected safe house, and if the situation escalated dramatically an Emergency Forces unit would be called in to respond to it. Because the Mabahith were gathering new evidence all the time and chasing up new leads, and because AQAP members always refused to parlay with their pursuers, the MOI could rarely be sure beforehand which knock on the door or attempted arrest would lead to violence. So the men of the Special Forces bided their time and focused on training for the day when they would be called upon to do their part.

On the morning of 29 May, the Special Forces based in Riyadh were in the middle of daily exercises when a call came in from the eastern oil city of Khobar. 'They told us that a group of terrorists had stormed a compound and taken over a hotel in the Eastern Province,' Major Nayef al-Tuwayr recalls. It was a hostage situation. 'We were ordered to come to Khobar at once.'[15]

Tuwayr and his fellow Special Forces officers equipped themselves and at around noon set off in trucks on the three-hour journey. Armoured cars went with them. During the journey, Major Khalid al-Muhaya mulled the situation over.[16] 'We had been told that there were no fewer than eighty or ninety hostages inside the hotel.' In fact there were just over forty hostages, although two hundred people inside the compound were trapped in their houses. 'I kept thinking, "Why them?" I mean, they had come to Khobar to work. They had contracts, the government had authorized them to be here. What had they done to deserve this?'

When they arrived, the soldiers passed through the security cordon which the local Emergency Forces had erected around the Soha Tower Hotel, part of a larger development of residential compounds called Oasis Residential Resorts. 'The forces there were already engaging the enemy,' Tuwayr says. 'But they could not get close to the hotel, let alone enter it.' The Emergency Forces had tried to storm the building, but were met with intense gunfire and had no choice but to retreat. 'They suffered casualties and needed to withdraw in order to get the wounded to hospital.'

The officers deployed from their vehicles eight hundred metres away from the hotel. The six-storey building was not exceedingly tall, but it was the tallest around, and even from that distance they could see that large chunks of concrete had been shot off the external wall. 'There were several units present, each with its own commander,' recalls Muhaya. 'We knew we would be called on to rescue the hostages, but for the moment we had to wait.'

Snippets of information trickled in about what had happened. Earlier that morning the terrorists had shot up a couple of office buildings on their way to Oasis. They were specifically targeting non-Muslims. Several people had been killed, possibly including a child. It was reminiscent of the massacre at Yanbu.

Like Yanbu, Khobar was an oil boom-town. It had once been a small Gulf fishing village, but then Aramco – headquartered nearby – attracted millions to the area and transformed that stretch of coastline into the Dhahran-Dammam-Khobar 'mega-city'. For expatriates, and especially Americans, that part of the Kingdom felt a lot like home. It was largely American-designed and -built, dating from the days when Aramco was a US concern and oil engineers from Texas and elsewhere flocked to the Gulf to build not only oil wells and pipelines, but also golf courses and housing estates for themselves and their workers.

The afternoon wore on. Periodic bursts of gunfire were heard from inside the hotel. It was frustrating for the Special Forces, who were keen to intervene. A group of them piled into an armoured car and circled the compound. 'It was reconnaissance,' explains Tuwayr. 'We moved in close and made a detailed survey of the building's entrances and exits.' They carried cameras and filmed through the grille of the bullet-proof windows.

When the reconnaissance team returned to their unit, blueprints of the hotel were delivered and the officers studied them thoroughly. A bit later, videotapes from the compound's CCTV were also handed over. 'The footage was pretty fuzzy,' Tuwayr remembers. 'We couldn't make out much. It looked like there were three guys. Nobody recognized them.' The first clip in fact shows four young men, dressed in simple tracksuits and carrying assault rifles. They arrive at the main gatehouse and talk briefly to the guard, who lets them in.

The CCTV is not a continuous video stream. It is a series of still photos taken every two seconds. In one still, taken from a camera inside the compound, a middle-aged woman is shown knocked onto the ground; in the next, she is crawling out of the frame, leaving behind a trail of blood. Another camera shows staff coming and going through the door to a restaurant kitchen. The terrorists follow one inside. Next, a kitchen worker's body can just be seen crumpled on the kitchen floor. The footage switches to another camera, this one filming the hotel's back entrance, which is surrounded by a tall fence. One of the terrorists tosses his rucksack over. Then they tip some fast-food delivery bikes on their sides and use them as a boost to scale the fence. The camera from inside the entrance shows them hopping down. They are remarkably relaxed. One of them peers through the glass doorway. Then the frame is empty. They are inside, where there were no CCTV cameras, as far as is known. However, there was one pointing toward the hotel's main entrance. A large mat lies in front of the sliding door: WELCOME, it reads. People can be seen running inside, including someone wearing desert camouflage trousers who is clearly an American. A while later, one of the terrorists emerges. The camera angle is awkward, but his reflection can be seen on the door: he sits by the steps, at his ease, taking the air.

Night fell and still the Special Forces waited. 'Throughout the night, we could hear gunfire,' Tuwayr recalls. 'Every now and then you'd hear a shot or two, then another shot. It was coming from inside the hotel. To be honest, we wanted to storm the building as soon as possible. The situation was critical.' There was a flurry of excitement when higher-ups decided to evacuate the residents hiding inside the compound's villas. Armoured cars and vans were sent in and 201 frightened people were evacuated.[17] But the hotel was still full of hostages.

Then at around 4 a.m., just after dawn prayer, they heard a tremendous burst of gunfire. 'We could tell it was coming from the terrorists and directed at the security cordon. It was really something.' The gunfire appeared to be the cue the commanders of the Special Forces were waiting for. Not long after, the order finally came in.

It was primarily to be a hostage rescue operation, although they were prepared to engage the enemy. The officers would enter the hotel from the roof by helicopter. 'It was impossible to storm the hotel from the ground floor because the enemy was in by far the dominant position,' explains Tuwayr. 'But if you are coming down from the upper floors, you are in control. So we brought in three helicopters and the units were divided among them.' The plan was to stage a touch-and-go operation.

The helicopters were vulnerable to gunfire and needed to be able to back off quickly. They would get as close as possible to the roof of the hotel and, after disembarking, the Special Forces would make their way floor by floor down to the hotel lobby. Meanwhile, the security cordon would move in close, and sharpshooters would be positioned to take out the terrorists should they attempt to flee.

It would not be easy. The officers had never trained in the Chinooks they had been given to use. Muhaya explains, 'We got them from the Civil Defence. Even though they are huge and difficult to manoeuvre, they were what was available and we were in no position to wait for an alternative.

'It was around six in the morning; the sun had already come out. I was in the first helicopter.' Potentially they were exposed to enemy fire, so speed was of the essence, and before long all three helicopters had disgorged their men and the roof was secure.

The building was a long thin rectangle. 'It had two internal staircases, one on the east side of the building, and one on the west.' The units gathered into two groups. Each group took a staircase. They swept the top floor. Finding no one, they secured the floor as a base of operations for the duration of the rescue. Any hostages they found on their way down would be taken here, checked over, and then taken to the roof in groups for removal by helicopter.

'As we went from floor to floor,' relates Tuwayr, 'we kept in touch with the other teams and made sure each floor was free of terrorists. We found people who had been killed, people from among the hotel staff mainly. Every time we moved to the next floor, the commander of the other assault team would say on the radio, "We have found a corpse or two." They stick in your mind, these scenes. I cannot forget them. They were horrid. Unarmed people, workers. They had killed them on the stairs, or had killed them elsewhere and piled them up in the stairwell.

'The corpses had clearly been shot at point-blank range. We found people face down who had been shot in the back of the head. We also found people slumped in a kneeling position who had been shot in the forehead. The people killed in the toilets, that was the worse. They had thrown the bodies on top of each other.' Forensic footage shows smashed bathroom mirrors and blood-streaked tiles. One door opens onto a particularly gruesome scene. A room service card hangs off the handle: 'Please clean this room.'

'As we went, we were at the ready for the terrorists. We knew that we were forcing them downstairs, into a sort of trap. Our hope was, eventually, to capture them.'

On each floor the soldiers methodically went from room to room. 'We also found hotel guests. They were in a horrible state of terror and fear. We talked to them and assured them that they were safe now, but they were so scared that they did not trust us.

'I remember one guy in particular. Most of the doors were locked, of course. In order to storm the rooms properly we needed to smash the door down quickly, before announcing our presence to anyone inside. There was no way of knowing beforehand if they were hostages or terrorists. Unfortunately it meant that our arrival could, at first, make someone even more scared. But we had no choice. And we had to deal with everyone, even if they looked like a civilian, as if they were a dangerous person. Terrorists often wear civilian clothes, after all.

'So this guy. Immediately we realized he was a hostage. He was having a breakdown. Tears were pouring from his eyes. We made him sit down and brought him water. I held his hand, cradled his head in my arms, embraced him round the shoulder. We put down our weapons to help him collect himself. I tried wiping his tears away. Of course he was speaking English. He just repeated "shots" – that means gunfire – and the word "terrorist" over and over. Eventually he did calm down and we were able to move him up to the safe area.'

Major Muhaya's experience was much the same. 'I was coming down the stairs and I saw one guy, a Bangladeshi or a Sri Lankan, I cannot be sure. He worked there. I still remember it, as God is my witness. It was like he had not died, he was so casual. Just lying on the stairs. They must have surprised him suddenly, because he still had his hands in his pockets.'

The second team also found Westerners cowering in their rooms.[18] 'There was a Frenchman ... no, not French, a Dutchman. We broke down his door and asked him if there was anyone in the room next door. He said there was, and we knocked but there was no response. The guy inside was too scared to reply. So I climbed up to the air-conditioning duct and called to him through it. I explained we were the police. Eventually he came out and said, "We thought no one would come. Those people ... they are crazy! We heard the shooting ..." He was clearly shaken, the poor man. He must have been thinking, "This is it. I'm finished. It's all over."'

The two teams snaked down towards the lobby. 'You have to understand, we were all really tense, expecting to encounter the enemy at any moment. At one point I turned down a corridor just as one of my colleagues turned into it from the other end. That spooked us. Thankfully our fingers aren't constantly on the trigger.'

On the first floor, they discovered an ammunition cache and some mobile phones in one of the suites. The terrorists had certainly been there. Finally, they made it to the ground floor.

'In the lobby,' Tuwayr continues, 'we found bombs at all the entrances set up as booby traps. They had thought we would storm them from below. The bombs were primed and ready to go off the moment a door was opened.' There were signs of the Emergency Forces' failed raid on the hotel. 'There was a lot of blood. Pools of blood, really, from the Emergency Forces guys.'

One assault team continued down into the basement. 'Something I will never forget is that some people were so scared that they had climbed into the hotel's septic tank and hid there. We had to coax them into coming out. They couldn't believe they were safe.' Inside a boiler room they found further evidence that the terrorists had used it as a sort of base. Another team cleared the hotel kitchens, where they found more bodies. Outside in the loading area beside the kitchen entrance, there was still no sign of the attackers.

Back up in the lobby, the men discovered that the terrorists had jammed the lift doors open with chairs. The booby traps, the ammunition cache, the disabled lifts. It had all been thought out.

But where were they?

11

The Khobar Massacre

What exactly occurred during the Khobar massacre, as the horrific events of 29 May 2004 came to be called, is to this day hard to discern. Confused eyewitness accounts have proliferated. Reports have it that fourteen terrorists were involved and that six men stormed Oasis Residential Resorts. Others say that several terrorists were killed and several more arrested. The attackers are supposed to have been wearing military clothes and driving military vehicles. These accounts were all products of a widespread game of Chinese Whispers played not only by the media but also by compound residents and other foreign workers in Khobar. The expatriates were scared and – especially because the attacks ended with a whimper instead of a bang – their fear quickly turned to anger. Accusations abounded that justice had been intentionally subverted to save the government's reputation.

AQAP published its own account in the form of an interview with **Turki al-Mutayri**, who led the team of terrorists during the massacre. It appeared in *Voice of Jihad* and is shot through with clear embellishments and outright fabrications. As for the MOI, its media liaisons were understandably tight-lipped during the massacre. Eventually two of the terrorists involved were arrested, and the Mabahith say that they were among the least cooperative of all those detained during the war.[1] That rings true. However, the episode was a significant embarrassment to the government and the MOI remains taciturn. It is possible that the MOI would rather the details remain obscure.

What follows is based on a balance of all these partial sources, plus the more straightforward CCTV footage, interviews with the security officers, and forensic analysis of the crime scene. Also, as described in the previous chapter, MOI film crews were present during the siege. The footage they shot has been an additional help.

Mutayri was a member of Abu Ayub's assassination cell and had been a close associate of Muqrin for many years. He was born in Riyadh in 1984. According to an interview he gave to *Voice of Jihad*, he travelled to Afghanistan about six months before 9/11 and met Bin Laden in Kandahar.[2] He asked the Sheikh if he could have his blessing to martyr himself in a suicide operation. 'I am pleased to say,' Bin Laden replied, 'that, God willing, you will now be trained with the brothers. Then you shall have your wish.' Bin Laden sent him to Camp Farouq where he met Muqrin, and he was one of the many candidates to play the role of 'twentieth hijacker' on 9/11.[3] He was given special training for it, but then, according to his account, the date of the operation was moved forward and he was passed over. When he heard how successful the attacks were, 'I was very glad, and very sad.' Sad, that is, to have been left out.

After America's invasion of Afghanistan he participated in several battles, during which he met a number of other future AQAP members, and was only seventeen when he received the order to return home.[4] Back in Saudi Arabia he lost contact with Muqrin and started planning a suicide operation on his own. But then Muqrin got in touch and Mutayri became his 'assistant', accompanying the older commander on recruitment and training operations across the Kingdom. He appears never to have been far from Muqrin's side: he was present at many of Muqrin's near arrests during raids, participated in Muhaya, killed two policemen at the Khalid al-Farraj rescue attempt, and was put in charge of surveilling Mabahith officers and planning their assassinations. In short, he was the perfect operative: competent, committed, and loyal.

As has been explained, though Muqrin claimed them as his own, the men who carried out the Yanbu massacre on 1 May were not Muqrin's men. There is little doubt, however, that the media impact from Yanbu inspired Muqrin to copy his own copycats. Also, the security situation in Riyadh had become even more oppressive following the Washm Street bombing. Muqrin needed to shift focus elsewhere. The oil-rich Eastern Province was a natural choice. He had sent an operative called **Nimr al-Baqami** there back in March or April to establish a cell and scout potential bombing locations.[5] Now he told him to gather information on suitable targets for a Yanbu-like mass shooting.

He soon received Baqami's report. Baqami suggested three locations in Khobar: the headquarters of the Arab Petroleum Investment Corporation, known as Apicorp; the Petroleum Centre, a business park where several international companies had offices; and the Oasis Residential Resorts. Muqrin then called a meeting at a safe house in Riyadh, a villa in the Wuroud district, where he and Abu Ayub selected four members from the assassination cell to carry out the operation. Mutayri was the leader. Baqami was also chosen, along with Adel al-Dhubayti and Abdullah al-Subaei. The foursome were christened the Jerusalem Squadron.

Nothing is known about Dhubayti or Subaei apart from the fact that they had been among the participants in Operation Volcano. Baqami's background is similarly obscure. However, his video will is revealing. He sits in front of a blue curtain, an imposing hulk of a man, probably in his mid-twenties. His moustache is neatly trimmed and he wears a military jacket over his white thobe. That he considered himself a fierce warrior is evinced not only by his dress but also by the aggressive swagger with which he addresses the camera. He also recites from memory a long poem about Umar ibn al-Khattab, a companion of the Prophet who became the second caliph of the Muslim empire and is revered as an exacting law enforcer and brilliant military commander. Perhaps Baqami modelled himself on his hero.

The Jerusalem Squadron were driven to the Eastern Province by a fellow cell member. They wore women's clothes to disguise themselves, a common practice of AQAP. Before leaving they purchased a light-green Toyota Maxima using a forged ID card and hired a shipping company to transport it to Khobar for them. In Khobar they spent several days at the flat Baqami had rented, venturing out to do more surveillance of the three targets and readying themselves for the operation.

Mutayri would later claim that all four expected to die. Apparently he penned a letter to Osama bin Laden and asked Muqrin to deliver it to him. It was later published in *Voice of Jihad*.[6] '*Salaam alaykum*,' he writes, followed by the usual best wishes and pious exhortations. Then,

> The pledge I made to you in the Nabras guesthouse in Kandahar four months before 9/11 has been carried out ... When the Taliban fell, we returned to the Arabian Peninsula and I met up with Abu Hajer [Muqrin], may God reward him. He made the necessary arrangements and made every effort to gather the forces, organize the troops, and rally the Muslims to join our ranks.
>
> As for me, I have accepted a martyrdom operation along with three lions of Islam. May God grant us victory and

enable us to slit the necks of Jews, Christians, and apostates. May He grant that our blood be fuel for this blessed convoy and a light to illuminate its path ...

We ask you and our mujahideen brothers to pray that we be accepted in heaven. God willing, we shall meet again there.

The Jerusalem Squadron set out at 5:45 a.m. Mutayri was driving and Baqami was seated beside him. Subaei and Dhubayti were in the back; throughout Mutayri's account they are referred to by their *noms de guerre*, Hussein and Nadir respectively. When they neared the first target, they stopped the car, changed into black tracksuits and strapped on their tactical vests and their weapons. 'The first company was the Arab Oil Investment Company. It belongs to the American company Halliburton, which is involved in Iraq.' In fact, Apicorp is essentially a bank for the Arab energy industry and was founded by the Organization of Arab Petroleum Exporting Countries.

'The company had two gates. We arrived at the first gate and Nimr and the other brothers got out of the car ... There was one guy behind the gate on the other side of the fence, two more outside the gatehouse and another inside whom Nimr ordered to open the gate. He refused.' The guard hid underneath his desk, and as they were making no progress there, Nimr and the others got back in the car and drove to the second gate. Though Mutayri's account fails to mention precisely what happened next, an AQAP propaganda video released several months later included an audio recording which the terrorists recorded using a mobile phone. They shouted at the guards to open the gate – there were two of them, both Saudis – and apparently they refused because someone shouted 'Shoot! Shoot!' and they opened fire. Both guards were killed. During the shooting, a bullet hit the fuel tank of a GMC Suburban as it drove past the gates. The four children inside were being driven to one of the many international schools in the neighbourhood. The car caught fire.

Three of the children managed to escape along with the driver, but a 10-year-old Egyptian boy was trapped and burnt to death.[7]

The audio recording continues as the attackers walk up to the building. Sixty-two-year-old Michael Hamilton, a Scottish executive who had been living in the Kingdom for twelve years, had pulled into the car park shortly before their arrival. They shot him in his car.[8] Mutayri would point out that 'the mobile phone on a bloodied car seat which appeared on the news – that was his'. On their way inside the building, they fired at random and shot up the spacious lobby and several offices – but no one inside was killed. 'Where are you, infidels?' they shouted. 'Where are you?' In the telephone recording, they can be heard ordering people to tell them where the Americans are. They made them recite the first half of the Shahada – 'There is no god but God', the primary Islamic declaration of faith – to prove that they were Muslims. A Filipino employee was shot, but luckily he was hit only in the leg and survived.[9]

'Come on, brothers, it's time to go!' the attacker with the mobile phone called out, and they headed back outside, shooting as they went. They passed Hamilton's body and had an idea probably inspired by the attackers at Yanbu. 'We tied the infidel to our car by one of his legs and drove off.'

They soon encountered the Security Patrols. A jeep approached and they fired at it, killing the soldier inside. The other patrol cars returned fire, but the terrorists slipped through and continued on their way. 'Praise be to God, we had memorized several routes to the second target, so even though the patrols had cut off the road we'd initially come down, we were able to take another street.' They raced to the Dammam–Khobar highway. In the recording, one of them says, 'Brothers, if you find an infidel, shoot him.'

Hamilton's body was still attached to the car. They dragged it for 4 kilometres. 'His clothes ripped off and his body was naked. It was during working hours and the streets were full of people.

Everyone saw the infidel being dragged along, praise God.' Nearing a highway overpass, they were ambushed by another security patrol. They fired at them and sped across the bridge. 'When we reached the middle, the rope snapped and the infidel's corpse fell down into the intersection below. Everyone waiting at the traffic lights witnessed it.'[10] Once again they managed to escape the patrolmen. (Though Mutayri interprets the Jerusalem Squadron's supposedly effortless escapes as evidence of the patrolmen's cowardice, it must be remembered that the soldiers will have suspected that the terrorists' car was wired to explode, and so kept their distance.)

As they passed the Ha'il Centre Compound, situated along the highway, they fired upon a passing car and killed the Indian driver, Lawrence Monis – though Mutayri leaves that episode out. The car, out of control, swerved and crashed into another car. Continuing south, they turned west onto Prince Sultan Road and at around 7:55 a.m. drove up to the Petroleum Centre, two bulky buildings connected by an entrance hall surmounted by a distinctive glass pyramid. Companies such as Royal Dutch Shell and Lukoil had offices there. 'We got out of the car and, praise God, the brothers felt a profound sense of peace and miraculous tranquillity.'

They walked up to the gate on foot. 'We found four young men from the Arabian Peninsula' – AQAP do not use the word Saudi, because of its links to the House of Saud – 'who were wearing Aramco uniforms. They asked us, "What's going on? What has happened?" We told them they had nothing to fear, that we were not coming for them but for the Americans.' The security guards would later tell the MOI that the terrorists had threatened to kill them if they didn't let them through.

Once inside the building, less trigger-happy than before, they encountered several Arab employees. 'They were in shock and kept saying, "What's happening? Who are you?" We told them, "We are mujahideen and we want the Americans. We have not come to raise our weapons against Muslims, but rather to purify the Arabian Peninsula of infidels and apostates ... We need you to tell us where they are."' The audio recording broadly backs up this account. The terrorists can be heard shouting, 'Where are the Americans? Quickly! Come on!' and one of them tells someone, 'Go with God's protection. God alone is to be feared. Do not report anything.' Then he tells someone else, perhaps a security guard, 'If anyone wants to go, let them. We have nothing to do with you guys.'

Mutayri's account continues. 'We headed to the top floor. The building contained several companies and so there were many doors. Behind every door we found a large hall with lots of desks and a main office behind a glass facade. Inside one office we found an American infidel. It seemed that he was a company director. We entered and called out to him, and when he turned towards us in response I shot him in the head. His head exploded.' The man was Frank Floyd. He was from Kentucky and had lived in Saudi Arabia for over twenty-five years.[11]

Entering another office, they encountered another man. 'Brother Hussein slit his throat. He was a South African infidel.' His name was Abraham Bayar. Above his corpse, his computer's screensaver displayed a photograph of his family.

They went back out to the main corridor. 'Brother Nimr was standing guard, calmly sipping water as if at a picnic, so intense was his courage. Then we left the building and got back into our car.' Mutayri does not mention that they had also killed two Filipinos.[12]

The death toll had reached nine. The Jerusalem Squadron set off towards its third and final target: the Oasis Residential Resorts.

The Oasis Residential Resorts were situated in the swanky Golden Belt neighbourhood. 'It is a well-known centre of licentiousness and prostitution,' Mutayri wrote. A more charitable description is that it was home to many well-to-do expatriates and Saudis, including the governor of the Eastern Province, Prince Muhammad bin Fahd, who had a palace nearby. The section the Jerusalem Squadron targeted covered around twenty-five acres and comprised two residential compounds, the Soha Oasis and the Abdulaziz, containing about two hundred semi-detached luxury villas. In addition, the Soha Oasis featured the five-star Soha Tower Hotel, a lavish Italian restaurant called Casa Mia, and a full-sized ice hockey rink.

Mutayri claims that the car had been wired to explode. In the original plan, he explains, he was going to detonate the car at the gate after dropping the others off to allow them inside, but that on the day itself they noticed a smaller, less highly guarded entrance along the northern wall and decided instead to enter through it on foot. This is definitely a lie. The car was thoroughly investigated later – the investigation was recorded on videotape – and no explosive material was found inside. Mutayri's dissembling is odd. Most likely the fabrication was intended to bolster their image as fearless martyrdom-seekers. In any case, it is a reminder that AQAP's accounts cannot be wholly trusted.

What really happened is that they pulled up alongside the armoured car guarding the main entrance and fired at it. 'The soldier seated behind the gun, I saw his skull explode, praise God,' Mutayri recalls.[13] Then they drove up the street and around the corner to the northern service entrance right beside the recreation centre and parked the car in the street. A small gatehouse containing only one unarmed security guard stood beside a closed gate and an entrance door for pedestrians. Baqami got out, calmly climbed over the two rows of Jersey barriers and sauntered up to the gatehouse. From what can be ascertained from the CCTV footage, Baqami did not threaten the guard, at least not with his weapon, who in no time at all had opened the door.

Over the next five minutes the Squadron nonchalantly unloaded the car. One at a time, bags full of grenades and ammunition were heaved over the barriers and carried into the compound. It is extraordinary how relaxed they were. How they could have been left unmolested by the police after all the death and destruction they had already caused, is a mystery. Perhaps, again, the authorities assumed the car was going to detonate and so stayed well clear.[14]

The four men now stood at the northern end of a street that bisected the compound. The large villas of the Soha Oasis lay on their left. Immediately to their right stood the delivery entrance to the kitchens of the Abdulaziz compound's recreation centre. They walked over and hid behind a delivery truck. Kitchen workers came and went. Two of the attackers approached the door. They asked the workers inside if they were Muslims. One of them was not, and they shot him.[15] The Muslim workers looked on. 'We took advantage of the situation to preach to them and to reassure them about who our targets were,' Mutayri later reported.

They circled round the building and entered the sales office. Two employees were inside. Mutayri asked them to present their identity cards – Muslims' cards are green, non-Muslims' are brown – and luckily for them, theirs were green. So the squadron moved on. They crossed the street and passed through the gate into the Soha Oasis.

For the next hour or so, the Jerusalem Squadron roamed the compound, breaking into villas, shooting up some and setting fire to others. Mutayri's account of this phase of the operation is vague and confused. Eyewitness reports and CCTV are more reliable. In one villa they encountered a 7-year-old Iraqi-American boy.[16] Subaei had cut his arm on some glass and despite the fact that blood from the wound was dripping onto the entrance floor, the boy remained remarkably calm. 'Are you a Muslim?' they asked him. He said he was, and they left.

A little later the boy's father, Abu Hashim – he went by the name of Mike in America – came downstairs and, seeing the blood, got in his car and drove to the security gate to see what was going on.[17] On the way he encountered the gunmen at an intersection. At first he thought they were security guards, so he pulled over to talk to them. When they asked him his religion, he realized the truth. He showed them his ID card and when they discovered that he was both a Muslim and an American, they discussed among themselves whether or not to kill him. They decided to let him go. 'They gave me a lecture on Islam and said they were defending their country and ridding it of infidels,' Abu Hashim later told reporters. 'They were so polite. I cannot comprehend the politeness they showed me because I am a Muslim, and the cruelty [they showed] to others.'

Shaken, Abu Hashim was about to pull away and return to his family when he noticed walking towards them the 50-year-old head chef of the Casa Mia restaurant, a Swede called Magnus Johansson. The terrorists did not bother enquiring about Johansson's religion; they shot him on the spot. As Abu Hashim sped away, Baqami crouched down beside the Swede's body and began slicing his neck before giving up.[18]

A little later on, they spied a woman running out of her house and towards the front gate. She was Dianne Reed, a 47-year-old substitute teacher from Tennessee.[19] Her villa had been set on fire and after dousing the flames she decided to leave. One of the terrorists fired at her from a distance and a bullet struck her in the leg. She fell onto the ground and, bleeding copiously, crawled away. A passing Dutch woman, also fleeing, helped her to safety. Luckily for them, the terrorists decided not to pursue them.

The terrorists continued on their way. 'We heard the sound of the Security Patrols and crowds of men gathering outside,' Mutayri recalled. They took cover, one at each corner of the intersection. They waited, but nothing happened. 'The cowards didn't dare storm the compound!' The security services had in fact begun arriving in force; they surrounded the site, but did not enter.

The four gunmen headed in the direction of the Soha Tower Hotel. On their way, they shot dead an Indian facilities manager in his office.[20] The compound's residents were now in a panic. Families were fleeing burnt and shot-up houses, seeking refuge with neighbours. Those with villas just inside the external wall used ladders to climb over. Most locked themselves in their upstairs bedrooms and waited for the security services to get there. They would wait for hours.

That day the hotel was playing host to twenty-six guests from all around the world. The receptionist, a 34-year-old Filipino called Camilo Tinaco, heard the shooting in the street and told the guests to go up to their rooms and lock the doors. He himself grabbed the guest list and the hotel's master key, and locked himself inside a room on the fourth floor.[21]

The terrorists arrived – they did not come in through the main entrance, but climbed the back fence – and went towards the restaurant. A junior staff member, Marvin Mereno, also Filipino, was standing near the welcome desk when one of the terrorists approached him and asked, 'Are you a Christian?' Mereno did not reply right away, but eventually said, 'Yes I am.' He was shot in the face and left for dead.[22] Another Filipino, a 24-year-old head cook called Mariano Cabasag, was not so lucky.[23] 'We found Filipino Christians and cut their throats,' Mutayri would gloat. 'They were killed as gifts for our brother mujahideen in the Philippines.'

The terrorists were hungry. 'We found a restaurant' – whether Mutayri means the luxurious Casa Mia or the smaller café by the hotel lobby is not clear – 'and ate breakfast. We rested there a while, then went upstairs. We found a number of Hindu dogs and cut their throats. I told the brothers to put their bodies on the stairwell, so that the tyrant's soldiers would see them when they stormed the building and be filled with terror. But it appears that we overestimated those cowards, because they didn't enter until after we'd gone.' That is not quite true, as Mutayri himself goes on to relate.

For four hours the Jerusalem Squadron remained completely unmolested as they roamed the hotel and recreation centre. They spent much of that time rounding up the Muslims they encountered and moving them to the upper floor of the ice rink. There were thirty-seven in all. Once they had gathered them together, they did something rather unexpected. 'We took advantage of all that time to teach them the Qur'an. We taught them how to recite the Fatiha properly. They were astounded. "How can you do this in the heat of battle?" Praise God, it is He who enabled us to do it.'

Mutayri says that the restaurant workers among his Muslim captives told him their boss was a Hindu who did not give them breaks to pray. They were referring to E. Carlos Cleopas, the hotel's food and beverage manager.[24] 'They said he would be coming soon, and when he arrived we checked his religion on his ID card and kept him with us. We called Al Jazeera [the satellite news network] and they did an interview with us, though they did not broadcast it. I told them we were speaking to them from inside the compound, and that we were only targeting infidels.' Mutayri says he killed Cleopas later. He was the man the Special Forces officers found dead at the bottom of a staircase with his hands still in his pockets.

Mutayri then went into one of the hotel rooms and turned on the TV. The news was reporting the attacks. He must have been gratified to see the coverage. 'The news was saying that the Emergency Forces were at that very minute invading the compound! I planted the brothers in specific locations around the hotel, and we prepared to repel these dogs of the state, should they try to storm us.'

It was now around 1:30 p.m. It seems that Mutayri and Baqami went down to the lobby; the other two were stationed at windows on the second floor. When the Emergency Forces arrived, the gunmen upstairs fired at them. Baqami and Mutayri threw pipe bombs, wounding several, and although Mutayri claimed later that Baqami killed the soldiers' 'commanding officer', that is not true. However, it was a victory for the Jerusalem Squadron. The Emergency Forces fled. They would not make another attempt to take the hotel by force.[25]

The security services began to fire at the hotel from the street. Mutayri then moved his Muslim hostages up to the fourth floor of the hotel, where they would be safe from the MOI's bombardment.[26] One of the hostages, a Jordanian who was apparently in touch via mobile phone with government forces outside, would later say that they were put into different hotel rooms based on their nationalities.[27] Mutayri then ordered his men to set up crude booby traps in case the soldiers returned. Pipe bombs were placed at the entrances in such a way so that anyone opening the doors would set them off. Then they went back to hunting infidels.

Tinaco the receptionist was still locked in his room. He had been keeping in constant touch with the Filipino ambassador by mobile phone, who had been passing on the information to the authorities. The terrorists banged on the door but, because Tinaco had pushed the bed up against it, they could not force their way in. That appears to be the case in general. The hotel guests who stayed in their rooms were not harmed.

An Italian chef called Antonio Amato was, unfortunately for him, not one of them. He appears to have attempted an escape down the stairs, but was spotted. 'We pointed our weapons at him and told him to come over. The infidel did so. We checked his ID card and decided to call Al Jazeera again and send his compatriots a message warning them away from their war on Islam and its people. Then we would slit his throat as a gift to those Italians who are killing our brothers in Iraq, and to their buffoonish president' – he was referring to Silvio Berlusconi – 'who wants to enter into confrontations with the lions of Islam.' Apparently they got through to an Italian speaker at the network, who spoke to Amato over the phone for several minutes.[28] 'Did you record that?' Mutayri asked the man down the phone.

'Yes, I did.'

'Good,' was Mutayri's reply, then he claims that Baqami slit Amato's throat. Again, this does not appear to be true. Amato's corpse was found face-down in the hotel's boiler room. He had been shot execution-style in the back of his head.

Amato was the last hostage to be killed. The Jerusalem Squadron had slaughtered twenty-five people that day, sixteen of them inside the Oasis Residential Resorts.[29] Many more had been wounded. And they had achieved that without sustaining anything greater than a single superficial flesh wound.

But that black day still held a surprise in store.

Sometime very early in the morning of 30 May 2004, fifteen hours after entering the Soha Tower Hotel, three members of the Jerusalem Squadron managed to leave the hotel, climb over the compound's external wall, steal a car, and shoot their way through the security cordon. That much is clear. What is also clear is that Nimr al-Baqami did not make it. He was wounded and arrested.

However, the details are less clear. Most news reports stated that the MOI let the terrorists go in exchange for not blowing up the hotel. Nawaf Obaid, a Saudi security analyst who at that time had close connections inside the court, confirmed that narrative.[30] 'It was a deal,' he told reporters, 'and the orders came from senior people who said, "Let them out."' A compound employee claimed that one of the hostages overheard phone conversations between their captors and the government, hashing out a deal. 'The security forces refused at the beginning but apparently relented,' he said.[31] CNN reported that Prince Nayef himself admitted they let the terrorists go, to prevent any further killing.[32] We know now that if the Jerusalem Squadron did threaten to blow up the building, they did not have the explosives to do it. But the MOI could not have been certain of that at the time.

The MOI still deny that a deal was made. They claim that, in line with their usual practice, they did try to coerce the terrorists out of the hotel, promising they would receive fair treatment at their hands. This is what a police spokesman meant when he told news reporters at around midnight that the authorities were 'trying to negotiate'.[33] However, the terrorists refused and at around 2:30 a.m. the four gunmen broke through a line of Emergency Forces officers outside the hotel, firing their guns and using hostages as human shields. This was the gunfire which the Special Forces officers, waiting for their orders, recall having heard. The Emergency Forces returned fire and Nimr al-Baqami was shot and collapsed. His fellow terrorists abandoned him, ran across the compound, and climbed the wall close to where they had parked their car (the MOI still suspected the car was wired to explode, so stayed away). They then stole a pickup truck parked somewhere nearby. Firing at various security cordons that had been set up around the city, they dumped the pickup, hijacked a passing car, and made their way to a mosque where they hid for several hours – perhaps up to a day – before fleeing to Riyadh. The imam of the mosque was later arrested.[34]

AQAP also denied making a deal, but they gave a very different version of their escape. Mutayri said it began at 9 p.m., when, after praying three times to God for guidance, all four sneaked out of the hotel. They walked back to the recreation centre and climbed up a tall decorative water feature to gain access to the external wall. 'Brother Hussein was the first to jump,' Mutayri explained. 'He threw down his ammunition bag, flung his Kalashnikov across his back and tightened the strap, said a *bismillah* and jumped. When he landed, he lay stretched out on the ground, so one of the brothers thought he had died. But when we called out to him, he replied and said he was fine. We were convinced then that it was a great miracle from God, because the wall was thirteen metres high!' (The wall was nearer four metres high.) Encouraged by Subaei's survival, the other three jumped down as well.

Then Mutayri's account gets really weird. 'We were now in the street, where trees hid us from view. All the forces gathered outside thought we were still inside the hotel. The time was almost 10:30 p.m. and we were very tired ... We decided to rest before attacking them. There were only a few metres between us and them, but God in his mercy diverted their attention towards the hotel and had prepared the tall trees for us to hide behind ... The brothers slept for an hour as I stood watch ... Then I slept a sleep the likes of which I had never slept in my life, God be praised.' This beggars belief. There were odd trees dotted along the street side of the wall, but hardly enough to shelter four armed men from the eyes of numerous soldiers. Mutayri probably created the fiction to stress God's intervention in their favour.

He strikes that note again and again during the rest of his account. It reads like something out of a Hollywood action movie. The Jerusalem Squadron burst out of their hiding place, guns blazing, and confront wave upon wave of armed resistance. Soldiers are slaughtered, cars explode or are overturned in the fighting, and throughout it all the four jihadists are desperate for martyrdom – but God withholds that particular blessing from them.[35] That is, until Baqami is shot down in a blaze of glory. 'A bullet struck him in the middle of the chest, but despite it, the valiant lion kept firing ... His blood was flowing ... Back inside the car, he pointed to heaven. Then we shook him but he did not move, so we knew beyond a doubt that he had been killed.' Mutayri does not say so, but the implication is that they dumped the body.[36] He had to stress how sure he was that Baqami was dead, otherwise people would accuse him of abandoning a wounded comrade. In reality, however, Mutayri's tale of Baqami's fall is yet another exaggeration. The only wound Baqami sustained was a bullet to the knee; it was so bad that the leg was later amputated.

Mutayri sums up the twenty-four hours of cold-blooded killing:

> By the grace of God we arrived at the centre of town. It was as if what we had passed through had been a dream, because of the many miracles we had seen and the divine support we had been granted ...
>
> The truth is, we consider the operation a great victory from God. Many people learnt about what the mujahideen are demanding and saw it with their own eyes.[37] Many of them prayed for our victory and success. Some of the Pakistani and Indian Muslims shouted 'Allahu akbar!' with us, and when they found out we were called the Jerusalem Squadron, they said, 'We want to go with you to Jerusalem!'
>
> ... I and the other members of the squadron swear before God that we will participate again in a raid like this one.

12

The Assassination Cell

Prince Muhammad walked among the blood-stained corridors and stairwells of the Soha Tower Hotel and contemplated this latest assault on the sovereignty and hospitality of the Saudi state. The MOI's public relations team were being bombarded with questions from all sides, but as verifiable information was slow in coming, the temptation was to keep mum until they could release an official account; that was their usual practice. But speculation and exaggeration were already proliferating, as were accusations – which had been voiced before – of Saudi duplicity and incompetence.

The prince was able to see that there was some justice in the latter charge. The terrorists had managed both to circumvent and to break through the cordons with humiliating ease. It was not the first time, either. The Security Patrols were a major weak spot in the Kingdom's counterterrorism defences. Something would have to be done about that.

More importantly, Prince Muhammad had not yet resolved the problem of communication between the forces, which had dogged him from the very beginning. He was in charge, that much the crown prince had made clear. But the ministry's formidable bureaucracy was an obstacle to streamlining the chain of command.

These observations had not been lost on the diplomatic community. Ambassador Oberwetter – who was out of the country during the Khobar massacre, but had kept in close contact with his Riyadh staff – summarizes the prevailing view at the time. 'The way the government went about inserting its forces into the situation showed that they needed a lot more training in terms of how to react to a hostage situation, especially inside compounds and tall buildings. But what was even clearer, the Saudis were not fully coordinated within their own government. Nobody knew who was – as we Americans would put it – on first base.'

Oberwetter raised this issue with the Saudi government and was reassured, at least, that they knew there was a problem. 'The group in charge during a terrorist attack was supposed to be the MOI. We thought that was a good thing, because the MOI had already undergone a steep learning curve and was putting improvements in place.' But there was still some way to go. 'Khobar was a serious incident. If they had got their act together, it would have been less serious.'[1]

Sir Sherard Cowper-Coles, the British ambassador, travelled to Khobar immediately following the end of the siege, in order to deal with the British casualties. He also visited the crime scene at the hotel, where he bumped into Prince Muhammad. They knew each other; the British had been providing the Kingdom with training and other counterterrorism assistance. 'I was full of admiration for Prince Muhammad,' Cowper-Coles recalls. 'He is a highly intelligent, very serious man. And he is a workaholic. He works through the night. When I would go to see him, it was often in the evening or in the early hours of the morning.' That particular morning, however, the prince was in a reflective mood. '"The Kingdom's safety is ultimately in the hands of God," I remember him saying. He was thoughtful like that. And most importantly, he knew that terrorism needed to be tackled by carrot as well as stick.'[2]

The prince had been developing the Kingdom's 'carrot' response for months and would soon roll out an amnesty programme that would prove very controversial. However, it is difficult to imagine that he had carrots on his mind in the aftermath of Khobar. A nationwide dragnet was launched: those responsible for the massacre must be found – if for no other reason than that the eyes of the world were fixed on the Kingdom. On 1 June 2004 two militants were chased into the mountains near Mecca after firing on a checkpoint and, in the resulting stand-off, they were killed. The MOI reported that they had participated in Khobar. They had not. But the announcement indicates the pressure the MOI was under to produce results.[3]

Muqrin crowed to the skies. In an Internet press release published on 30 May, he praised the Jerusalem Squadron's valour and courage. 'These heroes are a worthy model for the young men of the Arabian Peninsula, and there are many more like them. They are racing towards martyrdom, eager to fight the enemies of God: the Jews and the Crusaders, and their henchman among our apostate rulers. Each of them feels in his heart the pain of his Muslim brethren in Palestine, Afghanistan, Iraq, and everywhere; and the cure to this pain, this is what they will show you.'[4]

No doubt Prince Muhammad found it hard to understand how killing foreign workers, rich and poor, upon whom the economy of his country and therefore the welfare of its people depended, did anything to alleviate the suffering of their Muslim brethren. Unfortunately, he and other members of elite Saudi society could not ignore the fact that Muqrin had an audience among the populace. Anti-American sentiment had been high enough in the run-up to the invasion of Iraq. But in late April 2004 the whole world had been shocked by reports of horrendous prisoner abuse at Abu Ghraib prison outside Baghdad. The photos of American military personnel subjecting Muslims to degrading treatment, and descriptions of the 'enhanced interrogation techniques' practised upon them, had been playing on loop throughout the Arab world. The backlash was driving Saudis further into anti-Americanism.

It was time for plain speaking. Prince Bandar, the Saudi ambassador to Washington, penned an op-ed for the Arabic daily *Al Watan* on 1 June. He did not mince his words. In a bold move, he compared AQAP not only to the fanatical Ikhwan who launched a similar campaign of violence in the 1920s, but he went even further. Violent takfeerism, he said, was as old as Islam itself. 'Deviants did not appear for the first time in our era,' he wrote. 'They did not appear because our nation has connections with America or with Christians and Jews, or because of Israel's aggression against the Palestinian brethren, or because of events in Fallujah or Chechnya. They emerged for the first time during the era of the Companions of the Prophet Muhammad. Those who assassinated the third caliph, Uthman ibn Affan, were neither Christians nor Jews. They were descendants of the Companions.'

Muslims, in Prince Bandar's view, needed to rally in opposition to such misguided bloodshed. 'Enough of this futile vindication of what these criminals do. We should stop blaming others. What ails us lies within our own ranks. Enough of demagoguery and confusion at this critical stage in our history. We should all, as a state and a people, expose these criminals. They are disseminating corruption in the land, and we are obligated, as rulers, clerics and citizens, to follow and implement the words of God: *The recompense of those who wage war against God and His Messenger and do mischief in the land is only that they shall be killed.*[5] Period. No deliberation or hesitation.'[6]

Abdulrahman Alrashed, managing director of the satellite news broadcaster Al Arabiya, wrote a piece for *Asharq Al-Awsat* in which he listed the Khobar massacre as just one in a long line of terrorist atrocities committed by Muslims. 'The majority of those who have carried out suicide bombings against buses, vehicles, schools, houses and buildings, all over the world, have been Muslim,' he wrote. 'What a pathetic record. What an abominable "achievement". Does this not tell us something about ourselves, our societies, and our culture?' Once upon a time it was the regimes of Arab national-socialists who were the main cause of violence in the region. 'Then came the neo-Islamists. An innocent and benevolent religion, whose verses prohibit the felling of trees in the absence of urgent necessity, that calls murder the most heinous of crimes, that says explicitly that if you kill one person you have killed all humanity, has been turned into a global message of hate and a universal war cry.'[7]

Arab News joined the refrain. 'This battle will take years to finish, but there is no other option. Sitting back and sticking our heads into the sand is the worst thing we can do. The devil is here, and he's knocking hard on our door.'[8]

This soul-searching was, again, precisely what Crown Prince Abdullah had emphasized in the wake of the Riyadh compound bombings. It was an uphill battle, but the tragedy at Khobar had generated a renewed sense of urgency among the Kingdom's reformist voices. Their project – to shift Saudi society away from narrow-mindedness and towards greater openness, from ignorance and dogmatism to tolerance and respect for religious and cultural expressions other than their own – would remain a pressing issue long after the last shovelful of sand consigned the Organization to the grave.

The Western press were primarily fixated on the effect the Khobar massacre would have on the price of oil, which had already been rising. A week before the attack Saudi Arabia had announced it would pump more to offset the rise, a move which had helped a little. But the attack spooked the oil markets and on 2 June the *New York Times* reported not only that the price of crude for July delivery had shot up over 6 per cent, but that fear of a disruption to supply was placing a 'risk premium' of between six and ten dollars on every barrel.[9] Also, there were fears that the Kingdom's oil industry would be crippled by the number of expatriates fleeing the country.

Fortunately, the price of oil is a complicated beast, and the spike following Khobar was short-lived. The price would continue to rise and rise, but that had little to do with terrorism and more to do with increasing demand from the Far East, the falling value of the US dollar, and a general commodities bubble in the run-up to the 2008 global financial crisis. Fears of an Al Qaeda attack on Saudi oil installations, while not misplaced, were also exaggerated, and Aramco was confident that its security measures were robust enough to repel any attempted terrorist attack.

The government was keen to get that message out. It invited journalists to the Eastern Province to report on the security of the Kingdom's oil installations. Frank Gardner, the BBC's security correspondent, was sent to Khobar where he and his Irish cameraman Simon Cumbers were granted unprecedented access to closely guarded locations around the region. Gardner had worked as an investment banker for a Saudi bank before becoming a journalist, and spoke good Arabic. He and Cumbers filed a particularly dramatic report outside a petrochemical plant; flames from the plant's gas vents flared up behind him. 'In my TV reports,' Gardner would later write, 'I made the point that while Al Qaeda-linked groups had successfully attacked a relatively small number of Westerners and other non-Muslims living here, they had so far failed to make any impact on Saudi Arabia's oil production itself. I wanted to dispel the myth that the Saudi oil industry would collapse the day after Western expertise departed.'[10]

During his trip, Gardner interviewed Cowper-Coles at his Khobar hotel and was invited to attend the memorial service to

Michael Hamilton, the Scottish expatriate who had been killed at the outset of the massacre. Cowper-Coles spoke at the service and warned the mourners that there were likely to be more attacks on Westerners.

In fact, a week before Khobar a German in Riyadh had been gunned down in a drive-by shooting.[11] He was just the first. On 2 June two American army officers were fired at while riding in a car near a military compound in southern Riyadh. Most American soldiers had been withdrawn from the country the previous year, but some remained as trainers of the Saudi National Guard. AQAP claimed to have killed them, but in fact only their Saudi driver was wounded.[12]

Then on 6 June, Gardner and Cumbers themselves became victims of the terrorists they were covering in their reports. They had travelled to Riyadh from the Eastern Province a couple of days before to delve deeper into the Kingdom's counterterrorism campaign. On the afternoon of the 6th, accompanied by a Saudi driver and an official minder from the Ministry of Information, they went to the infamous Suwaydi neighbourhood to shoot pieces-to-camera.[13] Had the two of them been content with something quick and easy, they probably would not have come to grief. But as the neighbourhood seemed peaceful enough, they spent half an hour filming different takes.

They were packing up their van when tragedy struck.[14] A car pulled up and a young Saudi got out. It was Abdullah al-Subaei, one of the Jerusalem Squadron, fresh from his 'victory' in Khobar. Subaei called out *'Salaam alaykum'* and Gardner responded in the customary way, but the words were barely out of his mouth when he saw Subaei pull out a 9mm automatic pistol from underneath his thobe. Gardner instinctively shouted, 'No! Don't do this!' and started to run.

But Subaei had not come alone. Abu Ayub was with him, as were fellow Khobar team member Adel al-Dhubayti and two others.[15] They had come to Suwaydi for a rendezvous with

Muqrin and were following Muqrin's car through the neighbourhood when they noticed Gardner and Cumbers filming. After pulling over to a side street, they had discussed what to do and Abu Ayub decided to lead an ambush. Muqrin stayed in his car within view of the attack and Abu Ayub and the others drove up to the BBC crew.

Abu Ayub and perhaps one or two others got out of the car, chased Gardner into the neighbourhood, and shot him several times. Gardner played dead while his attackers went through his pockets. In his back pocket they found a small copy of the Qur'an which Gardner always carried with him on location, and Gardner supposes it may be the reason why they did not finish him off with a bullet to the head.

As for Cumbers, he threw himself into the van, but was shot before the driver could speed away, probably by Subaei. The van then raced down the street. After driving a kilometre or so, the driver pulled over and checked on Cumbers's condition. He was dead. Cowper-Coles would later confirm the Irishman's identity at the morgue.

Gardner lay in the street for over half an hour before the police came. A crowd of onlookers gathered around, but despite his pleas for help, no one stepped forward. When the police finally did arrive, he was carried into the back seat of their car and rushed to hospital. Given what had happened, he was very fortunate that a South African doctor specializing in gunshot wounds was on the hospital staff. Gardner had been shot six times; his major organs had mercifully been missed, but a bullet had hit his spinal cord and he was left partially paralysed and dependent on a wheelchair.

But he was alive.

As head of Riyadh's Security Patrols, Major-General Saud al-Halal was at the forefront of the effort to hunt down Muqrin and bring the killing to an end. 'It was a painful time,' he recalls.

'The situation for foreigners was so bleak that they were beginning to leave. It was all part of the Organization's plan. They were trying to destroy our morale, as members of the security services, and to shake our resolve in confronting them.'[16]

Halal was one of the first to be informed of the Suwaydi shooting. Eyewitnesses at the scene described the two vehicles implicated in the attack: Abu Ayub's minivan and, parked a distance away, a green Nissan SUV. The SUV had been spotted a number of times and the MOI had its number plate on record. It was clearly linked to the minivan because the two cars had arrived and driven off together. But it had not participated in the actual assault, an indication that whoever was inside was important. Could it be Muqrin? Halal alerted the traffic police. The SUV was to be found at all costs.

'Similar assaults followed,' Halal says. 'It was depressing. They were able to go undercover and choose their victims freely. They would use a normal car, they would pull up alongside the person they had targeted, force him to stop, and then they'd shoot him. Incidents like this came one after the other. As I say, it was a depressing picture.'

Two days after the Gardner incident, a 63-year-old American called Robert Jacobs was killed at his Riyadh villa. He worked for the Vinnell Corporation but had refused to live in a walled compound. He loved Saudi Arabia – he was particularly fond of camel races – and preferred to live in an ordinary house among ordinary Saudis.[17] It cost him his life. On 8 June, Jacobs was walking out of his villa when he spotted two gunmen running towards him. 'Please! Please!' he cried, but it was no use. A shot rang out and he fell to the ground. His attackers raced over and fired another nine bullets into his prostrate body. One of the gunmen, a bulky man, crouched down beside Jacobs and slit his throat. The MOI would later discover that his slaughterer was Abu Ayub.[18]

Then on 12 June yet another American was killed in his home.

Forty-nine-year-old Kenneth Scroggs worked for a British-Saudi electronics company. He had just pulled into his garage and was stepping out of his car when gunmen sprayed him with bullets. His body was found slumped beside the open car door, covered in pieces of shattered glass.

On that very same day, an American was kidnapped and held for ransom. **Paul Marshall Johnson, Jr** was born in 1955 in a small working-class town in New Jersey. His father died when he was a teenager and so Johnson was forced to provide for his mother and younger siblings. He joined the US Air Force and trained as an aviation engineer. After leaving the service he went to work for AEC in Saudi Arabia, training Saudi engineers in repairing and upgrading the targeting and night-vision systems on the Kingdom's Apache helicopters. He had lived in the Kingdom for over a decade. Easy-going, he cut a distinctive figure. He was frequently seen wearing a large cowboy hat, which endeared him to his friends in the Kingdom, both Saudis and expatriates. He was also a doting husband to his wife Thanom, a Thai citizen.

It is not clear how Johnson came to the attention of AQAP, but somehow he was put on Abu Ayub's list of targets. However, instead of assassinating him, Abu Ayub ordered his sub-cell to kidnap him. They spent several days tracking his movements. On the morning of 9 June, Johnson left home for work. Four AQAP operatives followed him, including Mishaal al-Farraj and Fahd al-Juwayr, two of the cell members who had had so much fun learning to drive oil tankers in preparation for Operation Volcano.[19] However, before they could carry out the kidnapping, their car broke down and they were forced to return to their safe house.

At noon on the 12th they set out again, this time accompanied by three more cell members. They had refined their plan. Instead of trailing Johnson, they set up a fake checkpoint on the road he took from King Khalid International Airport, where he worked. To look the part, they wore police uniforms. Ambassador Oberwetter recalls how, from the Westerners' point of view, this new tactic was especially unnerving. 'If you can't drive down the street,' he explains, 'and stop at a police checkpoint trusting that they are in fact police and not kidnappers, well, that's a big problem.'

Because of the sense of threat circulating among the expatriate community, Johnson had taken to wearing a thobe over his orange jumpsuit uniform, the better to blend in. When he drove up, he saw what looked to him like an ordinary checkpoint, so he stopped. They beckoned him to get out of the car and he obeyed. That's when they pounced. They held him down and injected him with a narcotic substance normally given to sedate livestock before slaughter.[20] Johnson passed out and they carried him to their car. Before driving off, they tossed a Molotov cocktail through Johnson's car window. It burst into flames.

That very evening Muqrin released a statement on the Internet. It included a photocopy of Johnson's passport and his Lockheed Martin employee badge. 'The mujahideen of the Fallujah Squadron have kidnapped an American infidel, a Christian called Paul George Marshall' – Muqrin got Johnson's name wrong – 'who works as an engineer developing Apache helicopters, one of four such specialists working on this helicopter in the Arabian Peninsula. Everyone knows that these helicopters are used by America and its Zionist and apostate allies to kill, terrorize, and displace Muslims in Palestine, Afghanistan, and Iraq. The mujahideen reserve the right to do to him what Americans have done to our brothers in Guantánamo and Abu Ghraib.' Muqrin promised to release a video confirming Johnson's captivity and to publish another statement outlining AQAP's demands.

This was something new. Their war on terror had not yet presented the Saudi government with this sort of hostage negotiation. An online video showing AQAP mistreating a helpless and innocent American citizen would do little to improve the Kingdom's reputation among Westerners. At the same time, whatever Muqrin's demands turned out to be, the government could not and would not negotiate with terrorists. Thousands of policemen were sent to search flats around Riyadh in search of Johnson. They focused mainly on Suwaydi, but made no arrests.[21]

Ironically, the MOI had never been so close to capturing Muqrin. As Halal explains, 'Muqrin regularly moved between certain locations in the Riyadh area. He lay low in safe houses and would adopt disguises. He had many. And the way he would communicate with other Organization members was, well, I can only call it ingenious.' But the Mabahith had a fair understanding of it by now. Lists containing complicated code names – both for individuals and for various activities – had been seized at several safe houses. Also, they had compiled a list of vehicles known to be used by the Organization and were keeping them under regular surveillance.

On Monday 14 June, two days after Johnson's disappearance, they had a run-in with two such vehicles. 'This was not made public at the time,' Halal recalls. 'We were tracking the leadership, and on that Monday they were spotted meeting on Olaya Street.' Olaya Street runs north–south, parallel to the busy King Fahd Road. It was fast becoming the city's new commercial and entertainment hub. 'They were in a Mercedes and a black Caprice. We followed them down some back streets. At the same time we were preparing to ambush them between Prince Sultan bin Salman Road and Arouba Road.'

It was a relatively swanky neighbourhood. Large walled villas lined quiet streets. 'But they realized they were being followed and the driver of the Mercedes panicked and crashed the car. They all got out and piled into the Caprice, which sped off. They fired at us out of the windows and we fired back.

Eventually their car broke down and they forced a doctor out of his car at gunpoint and drove off in it. It was later located in the King Fahd neighbourhood.' Muqrin had been in one of the cars. The abandoned Caprice was searched; inside they found explosives, weapons, and communication devices. 'The car had been rented under the name of someone affiliated to the Organization – what we call their "invisible logistical support network".'[22] Muqrin got away, but the MOI was getting closer.

Inside a villa in the Wuroud neighbourhood, Paul Marshall Johnson was being subjected to an extended, videotaped interrogation. He was seated on the floor. A white blindfold had been wrapped around his head and secured with packing tape, and his hands and feet had been bound with plastic ties. The left sleeve of his orange jumpsuit had been ripped off, exposing the tattoo of a phoenix that he had had inked on the upper part of his arm. Just below it was a small streak of dried blood from the injection they had given him, and he was still a little groggy from the sedative.

The villa was Muqrin's temporary headquarters and was home to several cell members. Muqrin stood at the back of the room and watched as four subordinates carried out the interrogation. One stood behind Johnson, and another holding a cable whip sat next to his outstretched legs. Abu Ayub was operating the camera, beside which crouched a jihadist called Ismael al-Khuzaim. Little is known about him, but because he knew some English, he had been put in charge of the interrogation. Khuzaim shot off questions rapidly in a high-pitched, piercing voice. He was trying to get the American to implicate himself in the crimes they believed he was guilty of.

'You said assembling. But what kinds of projects in general? What's the major name?' Khuzaim's English was very basic. Not only did Johnson struggle to understand his questions, but Khuzaim could not always understand Johnson's answers.

'I have to teach three students ...' Johnson slurred, perhaps from the sedative.

'I know, I know.'

'... on how to repair ...'

'I know. Every project has three or four or six Saudi men, all of them.'

'Right.'

'But you said, "I'm the instructor." You are lying. You are not an instructor.' Khuzaim talked to the others in Arabic. 'In the beginning he said he was a teacher!' Then he barked at Johnson, 'Are you a manager or not?'

'Well, I'm both. I'm an instructor and a manager ...' Despite his fear and frustration, Johnson was docile, even polite.

'I don't care if you have another job. But are you the manager? Say yes or no.'

Johnson nodded his head. 'Yes. Okay?'

'I have special report. If you are lying, I will break your head. If you are in the right way, you will see another thing.'

'Okay.'

This went on for some time. Their questioning went round in circles. 'How do we know if you are Jewish or not?' Khuzaim asked Johnson.

'Give him one of our slaps,' someone whispered in Arabic. The man standing behind Johnson slapped him hard in the face.

'If you call someone at the office, they can tell you ...' Johnson said. They slapped him hard again.

A little later, a shemagh was tied around Johnson's neck. If necessary, they could quickly gag his mouth with it.

'What is your work in Saudi Arabia?'

'The Apache helicopter ...' He was thirsty.

'Wait, wait. From the start.'

Johnson waited a second, and then began again. 'In the front end of the Apache helicopter ...'

'Speak slowly. Speak slowly.' Someone moved to slap

Johnson, but Khuzaim said in Arabic, 'No, don't hit him again,' and then in English, 'Speak slowly.'

'Okay. On the front end of the Apache helicopter, there's some electronics. Optical stuff.'

'Yes?'

'That's what we work on. AEC has a contract to do with optical stuff.'

'What did you say, "optical"? What kind of optical? And like you say, "I train three people." What kind of training?'

Johnson carefully enunciated each word. 'Electronic optical training . . .'

'He's lying,' the other man said. 'Tell him he's lying.'

'You are lying!' The man at his feet whipped Johnson.

'No, sir,' he whimpered. 'Electronic optical training. We teach them to repair boxes . . .'

'See? Now you say there is repair!'

'Right,' Johnson nodded. 'True.'

'Before you didn't say "repair".'

The others began to grow restless. Someone whispered in Arabic, 'We should just break him.' The man behind Johnson started to tie the gag over his mouth.

Johnson shouted through the cloth, and Khuzaim stretched out his arm. 'Wait, wait, wait.' The gag was removed. 'How much you take, your salary, by dollar?' Khuzaim barked. 'Everything, with housing, and there is some benefit for you. How much every month, by dollar?'

'By dollars?'

'Yes, quickly!'

'Er, eight . . . seventeen . . .' Before Johnson finished tallying the figure, one of them smacked him hard with the back of his hand.

'Come on, he's playing with us.'

They stood up one by one. 'Take this as a gift from us!' The one at Johnson's feet flicked him with the whip, while the one behind gripped his hands tightly over Johnson's gagged nose and mouth. Unable to breathe, he started to scream and struggle.

Alarmed that Johnson's cries would be heard, Khuzaim ordered him in a whisper, 'Shut your mouth!' and then to the others, 'Hit him!' They whipped his legs more vigorously. His groans were muffled.

'Hit him harder!' Smack. 'Harder!' Smack. 'Harder!'

The following day Muqrin made good on his promise and released a video outlining his demands. Brief snippets of the interrogation had been edited together to show Johnson 'confessing' to his 'crimes'. Muqrin stood before a sinister red curtain, the archetype of a terrorist guerrilla. He had slung an RPG across his back and wore a tactical vest across his chest. Adjusting his black balaclava, he raised an MP5 submachine gun up beside his head. 'If the tyrants of the Saudi government want us to release Paul Marshall Johnson,' he exclaimed, 'then they must release the mujahideen held in Ha'ir, Ruways, and Ulaysha prisons within seventy-two hours of this message.'

The Saudi government's reply was clear. They would not negotiate with terrorists, and releasing Al Qaeda suspects was out of the question. 'Our position has been the same for thirty years,' the crown prince's foreign affairs adviser Adel al-Jubeir told CNN. 'We do not negotiate with hostage-takers because then you open the door to more hostage-taking and more terrorism.'[23] The American embassy gave the government its full backing.[24] At the same time, they repeated their warnings to American citizens to stay away from the Kingdom. All citizens currently there were urged to leave immediately.[25]

Americans were following the story closely. Johnson's family went on the news and pleaded for the terrorists to let him go.[26] 'He's an innocent man,' Johnson's sister said. 'Killing him is not going to solve anything. Please don't murder him.' It came out that, though he was now being offered up as a sacrifice to atone for the Bush administration's sins in Iraq, he had in fact opposed the invasion. Johnson's son was shown with his own infant son on his lap – the grandson Johnson had never met. He addressed his father's kidnappers directly. 'You guys are probably fathers,' he said. 'Just please let him come home and be a grandfather.'

The White House said it was working closely with Saudi officials and keeping a close eye on the situation.[27] At the same time, Colin Powell said publicly that the Kingdom was not doing enough to counter the rise of terrorism which now threatened to topple the royal family. He called on the Kingdom to work more closely with the United States, and took advantage of the situation to reiterate the need to close down Islamic charities channelling funds to Al Qaeda.[28]

But Crown Prince Abdullah was not sitting idly by. On Saudi TV he said that it was the duty of all Saudis to protect the Westerners in their midst. 'Foreigners are under our protection, under your protection. All of you, not only the king or the crown prince or the defence minister.' He went on to say that the government had been exercising a certain restraint out of compassion for those members of AQAP who had been deluded. 'But patience has its limits.'[29]

The Mabahith studied the ransom video closely and noticed an electrical socket in the corner of the frame which, based on its make, could only have been in a building built over a particular period. This did not narrow the search dramatically, but it did allow them to rule out certain neighbourhoods. They began to comb the city, looking for Johnson.

Meanwhile, the hunt for Muqrin continued. On 16 June the MOI had another run-in with him. 'We witnessed a meeting between Muqrin, Abu Ayub, and several other cell members in north Riyadh,' Halal explains. 'The meeting was only fleeting and didn't give us opportunity to engage them because, as it happens, it was the last day of school before the summer holidays and the roads were jammed with people. If they had opened fire on us we would have been forced to shoot back, and there would have been many civilian casualties. So we let them go and kept up the surveillance.'

It was an extremely frustrating time for the MOI. Every time they closed in on Muqrin, he wiggled free. And the seventy-two-hour deadline for Johnson's execution was fast approaching. Halal and his colleagues were near despair. Muqrin, on the other hand, must have been feeling pretty good. The Organization had suffered many setbacks, but despite that, his own profile had never been higher; Khobar, the string of assassinations, and now Johnson had occasioned the kind of media exposure he had long been looking for. In his mind, the valour of the mujahideen would inspire more and more Saudis to flock to Al Qaeda's banner. And he would be their leader.

Friday the 18th dawned. Johnson, seated in a corner of the Wuroud safe house, after several hours of patient wriggling, finally slipped his hands out of the plastic ties which bound his wrists. Across the room, his guard Sultan Bijad, the smooth talker who had featured so prominently in the Muhaya propaganda footage, sat nearby, noticing nothing. Whether or not Johnson knew he was to be executed that day, one thing was on his mind: escape.

They had put him in a room on the ground floor with access to the outside, and he could see sunlight around the edges of the door. Only Sultan Bijad stood between himself and freedom. Mustering as much stealth as possible, he stood up. It would have been a strain after three days of sitting, but the adrenaline took over and he suddenly lunged at his gaoler. Johnson was a large, powerful man, and Sultan Bijad was taken by surprise. The American knocked him to the ground. Sitting on top of him, Johnson tried his best to cover Sultan Bijad's mouth with his hands, to prevent him from raising the alarm. The two men struggled. Sultan Bijad thrashed around, trying to

Children with guns 'One day the adults dressed up two toddlers who lived there in military fatigues and made them perform for the camera . . . "They're getting the hang of it!"'

Abdulaziz al-Mudayhish before the Washm Street bombing 'His baby-face was still not able to grow a proper beard and he had a teenage twinkle in his eye and a teenager's vanity. What he lacked in intelligence he made up for in charm.'

The 72 Heavenly Virgins Mudayhish covers his eyes with a paper number plate reading '72 Virgins'. 'He moved forward slowly, eerily, completely overwhelmed by the glorious destiny that was about to overwhelm him.'

The Washm Street bombing, 21 April 2004 'The explosion resulted in only minor damage to the attackers' primary target, yet it totally demolished the eastern side of a building used by the General Directorate of Traffic.'

Crowd cheering in the aftermath of the Safa neighbourhood raid, 22 April 2004 '"Long live the Emergency Forces! Long live the Umma!" they cried. They were whistling too, and hanging out of windows. There was a tremendous excitement in the air.'

Police questioning a young man after the Safa raid At the morgue, a young Al Qaeda recruit identifies bodies from the Safa neighbourhood raid. 'He stared at them with little emotion; it is likely he was feeling the shock of the cell's sudden collapse.'

An Al Qaeda cell at prayer *At the end of time, young men with foolish dreams will appear. They will speak of goodness but, like an arrow missing its target, they will stray from Islam. Their faith will go no further than their throats.* – Prophetic hadith

The Khobar massacre, 29 May 2004 CCTV image from inside the Soha Oasis compound. 'One of the terrorists fired at her from a distance and a bullet struck her in the leg.'

The Soha Oasis Hotel, Khobar 'A group of Special Forces officers piled into an armoured car and circled the compound. They carried cameras and filmed through the grille of the bullet-proof windows.'

Victims of the Khobar massacre in a stairwell 'They stick in your mind, these scenes. I cannot forget them. Unarmed people, workers. They had killed them on the stairs, or had killed them elsewhere and piled them up in the stairwell.'

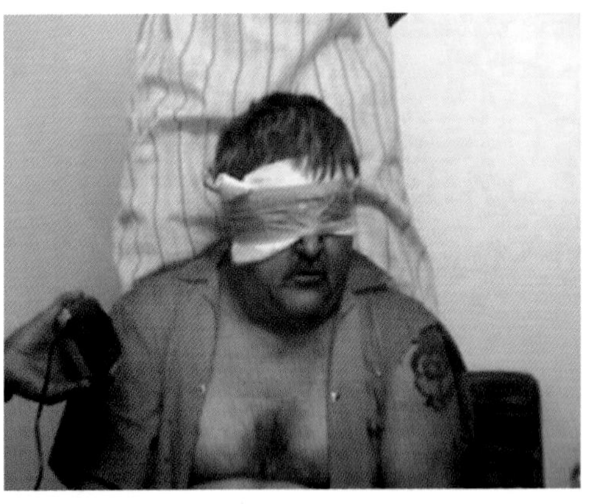

Kidnapping victim Paul Johnson, Riyadh, June 2004 'Inside a villa in the Wuroud district, Paul Marshall Johnson was being subjected to an extended, videotaped interrogation.'

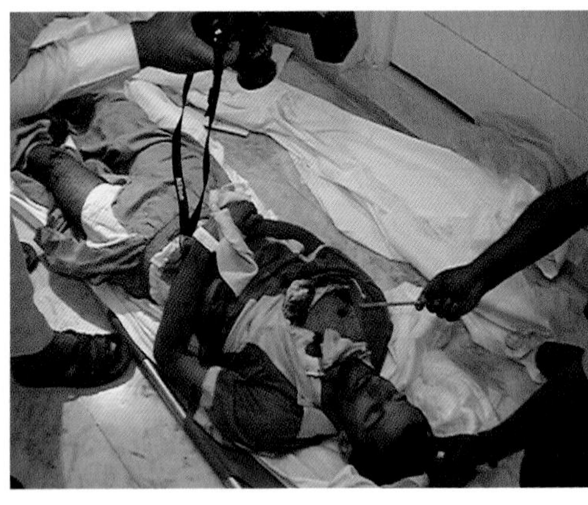

The body of Abdulaziz al-Muqrin, 18 June 2004 'Using a thin stick, an officer pointed out the wounds Muqrin had sustained. "The dog," muttered the cameraman. "He messed up the whole world."'

The MOI headquarters attack, 29 December 2004 'Security was so heavy that the bombers simply drove past and detonated ninety metres from the gate. The explosion caused only minor damage to the eastern facade.'

MOI snipers scramble to safety: the battle of Rass, 3–5 April 2005 'They had run out of ammunition and because there were terrorists inside the villa below them, they couldn't come downstairs. So we brought a ladder and laid it across the gap between the rooftops.'

The battle of Rass, day three 'The order was given to turn the big guns on them.'

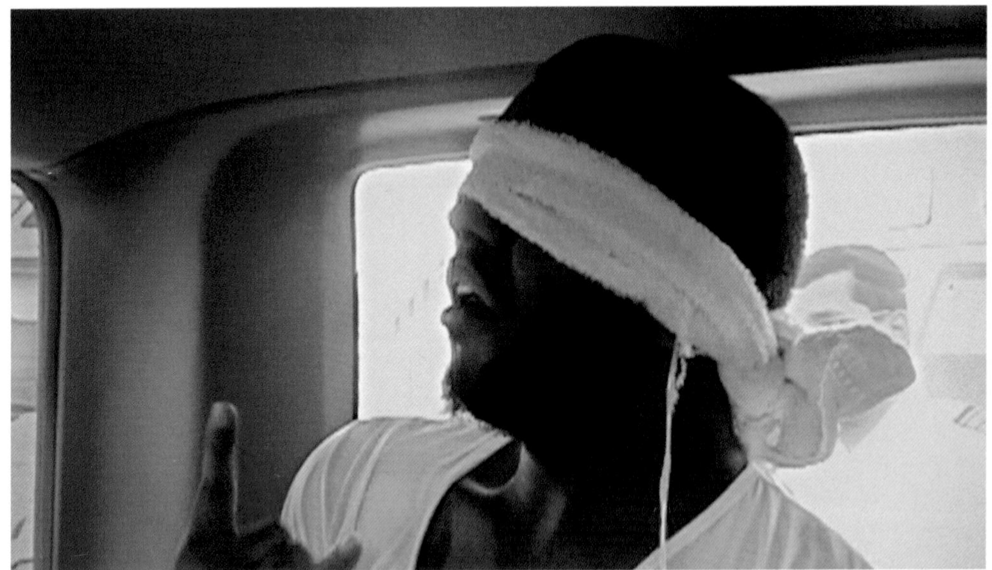

Captured AQ member Osama al-Wahaybi in a police car, 3 July 2005 A Mabahith officer grills him: 'Enough, you dog! No more lies! Tell me who he is!'

The Dammam siege, 3–5 September 2005 'For three days the MOI laid siege to the cell's safe house in the Mubarikiya neighbourhood. Four officers were killed and over seventy wounded.'

Fahd al-Juwayr 'The 34-year-old simpleton whom Muqrin had once deemed fit only for suicide martyrdom now found himself standing in Muqrin's place as leader.'

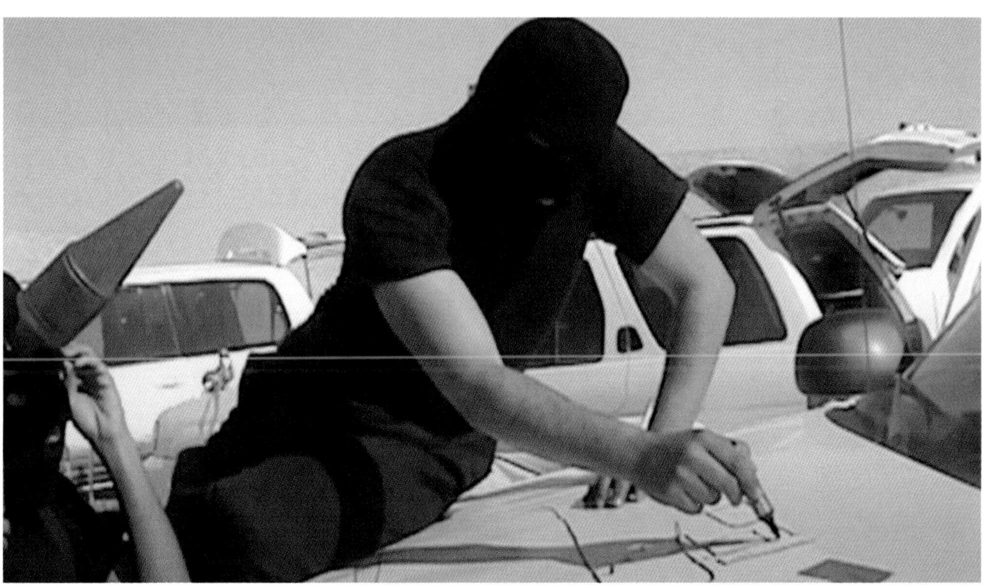

Preparation for the Abqaiq oil refinery attack, 24 February 2006 'In the morning, Juwayr gathered everyone round one of the truck bombs and started drawing a map of the town, the refinery and the roads they would use to approach one of the remote service gates.'

The Munasaha programme 'Candidates for the programme were moved from prison into a low-security residential campus on the outskirts of Riyadh. There they lived a communal life of work, study, and prayer.'

Abdullah al-Asiri, the would-be assassin of Prince Muhammad 'He picked up a hand grenade to symbolize the new kind of bomb his brother had invented for him. "God willing, this will reach him. We shall give it to him, and by God, we shall perfume it before we do."'

Assassination attempt on Prince Muhammad, 28 August 2009 'Most of the bomb's force was absorbed by Abdullah's body. His torso separated from his legs, and his left arm, which was ripped off, shot straight upwards. Investigators removed it later from a hole in the ceiling.'

slip from the larger man's grasp, and filled the air with his muffled cries.

Johnson's strength failed him. Sultan Bijad wrestled his arms away and with a frantic shout called out to his comrades. In a flash the rest of the cell burst into the room.[30] Muqrin was among them. They dragged Johnson off their flummoxed comrade and pinned him to the ground. Calls went up for someone to fetch another set of ties with which to re-bind his hands. But the American began to scream and shout for help at the top of his lungs, desperately hoping someone on the outside would hear. Fearing precisely that, they grabbed a discarded sock, bunched it up into a ball, and shoved it into his mouth. He continued to struggle, yet soon began to shake. A more and more desperate gagging sound came from his gasping mouth as the sock slipped further and further back in his throat.

Then his body went limp. Someone checked to see if he had passed out. With a shock they all realized that he had died from asphyxiation.

In a way it was a mercy for Johnson. He went down fighting and was spared what would have been an even more agonizing death. However, Johnson's premature end left Muqrin in something of a bind. He had sworn to behead him unless the government gave in to their demands. Beheading a corpse would have much less impact.

Muqrin came up with a solution. The execution and the filming would go ahead as planned. The cell members laid Johnson's limp body face down on a white sheet. Muqrin ordered Abu Hassan, a member of Awshen's media team and number sixteen on the List of Twenty-Six, to carry out the beheading.[31] Two others were ordered to crouch beside Johnson's legs and, as soon as the operation began, to shake the body as discreetly as possible to make it look as if Johnson was alive and shuddering from the pain.

And so it went. Abu Hassan pulled out a long knife, placed it on Johnson's cold neck, and in a rather workmanlike fashion began to slice. Abu Ayub, filming nearby, said rhythmically under his breath, 'Abu Hassan, thanks and praise be unto you, and good blessings. May God protect your hands and reward you for this glory.' The other two shook the body as they had been instructed and to the casual observer it indeed seemed like Johnson was squirming in pain. However, his face, turned towards the camera, wore no expression and instead of spraying from the wound as it would have if his heart had still been beating, the blood seeped out gently onto the white sheet.

'Whoa, whoa, whoa!' Abu Hassan laughed as he slipped in the blood. 'I'm going to fall over.' Regaining his balance, he finished the job and lifted up his trophy by the hair. 'Allahu akbar!' exclaimed the assembled cell members and then again even louder, 'Allahu akbar!' They each took a turn holding it up. Snickering, they gawked at it and, betraying no hint of disgust or remorse, teased each other with it.

This was the consummation of AQAP's unthinking takfeerism. Abu Hassan placed the head beside the body and propped his knife up against it. Along with the others, he began to clean up the grisly scene. Johnson's body would have to be buried quickly.

Suddenly, from the back of the room, a new voice sounded. Its sweetness indicated the age of the speaker, no older than eight or nine. 'That's my daddy's knife,' the child exclaimed, bursting with filial pride. It was Abu Hassan's son. He had watched his father behead the corpse of Paul Marshall Johnson.

The King's Cup of Champions is the final tournament of Saudi Arabia's football season. That year the tournament fell on the 18th. Al-Shabaab, Riyadh's oldest football club, was playing Ittihad, a Jeddah-based club and the Kingdom's oldest, at King Fahd Stadium on the edge of town. Saudi Arabians are passionate football supporters, and the biggest cup of the year promised to attract the great and the good to the stadium. The crown prince himself was going to attend along with many other senior royals so the MOI had upped security in the neighbourhood. All eyes were on the stadium.

It is believed that for that reason, Muqrin arranged to meet with Abu Ayub that evening at a petrol station several miles away in the Melez district. Centrally located, Melez was the first modern neighbourhood in Riyadh and contained both handsome villas and government buildings. Usually security in Melez was tight, but because of the match on the other side of town, its streets would be empty. It helped that the other businesses in that area were mostly small hardware stores which stood closed on Friday nights. Muqrin would have felt relatively safe.

However, when he drove up to the petrol station that night, the MOI were waiting. They had realized that senior AQAP leaders were using it as a meeting place. A few days earlier they had spotted the green Nissan SUV from the Gardner shooting parked outside and put a trail on it. At the same time they spotted another AQAP vehicle, a white Jeep Cherokee, parked beside the petrol station's car wash. So when they intercepted an AQAP communication indicating that Organization leaders were meeting in Melez that night, they suspected they were going to the petrol station to retrieve the Cherokee. Perhaps Muqrin himself would be there, they thought.

To make sure nothing went wrong, three security cordons were set up covering the entire neighbourhood. The widest was manned by the regular police. Their job was to discreetly prevent ordinary civilians from entering the neighbourhood once the suspects were inside. Then there was a cordon manned by the Security Patrols. They were to ensure that the terrorists did not escape, should the third layer of security, made up of Emergency Forces and Mabahith officers, fail to capture or kill the targets.[32]

Finally, parked right beside the petrol station's minimart was an SUV carrying a number of undercover security men. They were monitoring the white Cherokee by the car wash on the other side of the car park. 'The signal to engage,' Halal explains, 'was when one or more of them made a move towards the Cherokee.'

Everything was in place. At around 9 p.m. the green Nissan drove into the station. Four people were inside. However, instead of pulling up beside the Cherokee as the MOI had expected, it drove up to the minimart and stopped only a metre or so from the undercover SUV. Brigadier-General Mudeef al-Talhi was on the scene. 'Of course, the terrorists did not know that the men in the SUV were from the security forces. Likewise, our guys did not know for sure that the men in the Nissan were terrorists.'[33]

One of the suspects got out; it was Ibrahim al-Durayhim. Extremely young-looking, Durayhim had started his terrorist career renting houses for Muqrin and had ended up as one of Paul Johnson's kidnappers. He began to move across the car park towards the car wash. 'There were many other vehicles parked at the car wash,' Talhi continues. 'We could not immediately tell whether the suspect was walking over to the Cherokee or not.' One of the plain-clothes officers nonchalantly got out of the SUV and followed the suspect, who did in fact walk over to the Cherokee. 'The security man drew his weapon and ordered him to give himself up.'

However, the altercation had been spotted. 'Abu Ayub – he was one of the three still in the Nissan – jumped out and fired at the SUV. At the same time, Durayhim started to run.' He ran towards what looked to him like a car full of civilians. Unfortunately for him they were more undercover officers. 'His intention was to carjack their vehicle but they rushed at him and opened fire.' The youth was killed by a bullet to the neck.

Abu Ayub had killed one security man inside the SUV and wounded two others. But yet another team of MOI officers, who had been hiding on the other side of the street, immediately ran up and confronted the three remaining gunmen head on. Abu Ayub was killed directly. His body lay splayed out on the pavement; his brains lay several feet away. The two remaining suspects, under fire, dashed toward the minimart. One of them collapsed on the doorstep before getting inside. It was Turki al-Mutayri, the leader of the Jerusalem Squadron. On his person would be found a box of syringes, presumably for injecting a sedative into victims, maybe even Johnson.

The other one managed to get through the door and barricaded himself inside. It was Muqrin. Eventually he shot his way out and ran across the car park. The security officers fired. Desperate to escape, Muqrin began to climb the petrol station's back wall. However, he had been shot several times and before he reached the top he fell backwards onto the black tarmac.

Officers rushed over. He was not dead. Neither was Mutayri. Medics were called. It would have been with some excitement that they loaded the still breathing Muqrin into the ambulance. He would be a source of invaluable intelligence and could tell them where he was holding Paul Johnson; they did not yet know that the American had been killed earlier that day.

But it was not to be. Muqrin and Mutayri both died en route.

At the morgue, the MOI's forensics camera crew was there to videotape the bodies. Using a thin stick, an officer pointed out the wounds Muqrin had sustained. It is easy to see why he did not die immediately. His torso and his legs were riddled with bullets but there were no bullet holes near vital organs. His handsome face was left without a blemish. His death mask expressed an unsettling serenity.

'The dog,' muttered the cameraman. 'He messed up the whole world.'

That evening a video confirming Johnson's execution was posted on the Internet by the Organization's media unit. It included stills which succeeded in giving the impression that he had been executed by beheading. Muqrin and the others had driven to the petrol station directly after burying Johnson's body and, because all four died, there was no one to tell the MOI where the body was. The government sealed off three neighbourhoods in Riyadh, including Melez, and police in armoured vehicles searched them extensively for signs of a grave but came up with nothing.[34] To this day the location of Johnson's body remains unknown.

Despite the disappointing conclusion to the Johnson affair, Ambassador Oberwetter acknowledged that the government had done everything they could. 'Allow me to praise in the highest possible terms the Saudi government,' he announced, 'for eliminating several of the worst Al Qaeda terrorists on the peninsula.'[35] His sentiments were echoed by several regional leaders, by President Bush, and by Tony Blair.[36] Oberwetter also passed along a message from Johnson's son in New Jersey. 'He asked me to say that he knows this act was not an act of the Saudi people, but of a few.'

The Saudi press was unanimous in its condemnation of Johnson's 'execution'. They expressed remorse and embarrassment that such an atrocity should have been carried out in their country, and tremendous satisfaction that Johnson's killers had themselves been killed. Al Arabiya, on its website, wrote that 'the reactions of the Saudi public have been made clear through Internet chat rooms dealing with Muqrin's death, where the majority of participants have expressed their great relief at Muqrin's death and that of his associates.' That is true enough. They felt relief, but messages posted on an ordinary Internet forum a week later revealed that many Saudis felt a range of confused and conflicting emotions. The site, called *Forum of Hearts: Arab Hearts in One House,* was a typical Middle Eastern web forum: pink fonts, flashing bits of text, and a liberal smattering of emoticons.[37] A woman called Wijdan al-Doha started things off. 'I implore you in God's name to be honest with yourselves and then to tell me truthfully: what did you feel when you heard that Abdulaziz al-Muqrin had been killed? How happy were you? How sad were you?'

Someone calling himself ForgiveMe replied. 'A few years ago our country was among the safest and most stable in the world. We were envied everywhere! I'd seen other countries, seen the problems they had. They were really scary! Then all of a sudden we started seeing the same thing here. And from whom? From our own people!'

BeautifulEyes was perplexed. 'This is a really confusing situation. Nobody knows what's right and what's wrong . . . If we say we are sad that he's dead we have to ask ourselves, "Okay, but why did they come here to Saudi to wage jihad, to terrorize peaceful people and to tarnish the image of Muslims?" But if we say his death makes us happy, then we have to think: he was a Saudi guy like millions of other Saudi guys. He dedicated his life to jihad and maybe his excuse for killing hostages in such a disgusting way is that Muslim blood is being shed in an even worse way. They are humiliated in Abu Ghraib and Guantánamo and of course in Palestine and Iraq. Maybe the aggression in their hearts was a response to the humiliation which Muslims experience all around the world. Don't forget that Al Qaeda said they weren't the ones who attacked the security building in Riyadh, and that they only targeted foreigners in Khobar and Yanbu. Of course the primary beneficiaries of terrorist acts are America and Israel. But the question remains: why did Muqrin die with a smile on his face?'

The twin ideals of pan-Islamism and obedience to established authority which King Faisal promoted in the 1960s had firmly taken root. Jihad in theory remained an ideal, and Muslim suffering anywhere demanded a response from Muslims everywhere. Furthermore, it was legitimate to categorize non-Muslims as infidels who are never entirely innocent and to interpret Western aims as essentially inimical to Islam in general. At the same time, the stability of Saudi society was imperative. To upset it was unforgivable. Consequently Muqrin's major error was not that he had killed innocent people but that he had killed innocent Muslims and disrupted the peace.

Of course, far less moderate Saudi voices were also in evidence online. The number of extremist websites had been proliferating; the Saudi government was already monitoring several thousand. In fact, the government was doing more than that. It was working with a small group of volunteers on developing a programme called Sakeena, from an Arabic word meaning 'tranquillity'. Sakeena's volunteer clerics, academics, psychologists, and others were trying to build a comprehensive archive of all extremist material emanating in or passing through Saudi Arabia. By getting to know the enemy better, they could better combat its ideology. At the same time, Sakeena members were beginning to infiltrate extremist chatrooms and forums. They were engaging directly with extremists, challenging their views, and facilitating private online discussions with those who were willing to talk. Over time, the Sakeena campaign would score many individual successes, though it would not succeed in stemming the overall tide of extremism on the Internet.[38]

As expected, Al Qaeda had something to say about Muqrin's death. 'Abdulaziz al-Muqrin – may God have mercy on him – is a name glittering with renown, a luminary on the path of surrender and self-sacrifice, and a shining star leading wayfarers through the wilderness. His deeds and his leadership shook the world. He caused the White House to tremble and even the mightiest Crusaders to shake and foam with rage. If my people only knew whom they had lost, whom they had killed, whom they had betrayed!'[39] Muqrin was not only mourned by jihadists inside Saudi Arabia. His writings and his reputation had resonated throughout the worldwide jihadist community. In Baghdad, imams at a mosque known for its radicalism declared a three-day mourning period.[40] Eventually Muqrin's writings on guerrilla warfare tactics for *Camp of the Sabre* were collected into a single volume called *A Practical Course for Guerrilla War*. To this day it is a key text for militant Islamists.

AQAP were no less keen to respond to the outcry following Johnson's execution. They laid the blame squarely on the government's shoulders. If only the MOI had acquiesced to the mujahideen's demands, the tragedy could have been averted. But no, the government had blathered on about negotiations. 'It is absolutely astonishing. Who are these people talking about negotiations? The word wasn't mentioned in any of our written statements or recordings. Our one condition was extremely clear – but apparently the serpentine language of politics cannot comprehend clarity. Our condition was that they release their prisoners, not that we negotiate over prisoners.'[41]

Voice of Jihad also published a letter by someone described as 'the wife of one of the Arabian Peninsula's martyrs' and addressed to 'the wife of slain infidel Paul Johnson'.

> I heard that you went on TV and like a little lamb asked what your husband's crime was. I think you are perfectly aware that he was a major criminal ... What do you think the purpose of your husband's work on the Apache helicopter was? Do you think these helicopters fly over Afghanistan, Palestine, and Iraq scattering roses and sweets on our children? Aren't you aware that they fire missiles and drop bombs, transforming streets and houses into piles of dust and charred corpses?
>
> So his work was righteous, was it? And he was innocent, was he? ...
>
> Hearts pound with love for our brothers incinerated by your husband's helicopters! Just as you loved your slain husband, so do we love them, in fact more so, more than you can imagine. For the blood of a Muslim is more precious to us even than the Kaaba. Whereas the blood of your

husband, an infidel and a polytheist, was no better than the blood of a dog . . .

Are you infidels aware just how much we hate you? We despise you to the bone. How could we not when you are preferred over us even inside our own country? . . .

I say this to the government lording itself over us: what you are doing to our young mujahideen is good. When you kill them, you send them straight to paradise. When you leave them be, it is even better. For they will continue to fight the infidels and expel them from the land of Islam.

On 20 June 2004, AQAP announced on an Islamist website that Saleh al-Oufi, one of only two surviving members on the Organization's Shura Council, had been elected leader in Muqrin's place. This was not entirely true. However, in the MOI's eyes Oufi was their new Public Enemy No. 1, and thus was he described by the world's media. The Mabahith and their colleagues in the security services set their sights on tracking Oufi down.

Two days later, in acknowledgement both of the MOI's successes and of the further work that needed to be done, the crown prince raised Prince Muhammad to ministerial rank. His title remained assistant interior minister, but it now carried the weight of a minister. Prince Muhammad's writ would run more smoothly throughout the MOI's labyrinthine bureaucracy, and the reforms he was making to the ministry's operations would experience fewer impediments.

The following day Crown Prince Abdullah made a startling announcement on state TV. 'My brothers,' he solemnly read out, 'God revealed in the Holy Qur'an: *If they repent before falling into your power, then know that God is forgiving and merciful.*[42] Therefore we announce – for the last time – that the door is open for forgiveness . . . We give all those who belong to that group, and who have not been arrested during terrorist operations, the chance to examine their consciences and return to God. Those who accept this and choose to surrender voluntarily within a period not exceeding one month from the date of this speech will be safe and will be treated in accordance to God's law.'

Fully aware of how this unexpected move might be perceived, the crown prince added, 'Fellow citizens, know that we do not make this announcement out of weakness. Rather, we give them this choice so that, by opening the door to a safe surrender, we will – both government and people – be absolved from guilt. For if the rational accept this, they will find safety. But if the arrogant reject it, then by God, our natural forbearance will not prevent us from striking them with all the power we derive from Almighty God.'[43]

The month-long amnesty was not met with unqualified approval, especially by Americans. Ambassador Oberwetter was placed in the position of having to explain the crown prince's motives to his American critics. 'Back in the US, there were lots of people with questions about this. They were saying, "There the Saudis go again! Letting bad guys go free!" We had a lot of explaining to do to our counterparts back on Capitol Hill, in the State Department, and in the White House, to get them to understand the way the word "amnesty" is understood in the Middle East. They thought the terrorists were being absolved from their crimes. But in Saudi Arabia it means this is your last chance. It's a sign: you'd better come in now, because if you don't, we'll come after you big time.'[44]

The Saudi embassy in Washington was careful to point out that the crown prince's offer was not a blanket amnesty. It was largely aimed at low-level AQAP operatives who had not participated in anything operational but who were too afraid to turn themselves in. By giving them the chance to do so, the Kingdom would potentially prevent sympathizers from becoming full-blown terrorists.[45]

Saudi clerics welcomed the idea. The government enlisted them to act as mediators, including Safar al-Hawali, who had helped convince Ali al-Faqasi to turn himself in the previous summer. The day after the announcement, the government received their first penitent. Saaban al-Shihri surrendered in Abha. He had been a weapons' smuggler for the Organization and had spent the previous year hiding in various locations in the south. He appeared on TV and expressed his regret at his actions. A few days later Uthman al-Amri, number nineteen on the List of Twenty-Six, also turned himself in. He told reporters that it had been a mistake to get involved with Al Qaeda, and that the exasperation of eighteen months on the run, mainly camping out in remote mountains, had inspired him to surrender.[46] (Later he would return to Al Qaeda and was eventually arrested.)

By the time the amnesty expired on 23 July, six men had turned themselves in, including two in Damascus and one in Tehran.[47] The MOI claimed that thirty or so had surrendered, but this was most likely a ploy to encourage more to do so. The low figure must have been a disappointment, but it did not come as a surprise to Oberwetter. 'I considered it just another sign of how deeply the terrorist mentality was dug in with those who wanted to carry out heinous acts.'

Perhaps. Or maybe, despite what they saw on television, they were too convinced that the MOI would mistreat and even torture them. AQAP certainly did everything in its power to convince operatives to reject the amnesty. On 19 July they published a video online celebrating the Washm Street bombing. *Echo of the Brigades* was released under the banner of the Haramain Brigades, the fake organization Muqrin had set up to take the blame for unpopular attacks. But jihadists in the know will not have been fooled. Also, six articles appeared in *Voice of Jihad* quoting scripture and authoritative fatwas to warn people that, should they surrender, they would be forfeiting paradise.

For most jihadists in the Kingdom, that argument trumped the crown prince's.

The amnesty did not mean the security services had reduced the pressure. Among the weapons, cash, and documents seized from Muqrin's car at the petrol station was a tantalizing lead. 'I consider this discovery to be the first real step towards eliminating the Organization,' Brigadier-General Talhi explains. 'It was a bundle of automatic garage-door openers. One of the security men had the idea of taking them around every district in Riyadh until we found the garage door for each particular opener.' The Mabahith did just that. 'In the end, we uncovered several safe houses using those garage-door openers.'[48] Most of them will have been empty or used only for storing equipment. However, some were placed under surveillance. In addition, on 1 July, the Emergency Forces raided the villa in Wuroud where Paul Johnson had been beheaded. It was empty, but still bore signs of the American's captivity.

At the same time, the Mabahith were monitoring a van which they suspected was linked to the Organization. They followed it to a villa in the King Fahd neighbourhood which further investigation revealed to be the media headquarters of Isa al-Awshen. Five days later, on 20 July, the villa was the target of what would be one of the war's most explosive raids – and which led to the gruesome discovery of Paul Johnson's head. For the first time, the Special Forces were called in to assist the Emergency Forces at a raid, so intense was the onslaught from AQAP members inside the villa. Awshen was killed, bringing the List of Twenty-Six down to eleven, and Mishaal al-Farraj and others were arrested.

Oufi had been in the villa as well, but had managed to escape, abandoning his wife Fawzia and their three sons, who were also living there. The MOI held them until they were convinced she could give up no more information, and then handed them over to her family in Medina.[49]

13

The Network Splits

'Ninety-five per cent of them were ignorant. Very ignorant. They had a sort of built-in ignorance.' Khalid al-Farraj, the captured AQAP member whose father had been gunned down by his own comrades, spoke candidly on television. 'The network had two muftis, Abdullah al-Rashoud and Faris al-Zahrani. But in my estimation, they didn't have the competence to issue fatwas. They had a certain amount of knowledge of the Sharia, some knowledge of Islamic jurisprudence, but their rulings on particularly thorny issues were clearly groundless.'

Farraj was one of several detainees who had agreed to give an interview to Saudi TV for *Inside the Cell*, which aired on 1 October 2004. Prince Muhammad and the Mabahith conceived the programme as part of the MOI's ongoing campaign to reach out to the Saudi people. Despite the deaths of Muqrin and Awshen early in the summer, a series of tit-for-tat engagements with their enemy over the previous two months had shown the MOI that the war was not yet over. AQAP was hobbled but it could still lash out in spasms of random violence. Three more Westerners had been shot in cold blood, and four police officers had been killed and several more seriously wounded in clashes across the country.[1] Several organized cells were still intact, and it was only a matter of time before they would start launching big operations again. The government decided it was a perfect opportunity for public engagement.

'One issue in particular reveals their ignorance,' Farraj continued. 'Takfeer. They said anyone in military uniform was an infidel. So, for example, whenever they passed a checkpoint, they would immediately fire upon the soldier stationed there. It didn't matter if he was an immigration officer, or a traffic cop, or whatever, they'd just shoot him. And any preacher who climbed up into a pulpit and denounced the Riyadh compound bombings, they'd consider him an unbeliever too. Sometimes I'd try to argue this point with them. I'd say, "Brother, surely it's difficult or even impossible to determine who is and who is not a believer." But they would not hear it. In their view not only are our rulers apostates, but anyone who supports them is an apostate. "But I'm very close to my grandfather," I'd say. "I love him very much, and he supports our rulers." "Well then," they'd respond, "he's an apostate!"'

The government was primarily interested in convincing Saudis not to believe AQAP's propaganda and to support the MOI's fightback. That is why Farraj and the other interviewees ticked off several government talking points: that the terrorists had been consciously targeting members of the security services, that Al Qaeda was directly behind the terrorist attacks, that suspects were not being mistreated by the MOI, and so on. They also emphasized Al Qaeda's immorality. Their acts of serial murder aside, they did not observe the normal prayer times, stole cars from fellow Muslims, implicated innocent people in crime by renting flats using stolen ID cards, and lied to donors about the true purpose of their charitable donations.

However, the programme was more than just counter-propaganda. It also allowed the penitent jihadists to air their personal grievances about how the Organization had treated them, and to offer something like an explanation for why they had got in so deep. 'They recruit in a backhanded way,' Farraj explained. 'They don't make it clear to new recruits that they will be working inside the Kingdom. Lots of the young guys in the cell were in trouble or had run away from home and were looking for a place to stay. Or maybe they were convinced mujahideen, but even then, what they really wanted was to go to Iraq or perhaps Afghanistan and needed money to get there.'

Once they were inside, the leadership would trick them into staying. 'A new guy would be asked to rent something for the Organization, or buy a car, and he'd do it in his own name. Then the leaders would tell him, "Now you're implicated. You'd better continue with us, or the government will arrest you, put you in prison, and torture you."' Sexual torture by the Mabahith was a common threat held over recruits. 'From that point on they'd be afraid to leave. Many people who joined the cell in this roundabout way came to me and said, "We want to leave, but we can't, we're scared of what the Mabahith will do to us."'

Abdul Rahman al-Rashoud was also interviewed for the programme. He was Abdullah al-Rashoud's cousin and the operative who had driven around the Diplomatic Quarter with a hidden camera fixed to the front of his car. 'Recruitment was mainly one-to-one. You might approach your cousin, say. You start hanging out with him, you become mates, and eventually you try to bring him inside.' Rashoud worked in recruitment. 'The Organization seeks a particular kind of young man, someone who doesn't have a firm grasp of Islamic law or intelligence enough to determine right from wrong; someone in love with the idea of adventure; and perhaps most importantly, someone who wants to prove himself. They all desperately want the approval of their peers.'

Once inside, recruits' access to information was strictly limited. 'The leadership practised what we called "intellectual deprivation",' Rashoud explained. 'Access to government media was restricted, as was any international media, of course. They only read Organization publications distributed internally.' The result was that none of the low-level operatives really knew what was going on. 'All their information came from the leadership, who always lied about the other side,' said Farraj. 'So the young guys didn't know the truth of who lived inside the compounds, or how many died, or their true nationalities.' Instead, said Rashoud, everything was spun to look as if victory was in sight. 'By trumpeting victory, the leaders tried to shore up the recruits' trust and strengthen their zeal. They needed to protect the recruits' original vision of the Organization. The vision may have been a figment of their imagination, but it was always presented as good and true.'

Nonetheless, the leadership feared their recruits might wobble, and so they put stratagems in place to make sure no one tried to escape. 'If one of the guys wanted to contact someone, his family or his wife, for example, he'd have to ask several times before being granted permission. And even then, someone else would always accompany him to the phone booth or the Internet café, to make sure he didn't run off. Letters from family were also opened and read, and if they contained appeals to leave and return home or to surrender, they would not be handed over.'

The interviewees did not miss the opportunity to exonerate themselves as well. 'I quickly became unwilling to recruit others,' Rashoud said. 'I felt bad for anyone who joined the cell.' He also claimed he had wanted to leave. 'I was looking for the right moment, but needed to make sure they didn't realize it. Because anyone who seemed to be on the verge of leaving would be identified and, well . . .'

Over the four months since Muqrin's death, the Mabahith had been able to form a clearer picture of the state the Organization was in. Saleh al-Oufi had proclaimed himself leader, but it had become obvious that a dispute over the leadership had resulted in Muqrin's network being split in two. Oufi established himself in Medina and oversaw an independent network in the Hijaz. The cells in the Najd and the Eastern Province, however, fell under the command of bomb-making expert Saud al-Qatayni. Oufi and Qatayni were both veteran jihadists, had served on Muqrin's Shura Council, and posed a significant threat, despite their now constricted circumstances. However, that autumn's sporadic attacks were evidence that neither leader, especially Qatayni, had yet managed to achieve total control over his cells.

That lack of strong central control had played into the MOI's hands. On 6 August, agents in Abha had arrested Faris al-Zahrani, one of the late Awshen's team of ideologues, who was setting up a new cell for Qatayni in the southwest. His arrest brought the List of Twenty-Six down to ten, and led to the detention of all sixteen members of his cell.[2] Then on 3 September, Abdullah al-Muqrin – a relative of the deceased leader who, from the sidelines, had helped facilitate the Khobar massacre – turned himself in. He led a cell in Dammam which had been carrying out surveillance on oil facilities along the east coast, and after the MOI contacted his parents, he realized they had him under surveillance and that it was no use carrying on. These arrests were significant, Zahrani's in particular. He had written many widely read texts justifying the killing of members of the security services, and was AQAP's last remaining mufti. (Abdullah al-Rashoud had fled to Iraq, and in June 2005 the MOI would learn that he had been killed by an American air strike there.)

It was imperative that the MOI maintain this momentum.

Some low-level operatives who expressed contrition were being granted early release from prison. They returned to their families and were expected to remain in constant contact with the Mabahith, who monitored their movements to make sure they did not break their parole by renewing their involvement with the Organization. One such operative was Assam al-Otaybi. Before his arrest, he had played an organizational role, renting flats and liaising between the cells, and had driven the Jerusalem Squadron from Riyadh to Khobar shortly before the massacre. After being granted parole, Mabahith agents received information that he had returned to his former affiliation, and so at midnight on 12 October they went to his house in the Nahda district of Riyadh to rearrest him. The house was empty, however, so they set up surveillance and waited.

At 11 p.m. the following day a car pulled into the villa's garage and half an hour later Otaybi's liaison officer rang him as usual. He did not answer. Two Mabahith agents from the surveillance team knocked on the front door. They were forced to knock several times before, finally, the door opened slightly. A veiled face peered through the crack. It was Otaybi's wife. She said her husband was sleeping and could not come to the door.

Just then, the officers were fired upon by a Ford saloon as it sped past the villa. They drew their weapons and fired back, but the car got away. However, bitter experience having taught them a thing or two about the Organization's tactics, the agents knew that the Ford was only a diversion to lure them away from the villa. So the Mabahith stayed put, and called in the Emergency Forces.

Brigadier-General Mudeef al-Talhi was among those who rushed to the scene. 'We planned the raid with cooperation from the neighbours,' he recalls. 'For the record, in all our counterterrorism operations, not once did anyone refuse us permission to make use of his home. On the contrary, everyone was always very welcoming. They threw open their doors to us. That's a fact.' The raid commenced and went remarkably smoothly. Too smoothly. 'No one on our wanted list was found inside, only seven women and a young boy.' The women said there was no one else in the house, but their behaviour aroused

Talhi's suspicion. 'I was apprehensive and afraid for my comrades,' he says. '"There is something in this," I told them.

'Just then a soldier came up to me and said one of the upstairs doors was locked.' Talhi politely asked one of the women to hand over the key. 'Of course, she refused. So I ordered them out of the house. Again, they refused. We didn't want to remove them by force, that would have been unseemly, but we were concerned for their safety. So we corralled them into a downstairs room on the opposite side of the house, and shut them inside. Then I gave the order for the door upstairs to be broken down.'

What happened next followed the usual pattern. Inside the room – which was actually an illegal, self-contained flat – three armed men waited to pounce. Facing a ferocious spray of gunfire, most of the officers were forced to retreat back downstairs. 'We couldn't attack them from where we were, but they were able to throw pipe bombs down on us. Twenty-two bombs, in fact.' Seven officers were wounded by the shrapnel, some of them critically. 'More than anything, we needed to get things under control. Our first concern was to evacuate the women and the child, then the injured.'

However, the firefight continued for over an hour. 'It was so loud, you couldn't hear the radio. Eventually a ceasefire was ordered, to give us a chance to evacuate, and a group of really brave guys – five officers and four soldiers – ran upstairs to draw the terrorists' fire.' It gave Talhi the breathing room he needed, and the women and the young boy were rushed outside. 'They were in a state of shock, really. They'd known the men upstairs were up to no good, but had no idea they had so much weaponry. They hadn't realized it was a terrorist den.' Talhi – who had himself sustained forty-five minor shrapnel injuries – oversaw the evacuation of the wounded, who now numbered twelve. Then he came up with a plan.

'There was a reserve team about two hundred metres from

the villa. After the withdrawal was complete, I ordered everyone to make it look like we were retreating completely. We hoped this would lure the terrorists out. They took the bait.' Two terrorists crept outside and were immediately cut down by sniper fire from the surrounding roofs.[3] The third remained holed up inside until just before sunrise, when the whole neighbourhood was rocked by an enormous explosion. He had detonated his suicide vest.

'When we searched the villa, we found stuff we never thought we would, given that we were fighting committed anti-secularists who trumpeted their own piety. There were pornographic films and pictures, drugs, that sort of thing. No one could believe it, but it was true, the exact truth.'

The terrorist who had blown himself up was later revealed to be Paul Johnson's 'executioner', Abu Hassan. The young boy was his son, the one who had witnessed the beheading. The MOI arranged for him to be adopted by a trustworthy relative.

In the Najd, attacks and arrests continued throughout October and November. In the early hours of 17 October, a man and a woman drove up to a checkpoint. The man got out to talk to the policemen, when suddenly the woman panicked, jumped into the driver's seat, and sped off. She was eventually apprehended after a long pursuit, though in fact 'she' was a he, and had disguised himself in women's clothes. On the 31st another militant was arrested after being wounded during a shootout at an Internet café in Buraydah. During a raid on a safe house in Unayzah on 16 November, one police officer was killed, eight were wounded, and five suspects were arrested. And on the 30th, a dramatic car chase in the Eastern Province resulted in injury to eight Emergency Forces officers when their vehicle overturned during the pursuit.

Things in the Hijaz were just as exciting. A man from Chad called Musa Shakila, who had fled the Khalidiya raid in June

2003, was arrested on 8 November in Jeddah. He informed the authorities of the location of a safe house in a large townhouse in the Jamia district. That evening, the street outside the house played host to a ferocious gun battle. A large detachment of Emergency Forces officers exchanged fire with three militants inside, two of whom had recently escaped from prison in Mecca. Despite riddling the house with bullet holes, killing one of the terrorists, the security services managed to capture the other two alive.[4] Then, the following day, the government announced they had intercepted a large boatload of weapons which were being smuggled in from Yemen. The boat contained 522 Kalashnikovs and 44,000 rounds of ammunition, and a Saudi at the Jazan quayside was arrested. And on the 27th, a man wanted in connection with the Muhaya bombing the year before was killed in Jeddah and another arrested when their car was ambushed by the security services.[5] This was followed by yet another smuggling bust on the 30th, in Asir province on the Yemeni border.

The MOI were confident that they were steadily and permanently dismantling AQAP on both sides of the country. Their confidence would soon be shaken.

'That morning, I was in my office in Riyadh,' James Oberwetter, the American ambassador, recalls.[6] 'It was the 6th of December, I believe. No, in fact I'm sure it was. That is a day I will not soon forget.' The ambassador's secretary rapped on the door in some distress and said that Gina Abercrombie-Winstanley was calling from the Jeddah consulate. 'Gina was our Consul General. I grabbed the phone. Emergency sirens were blaring in the background. "Mr. Ambassador, we're under attack and could use some assistance," she said calmly, though there was fear in her voice. The consulate had actually been invaded, and shots were being fired.'

Oberwetter wasted no time. 'I immediately called the heads

of all our bureaus and agencies and told them to come at once to my office. I'd never given them such a direct order, and wouldn't again throughout my tenure in office, so they knew there was a real emergency.' Before long the Americans had contacted their counterparts throughout the Saudi government. 'They assured us we would be given immediate support. In fact, the security forces in Jeddah had already been alerted and were rushing to the scene.'

They were not exactly speeding there. The midday traffic was heavy and it was some time before they arrived. Lieutenant-Colonel Bandar al-Akur of the Special Forces was among them. 'The situation was very difficult,' he explains. 'Live rounds were being fired from inside the consulate ground.' However, from what Akur and his men could tell, the terrorists had not managed to breach the main consulate building. 'We tried to gather intelligence from the security guards. They told us there were five terrorists involved, all heavily armed. They also gave us a plan of the grounds.'[7]

The site was extensive, covering about 20,000 square metres, and comprised several buildings. Security was pretty good. The National Guard had been assigned to man the outer gates, a private firm provided security inside the grounds, and the consulate also housed a detachment of US Marines.[8]

Enough information had trickled in to form a picture of what had happened.[9] Vice Consul Monica Lemieux was being driven to the consulate when, at 11:15 a.m., her Yemeni driver turned off Palestine Street and onto the much quieter Ha'il Street skirting the compound's eastern edge. They pulled up beside the gatehouse and, after passing through the normal security procedures, waited as the gate was raised and the anti-vehicle bollards lowered. A National Guardsman inside an armoured car waved them through.

Neither Lemieux nor her driver had noticed, but for some time a Nissan saloon had been trailing them. It waited patiently for Lemieux to be given the all-clear, and as soon as her driver started easing them through the open gate, it shot forward. Not fast enough, however. The bollards were quickly up again and the Nissan crashed into them. Five armed men jumped out. They tossed pipe bombs at the armoured car and at a machine-gun post. The guards were not injured by the small explosions, but they were startled and ran away. The five terrorists scrambled through the slowly closing gate.

Lemieux's driver told her to take cover, and she crouched down on the back seat. The gunmen shot up the car, killing the driver and wounding her, but were prevented from finishing her off by return fire from a Sri Lankan security guard inside the grounds called Jaufar Sadik. He felled one of the terrorists straightaway with a bullet to the head, and when the others ran off, he rushed over to the car and pulled Lemieux out. Shielding her with his body, he deposited her somewhere out of sight and returned to face the attackers. That act of bravery was his last. One of them jumped out at Sadik from behind and shot him in the back of the head.

By this time, the National Guard had re-secured the gate, and the detachment of US Marines, who had been alerted to the break-in, had managed to secure all American personnel inside the heavily fortified main building, which was called the chancery. The terrorists tossed a pipe bomb into the Marines' barracks, setting the temporary wooden building on fire and sending a huge plume of dark smoke rising up over Jeddah, but the barracks were empty. They then concentrated their fire on the chancery's bullet-proof doors. This did nothing, so they targeted the windows on the upper floor, wounding one American inside and causing a general panic throughout the building, but still they could not get in.

Thus thwarted, they began wandering the grounds, shooting haphazardly and calling out, 'Where are the Americans?' The scene became eerily reminiscent of the Khobar massacre. They rounded up seventeen civilians, mainly Saudi visa applicants, confiscated their mobile phones, and made them prove that they were Muslims. Three consular employees – a Sudanese, a Filipino, and a Pakistani – were killed. They then went around disconnecting all the other phones they found, except for one inside a guardroom, which they used to ring the security services. The hostages would only be released in exchange for female prisoners at Abu Ghraib. Next, they wandered over to the consulate's flagpole, lowered the American flag, and set it on fire.

Eighty minutes had elapsed since the beginning of the raid, and Lieutenant-Colonel Akur and the Special Forces had only just arrived. 'By the grace of God, we noticed the flag being lowered and knew that the terrorists must be there. So we immediately deployed and rushed to the southwest corner of the compound.' There they found not only the four remaining attackers, but their hostages as well. 'The terrorists were using them as human shields,' Akur says. Holding them in front, the gunmen began firing over their hostages' shoulders. Despite the danger, the Special Forces fired back. 'Praise God, we dealt with them directly, and the number of civilian wounded was kept to a minimum.' Ten civilians were wounded in the crossfire, along with one of the terrorists, who was rushed to the hospital next door.[10]

The other three gunmen were killed in the stand-off. Searching the bodies, the investigators realized how much more horrible the attack might have been: they found plastic ties which were intended to be used as handcuffs, and a machete. The militant who was killed at the onset of the attack was revealed to be Fayez al-Juhani, a 28-year-old from Jeddah who had been fired from the Mutaween for 'bad behaviour'. The previous April he had been arrested by the Mabahith on suspicion of terrorist connections, but had been released on bail, slipped into the underground, and eventually joined Saleh al-Oufi's Hijaz network.

A few months after the consulate attack, a group calling itself Jihad's Base in the Arabian Peninsula (Oufi may have given his network a new name to distinguish it from AQAP) released a propaganda video entitled *The Fallujah Squadron: The Raid on the Crusader Consulate in Jeddah*. In it, attack leader Juhani delivers a stern appeal to the Saudi security services to reject their tyrant masters and return to their religion. However, more unusually, the video shows Oufi himself delivering a presentation outlining his attack plan.

Oufi uses a laser pointer to take his men through video surveillance of the consulate which the cell filmed from the roof of the hospital next door. The small red dot moves confidently over the footage, which is being projected onto a wall. 'As you can see, brothers,' Oufi says. 'This is the American consulate in Jeddah. Here is one of the Pakistani guards who patrol the interior of the compound. This is a gas tank, as you can see, and here is the main building. The Consul General's residence is on this side. Behind these trees here is a church, and this is the barracks for the Marines.' Then Oufi stands in front of a white board on which he has drawn a crude map of the target. He points out the gate and the National Guard post. 'Our plan, O Sheikh Osama, is for the brothers to enter there. Diplomats' cars are not searched at that gate. So as soon as the infidel's car starts inside, our brothers will start shooting, to scare the soldiers who will likely run away or lie on the ground to avoid being killed.'

That part of Oufi's plan was remarkably prescient. However, he expected the Pakistani guard just inside the gate – who was actually Sri Lankan, as we have seen – to run away as well. Jaufar Sadik's heroism really did save the day. Not only did he kill the attack leader, but he bought the Marines enough time to secure the chancery. From that point on, the so-called Fallujah Squadron's failure was inevitable.

The audacious attack made it seem as if AQAP was experiencing a resurgence. But later, after weighing all the evidence, analysts realized that in fact it pointed to AQAP's continuing decline. The attackers had all been 'third-generation' Al Qaeda fighters: young, under-trained, and with no battlefield experience.[11] Oufi was a 'first-generation' veteran, but had only entirely green recruits at his disposal. It would mean that the abortive consulate attack was his network's sole fifteen minutes of fame. They would not attempt anything like it again.

In the nineteen months since the Riyadh compound bombings, not a word had been heard from Bin Laden about the campaign in Saudi Arabia. He had made several statements about Abu Musab al-Zarqawi's anti-American jihad in Iraq, but had been curiously silent about AQAP. However, on 17 December 2004 a seventy-minute audio tape was released on the website of the Global Islamic Media Front. In it, Bin Laden dispensed with the hints and allusions which had characterized his previous messages to the Saudi people. 'The Saudi regime,' he said,

> has committed very serious acts of disobedience – worse than the sins and offences forbidden by Islam, worse than oppressing slaves, depriving them of their rights and insulting their dignity, intelligence, and feelings, worse than squandering the general wealth of the nation. Millions of people suffer every day from poverty and deprivation, while millions of riyals flow into the bank accounts of the royals who wield executive power.

Bin Laden described in some detail the intrigues inside the court, including the power struggle between the Sudayri Seven and the crown prince which was discussed in chapter 2. He also criticized the changes to the school curriculum which the Americans had demanded, and the introduction of such reforms as the country's first municipal elections, which had been announced and would take place early the following year. Bin

Laden vilified the crown prince for his duplicitous support of the Iraq war, and dismissed the entire Saudi government as corrupt, ineffectual stooges of a tyrannical American empire.

> The solution to improve the situation is what has been made clear by God's law, and that is to remove the ruler. Even if he refuses to go, it is obligatory to depose him through force of arms ... Our countrymen who reject armed confrontation with the government in order to restore their rights are engaging in a huge fraud. Our rights will never be restored by a regime whose ruler is an apostate ... We do not pronounce takfeer on people in general, nor do we permit the shedding of Muslim blood. If some Muslims have been killed during the operations of the mujahideen, then we pray God has mercy on them; this is a case of accidental manslaughter, and we beg God's forgiveness for it ...
>
> God have mercy on our brother martyrs everywhere. God have mercy on Sheikh Yusuf al-Ayiri, Khalid al-Hajj, Abdulaziz al-Muqrin, Isa al-Awshen, and all their brothers, including the mujahideen who attacked the American consulate in Jeddah ... To righteous scholars, leaders, dignitaries, notables, and business leaders, I address the following statement: You must take the necessary steps before it is too late. For things are descending with extraordinary speed towards an explosion. Do whatever is in your power to defuse the crisis, in the knowledge that the mujahideen in Saudi Arabia have not yet even begun their fight against the regime.[12]

It was the most open and authoritative declaration of AQAP's aims yet, and the first time Bin Laden had personally acknowledged the involvement of his own senior lieutenants in the terrorist campaign. But from a strictly tactical perspective, it was too little, too late. Did Bin Laden know how incapacitated his Saudi network had become? Or was it a last-ditch attempt to rally support for a dying cause? Either way, twelve days later AQAP would prove beyond a shadow of a doubt that its days as an effective fighting force were over.

The Mabahith in Riyadh had determined the location of an AQAP safe house in the Rawda district, and by following cars to and from it they discovered another one in the Taawun neighbourhood. It was also placed under surveillance. Well-known terrorist suspects were soon spotted there, including Paul Johnson's gaoler Sultan Bijad, number seven on the List of Twenty-Six. Abu Ayub's younger brother Bandar al-Dukhayyel, number eighteen on the List of Twenty-Six, was also there. He had been on the run since the Marwa raid in November 2002 and had participated in every major Riyadh attack, including the botched rescue of Khalid al-Farraj.

Dukhayyel had won himself a certain renown back in July for an article he penned for *Voice of Jihad* describing the month he and a group of companions spent in the forbidding Ammariya mountains west of Riyadh while on the run from the security services. They were forced to seek shelter in caves and survived on only wild fruits and freshwater springs – which, Dukhayyel insists, would gush forth in abundance whenever they passed by, one of the many miracles sent by God to bolster their faith.[13] The tale is well written and peppered throughout with keen descriptions of how to survive in the desert. Members of the Mabahith recall how on reading it they could not help but respect Dukhayyel's fortitude.[14]

While the surveillance teams kept watch outside the Rawda and Taawun safe houses, the Security Patrols were on the lookout for a Toyota pickup which they had reason to believe was being used by yet another infamous jihadist, Khalid al-Sinan. He was the one who had started things off at Muhaya by firing an RPG at the compound's front gate, and he headed up a couple of cells of his own. At 9 a.m. on 28 December, the Security Patrols spotted his pickup and followed it to a petrol station in the Duwayba district. A gunfight ensued. In the crossfire, a Yemeni civilian was killed, as were two other suspects. Sinan himself was wounded and taken to hospital. He would die from his wounds before the day was out, but as far as his fellow AQAP members knew, he had been arrested. Their misapprehension would have explosive consequences.

The following morning at seven o'clock, a car with four passengers departed from the Rawda safe house. The Mabahith followed it. The car circled central Riyadh twice, then ended up outside the safe house in Taawun. The passengers disembarked and remained inside the house until 5 p.m., when Sultan Bijad and a companion got into the same car and drove off. All this coming and going was suspicious, and the Mabahith decided they could not afford to hold off any longer. They called the Emergency Forces.

Something was indeed wrong, although what was going on would only be pieced together later.

For several weeks, Sultan Bijad had been working closely with Khalid al-Sinan on a new plan. It was to be a return to form: two simultaneous truck-bomb attacks. This time, however, both targets were Saudi government buildings: a recruitment office for the Emergency Forces in the Sulay district and, most spectacularly, the headquarters of the Ministry of Interior itself, right in the centre of town. Sultan Bijad and Sinan had surveilled the targets together, and Sinan's cell had sourced the explosives, which were then transported to Riyadh and wired up to two GMC Supervans at a safe house in New Manfuha.

So when Sinan was arrested, Sultan Bijad panicked. He was certain the Mabahith would soon uncover the plan, and he decided to launch immediately. When he left the Taawun safe house on the evening of the 29th, he drove to New Manfuha and gave the bombing teams their orders. Three of the five chosen suicide bombers were familiar figures: Paul Johnson's interrogator Ismael al-Khuzaim; the hirsute, jovial Dakheel al-Ubayd who had learnt to drive a tanker truck for Operation Volcano; and Abdullah al-Subaei, the Khobar massacre killer who had gone on to shoot BBC cameraman Simon Cumbers.

At 7:50 that evening, the two truck bombs pulled out of the driveway. Khuzaim, Subaei, and one other drove north towards the city centre, while Ubayd and his co-bomber turned onto the Southern Ring Road in the direction of Sulay.[15] As for Sultan Bijad, he left New Manfuha and returned to the Taawun safe house with three others, unaware it was being watched.

'We had been warned that something might happen. It was stressful. We kept our phones on, messages were flying back and forth, and we were in a state of constant readiness.' Lieutenant-Colonel Bandar al-Duwaysh was an officer of the Security and Protection division of the Special Forces. The Special Forces had just been called in as backup for the raid on the Taawun safe house. 'We were at our headquarters getting ready when the explosion at the ministry building happened,' he recalls. 'It was not far away, and I could actually smell the gunpowder in the air.'

The raid on Taawun was ordered before AQAP launched the attack. It was sheer coincidence that they both occurred on the same evening. Had the Mabahith called in the raid a few hours before, it is possible the bombings would have been thwarted.

Not that they were particularly successful. Neither bomb got close enough to its target to cause major damage. Both facilities were too heavily guarded. Security was so heavy outside the MOI headquarters that, at around 9 p.m., the bombers simply drove past and detonated ninety metres from the gate. The explosion caused minor damage to the eastern facade of the building, and seriously damaged a passing taxi. But no one apart from the bombers themselves was killed.

The other team did an even worse job. Guards outside the recruitment office were alerted when they saw the van driving in the wrong direction down a one-way street. But, almost comically, when it was still 180 metres away, it suddenly exploded, again causing only minor damage to surrounding buildings and killing no one. Why it detonated so prematurely is a mystery the bombers took with them to the grave.

'The explosions had made the raid an even bigger priority,' Duwaysh continues. Major-General Khalid al-Harbi was also part of the Special Forces raiding party. 'We were heading toward Taawun – this is about thirty minutes after the bombings – when Prince Muhammad called. It affected us all deeply. In fact it is one of the proudest moments of my career. He told all of us commanders to bring our men back to him safely. Even if it meant sacrificing our own lives, the safety of the regular soldiers was paramount.'

The Taawun safe house was a ground-floor flat in a long, two-storey apartment block. The Mabahith had determined that there were seven terrorists inside. After the usual appeals to surrender, the Special Forces were told to launch a raid. 'We split into two teams,' Duwaysh explains. 'My team, team one, would carry out the raid itself, and team two would provide support from the roof. It felt like time had stopped completely, but in fact it didn't take long to open the door, four or five minutes only.' Before they had, however, the door to the flat opposite opened. 'A bearded man stepped out into the corridor and I thought he might be one of them, so a colleague and I quickly wrestled him to the ground and searched him. It turned out he was just a civilian.'

Meanwhile, the door had been smashed in and the raiding team prepared to enter the flat. Major Nayef al-Tuwayr, who had been part of the hostage rescue team during the Khobar massacre, was the first one in. 'I could see a person standing at the end of the hallway,' he recalls. 'He was wearing a dark robe and had taken cover behind something, so he was difficult to see in the darkness.' It was Sultan Bijad. He threw a grenade at Tuwayr, but it ricocheted off the door frame and bounced back inside, so he quickly chucked another one which rolled into the corridor, where Duwaysh was standing with the civilian. 'I shoved him and a couple of privates into the flat opposite and threw them to the ground,' Duwaysh says, but not everyone was so lucky. 'The impact on the units in the corridor was horrible. There was a lot of shrapnel, and several men were badly wounded.'

Tuwayr was one of them. 'I was injured, as was the man next to me. He was hurt really bad. So I ordered a tactical withdrawal.' The air was full of white plaster dust from the walls, and visibility was low. Soldiers on the street outside began firing at the ground-floor windows, and the terrorists shot back. Because the gunfire outside was so intense, Tuwayr could not retreat that way. 'I dragged my wounded colleague out of the flat and carried him up the stairs. We wanted to get up to the roof, which team two had secured.' However, Sultan Bijad was close on their heels. 'He chased after us. There was a brief altercation, and we dealt with him as the situation required.' They left his dead body where it lay on the staircase, and joined their colleagues on the roof.

As for Duwaysh, he was lying on top of the civilian, whose thobe was covered in blood. '"You are injured!" I cried out, but he said, "No I'm not, you are." That's when I noticed that I had sustained shrapnel wounds in my left wrist, and was bleeding all over him.' Duwaysh managed to get the civilian and himself outside by climbing out of the window. 'Right away I went back in. One of our colleagues inside had been shot, and the bullet had punctured his lung.' Duwaysh took him up to the roof with the others. They would have to find some way of getting them to the paramedics below.

The shooting continued back and forth. 'They could not get

out, because we had snipers pointed at every exit,' Tuwayr explains. 'So they decided to move up to the roof, where they had stashed part of their arsenal.' To create a diversion, Bandar al-Dukhayyel ran out the building's front door, but was immediately cut down by sniper fire. An unexploded live grenade was gripped tight in his dead hand. A member of the bomb squad would lose two fingers later that evening in an attempt to defuse it.

The other five terrorists began to make their way upstairs. Where the staircase reached the roof was in effect a small room, and Tuwayr was alerted to their ascent. 'The light on the landing suddenly switched off. We knew they were coming up, and that they had turned off the light so we wouldn't see them. After a few seconds, the door leading from the landing to the roof opened, and there they were.' Using the landing as a base, the terrorists threw three grenades and exchanged fire with the soldiers on the stairwell below and the ones on the roof, who had taken cover behind ventilation outlets and air-conditioning units. 'It was particularly dangerous as we noticed that one of them was wearing an explosive belt.'

It became even more imperative to evacuate the wounded. Major Khalid al-Muhaya, who had also been at Khobar, was with a unit on the roof of the building opposite. He came up with a plan. 'Sometimes you make a decision that, thinking about it afterwards, seems totally crazy,' he says. 'But I felt I had no choice. Could I just sit and watch my colleagues bleed to death?

'We brought up a long rescue ladder from the Civil Defence and laid it across the gap between the two buildings. The distance was at least six metres. A paramedic was with me, quite a strong guy, and he said, "I'll go," but I told him to wait. "Right now you're more important than I am. Let me go first to test it. If the ladder breaks and I fall, then you can find another way across." I crawled onto it. I was ten metres above the ground or more. And you know what went through my mind? My mother. I heard her telling me, "Why haven't you married? You must get married soon because I might lose you and I want a grandchild." Obviously I got across safely, as did the others.' With a twinkle in his eye, Muhaya adds, 'Incidentally, that experience might be the reason I got married shortly after. Thank God, I have now been given a son.'

The paramedics evacuated the wounded across the ladder while Muhaya joined Tuwayr, Duwaysh, and the other soldiers in the stand-off. They had managed to pick off three of the terrorists, but two remained, including the one with the explosive belt. 'They had run out of ammunition, and were scrambling over the corpses of their colleagues, trying to retrieve their weapons,' Muhaya says. 'We kept telling them to surrender. Up to the very last moment, they could have surrendered. But they refused.' Duwaysh will never forget what followed. 'Our bullets hit the guy's explosive belt and it went off. All five bodies were totally roasted by the blast. I mean, it was horrible. We found a complete brain by the landing door, and the ceiling inside was covered in pieces of flesh and bloody clumps of hair.'

Twelve AQAP members had died that evening, five in the bombings and seven at Taawun. Three of them had been on the List of Twenty-Six; only six names remained on it. Four soldiers were seriously wounded and several more sustained light injuries, but they all survived.[16]

'After Taawun, the Organization fled Riyadh,' Brigadier-General Mudeef al-Talhi recalls. 'They went to Kharj, and for a while there was what you might call a period of peace. Of course, we monitored all communications to and from Kharj, and launched a wide security sweep, checking all driving licences, rental records, and so on. We pretended it was an anti-drug operation, but we were really looking for the terrorists' hideout.'

It took the MOI only four days to uncover the safe house's

location, but it had been abandoned, and intelligence indicated the cell had relocated to Qaseem. On 9 January 2005, a four-member cell was broken in Zulfi, fifty kilometres east of Buraydah. All four were killed in a shootout, and three security officers were wounded. It was a step in the right direction, but network leader Saud al-Qatayni was still on the run. For several weeks, AQAP went completely silent.

The timing could not have been better. On 5 February, a three-day international counterterrorism conference convened in Riyadh. It had been announced back in September, and as usual the American press was sceptical. One contentious point was that, despite the Saudi government's claim that all countries which had suffered from terrorism were invited, Israel was left off the guest list. Riyadh explained that it did not consider actions described as 'resistance to occupation' to be acts of terrorism, but that did not wash.

Another stumbling block was that Syria and Iran had been invited. This put Frances Townsend, President Bush's homeland security advisor and by that time a close friend and colleague of Prince Muhammad's, in a difficult position. 'I'm heading the American delegation, one of the few women heads of delegation, but I'm not happy about having to sit in a room with representatives of countries which, under American law, had been designated state sponsors of terror. I mean, I'm going to be forced into a room with Iranians, who, it is important to remember, have never been forced to answer for their role in the bombing of our Beirut barracks in 1983. Two hundred and ninety-nine American and French servicemen were killed, but the Iranian officials responsible for the attack were never handed over. And now my Saudi friends had asked me to sit and listen to these people spout nonsense about being against terrorism.

'By this time, Prince Muhammad was a real friend. So in fairness to him I told him I was not comfortable with the situation.

My fear was that the Iranians would take advantage of the presence of a senior White House official and make a scene. I told the prince that I couldn't promise I wouldn't hit back if they did so.' It was a difficult conversation, and Townsend admits her emotions got the better of her. 'I'll never forget how he answered me. "You've got to put your emotions in the freezer," he said. "Don't worry. You won't have to meet them personally, and they won't make a fuss. I'll make sure they don't."

'So I walk into the hall. It's a bit like the UN, a vast semi-circular chamber. I'm seated on the far right-hand side, and the Iranians are on the far left-hand side, basically right in front of me. That didn't make me feel any less nervous, let me tell you. But then, just as it was my turn to speak, Prince Muhammad walks in and sits down, literally right behind the Iranian delegation. It was his way of telling me, without words, that I was free to say whatever I wanted. He could have seated anyone there to make sure the Iranians didn't misbehave. By sitting there himself, he was telling me that he was taking care of the situation personally.'

And Townsend did not pull her punches. 'State sponsors of terrorism are with the terrorists and therefore against all of us,' she said midway through her speech. 'They are the cowards who hide behind the hateful and murderous surrogates whom they arm, finance, and harbour. They seek influence through fear and intimidation. President Bush said this week, "Iran remains the world's primary state sponsor of terror." We must be unanimous in our strong condemnation of such state sponsorship of terrorism and demand its end.'[17]

However, it was the less bellicose parts of her speech which really made an impression, especially on her Saudi guests. 'I had not given them a copy of my speech beforehand. To be honest, I was rewriting it up to the last minute because I wanted it to redress some huge misconceptions. The break in US–Saudi relations in 2003 had played out publicly, but the two years that followed had largely been behind the scenes, and the world wasn't aware of how much progress we had made together. People thought America and Saudi Arabia were at odds over counterterrorism, but by 2005 this was dead wrong. The truth is, by the time I left office in 2007, American officials were exchanging as much intelligence with their Saudi counterparts as they were with the British, if not more so.'

She also wanted to express her country's gratitude for the work the Saudis were doing on the front lines. 'I must say,' she stated at the outset, 'the courage and bravery of all Saudi counterterrorism forces, most especially the Mabahith, is laudable and no doubt a source of enormous pride for all citizens of the Kingdom. Here in Saudi Arabia, many lives have been lost, and more have been wounded in the fight against evil. To the injured and to the families of the killed, I say "thank you". As a result of your sacrifice, the world is safer.'

As Townsend explains, 'The head of the Mabahith had been attacked, his brother had also almost been killed. I wanted to communicate that when a Saudi officer loses his life and sheds his blood for the security of his country, it is to me and to the United States as if an American officer's blood has been shed. We grieve the loss of a Saudi law enforcement officer as we grieve our own, and we stand as one together in the fight.'

Her speech went down very well. 'Prince Muhammad asked for a copy of the speech. I couldn't see why, to be honest. "You don't understand," he said. "Mabahith officers were there, and now your words are the talk of the services. You will never know what it means to us, what it means to me. I will never be able to thank you enough." I was stunned, but then it hit me. The Saudis were always hearing criticism. The epicentre of terrorist financing! Fifteen out of the 19 bombers on 9/11! They had taken it all to heart, and had never heard a senior American official stand up in public and be counted as their partner.

'I would have said it sooner if I had known what it would

mean to them. Even now, whenever I'm in the Kingdom a member of the Mabahith will say to me, "I'll never forget your speech," and Prince Muhammad frequently brings it up. It's become a source of extraordinary pride, both for me and, I think, for the Mabahith.'

14

Stamped Out

The period of quiet was bound to come to an end. On 3 April 2005, security services in Buraydah received a number of phone calls from concerned citizens in the nearby town of Rass. They lived in the Jawazat district, a newly developed area of family houses on the northwest edge of town. Two weeks earlier, a new family had moved into the neighbourhood. The fact that they did not introduce themselves to their neighbours was shrugged off as unfriendliness. But strange smells began emanating from their villa, as well as the sound of an electric drill late at night. It was too suspect to ignore.

The good people of Jawazat were right to be alarmed. After the Taawun disaster and the shut-down of the Zulfi cell, network leader Qatayni had sent word that all able-bodied cell members should regroup in Qaseem. Twenty responded to the summons. Among them were the Moroccan jihadist Karim al-Mejjati and his 11-year-old son Adam. Mejjati was one of Al Qaeda's top operatives. He had helped plan the Riyadh compound bombings, and was wanted internationally on suspicion of involvement in the 2003 Casablanca bombings and 2004

Madrid train bombings. He was also in touch with Al Qaeda sympathizers in the United Kingdom.[1]

The men gathered first at a safe house in Buraydah itself, but Qatayni felt the provincial capital was too well patrolled and so rented the villa in Rass, about 85 kilometres to the west. The move was carried out discreetly. They packed up their weaponry in normal packing cases and most of the cell members disguised themselves as women, so it would appear that a large family was moving in. A group of men all by themselves would have aroused too much suspicion. Whenever grocery shopping was needed, the men would send young Adam, and the rest seem to have seldom left the villa – although eyewitnesses would later claim to have seen one of them in the local mosque for Friday prayer.[2] He would come after everyone else had finished, and immediately after finishing his devotions would return home without speaking to anyone.

Acting on tip-offs from the concerned neighbours, the Mabahith discovered the villa had been rented using a fake military ID card. The local Emergency Forces were called in. Lieutenant-Colonel Umar al-Quwayz was director of their counterterrorism division. 'The call came in at around 9 p.m. on 2 April. The Mabahith asked us to reconnoitre the area, so the commander of the forces and I went to scope it out. We determined the best places to position the snipers, how the security cordon would be laid out, and planned our first assault.' Their plan involved armoured cars, so they called in support from Riyadh.

Colonel Fahd al-Harbi of the armoured security battalion remembers receiving the call. 'I was throwing a dinner party that evening. The guests had not yet arrived, and my commander rings to tell me something's going down in Rass and that I've got to get there. Whenever you're given an order to move, everyone in the house knows what to do. You go and put on your uniform, your wife brings your boots, your son brings your gun, someone else starts your car. Then you pull out of the driveway, and there they are, your loving family lined up in front of you. All you can do is leave them in the hands of God.' Harbi raced down the Qaseem highway. 'Some of my dinner guests didn't know the way to my house and kept calling me and asking for directions! I had to ring my son to make sure he served them well in my absence.'

He arrived at Rass at around 3 a.m. and incorporated his armoured units into the security cordon that was already being put in place. The neighbourhood began to wake up: shops were opening, men were departing for work, and children were leaving for school. The houses in the immediate vicinity were cleared, and a large detachment of Emergency Forces began to assemble near the target. It was one of four walled, salmon-coloured condominiums standing in a row opposite a large vacant lot.

Next door was a half-finished detached villa with a high roof, perfect for snipers. Two identical detached villas lay behind, and soldiers were stationed there to make sure the terrorists did not flee out the back, as had happened so many times before. To the west of the empty lot stood a mosque with a latticed perimeter wall, offering soldiers cover while still allowing them to fire. 'We were all carrying heavy weapons and soon took control of the entire neighbourhood,' Quwayz explains.

An armoured car drove up to the target and, over a loudspeaker, the terrorists were invited to give themselves up. There was no answer, so a detachment of soldiers opened the gate and went up to the front door. 'They surprised us with an onslaught of gunfire and grenades. Three or four of my guys were injured, so I ordered a tactical withdrawal.' The wounded were loaded into the armoured car. 'Then the engagement with the terrorists began.' No one had any idea there were twenty-one of them inside, all armed to the teeth.

The snipers on the roof next door noticed one group of

gunmen exit out the back and start climbing the wall into the villa the snipers were using. They began firing at them, and they fired back. Meanwhile, another group of terrorists had gone up to the top floor to provide cover for their comrades below. One of them – it was in fact Qatayni – took out a pipe bomb to lob at the snipers across the way, but it exploded in his hands. His injuries would prove fatal, and he knew it. He told the others to take his ammunition clips and they did, leaving him to bleed to death.

Two other AQAP members had also been killed in the initial gunfight. However, two managed to get over the wall and barricade themselves inside the next-door villa. At the same time, Quwayz launched a ground assault on the primary target. 'As soon as we entered, we encountered a lot of gunfire and had to withdraw immediately. More than once, we entered and were repulsed. Many of our men were injured.' Despite these difficulties, one terrorist was persuaded to give himself up: it was Hamad al-Humaydi, the sheikh from Zulfi who had been arrested in February 2003, the first cleric of many to be detained in the government's crackdown.

How Humaydi got away from his comrades is not clear; they would normally kill a defector before they let him hand himself over to the enemy. Perhaps he was sent out as a decoy. When asked how many terrorists were inside, he lied. 'He said that in addition to himself, there were seven,' Harbi reports. 'We knew we couldn't trust him, but even so, we relaxed.' Seven was not that many. 'At that very moment, however, a huge burst of gunfire erupted from an entirely new building.'

There were clearly more terrorists than Humaydi had indicated, and the fighting was spreading much further than the MOI had expected. The terrorists had blown holes into the interior walls separating their condominium from the others, and before long groups of them were dispersed throughout the block. Where exactly they were the soldiers could not tell. But some had jumped the back garden wall and were hiding inside the villas there as well. The Special Forces in Riyadh were urgently summoned.

Throughout the afternoon, gunfire and grenades came at the soldiers from every direction. But worse than that, the battlefield had now expanded to within fifteen metres of a local girls' school. Ninety-four students and thirteen teachers were inside. At the outbreak of hostilities, the school's principal, Nora al-Ghufayli, had rung the police and was told to gather everyone at the far end of the building. She told her girls that the sounds were just a military exercise, but they knew enough to doubt it and huddled there, terrified, waiting to be rescued. Yet so fierce was the fighting outside that the soldiers deemed it too dangerous to evacuate them.

There was another problem. 'We grew concerned for the snipers on the roof next door,' Quwayz says. 'They had run out of ammunition, and there were terrorists inside the villa below, so they couldn't come downstairs.' A trick from Taawun came in handy. 'We brought a ladder and laid it across the gap between the rooftops.' Soldiers below unloaded their ammunition clips over the wall offering covering fire as the trapped snipers scrambled across to safety.

It was sunset. As the call to prayer went up, the Special Forces arrived and a plan was hatched to finally rescue the trapped schoolgirls. An armoured car drove round to the back of the school and broke through the wall. Snipers placed near the wall turned towards the besieged villas and a long line of soldiers stood arm-in-arm, shielding the girls as, in groups of ten, they exited through the hole in the wall and were taken to safety by armed escort.

It was going to be a long night. 'We erected floodlights,' Harbi recalls. 'They would fire at the lights, hoping to extinguish them and make a run for it.' RPGs from the villas streaked across the night sky, return fire from the armoured cars pounded the walls, and thick clouds of plaster dust filled the air. Eventually, things grew quiet, and the battlefield was calm until late morning, when out of nowhere the fighting began again in earnest. Two armoured cars were taken out by grenade and RPG fire, wounding several officers.

'We tried again and again to negotiate with them,' says Quwayz. 'But they still refused.' A raiding party was assembled and ordered to start clearing the villas one by one. They started with the tall one next door to the safe house. 'There were six people inside. Several were killed and one injured.' The injured man was dragged out to the street and loaded into an ambulance; the soldiers shouted abuse at him as he passed – no surprise, given that so many of their comrades had been wounded. 'Then we moved on to the safe house itself. To our surprise, it was empty.' It was still full of explosives and ammunition, but apart from the dead bodies of Qatayni and the two others who had been killed at the outset, there was no one.

The afternoon on the second day was relatively calm as the raiding team made their way through the villas. They suspected they had put all of the terrorists out of action. 'It drew near sunset on day two,' Quwayz continues. 'We approached one of the condominiums down the row from the safe house, and suddenly for the first time in hours there was gunfire.' That came as a surprise. 'I led an attempt to storm them, with two colleagues for support.' Quwayz approached the building and readied himself. 'But as soon as I made a move toward the door, they fired off two shots. Of course that rather put me off going forward!'

One of the terrorists began to taunt him. 'He was underneath a stairwell about five or six metres away from the door. "Hey you!" he shouted. "Why don't you enter? Too cowardly, huh? Infidel!" That sort of thing. I remained calm. "I'm a member of the security forces and I am here only to uphold security. We have not come to shed your blood, but I can assure you, it is better for you if when I say surrender, you do so." "Nah, you're lying!" he shouted back. "All you apostates are liars. Be a man and come inside and fight me face to face!" "Even if I do come inside and you were to kill me," I replied, "there are a thousand more soldiers behind me." But it did no good.'

They fired back and forth a bit, and, making no headway, the soldiers withdrew. The order was given to turn the big guns on the terrorists. 'The gunfire was so heavy that it set the villa on fire. The smoke forced them outside, where we engaged them. One was killed.' The rest managed to flee the burning building and barricaded themselves inside another one. The MOI released a statement saying that eight militants had so far been killed, and a local hospital reported treating fifty-eight wounded servicemen.

'Then, just after evening prayer, one of the terrorists rang 990,' the Mabahith's emergency hotline. Remarkably, the militant's mobile phone was still functioning. '"I want to surrender," he said. "I'm inside the building and want to come out." His name was Saleh al-Shamsan. It turned out he was the guy who'd taunted me at the front door.' On surrender, Shamsan confirmed that their leader Qatayni had been killed, and told the officers that at the beginning there had been twenty-one men in total in the safe house. 'That meant there were still nine terrorists on the loose. The situation remained critical.'

That night was quieter than the one before. 'Launching a raid at night is dangerous,' Quwayz explains. 'Not only were we concerned about the safety of our own men, but we were worried about the terrorists as well. Our primary aim was still to capture them alive.'

As the sun rose on the third day of the battle, weary servicemen lay slumped along pavements and rooftops, trying their best to catch a few moments' sleep. Locals in the vicinity threw open their doors to the soldiers and gave them food and drink. 'Was I tired?' Harbi asks. 'I didn't sleep for three days, so yeah,

I was tired. But I couldn't sleep. When you know the mission isn't over, sleeping isn't really possible. When the mission is over, that's when you sleep.'

Later that morning, over one hundred soldiers advanced on the villas. Once again, they swept through them one by one. The aim was to corral the remaining terrorists into one location. 'By the end,' says Quwayz, 'we had pushed all nine into a room on the second floor of one of the villas. We decided to come at them from below and from the roof.'

Major Khalid al-Muhaya – a hero of Khobar and Taawun – was in the advance company. 'I was commander of the assault team and there were three other soldiers with me,' he recalls. 'Karim al-Mejjati was sitting by the back door. He had been wounded in the leg and was maybe waiting for one of his comrades to come downstairs to help him. He shot at me from where he was sitting, but luckily I'm not as tall as he thought, and the bullets passed over my head. "Surrender, Karim!" I called out. "We are your brothers. Cooperate with us!" But he only called us infidels and said he'd rather be martyred than give himself up.

'I threw a grenade at him, then another. The second blast hit him in the chest, and he was badly burned.' Muhaya advanced. It was a risk; Mejjati could have been wearing a suicide belt. 'I told him straight that he was finished. His life was over, but even so, he still had a chance to repent. He began to cry, and I told him to recite the Shahada before he died. But he couldn't speak, he was crying so hard. It was the first time I'd been so close to an enemy on the battlefield. Eventually he fell silent. We said a quick prayer and continued our sweep.'

Meanwhile, the soldiers from the roof had made their assault. 'There was no escape this time,' says Quwayz. 'We were above them, on the stairs, and had the advantage.' By now the terrorists were down to their pistols, which were no match for the MOI's superior firepower. 'Finally, there were only two left fighting. "We give up! We give up!" they said, and we went down and arrested them.'

The team had to carry out a routine sweep before giving the all-clear. 'They went into the room where the bodies lay. "Hold your fire!" someone called out. "There's a child in here! We need to get him to a secure location!"' It was the 11-year-old Adam, Mejjati's son. 'When the soldiers came towards him, he pointed a pistol at them and began to fire. He didn't want to be rescued. I'm afraid their training took over. Straight away one of the team members shot him and he was eliminated.'

It was a sad end to the battle of Rass. The bomb squad was called in to deal with the corpses. Once stripped of their bomb vests, the bodies were taken outside. Fifteen AQAP members had been killed, including two on the List of Twenty-Six: network leader Qatayni and Mejjati. Six were behind bars. Seven buildings had been shot to hell in the fighting and over a hundred soldiers had been injured – yet miraculously, none of them died.

Muhaya was among the wounded. 'It was during the final assault. They were firing pistols and one of our guys threw a grenade. I was busy fighting and didn't really notice that I'd been hit by the shrapnel. But I saw blood on my hand. "Your abdomen, your abdomen!" my colleagues shouted at me. "No, it's just my hand," I replied, but they shook their heads and pointed at me. "Look!" I glanced down and there was a lot of blood, it was flowing profusely. "I'll go bandage it and come back," I said. I didn't want to abandon the fight. But when I got downstairs, the paramedics rushed up to me and I felt cold all over my body.

'The next thing I know, I'm waking up in hospital. A colleague is sitting next to me. "Have there been any more injuries?" I asked.

'"No, Khalid, it's all over," he said. "The battle is over."'

*

The battle was over, but the war ground on. Two days after the events in Rass, during a stand-off with police in Sanaeiya in southern Riyadh, Abdul Rahman al-Yaziji, number four on the List of Twenty-Six, detonated his suicide vest. Another former member of the Mutaween, Yaziji had fought in Kashmir and Afghanistan. After the Riyadh compound bombings, he was held by the Mabahith for three months over his refusal to answer questions about his brother Abdul Kareem, one of the Vinnell compound bombers. As soon as he was out, he joined AQAP.

Yaziji's death meant there was effectively only one name left on the List of Twenty-Six: the leader of the Organization's Hijaz network, Saleh al-Oufi.[3] Throughout April the security services there kept his men on their toes. On the 21st, the day of the Hijaz's first-ever municipal elections, the Mabahith trailed a car carrying three suspects from Ha'il to Mecca. At a checkpoint, one of the suspects was arrested but the other two sped off. An extraordinary chase followed. The suspects, who were well armed, were eventually cornered and shot dead, but not before they had managed to shoot up or set fire to fourteen police vehicles, killing two security officers and wounding seventeen. The two militants were also killed; they had been dressed as women. On the 24th a man in Jeddah rang the authorities when he realized that tenants of his had stuffed their flat full of weaponry. When the security services arrived, the flat was found to be abandoned – in fact, its former occupants had already been killed in other confrontations – but among the weapons they seized was a large amount of explosives.

Things in the Najd were quieter. Rass had decimated what remained of Qatayni's network, and the man who emerged as his successor – a 35-year-old Moroccan called **Yunus al-Hayari** – was left with little to play with. Hayari was a veteran. He had fought in Bosnia in the early 1990s and in 2001 he went on Hajj with his wife and ended up settling in Riyadh. That is where he met Mejjati and began his association with what would become AQAP. Little is known of his activities before the King Fahd neighbourhood raid. However, it is known that he fled the raid with Oufi, and so it is possible that they were close. His assumption of the leadership may have been with an eye to healing whatever rift there was between the Najd-based network and Oufi's in the Hijaz. More likely, it was simply because he was the last veteran jihadist left.

Hayari's chief lieutenant in these straitened times was Fahd al-Juwayr. A rather cloddish figure, Juwayr had been a new recruit when he had received truck driving training for Operation Volcano, and the relentless attrition of more capable operatives had enabled him to rise through the ranks. Now he was put in charge of the remaining cells in Riyadh and Kharj and set about recruiting new members – not very successfully.

The other ace in Hayari's hand was Abdulaziz al-Anzi, a university graduate in forensic science and a whiz with computers. Ayiri had recruited him to the nascent propaganda team back in 2002, and after Isa al-Awshen's death in 2004, he was made editor-in-chief of *Voice of Jihad*. A very powerful writer, Anzi had done well to keep the Organization's propaganda output alive despite all the setbacks.

Yet Anzi had remained off the MOI's radar. Regular issues of *Voice of Jihad* had continued to be published over the four months following Awshen's death, but then in November 2004 they abruptly ceased. The Mabahith assumed their enemy's propaganda wing had been destroyed, and were therefore surprised when out of the blue another issue appeared two weeks after the battle of Rass. It contained a posthumous editorial by Qatayni, a non-specific description of the battle based on news reports, and a final page promising another issue soon.

On 9 May, the Security Patrols were trailing a suspect vehicle in the Rawabi district of Riyadh when the driver, realizing he was being followed, jumped out of his car and tried to carjack another. However, the car's owner fought him off, giving the patrolmen time enough to shoot him. The wound was not fatal, and the man was arrested. It was Anzi. Hayari had lost one of his few real assets, and *Voice of Jihad* was silenced.[4]

To the MOI, it truly seemed that the worst was over, and the United States agreed. On 18 May, the American embassy lifted the travel advisory warning for Saudi Arabia which had been in effect since April the previous year. All in all, things were looking up.

The trouble with terrorists, however, is that even when they are down, they are never entirely out. Ten days later terrorists sneaked into Qaseem airport and set three Cougar helicopters on fire with Molotov cocktails, and in the first week of June, two policemen at a checkpoint were wounded by passing gunfire. 'Then on the 19th,' recalls Lieutenant-Colonel Bandar al-Akur of the Special Forces in Jeddah, 'the services in Mecca rang to say that Lieutenant-Colonel Mubarak al-Sawat had been killed.' Sawat was a Mabahith interrogator at Ruways prison in Jeddah.

Sawat's name had been mentioned in connection to allegations of torture which former Saudi prisoners and human rights groups raised against the MOI in the late 1990s. According to Mabahith sources, Prince Nayef launched an internal investigation into the matter in 2000, and entrusted his son Prince Muhammad with rooting out these abuses. Although some would complain that the MOI was not doing enough, it is believed that conditions quickly improved.[5]

It had not been enough to save Sawat. The two men who killed him had suffered no abuse at his hands, but his reputation was well known to jihadists. 'They had been under suspicion so on the day before the killing he brought them in and took their statements. Then he let them go. They waited for him outside his office and followed him home.'

Sawat's wife Misbah would later describe what happened

the next morning. 'He left for work, just as he did every day. That morning, however, I heard a loud bang and rushed to the window.' Her husband's car was still parked outside, but he was nowhere to be seen. There were more loud noises. It was gunfire. 'I suddenly heard my husband shouting not to come outside.' She ignored him. 'I couldn't control myself, and soon I found myself in front of his body. Our neighbours reached the scene at the same time. I couldn't contain myself. He was covered in blood.'[6]

'The killers had brought a camera with them,' Akur continues. 'They'd intended to tie him up, carry him to the roof and film themselves killing him there. But Sawat fought back and they were forced to shoot him with their Kalashnikovs. Apparently his kids watched them do it. As if that was not bad enough, one of them then hacked at his body with an axe.' They left the axe behind, as well as their fingerprints. Forensics were able to trace the prints to a certain Kemal Fawdah, a 45-year-old ex-con who had exchanged his career in petty thievery for one in jihad. His photograph was widely distributed and police were on the lookout.

Two days later, the forces in Jeddah were told that Fawdah and his accomplice were spotted driving their way.[7] 'Security at the Prince Fawwaz checkpoint at the entrance to the city was beefed up. When the suspects drove up they saw that guards were inspecting every car, so they swerved off the road around the police cars, firing as they went.' Eventually they were forced to get out, and after failing to hijack one of the cars at the checkpoint, they fled into the surrounding neighbourhood. 'It was nighttime and they gave us the slip. It wasn't until dawn prayer that we tracked them down.' A local resident had alerted the police to their presence. 'He said, "There are individuals on the roof of my building. I am suspicious of them." So we mobilized and went to the scene.'

Both suspects were killed when they refused to give

themselves up. The entire country had been following the story, and eulogies for the 'martyred' Lieutenant-Colonel Sawat praised his courage and patriotism. However, his connection to the Mabahith's earlier brutal treatment of prisoners, particular in Jeddah, gives the story a more ambiguous slant.

Tragic though it was for his family and for the Mabahith, the Sawat episode was yet another reminder that 'enhanced interrogation techniques' often result in increased radicalization and violent resentments. The younger generation of Mabahith agents in particular want to turn the page on that unsavoury chapter in the Mabahith's history. They report that the Mabahith no longer uses torture in interrogations, though human rights groups maintain that, in the wider prison system, confessions are still sometimes extracted through such means. The government's often painfully slow drive to make the administration of justice fairer and more transparent is ongoing.[8]

By the summer of 2005 the List of Twenty-Six, posted in December 2003, had been whittled down to one: Saleh al-Oufi. On 28 June, the MOI released two updated most-wanted lists, one for terrorists wanted internally and the other for Saudis implicated in terrorism abroad. The suspects were almost all new 'third-generation' jihadists, which testified to the war on terror's successes in neutralizing most of Al Qaeda's veteran membership, both internationally and inside the Kingdom.

At the top of the domestic list was Yunus al-Hayari, though he did not remain there for long. On 3 July, Mabahith agents in Riyadh investigating a large villa in the swanky Rawda district decided it should be searched and called in the Special Forces. 'We set up two security cordons,' Major-General Khalid al-Harbi explains. 'Snipers took up their positions, and the raiding team walked up to the villa and rang the bell at the front gate.' They waited a minute or two, and then the door opened. 'A guy peered out, he looked normal. He wasn't wearing a thobe, just a

T-shirt and trousers.'[9] Only twenty-two years old, he had a bushy beard that did not yet reach his cheeks. They grabbed him and escorted him to their commanding officer.

'What is your name?' the officer asked as his men handcuffed the young man, who mumbled something in response. 'Eh?' the officer grunted.

'Osama.'

'Osama what?'

'Osama al-Wahaybi.'

'Who lives with you, Osama?'

'No one lives with me.'

'You're all by yourself, huh?'

'Yes.'

'So what's the arrangement, then? How many men are inside?'

'Um, my family's away at the moment.'

'Oh, they're away, I see. Travelling?'

'My brother was here, but he just left.'

The officer asked his questions quickly and confidently. He was used to AQAP members like Osama giving confused and contradictory answers. 'And your family?'

'They're not here! My mother and father live there . . .'

'But there are other families in the house, then?' the officer interrupted.

'No, nobody.'

'There's nobody at all in the house?'

'Yes, everybody's out.'

The officer gave him one last chance. 'So who did you say was in the house, then?'

Osama looked at his questioner with barely concealed contempt. 'There's no one. Everyone left shortly before I got here.'

The officer waved his hand. 'Okay, take him to the car.'

The raiding party regrouped and cautiously entered the front gate in formation. They then broke into two groups. Group one positioned themselves by the front door, and group two by the door to a servant's cottage which jutted out at an angle to the main house. A cameraman followed them. 'Get out!' a young soldier whispered. 'By God, it isn't safe for you. That's an order!' His order was ignored.

Group one kicked down the front door and swept the house, arresting two unarmed men. Group two, meanwhile, was having a harder time. The excitement in the air had got the better of them. 'Where is the axe? Bring the axe!' whispered the soldier nearest the door. His comrades looked around sheepishly. 'Doesn't anyone have an axe?' After a brief moment of panic, an axe was passed across, and the rest of the team moved forward. 'Come on, stand back!' he said. 'Let's not all bunch together.'

Two swings of the axe snapped off the door handle but otherwise made little headway. 'Here, use this, brother,' one of the team said and handed a crowbar over, but it too failed to force the door open. Glancing around nervously, a young soldier pointed his weapon towards a window on the upper floor.

'Let me give it a try,' another soldier said, and after several mighty swings of the axe, the door flew open. However, someone on the other side was ready to fight. No sooner was the door open than a furious barrage of gunfire exploded in the direction of the soldiers. The cameraman fled in panic.

As the soldiers outside the servant's cottage regrouped, a Mabahith officer grilled Osama, who sat blindfolded in the back seat of a police car. 'Tell us! Who is shooting at us? Is it Yunus?' the officer shouted.

'I don't know!'

The officer slapped him. 'Enough, you dog! No more lies! Tell me who he is!'

Osama's earlier defiance had become much less confident. 'I swear, I don't know.'

'He knows, he knows,' another officer tutted.

'You say you live there?'

'Yeah, but I'm not the only one. I live with my mum and dad . . .'

'Then how can you not know who he is?'

'I don't know, I just don't . . .'

'I swear to God, you'd better tell us. Who is he?'

They got no further with Osama that afternoon and he was taken away.

Meanwhile, upon hearing the gunfire, the Special Forces team inside the villa itself had rushed downstairs. 'Careful, the window!' one of their colleagues in team two shouted at them and they stopped just inside the front door. The gunman, who was shooting out the cottage window, had a clear line of sight to them. They backed up and took up defensive positions. Two officers ran into the villa's majlis off the central corridor. One of them ripped down the curtains and, squatting on the sofa, took aim through the window.

'Surrender yourself!' an officer at the door shouted. He turned and barked at his comrades, who were crowding him. 'Get back! Jassem, Musab, upstairs!' They withdrew to provide cover from above. Gunfire erupted from the cottage. 'Is he shooting?'

'Open fire!' the commander yelled. They emptied their weapons into the cottage. The order to surrender went out again, but the gunman in the cottage only fired back in reply.

'Grenade, grenade!' someone called out. An officer had carried one into the garden from the street. 'Stand back, brothers!' The grenade was tossed at the cottage and a momentary flash illuminated the villa's front porch. Smoke began to pour out of the cottage's window. The building was on fire.

'Be careful!' an officer watching from the majlis shouted. 'He'll be forced to come out!'

'Is he wearing a belt? Can you tell?'

'You are surrounded on all sides. Come out and surrender!'

There was no more shooting. Fire poured out of the cottage

door, and after two or three minutes a man crawled out of the burning cottage and lay on the concrete patio; blood covered the left side of his body and he writhed in pain. 'There is no god but God!' he cried.

The soldiers kept their distance; they could not be sure whether the dark-green tactical vest strapped across the man's chest held a bomb or not. 'Hold your fire!' the commander shouted at his men. Then to the fallen figure he shouted out, 'Take off the belt, man! Toss it aside so we can come to help you!'

'No, I take refuge in God!' the man shouted back. Several minutes passed. Eventually, he withdrew a grenade from the belt, pulled the pin, and lay on it. It blew a large chunk out of his upper arm, and he died.

'He's dead,' an officer spoke into his CB radio. 'He chose suicide.'

'That's nice,' someone standing nearby muttered. 'I ask God that they all make the same choice.'

It was left to the bomb squad to ready the corpse for transport to the morgue, where it was confirmed that he was indeed Yunus al-Hayari. His tenure as AQAP leader had lasted just under three months. The fact that he had been all alone in the servant's cottage, barely protected by three unarmed men in the main house, shows just how diminished the Riyadh cell had become.

As for the young man Osama, those who knew him were shocked to discover he was involved in terrorism, no one more so than his father Abdul Rahman, a well-respected sheikh. However, any doubts as to Osama's commitment to jihad were dispelled two years later when he escaped from Melez prison and joined Zarqawi's Al Qaeda franchise in Iraq. He was reported killed in October 2007.[10]

The rest of July 2005 was overshadowed by the 7/7 suicide bombings in London, which killed fifty-two people and injured over seven hundred. 'I happened to be in London that day,' recalls Sir Sherard Cowper-Coles, the British ambassador to Saudi Arabia at the time. 'It is a measure of just how much cooperation we'd established with Saudi intelligence in the war on terror that Prince Muhammad immediately rang me on my personal mobile to express his solidarity and to extend whatever help he could. It was gratifying to be able to report back to the Cabinet that the first person to offer his support was Prince Muhammad.'[11]

However, the Kingdom's involvement in the 7/7 story does not end there. On 1 August, King Fahd finally succumbed to his long illness, and Crown Prince Abdullah ascended the throne. Tucked in among the news stories about the smooth succession was a report by the *Guardian* newspaper alleging that 'senior Saudi security sources' were claiming that in the weeks preceding the 7/7 bombings, the Kingdom had warned MI5 and MI6 than an attack was imminent.[12] Both Karim al-Mejjati and Yunus al-Hayari, the article claimed, had been in contact with Al Qaeda operatives in Britain earlier in the year, and the information had been passed along to British intelligence. Prince Turki al-Faisal, Saudi ambassador in London and former head of the GIP, the Saudi foreign intelligence agency, confirmed the report.

The British categorically denied they had received any information which could have averted the attacks. Six months later, however, similar allegations emerged. In December 2004, Saudi security had arrested a man called Adel at the airport in Buraydah; he had been trying to enter the country on a forged passport. Under questioning, he revealed that Al Qaeda was planning an attack in London, to take place in about six months' time, the details of which were remarkably similar to what transpired on 7/7. He said it was to involve four men who were being coordinated by a Libyan businessman in London, and that the bombings were targeting locations near 'Edgewood Road' – his knowledge of London geography may have been faulty, but one of the bombers did attack a train at Edgware Road Underground station. Adel also confessed that he had come to the Kingdom to drum up $500,000 in financing for the operation, and was to contact a Syrian telephone number once he had acquired the funds.[13] The Saudis claimed they had passed all this information on to their counterparts in America and Britain.

The revelation caused a minor furore in the United Kingdom. People wanted to know why, despite the warnings, the threat level in Britain had been lowered only three weeks before the attack. The White House confirmed the story, as did British intelligence, grudgingly; they said they had followed up on the information provided by the Saudis, but that it had not been the sort of concrete, actionable intelligence which might have enabled them to stop the terrorists. The Saudis were pressing the issue, or so the thinking went, because they wanted to make a point: that despite their reputation, they were an equal partner in the war on terror.

Ironically, the British found themselves in the position the Saudis had been in in the aftermath of the Riyadh compound bombings, accused of 'ignoring warnings' and 'not doing enough' – charges which were once again levelled at King Abdullah during an interview with BBC News in October. 'I believe most countries are not taking this issue too seriously, including unfortunately Great Britain,' the king said. Given what his country had gone through, the king was understandably offended. 'We sent information to Great Britain before the terrorist attacks in London, but unfortunately no action was taken, and it may have been able to avert the tragedy.'[14]

Once again, British intelligence denied the allegations and the back-and-forth continued. Non-politicos like Prince Muhammad, engaged in the daily business of cooperating with allies in the fight against terrorism, were not impressed by the flap. It was yet another lesson that an amorphous threat like terrorism is extremely difficult to police, and that trying to score political points over allies' failures to achieve the impossible only detracts from the hard and often thankless task of achieving what is possible.

The war back in Saudi Arabia was drawing to a close. Suspects arrested in a series of raids in the Hijaz had revealed Saleh al-Oufi's location. He was in Medina, in a flat on the fourth floor of an apartment block in the Bahar district. At the same time, one of Oufi's principal operatives, a 29-year-old called Majid al-Hasiri, had been spotted driving from Medina to Riyadh, where agents followed him to a villa in the Maseef district. Married and the father of a 2-year-old daughter, Hasiri had been reported by his family when he had disappeared eighteen months earlier. The MOI decided to apprehend both Oufi and Hasiri on 18 August.

'The operation was synchronized between Riyadh and Medina,' explains Brigadier-General Mudeef al-Talhi. He had helped coordinate the operation that led to Muqrin's death, and was sent off to nab Hasiri in Riyadh. 'Zero hour was 4 a.m. Now, in any operation, the team is made up of two different kinds of people, those who are pumped up and ready for action, and those who are calmer. Me personally, I'm what you might call impetuous. I don't like to wait around. "Right, let's go!" is my mantra. When it comes to drawing up a plan, I'd just rather play it by ear and put my trust in God.' Talhi chuckles. 'Thank goodness one of my comrades that morning was of the calmer sort. "Let's wait until dawn prayer," he cautioned. "Perhaps someone will leave the flat to go to mosque, and we can question him."'

The call to prayer went out, and a few minutes later, a young man emerged from the villa. 'We detained him. Then, a minute later, another young man came out, then another, and we detained them as well. They were brothers. All three were westernized. I mean, they didn't have beards, they didn't look like takfeeris.'

Talhi questioned the eldest, who was in his late teens. 'Who else is in the villa?' he asked him.

'Only my father,' the young man replied. 'No one else.'

Talhi took out a mobile phone. 'Okay, call your father and tell him to come outside.' The young man did so, and before long an old man stepped out into the street. 'He had a very dignified bearing,' Talhi recalls. 'So much so, in fact, that we all kissed him on the forehead.' There is no greater mark of respect in Saudi culture.

However, the old man was surprised to see his three sons in police custody. 'What is going on?' he asked.

'Nothing at all, sir,' Talhi replied. 'Are these your children?'

'Yes they are.'

'Have you any others? If so, where are they?'

'Well, there is Saad,' the old man offered.

'And where is Saad?'

'He's in that villa, over there.' The family owned several on the street.

The cordon they had set up was modified to incorporate this new information. Talhi explained to the old man that he hoped he could count on his full cooperation.

'Anything, just ask,' he replied.

'Well then, I'd like you to ring that doorbell and say, "Saad, it is your father. Please come outside." Can you do that for me?'

They walked up to the door and the old man rang the bell. His son Saad answered the door in his pyjamas and was immediately escorted to the street. Talhi threw the usual questions at him, and Saad replied with the usual denials.

'Okay, you say there's no one else in the house. Fine. But then what happened to the guys who were with you in the car when you arrived last night?'

Saad skipped a beat. 'Um, they're just guests.'

'My son!' his father said. 'First you say no one is with you, then you say you've got guests inside? Are you still asleep or something? What kind of talk is this?'

Talhi calmed the old man and turned to Saad. 'Okay then, would you kindly ask your guests to come outside?'

Saad refused. His father grew even more exasperated. 'Good God! I'll go and get them,' he said and set off towards the house. Four or five steps was as far as the old man got before Saad called out, 'Father, no! They'll kill you!'

That was all Talhi needed to hear. Saad was arrested. 'Of course I never would have allowed the old man to actually go inside,' Talhi explains. 'But I thought it'd put pressure on Saad, watching his father walk into harm's way.' The rest of his family was instructed to evacuate and the raid commenced. 'When Hasiri realized he was about to be caught and that there was no escape, he blew himself up. Thank God, no one but me was injured, and even that was just a light wound on my hand.'

In Medina, meanwhile, the MOI had closed in on Saleh al-Oufi. 'It was imperative that we dealt with him when we did, as King Abdullah was arriving in Medina that very day and we were afraid he might be targeted,' recalls Major-General Khalid al-Harbi. 'When we arrived at the apartment building, we were concerned for the safety of the people in the neighbourhood, as it was densely populated and the streets round about were very narrow.'

What is more, they discovered that there were elderly people living in the building, some of them in wheelchairs. 'We called them over the building's intercom and told them to prepare to be evacuated, but at that very moment Oufi and the two men with him upstairs opened fire on us.' One of Harbi's men was struck in the upper back. 'It was a deadly blow. He was only in his early twenties, poor man, married and with a year-old child.'

Oufi, who had given the security services the slip several times, hoped the gunfire would facilitate an escape. 'He went downstairs to a window on the first floor and jumped down to a courtyard in the back. The street behind was narrow, and he thought he could easily sneak away.' However, the soldiers were prepared for precisely that. 'He was surprised by the tight cordon we had set up, and began firing.' The gunfight did not last long. 'He was quickly shot, and as was so often the case, instead of capture he chose to detonate his suicide belt.' One of Oufi's men was also killed and another arrested.[15] Apart from the soldier shot at the outset, there were no other MOI or civilian casualties.

The last name on the List of Twenty-Six had been scratched out. The rest of 2005 was devoted to mopping up what was left of Hayari's network. A cell he had established in Dammam to carry out attacks on oil installations was uncovered on 3 September. As they had at the battle of Rass, for three days the MOI laid siege to the cell's safe house in the Mubarikiya neighbourhood, reducing it to rubble and killing all five cell members. Four officers were also killed, and over seventy wounded.

A number of unoccupied safe houses were then raided in September and October, and on 3 December seventeen terrorist suspects were arrested in raids throughout the Najd. Finally, on 18 December, two more top members of Hayari's network were killed in a long shootout with road security in Qaseem. Five police officers died.

As the year drew to a close, the Kingdom had survived twelve months without a major terrorist attack. The MOI in particular heaved a sigh of relief. To all intents and purposes, Prince Muhammad and his men had crushed AQAP.

With one final exception: Fahd al-Juwayr, Hayari's deputy. Somehow he had evaded detection and watched from the sidelines as one by one his comrades were killed or apprehended. The 34-year-old simpleton whom Muqrin had once deemed fit only for suicide martyrdom now found himself standing in

Muqrin's place as leader. At the beginning of 2006, he gathered together a motley collection of survivors and new recruits at a small warehouse in Riyadh's Faisaliya district, the last functioning cell of the original AQAP. 'I've got a new plan,' he announced. 'It's gonna be big, even bigger than 9/11.'[16]

From the very beginning, AQAP had nursed an ambition to disable the Kingdom's oil infrastructure. They knew along with everyone that the key to Saudi Arabia's prosperity and the means by which the royal family lubricated their claims to power lay in the country's immense reserves of black gold. Several 'oil cells' were established in the Eastern Province over the course of the Organization's history, which focused mainly on the Abqaiq refinery located 60 kilometres southwest of Dhahran. The largest refinery in the world, Abqaiq produced over 6 million barrels of oil each day. The cells had thoroughly surveilled its perimeter several times, and now, hard-pressed on all sides by the MOI's relentlessness, Juwayr decided the time had come to bomb it.

The operational core of the cell comprised seven men in addition to Juwayr.[17] Four had been in AQAP for a year or two, but they were all inexperienced, and none had much expertise in explosives. Not long before the meeting in Faisaliya, a few cell members went to the desert to practise setting off small bombs they had built, which were attached to simple timers constructed from Casio watches. 'What time is it?' one of them asked as they waited a distance away from where they had left one of the bombs underneath an upturned bucket.

'It's ten to two,' his comrade replied. 'I set it to go off at five to two. Be patient.' The spindly Cornulaca bushes rustled in the desert wind and the two young men prayed under their breaths. Right on cue, there was a loud pop and the bucket shot up into the air. 'Allahu akbar!' they cried and ran over to the patch of blackened sand.

'It didn't explode,' one of them said. Large chunks of the bomb were in his hand.

'Really? There was a flash.'

'Yeah, but it didn't explode. Look, here is the charge.'

Despite his crew's ominous lack of experience, Juwayr pressed on. He brought two white GMC pickup trucks to the Faisaliya warehouse and, probably working from a manual, the team wired them up. On the hood they wrote 'Under your orders, Osama! Say goodbye to the biggest thievery in history!' Muhammad al-Ghaith – who like Juwayr had been given tanker truck training for Operation Volcano and had purchased the bulldozer for the aborted attack on the ROC compound – was selected to be a suicide bomber along with a particularly laddish charmer called Abdullah al-Tuwayjiri.

'Honestly I don't know what to say,' Tuwayjiri averred with a cheeky grin. The warehouse lights were off and he sat in the cab of his truck bomb, illuminated only by the light from a video camera. 'I praise God that He has permitted us to prepare this truck and I dedicate this operation to our sheikh and dear friend Osama bin Laden,' he said, stroking the detonator. 'May God allow me to press this button, this noble button.' He raised his eyes up to heaven and spoke in an ecstatic whisper. 'What do I feel? I feel what anyone would, whose faith is strong in the Lord.'

The attack was set for 24 February. The day before, the cell left the warehouse and took desert roads to the Eastern Province. Juwayr's thoughts were on the failure of his fellow Saudis to rise up. 'To Muslim people everywhere, how long will you stay silent?' he had thundered during the filming of the propaganda video intended for release after the attack. 'You are sunk in oppression and degradation! You are ruled by idolaters! And yet you stay silent. Where is your Islam? Where is your worship of God? Arise, I say! Mount your steeds and fly to us in our distress. Join us in our fight along the path of

God. For there are only two deeds worth striving for. Victory, or martyrdom.'

They set up camp somewhere in the desert outside Abqaiq town, which was mainly home to employees of the state-owned oil company Saudi Aramco. Juwayr had originally thought to disguise the truck bombs as Aramco vehicles, which he had studied outside the homes of Aramco employees. In the end he ditched that idea in favour of a straightforward assault, and as the sun set on the day before the attack he led his men in a final round of weapons training. Tuwayjiri squatted on a sand bank and fired several rounds into the dunes beyond. 'I can't stop thinking of my mother and brother,' he said between rounds. 'We will meet together in paradise, God willing.'

Later that night, they sat around a small fire. Ghaith, the other suicide bomber, sat and fidgeted, a still-wet, homemade cast wrapped around his left leg. He had broken it a few weeks before, when he and two other recruits had unintentionally flipped their car while doing some daredevil driving in the desert. By sheer coincidence, just as they were pulling themselves out of the overturned car, a Mabahith officer drove up. He had merely been driving past, and enquired if he could be of service. Ghaith, who was in great pain, masked it as best he could and told the officer, yes, they could use his help. The officer got out, and as he bent down to examine the upturned car, they quickly got into his vehicle and sped off, abandoning him in the desert.

Such jollities were far from Ghaith's mind that night, however. He was as pensive as he had been at Camp of the Sabre just under two years ago, when Muqrin had pressed him to describe how excited he felt to be meeting his maker. Now he simply stared at the flaming embers. 'What's with you?' Tuwayjiri asked him.

'Leave me alone,' Ghaith replied.

Dawn broke. Tufts of cirrocumulus glowed light pink in

the azure sky. Tuwayjiri was up early. Softly to himself, he sang a song.

Where are our days, where?
Where are the days we spent?
They went in the blink of an eye.
How beautiful is our memory of them.

Juwayr gathered everyone round one of the truck bombs. He had laid out a large blank piece of paper on the bonnet. 'Hey Waleed!' he called out, using Ghaith's cell nickname. 'Can you hobble over here?'

'The cast is still soft.'

'It didn't dry? Well, it'll dry in the wind, if you stand up.' Ghaith stood a distance away, and Juwayr raised his voice to make sure he could hear. 'Okay, everyone,' he began and started drawing a map of the town, the refinery, and the roads they would use to approach one of the remote service gates. 'We'll set off together. I'll be with the team in the SUV, and we'll drive in front. The two pickups will follow behind at a distance.'

'You'll keep us informed of what's happening?' Tuwayjiri asked.

'Yeah, we'll use our walkie-talkies. Now, when we approach the refinery at this point here, there'll be a checkpoint. If the guards tell us to stop, we'll keep driving. They'll follow us to the gate, and we'll deal with them there. It'll have an armoured truck, and I reckon there'll be a few soldiers either to the left or right, but those of us in the SUV will be ready with our weapons. If possible, we should just capture them. We don't want to draw attention to ourselves by shooting.' The Organization's earlier surveillance had given them an impressive understanding of the refinery's perimeter. Juwayr explained in detail exactly what they would have to do to neutralize the guards: one at the truck, a couple more inside a tent a short distance away, a few more inside a Portakabin behind the tent.

'Now,' Juwayr turned to Tuwayjiri, 'you and Waleed will have pulled over a few hundred metres before the gate. We'll let you know when we've got it open, and then you can enter. Because of Waleed's cast, you should drive in front, in case you need to use your weapon. Once you're inside, take your time and find the best place to detonate. Are you listening, Waleed?'

'Yeah, I can hear you.'

'Shall I tell you a secret?' Tuwayjiri's voice crackled over the walkie-talkie. The SUV carrying Juwayr and the four other members of the assault team sped down the highway.

'Tell us,' Juwayr replied.

'I love you all.'

'Ah, what a nice secret.' The desert flashed by. A huge oil storage tower loomed into view, SAUDI ARAMCO blazoned on its side.

The walkie-talkie crackled again. 'What about me? Do you love me?'

'Never mind,' said Juwayr.

'Well, our happiness will be doubled when we all meet again in heaven!'

'Okay, okay. No more nonsense.'

When they reached Abqaiq town, Tuwayjiri got on the walkie-talkie again. 'I've run out of petrol. The light on the dash has come on.'

Juwayr remained remarkably composed. 'Is it really really empty, or is there a tiny bit left?'

'Well, the low-fuel light is on, and the gauge is in the red.'

'Really?' If it had not been down to his own poor planning, Juwayr would have wondered what kind of idiot forgets to fill up before a truck bombing. 'Okay, no problem. See that petrol station over there? Go and fill up.'

'Right,' Tuwayjiri replied. A moment later, he added, 'Have you got some money?'

'You don't have any with you?' Juwayr sighed and began to pray. Between a jihadist's inflated sense of self and the imbecilic reality of his actions there lies a wide gulf.

They filled up and drove on. They reached the outskirts of the refinery complex without anyone stopping them. Tuwayjiri and Ghaith pulled over and awaited Juwayr's all-clear. The assault team prayed rhythmically together. One was in tears, overcome by a feeling of closeness to God.

It was 2:55 p.m. 'Look, there's the gate,' one of them pointed. A thick black and yellow barrier was chained fast to the asphalt road. The armoured truck stood beside it.

'But where's the Portakabin? Where's the room you told us about?' A militant in the back seat began to panic slightly.

'It's just there. Don't worry,' Juwayr silenced him. They got closer. 'I'll spray the guards with bullets, and you'll attack them too, right?' There was no answer from the back. 'You'll attack them too, won't you?' He received a nod in reply.

The car slowed down. 'No no, pull up right beside them,' Juwayr commanded. A guard was standing beside the truck. 'It's a soldier,' he said. 'I'll put a bullet in his head. Quickly, quickly!'

'Allahu akbar!' The five gunmen leapt out of the car and immediately began to shoot. Juwayr killed the guard and, with two others, ran to the tent. Inside it an old man in uniform was on his tea break. He was also killed. They then shot at the Portakabin, wounding four men, but instead of proceeding inside to finish them off, they withdrew back to the gate.

'We can't open it,' Juwayr was told. 'The chains are too strong!'

Ghaith radioed, asking if he and Tuwayjiri should begin their approach. 'No, Waleed!' Juwayr shouted back at him. 'Don't move.'

'Oh my God, we're going to fail . . .' someone moaned.

'Oy, listen!' Juwayr barked. 'You, shoot the gate. Shoot at the chains!'

The sound of the bullets against the metal barrier was deafening. 'These Kalashnikovs are useless!' the shooter yelled, so Juwayr took over.

For three minutes they alternated between shooting the chain and hacking at the asphalt to which it was attached. Finally, the chain began to loosen. 'Lift the bar, lift it!'

'Allahu akbar!'

The way into the refinery was free and the two pickup trucks drove up. 'Don't stop!' Juwayr shouted. 'Go, quickly! God bless you!' he called after them as they rushed inside. He ordered the others back into the SUV and, turning around, they sped off.

Juwayr's knowledge of the refinery beyond the perimeter fence had been much less certain. The two truck bombers soon had to stop at the locked chain-link gate of another layer of fencing further in. Tuwayjiri radioed Juwayr and asked him to come and help them open it, but Juwayr told him to ram it. Three times the wired-up pickup smashed into the gate, and on the fourth it swung open.

Meanwhile, Juwayr and the assault team raced away down the highway and prayed. 'O Lord, O Lord, O Lord!'

'One of the guards, I killed him!' one of them boasted.

'Which one?' his comrade asked.

'The one in the tent. He was an old man, blubbering something about Islam or I don't know what. He said we'd never get through, and before I shot him, I told him yes we would. And we did!'

They all looked nervously back in the direction of the refinery, which was receding from view. 'I guess it didn't explode,' one of them ventured, but he spoke too soon. Two thin plumes of smoke suddenly rose into the air.

'Allahu akbar!'

'It exploded!'

'Two explosions!'

'Allahu akbar!'

To the sound of his comrades' cries of joy, a lion of Islam stood up through the sunroof and ecstatically fired his Kalashnikov into the air. It was perhaps not the wisest thing to do, seeing as every police car in the vicinity was on the lookout for them. But they had just destroyed the world's largest oil refinery, tipped the global economy into permanent meltdown mode, and ushered in a period of peace, justice, and eternal righteousness.

Or so they thought. In fact, the truck bombs had encountered yet another layer of security, this time a row of low metal bollards circling the facility at a distance of about 30 metres from the refinery itself. There was no getting through, so they detonated where they were. It caused a certain amount of superficial damage to some nearby auxiliary buildings, but no one was killed or even injured and not a single drop of oil was prevented from making its way to market.

What is more, even if they had managed to get closer, the bombs could never have made the impact they thought they would. Abqaiq is a huge facility, covering nearly 100 square kilometres, and because they are intrinsically unstable environments, oil refineries are designed to deal with explosions. Had the terrorists disabled a part of the system, as they well might have, fail-safe mechanisms would have instantly isolated the damaged area and cut it off from the rest of the network. Barring a sustained military assault from the air, fatally undermining the ability of Abqaiq to keep the petrol flowing is near on impossible.[18]

The SUV's number plate was captured by the refinery's CCTV camera and, three days later, the Mabahith tracked the cell down to a safe house in northeast Riyadh, where they had fled after the attack. It was a large, walled rest house in the Yarmouk neighbourhood – as it happens, not far from where the Organization had carried out the Riyadh compound bombings three years before. The raid played out in the usual way. The terrorists refused to surrender and, after a fierce firefight, all five were killed.

The corpses of Juwayr and his men were carried out to the front lawn. Forensics officers took DNA samples and investigators combed through their personal effects. The scene was sombre and professional, a far cry from the apocalyptic vision Bin Laden and Ayiri had fantasized about in Afghanistan, back when the jihadists were confident that the Saudi people would rise up in revolt.

'The blood of our martyred brothers has watered the land of Muhammad,' a surprise thirtieth issue of *Voice of Jihad* would lament the following year. 'Their sacrifice is a testament to the true path in this time when supporters are few. No jihad front has been as abandoned as has the jihad front in the Arabian Peninsula. To those who have refused the call, we say: continue in your deep slumber if you will. But know this. Jihad will not cease, not until the Last Hour.'

Epilogue: A New Kind of Assassin

August 2009, three-and-a-half years later

Northern Yemen – mountainous, undeveloped, and lawless – had never been at the cutting edge of anything. But in summer 2009, it was catapulted into the cutting edge of advanced chemistry – specifically, the chemistry of blowing things up. The catalyst for this remarkable change in the region's global profile was that Al Qaeda's fighters there had grown active once again and had recently even started adopting Muqrin's old brand. Al Qaeda in the Arabian Peninsula was back from the dead.

Inside a remote Yemeni safe house, a handsome 27-year-old from Riyadh sat at a table strewn with bomb-making materials. Ibrahim al-Asiri was fast becoming one of the new AQAP's most prominent Saudi members. He had brought only a rudimentary knowledge of chemistry with him when he arrived in Yemen nearly three years before. However, the leader of the jihadists in Yemen, Osama bin Laden's former private secretary Nasser al-Wuhayshi, encouraged him to study it more deeply. He assigned Asiri to the network's explosives division.

Asiri's experiments focused on pentaerythritol tetranitrate, an extremely explosive substance called PETN for short. RDX had always been Al Qaeda's explosive-of-choice, but Asiri thought PETN was the future. In appearance a crystalline white powder, PETN had a lower vapour pressure than RDX. This meant far fewer of its molecules sublimated into the surrounding air, making a PETN bomb much easier to get past sniffer dogs. Also, a lower critical diameter meant a suicide bomber, for example, did not have to carry much of it to cause a tremendous amount of damage.

Asiri had been working on several ideas incorporating PETN. One was to hide a small but powerful charge inside an otherwise innocuous piece of machinery, such as an ordinary laser printer. Another was to manufacture an undergarment lined with PETN; lacking metal parts, it would enable a suicide bomber to pass through X-ray scanners undetected. But it was a third idea that had particularly impressed the leadership. By carrying explosives on their person, suicide bombers are relatively easy to spot at close quarters. If, however, they had no explosive vest and no visible wires, they would be much more effective assassins. To achieve this, Asiri was putting the finishing touches to a bomb capable of being hidden inside the bomber's rectum and triggered remotely by mobile phone. Made out of PETN and about six to eight inches long, apart from a small detonator and a mobile phone receiver the bomb had a bare minimum of electronic wiring. The bomber would pass through any security undeterred.

And Asiri's masters higher up the chain had determined who the first target was to be: Prince Muhammad bin Nayef.

The last vestiges of the first AQAP – the organization built up by Yusuf al-Ayiri and which reached its apogee under Abdulaziz al-Muqrin – may have been smothered at the Yarmouk neighbourhood raid after the abortive Abqaiq attack in February 2006. But Prince Muhammad had remained a painful thorn in the side of all the jihadists on the Peninsula. Asiri frequently recounted to himself the litany of abuses the brethren had suffered at the prince's hands. The MOI had been rounding up and imprisoning Saudi mujahideen returning from fighting in Iraq. When a group of them managed to escape from prison in Kharj in March 2006, the Mabahith tracked them down and, on 23 June, raided their safe house in Riyadh's Nakheel district. All six cell members were killed.[1] There was then another prison break in July 2006, this time from the Melez gaol in central Riyadh. Some of the escapees succeeded in leaving the country and carrying out terrorist attacks in Iraq and Lebanon. The others, however, were again hunted down by the Mabahith, who tracked them from safe house to safe house, rounding up twenty-one collaborators as they went.[2] The fugitives were finally coerced into giving themselves up during a showdown in Jeddah on 21 August, and by December 2006, Prince Muhammad's men had arrested a further 180 suspects.[3]

It was around that time that Asiri went to Yemen. He had grown up in a very strict home in Riyadh, and after dropping out of his university chemistry degree he joined a cell destined for Iraq. But the cell was uncovered in 2004 and he spent several months behind bars. During his incarceration he met other jihadists with whom he kept in touch after his release. He was on his way to join the group who had escaped from Kharj prison when he learned of their deaths in the Nakheel raid. That is when he decided to flee south.

He took his younger brother Abdullah with him. They were among the first Saudi Al Qaeda members to cross the border. For five weeks they negotiated the difficult mountain passes on foot, several times narrowly escaping detection from the Security Patrols that criss-crossed their route. The journey was particularly gruelling for the 20-year-old Abdullah. Unlike his well-built, academic older brother, Abdullah was slight of body and mind. Once in Yemen, therefore, when Ibrahim was told to hit the chemistry books and start building bombs, Abdullah was assigned to the kitchen. Yet he was well liked and praised for his piety.

That was over two years ago. Ever since, as the network in Yemen grew in strength and sophistication, both brothers had nursed a powerful hatred for Prince Muhammad. Everyone in the network had. The prince had thwarted their ambitions to achieve martyrdom in Iraq, had forced them to go on the run, and had caused hundreds of others to suffer in the same way. 'The brothers in Yemen have sworn an oath, pledging revenge on you for what you have done to our brothers in the Arabian Peninsula, Abdulaziz al-Muqrin, Yusuf al-Ayiri, and all the others,' exclaimed a fellow Saudi exile who shortly afterwards was killed in a confrontation with the Yemeni security services, assisted by Mabahith agents. 'God willing, we will relieve the hearts of believers, east and west, by cutting off your head, you pig!'[4]

Asiri reflected on the sophisticated plan that the leadership had come up with to assassinate the prince. The first stage was already in play and the cell awaited the return of a Yemeni operative, Muhammad al-Ghazali, who had been charged with gaining access to the prince and recording the MOI's security measures between the border and the prince's office. Ghazali had duly contacted some Yemenis who were known collaborators with the Saudi MOI and told them he spoke on behalf of prominent Al Qaeda members who had decided to hand themselves in. But they would only do so once Ghazali had negotiated the terms of their surrender with the prince in person. The Yemenis were suspicious, but put Ghazali in contact with an officer of the Saudi border guards. He in turn got in touch with the prince, who agreed to a meeting. Ghazali had then gone to the border and boarded a private jet for Jeddah.

The elder Asiri picked up the prototype suppository bomb and raised it into the lamplight. He felt confident that it was ready. Once Ghazali returned with his description of the prince's security measures and the bomber was sent on his way, the assassination would be a matter of a simple handshake. The question was, who was the best candidate for the job?

There was a knock on the door and the young Abdullah ventured in. He told his older brother that Ghazali had got in touch. The meeting with the prince had gone well. Everything was unfolding according to plan.

Not long afterwards, on the evening of 28 August, Prince Muhammad was still in Jeddah, struggling with the heat, the humidity, and the narrow streets thick with fumes. In 2009, however, Ramadan began in August, and because the Hijaz becomes such a hive of activity during Ramadan, the prince felt he was needed there more than he was in Riyadh. His Jeddah headquarters were relatively modest, two rows of cream-coloured offices, residential suites, and meeting rooms. He sat at his desk and considered how much had changed about his job over the years.

He had joined the MOI to streamline its administration, back in the years before Al Qaeda. However, counterterrorism was now a permanent feature of the prince's work. Ayiri's Al Qaeda franchise inside Saudi Arabia may have been no more, but the parent organization still remained, along with its sympathizers. And though the MOI was doing its best to prevent attacks, some terrorists had managed to slip through the net. In February 2007, the first fatal attack on Westerners in eighteen months occurred when four French tourists were killed north of Medina. Two of them were in fact Muslims, but their attackers – their ringleader Waleed al-Radadi was a known member of Al Qaeda – panicked before enquiring about their religion and opened fire immediately. Radadi and his accomplices were eventually hunted down. Then on 17 April of that year, the head of the Mabahith in Qaseem, Brigadier-General Nasser al-Othman, was killed at his farm in Buraydah after Al Qaeda members, assisted by Othman's own nephew, dug a small tunnel underneath the farm's security wall.

But in general, Prince Muhammad's focus had shifted to Yemen. Al Qaeda had always used that ill-governed country as a base, but between 2002 and 2006, when things were hottest in Saudi Arabia, President Saleh had managed to keep terrorist activity in Yemen to a minimum. Then, after President Bush's 'surge' deprived them of their Iraqi safe haven, and in response to better policing throughout the Muslim world, Al Qaeda again began looking to Yemen to fill the void.

In response, the Mabahith had cultivated close relations with the Yemeni security services and had even put undercover agents on the ground there. But the Yemeni situation had grown even more worrying when, earlier in 2009, on 12 January, a propaganda video celebrating the rebirth of Al Qaeda in the Arabian Peninsula appeared online. Seated on either side of AQAP's new leader Nasser al-Wuhayshi were two Saudis, Abu Sufyan (whose real name was Saeed al-Shihri) and Muhammad al-Oufi. Seeing them there gave Prince Muhammad a terrible shock. Both had been held at Guantánamo, but more importantly from the prince's point of view, after being transferred to Saudi custody at the end of 2007 they had participated in and graduated from a rehabilitation programme for extremists which the prince had founded at the end of 2006.

Called the Muhammad bin Nayef Centre for Counselling and Care – known as the Munasaha programme, from an Arabic word connoting both 'dialogue' and 'guidance' – it had been designed to bring the MOI's different rehabilitation programmes, in place from early 2004, under one umbrella. Its guiding principle was that, for all but the most radicalized, Al Qaeda's takfeeri ideology was treatable. In Prince Muhammad's view, jihadists were first and foremost victims of a sociological disorder and therefore patients in need of therapy.

Candidates for the programme were moved from prison into

a low-security residential campus on the outskirts of Riyadh. There they lived a communal life of work, study, and prayer, and were given regular access to their families and, when applicable, their wives. Religious re-education was a main ingredient in their treatment, but beyond questions of doctrine, what really made the programme stand out was its focus on psychological counselling. Life inside AQAP would often leave former members feeling depressed and paranoid, or, on the other side of the spectrum, with delusions of grandeur. Their families, too, were sometimes at a loss about how to deal with them and were offered counselling as well. The entire programme was oriented towards keeping graduates from reverting to Al Qaeda once they were allowed to return to their families. Counselling would continue and the MOI would help ease their way back into society, even providing employment or arranging marriage.

Prince Muhammad had assumed Abu Sufyan and Muhammad al-Oufi had become upstanding members of Saudi society. So he flew into a rage when he discovered that no one inside the Mabahith knew the two Munasaha graduates had even left the country. He subjected the Munasaha programme to an immediate review. It turned out that eighty-three graduates, including eleven former Guantánamo detainees, had relapsed. Most were in Yemen working on terrorist attacks with the newly resurrected AQAP.

Eighty-three out of the more than 2500 who had already passed through the programme or would go on to do so is in fact a statistically low rate of recidivism. Nevertheless, Abu Sufyan's and Oufi's backsliding had been a public embarrassment to the MOI, and Prince Muhammad responded with his customary combination of carrot and stick. The border police at the Yemeni border were beefed up and militarized, but even more importantly, the Saudi government announced another general amnesty which, in one very important case at least, worked: just over a month after the video's appearance, Muhammad al-Oufi turned himself in to Saudi officers at the border.[5]

That was six months ago, during which time the amnesty had remained in effect. Some people thought it was being extended beyond what was reasonable. The prince had therefore been gratified by a call from his border officers earlier that month. A young Yemeni AQAP member called Muhammad al-Ghazali, they had told him, wanted to negotiate the terms of surrender for Abu Sufyan and nine others who had split off from AQAP. Abu Sufyan wanted assurances that they would not be imprisoned or forced to appear on television. Ghazali was insisting, however, that he would only speak to the prince himself, and only in person.

In line with his custom from the very beginning, the prince had readily agreed to the face-to-face meeting. It was the Saudi way. And at the meeting with Ghazali a few days later, he had agreed that the ten penitents, who insisted on offering themselves up one by one, could return to their parole and that he would personally welcome them back into the fold of the faithful. The Mabahith were wary of the plan and advised the prince that the fugitives should be handed over to them first. But no, the prince was confident in the security measures his own team had in place. It was a matter of honour. He would meet them in person straight away.

He was waiting for the first penitent now. Ghazali had rung on 26 August to give the prince the penitent's name, Abdullah al-Asiri, and to say he would be waiting at the border. The prince had then sent his security officers to meet Abdullah at the border and fly him to Jeddah. After searching him thoroughly, they had given him the all-clear. As soon as everyone had broken their fast, Abdullah would be shown into the prince's majlis and the formal surrender would take place.

Skinny, trusting Abdullah stiffly leaned down and slipped into the back seat of the waiting car. Placing his hands on the black leather either side of his hips, he raised himself up a bit and slid into position. To bend as little at the waist as possible, he stretched out his legs awkwardly. He was not only uncomfortable, but he was suffering from hunger pangs as well. His brother had told him to eat as little as possible during the operation, to keep the bomb secure.

Not that any of that bothered him. He was on his way to his Lord. That was all that mattered.

The car pulled away from the kerb and Abdullah beamed. When Ibrahim had put him forward as a candidate for carrying out the assassination, he had felt so honoured. From childhood he had dreamed of passing over into the ultimate glory, of being a tool of God's justice and a receptacle of His mercy. 'God willing, in a few hours I will go to meet the Almighty,' he had stated in the impromptu suicide will he filmed just before the prince's agents met him at the border. 'I am setting off to harvest the head of that vicious man who fights against God day and night. I ask Him to accept me and to ease my path to Him.'

The streetlights of Jeddah whizzed past. Silently in his head, Abdullah recited a poem which his fellow martyr Saleh al-Oufi had composed for his mother.

A patient heart in the face of fate
  is a virtue deserving great reward.
I have never, God knows, muddied my feet
  with any disgraceful act.
I have to meet God sometime, mother.
  I am, after all, mortal.

He thought of the brethren he was leaving behind and of his older brother. They had shown him such favour, entrusting him with this task. He hoped they would join him soon.

The car pulled up to the prince's office. Thick foliage covered the broad arched portico lining the complex. Abdullah shifted in his seat, pushed the car door open, and heaved himself out. As he nimbly stepped towards the front door, he reflected on a promise he had made back in Yemen. 'This is my ammunition,' he had proclaimed, indicating a table of beakers filled with chemicals. Then he had picked up a hand grenade to symbolize the new kind of bomb his brother had invented for him. 'God willing, this will reach him. We shall give it to him, that is certain, and by God, we shall perfume it before we do.'

The majlis was very plain. The cream-coloured walls were lined with olive-green cushions and the floor was covered with Persian rugs. To one side sat an ordinary television set. It was a room not unlike millions of others throughout the Gulf.

Prince Muhammad greeted Abdullah warmly. He placed a friendly hand on his shoulder and showed him to his seat. The two men chatted amiably. The prince emphasized just how overjoyed he was that Abdullah had seen the light and decided to come home, and assured him that the others would receive a similar welcome. He was particularly looking forward to welcoming Abu Sufyan, he said, as well as Abdullah's brother Ibrahim.

'Well, sir,' Abdullah replied, 'in fact my brother asked me to ring him once you and I were finished with our discussions. He would like to send you his greetings.' The prince was more than happy to speak with Ibrahim and offered Abdullah the use of his own mobile phone.

'The meeting is going well,' the prince heard Abdullah say into the phone once Ibrahim was on the line. 'We're having a friendly chat. Prince Muhammad has confirmed everything. As soon as you arrive, a plane will bring you to Jeddah and we'll go to Mecca for *umra*. Our families will join us as well.' Abdullah smiled at the prince.

'As for any interrogation,' he continued. 'It'll be no different from before. Normal. And you can live wherever you like. If you decide you don't like a particular neighbourhood, they'll move you to a better one.' The line was bad and Abdullah had to raise his voice to be heard. 'Anyway, everything is fine. I'll give you to the prince.' Prince Muhammad extended his hand, but Abdullah was not quite finished. 'I would like to say one thing, though. Trust in God is the key to success in this life and the next.'

A soft beep then sounded from the other end of the line.

'Trust in God is the key to success in this life and the next,' Abdullah repeated. He exhaled calmly. 'Okay, I'll hand you over to the prince.'

Prince Muhammad took the phone. '*Salaam alaykum*!' he said heartily.

'*Wa alaykum as-salaam*,' crackled Ibrahim's reply.

'How are you, my brother? Are you well?'

'I am well, praise God. And you, sir? How are you?'

'All is well, all is well. But give me news of your health. How are you feeling?'

'All praise belongs to God, all is well.'

'I am truly delighted to be speaking to you . . .'

Before the prince was able to finish his sentence, Abdullah exploded.

The Saudi press called it a miracle. Despite being less than five feet away from the bomber, Prince Muhammad escaped with only minor injuries on his left hand. AQAP immediately trumpeted the prince's assassination, so he made sure to show himself in public the next day to dispel the rumour. He also rang Abdullah and Ibrahim's father to offer his condolences on the death of his son.

In the immediate aftermath, however, there was great confusion. The walls of the smoking majlis were spotted with pieces of flesh and specks of blood. The security services had no idea how the bomb had been smuggled in. Everyone was a suspect. The prince's men were taken outside and questioned. They sat slumped on the pavement in shock. Some were in tears.

In time, the truth was discovered and news of the suppository bomb spread like wildfire. The world contemplated this newest horror with a combination of fear and macabre fascination. But because the bomb was metal-free, it had no shrapnel, and most of the bomb's force had been absorbed by Abdullah's body. His torso had separated from his legs and his left arm had been ripped off, shooting straight upwards. Investigators removed it later from a hole in the ceiling.

Before long, AQAP released a video that claimed the assassination attempt, despite its apparent failure, had actually been a great success. 'To God belongs all praise,' thundered Abu Sufyan's weathered, wrathful face, 'for he has enabled the mujahideen to penetrate your security bubble. You may have succeeded in restricting our activities inside our homeland, but by God we swear we shall spare no effort in our war with you. Our special operations will continue, operations so terrifying that they will whiten the hair of your youngest children.

'I say to you, O prince: You once declared you had put an end to Al Qaeda, that it no longer existed. Yet not only do your most-wanted lists continue to grow along with the number of mujahideen embarking upon the path of jihad. But it is also now known throughout the world that we are able to cross the threshold of your own palaces.'

The war with Al Qaeda is not over.

Ibrahim al-Asiri, from his hideout in the mountains of Yemen, has been behind a number of similarly bold bombing attempts. He is suspected of being behind the infamous underpants bomb on Northwest Airlines Flight 253, which failed to go off on Christmas Day 2009 when the bomber, a Nigerian called Umar Farouk Abdulmutallab, botched the detonation in flight. He is also thought to have been behind the bombs in the failed October 2010 cargo planes bomb plot, in which PETN explosives hidden inside Hewlett-Packard laser printers and smuggled on board planes bound from Yemen to the United States were located and defused before they reached their destination, largely thanks to the Mabahith's intelligence work. These inventions spooked the world counterterrorism community and are the reason why air passengers are now frequently subjected to full-body X-ray scanners at airports.[6]

The thwarted attacks proved that AQAP, though it continued to harass the Saudi authorities and was still working toward revolution in the Kingdom, had matured into a genuinely international branch of Al Qaeda. The increasingly popular English-language lectures of Anwar al-Awlaki, a Yemeni-American ideologue close to the leadership, made AQAP the destination of choice for Western jihadists. As such, it became an increasingly important battleground in America's war on terror. The Obama administration's controversial programme of drone strikes in Yemen – controversial not only because of civilian collateral damage but also because they have targeted American citizens without trial, including Awlaki himself, who was killed in 2011 – has been relatively effective at containing the threat. That effort has received invaluable assistance from the Saudis, whose undercover Mabahith agents inside Yemen are frequently sources of vital intelligence.

Prince Muhammad was made interior minister in November 2012, a few months after the death of his father Prince Nayef. In just over a decade, Prince Muhammad had managed to make great strides in transforming the MOI into an effective terrorist-fighting force. At the same time, his efforts to rehabilitate terrorists began to be emulated in countries across the Middle East and beyond, including by the United States, which drew on the Munasaha programme when redesigning their detainee policies in Iraq.[7] For these and many other reasons, the prince's tenure as head of Saudi counterterrorism has been a success.

Of course, the future is always an open question. For the ever-adaptive Al Qaeda, control of the Holy Places and the Kingdom's oil reserves remains the Big Prize. At the time of writing, however, Al Qaeda no longer poses a serious immediate threat to the Saudi state or its people. AQAP in Yemen has suffered many losses. Security at the borders is much more robust than in the past and the MOI's security services as a whole have over a decade's worth of counterterrorism experience behind them.

More than anything, it is Syria that looms largest on the Mabahith's horizon. Once again, Saudi citizens are at the front lines of a foreign jihad, parts of which are dominated by Al Qaeda affiliates. Once again, as the most outspoken supporter of the Syrian opposition, the Saudi government is politically and financially involved in international Islamist militancy, just as it was in the 1980s and 1990s in Afghanistan. And once again, battle-hardened Saudi fighters are returning home.

However, the men of the Mabahith – no longer naïvely quiescent as they were in the run-up to the Riyadh compound bombings – are confident that they have the necessary systems in place to deal with any potential threat. And the Saudi people – torn, as ever, between liberalizing moderates and cast-iron reactionaries – are determined that the spectre of Islamist terrorism will never again be raised inside Saudi Arabia.

Was Al Qaeda in the Arabian Peninsula's campaign to overthrow the Saudi government bound to fail? Almost certainly.

The Organization's strategy assumed that the majority of Saudis seethed with rage at what they considered to be a pro-Western, irreligious establishment. It believed it could harness and direct that rage towards revolution by attacking first Western and then government targets. However, the Saudi people were not as anti-House of Saud or anti-Western as the Organization supposed. They did not regard the presence of Westerners inside the Kingdom, even American military personnel, a significant insult to the sovereignty or sanctity of the state, a position which was only strengthened by the withdrawal of most American servicemen in August 2003, three months into AQAP's campaign. So the numerous recruits Ayiri and Muqrin assumed would flock to Al Qaeda's banner never materialized. Instead, public opinion was quick to turn against AQAP, and ordinary Saudis ended up making an invaluable contribution to the fight against them. This was the major reason for the Organization's failure.

This lack of wider public support shows that Saudi Arabia's state-sanctioned Wahhabism – fundamentalist though it is and therefore linked to the spread of Islamic fundamentalism internationally – is not synonymous with Al Qaeda's brand of takfeerist jihadism. Ironically, Western commentators often view Saudi Arabians much as Bin Laden did, as angry extremists ready to rush into violence. But like most people, Saudis actually prioritize security and the rule of law and so, when terrorism reared its head at home, they stood firmly behind their government.

The government's counter-propaganda campaign played a role in this, along with their crackdown on extremist preachers. So did initiatives like the Center for National Dialogue which, however superficially, encouraged moderation and tolerance and widened the scope for public participation in social issues. But perhaps more than anything, keeping the citizenry on side was simply a matter of luck. Between 2003 and 2008, the price of oil reached unprecedented heights. Had the oil price remained as stagnant as it had been in the 1990s, when at one time state revenues sank so low that the government could not afford to put petrol in police cars, then an impoverished and discontented Saudi populace might have been much more receptive to AQAP's message.

For civil unrest is not wholly unimaginable in Saudi Arabia. Protests inspired by the Arab Spring have occurred inside the country, mainly staged by discontented Shi'ites in the Eastern Province. Indeed, the threat was deemed significant enough for King Abdullah to introduce a package of benefits amounting to

$10.7 billion in February 2011. It proved once again that as long as the House of Saud spreads the wealth around enough to keep people happy, their rule is secure.

There is another reason for AQAP's failure: incompetence. The leadership did not know how to carry out a revolution. Their bag of tricks was limited to urban, guerrilla-style terrorism, and their strategy never progressed beyond the vague fantasy, inspired by apocalyptic expectations, that a mass uprising was imminent. High-level Mabahith officers believe Ayiri's early death was the movement's death knell; he was the only serious strategic thinker among AQAP's leaders. Had Ayiri been in more direct control and survived longer, the Organization's approach might have been more canny.

As it happened, the means by which most successful revolutionaries realize their aims – patient cultivation of public opinion; infiltration of one or more of the most vital arms of the state, especially the military; recruitment of respected establishment figures, perhaps a prominent member of the royal family; and politically savvy acts of violence and targeted assassinations – were not well pursued by AQAP. Such considerations were not wholly absent; the Organization adopted a propaganda programme, tried to enlist clerics with authority, and thought that its targets were of strategic value, especially at the outset. But their moves had not been properly thought through. As explained above, they misjudged public opinion, and the clerics were also quick to distance themselves from takfeerism as soon as it manifested itself in terrorist attacks. Locked into a failing strategy, the Organization's leaders were not cunning enough to formulate something more workable. It did not help that their recruits were unintelligent, undisciplined, and often buffoonish. AQAP never evolved into anything more than a well-armed criminal gang, murderous but ineffectual.

The war in Iraq also played a role. There the case for jihad was more straightforward: a Muslim country had been invaded by a non-Muslim army. Saudis predisposed to jihad were able to sign up for Zarqawi's Al Qaeda franchise with fewer scruples. Not that Al Qaeda in Mesopotamia pursued a radically different strategy from the one adopted by AQAP. They did not, and it had similar consequences, at least in the short term: the Iraqi people by and large turned against them and they lost whatever religious legitimacy they had had in the eyes of mainstream clerics. Nevertheless, the Iraqi jihad did syphon off potential fighters from the pool of recruits targeted by AQAP, which was another factor in the Organization's failure.

None of this would have mattered, however, had the MOI's counterterrorism campaign, led by Prince Muhammad, been less well conducted. Though the government was initially slow to perceive the terrorist threat within its borders, despite warnings from their American allies and others, then-Crown Prince Abdullah summoned the political will to deal with the problem. He gave Prince Muhammad the authority to act in his name, which was an immense help. In a culture which prioritizes consensus over unilateral action, Prince Muhammad could have seen his counterterrorism strategy hobbled by fraternal infighting and bureaucratic obstructionism had he not received the crown prince's imprimatur.

That strategy was multi-faceted. The MOI's police and paramilitary units needed better equipment and specialist training, and they got it. Even more vitally, Prince Muhammad refocused the Mabahith's expertise, from merely keeping tabs on internal dissent and countering domestic threats to the royal family's rule, to collecting actionable intelligence on an international terrorist organization bent on attacking not only government targets, but also Saudi and non-Saudi civilians. This entailed forging creative intelligence-sharing partnerships with key allies, especially Britain, France, and, above all, the United States.

The fallout over 9/11 had strained US–Saudi relations, and politics always threatened to get in the way of productive cooperation. Had Prince Muhammad not found sympathetic partners within the Bush Administration who were willing to work creatively with the Saudis, not only on intelligence but also on the ever-important question of terrorist financing, things might have turned out differently.[8] The relationship the prince forged with Frances Townsend, President Bush's homeland security advisor, was vital to the success of that important partnership, as was her work, along with others, to facilitate a joint CIA–Mabahith intelligence-sharing task force.

For the actual fight, Prince Muhammad pursued a robust policy of carrot and stick. The stick he wielded was well financed – over the course of the war, the state spent over $30 billion on counterterrorism. There was little shortage of either manpower or weaponry. Although the MOI's soldiers were instructed never to initiate violence against the enemy, they did not hesitate to meet violence in kind. They also felt fewer misgivings than their counterparts in Western agencies about collateral damage to persons or property. Undoubtedly mistakes were made, but Prince Muhammad's response to them was no less robust: admit them and learn from them, yes, but do not flagellate yourself over them. Fear of public criticism, he believed, destroys morale and cripples the security services' willingness to take the risks that are necessary when facing an enemy like Al Qaeda.[9]

That enemy Prince Muhammad refused to dehumanize or demonize, an approach which was largely mirrored by Saudi society at large. The Munasaha programme was the most concrete manifestation of this benevolent, paternal attitude, but it coloured the MOI's entire 'soft' counterterrorism strategy and also informed initiatives like the Sakeena campaign to combat extremism online. It must be borne in mind that Al Qaeda members are perceived differently in the Kingdom from how they are perceived elsewhere. To Westerners in particular, jihadists are an entirely foreign enemy; everything about them – their dress, their language, their religion, everything – is alien, an impression which has surely informed penal policy in places like Abu Ghraib and Guantánamo Bay. To other Saudis, however, Saudi jihadists are brothers, cousins, neighbours; they inspire immediate sympathy, not for their ideas or actions, but for the culture they share.

This is plainly evident from the way Mabahith officers talk about them. As of 2013, the security services had detained around 11,000 terrorist suspects and held 2,772 in prison awaiting trial.[10] But to the MOI's intelligence officers, Al Qaeda's recruits are not demons. They are wayward youths in need of rehabilitation. More than anger or disgust, their misguided brothers provoke in the Mabahith a profound sense of sadness.

Glossary

Abaya (عباءة / عباية) Loose, full-length over-garment, normally black, worn by women across the Muslim world. It is sometimes combined with other garments (such as the *niqab*, a type of face veil), and is compulsory for all women in Saudi Arabia.

Adab (الأدب) Concept that originally referred to the customs that the Arabs inherited from their ancestors; *adab* came to refer to good manners, eloquence in speech, and fluency in writing, and thus also literature.

Al-Nida (النداء, lit. *The Summons*) The name given to an Al Qaeda website founded by Yusuf al-Ayiri and Isa al-Awshen in 2001.

Al Qaeda (القاعدة, lit. *the base*) Global militant Islamist organization founded in the late 1980s by Osama bin Laden.

Al Qaeda in the Arabian Peninsula (AQAP) (القاعدة في جزيرة العرب) Franchise of the Al Qaeda network within the Arabian Peninsula, known simply as 'the Organization' by the Saudi security services. Al Qaeda members reject the authority of the House of Saud, so they use the term 'Arabian Peninsula' instead of Saudi Arabia, where AQAP was founded. After AQAP's failure in the Kingdom, the franchise relocated to Yemen, where it remains active today.

Allahu akbar (الله أكبر, lit. *God is greater*) A common Arabic expression used in the call to prayer, during the prayer, and as a pious exclamation (e.g. of joy, distress, or determination).

Awakening, the (الصحوة, pronounced *as-sahwa*) A non-violent clerical reformist movement which developed in the 1980s and early 1990s in Saudi Arabia. The Awakening clerics criticized the Saudi government for not conforming to traditional Islamic values and for subservience to the West. The movement was subject to a severe crackdown by Saudi authorities in the mid-1990s, during which time many of its leaders were imprisoned. Osama bin Laden drew on the writings of Awakening clerics such as Safar al-Hawali as he developed Al Qaeda's distinctive ideology.

Badr, Battle of (غزوة بدر) A battle fought in AD 624 in which vastly outnumbered Muslim forces led by the Prophet Muhammad defeated pagan forces from the Quraysh tribe of Mecca. Two years before, persecution of the early Muslim community by the Quraysh had compelled Muhammad to flee Mecca for Medina.

Baraka (بركة, lit. *blessing*) In Islam, a blessing from God.

Bismillah (بسم الله , lit. *in the name of God*) The first words of the opening phrase of all but one chapter of the Qur'an: 'In the name of God, the Merciful, the Compassionate.' The *bismillah* is invoked in numerous contexts by Muslims, both in prayer and as a blessing (e.g. before eating).

Caliphate (الخلافة) An Islamic state led by a supreme religious as well as political leader known as a caliph, from an Arabic word meaning 'successor', i.e. a successor to the Prophet Muhammad.

Camp of the Sabre (معسكر البتّار) Name of an AQAP training camp established in Saudi Arabia, attended by members of the Organization and featured in propaganda material. Also, the name of a magazine published by the Organization detailing military tactics and training.

Clerics (العلماء, pronounced *ulama,* lit. *those who are knowledgeable*) The community of Islamic scholars, including those qualified to issue religious judgements such as fatwas.

Eid al-Adha (عيد الأضحى, lit. *feast of the sacrifice*) An important Muslim festival which commemorates Abraham's willingness to sacrifice his son Ishmael to God. Sometimes referred to as 'Greater Eid', it falls on the tenth day of the twelfth month in the Islamic calendar. Another festival of a similar name, *Eid al-Fitr* (or 'Lesser Eid'), takes place at the end of Ramadan.

Emir (أمير) An Arabic title. In a military context, the title refers to a commander or a general; in the context of royalty, the title normally refers to a prince.

Fatiha, the (الفاتحة, lit. *the Opening*) The first chapter of the Qur'an, made up of seven verses. The Fatiha forms the basis of Muslim prayer rituals.

Fatwa (فتوى) A legal judgement or ruling issued by a qualified religious scholar. A fatwa can respond to an individual Muslim's request for guidance from a scholar, or may be a command for the Muslim community as a whole.

Fitna (فتنة, lit. *strife*) The concept of *fitna* refers to civil strife or discord, and the term is used historically to refer to periods of internal conflict or upheaval within the Muslim community.

Hadith (الحديث, lit. *piece of information, tradition*) In Islam, reports of the sayings and doings of the Prophet Muhammad, as recorded and passed on by members of the early Muslim community. *Hadith* form the basis of Islamic law and Qur'anic exegesis.

Hajj (الحجّ) The pilgrimage to Mecca which takes place in the twelfth month of the Islamic calendar. One of the Five Pillars of Islam, the Hajj is obligatory at least once in a lifetime for all Muslims who are physically and financially able to perfom it.

Haram (حــرام, lit. *forbidden*) Term designating actions that are forbidden under Islamic law. Its opposite is *halal*.

Houris (حورية، حوريات، حور العين) Companions for pious Muslim men in the afterlife, commonly referred to as the Heavenly Virgins. Accounts as to their physical characteristics, number (often seventy-two), and role differ in Islamic sources. The etymology of the word is not precisely known; it may come from a word signifying the contrast between the white of the eye and the black of the iris.

House of Saud (آل سـعود, in Arabic *Al Saud*) The ruling family of Saudi Arabia. The Kingdom is the only country in the world to be named after its royal family. The dynasty stretches back to the eighteenth century, but reached international prominence in 1932 when King Abdulaziz, often referred to as Ibn Saud, founded the modern Kingdom after unifying much of the Arabian Peninsula.

Iftar (إفــطار, lit. *breakfast*) Specifically, the evening meal with which Muslims break their fast at sunset during Ramadan.

Imam (إمام) In Sunni Islam, the worship leader of a mosque.

Inshallah (إن شــاء الله, lit. *if God wills*) A common Arabic phrase used to express a desire that an event will occur in the future.

Intifada (انتفاضة, lit. *shaking off*) A twentieth-century neologism used to describe an uprising against perceived tyranny, most famously used to describe the mass Palestinian uprisings against the Israeli state from 1987 to 1993 and from 2000 to 2005.

Islamism/Islamist (الإسـلامـية/الإسـلامي) Generally, terms used to describe the extension and application of Islamic beliefs and principles in the political and social spheres, and those who practise such application. Often referred to as 'political Islam', Islamism is a wide-ranging spectrum of ideas; more extreme Islamists call for the complete reworking of society and government based around Islamic principles. In the West, Islamism usually carries connotations of Islamic fundamentalist ideology and, often, the militancy and violence associated with this phenomenon.

Istiraha (استراحة) Translated as *rest house*, an *istiraha* is a detached building with basic amenities for cooking and usually an outside space, typically rented by families in the Gulf to host large family gatherings. Al Qaeda would rent them as hideouts on the outskirts of urban areas.

Jihad (جهاد, lit. *struggle*) In Islam, jihad refers to numerous struggles, ranging from a Muslim's internal struggle to practise his faith, to the struggle to build a cohesive Muslim community. The term has taken on wider connotations of violent struggle by Muslims against non-Muslims and is therefore sometimes translated as 'holy war'. *See also* Mujahideen.

Karamat (كرامات, lit. *marks of honour*) In Islam, miracles, particularly those occurring around martyrs.

Mabahith, the (المباحث, lit. *investigations*) The name by which the General Investigation Directorate, the Saudi Ministry of Interior's internal security service, is popularly known.

Majlis (مجلس, lit. *place for sitting*) A seating area, usually in a home, and traditionally provided with cushions on the floor.

Miswak (مسواك) A small twig from the *salvadora persica* tree used as both a toothpick and, traditionally, a toothbrush.

Muezzin (مؤذّن) A person appointed to recite the Muslim call to prayer.

Mufti (مفتي) In general, someone who issues a legal judgement or ruling known as a fatwa. In countries such as Saudi Arabia, the Grand Mufti is appointed by the king and occupies the most senior position of religious authority, issuing judgements on both legal and social issues.

Mujahideen (مجاهدون, lit. *those who struggle*, sing. *mujahid*) The name applied to those Muslims who participate in military jihad. The term was used to describe the opposition groups who fought against the Soviet-backed government in Afghanistan, and in other instances of jihad such as Bosnia and Chechnya. The term is now closely associated with radical, militant Islamists.

Muslim Brotherhood, the (الإخوان المسلمون) An Islamist political organization founded by Hassan al-Banna in Egypt in 1928, the movement was violently suppressed by the rulers of both Egypt and Syria, but supported in many quarters in Saudi Arabia. The Brotherhood is officially banned in the Kingdom, though its presence has long been tolerated.

Mutaween (المطوّعين) Agents for the Committee for the Promotion of Virtue and Prosecution of Vice, a volunteer police force tasked with enforcing Sharia law across Saudi Arabia, including dress codes and the separation of men and women in public spaces.

Northern Alliance (التحالف الشمالي الأفغاني) Military front formed by leaders of the Islamic State of Afghanistan in late 1996. The multi-ethnic group fought against the predominantly Pashtun Taliban. The Northern Alliance split into distinct political entities after the US-led invasion of Afghanistan in 2001.

Ottoman Empire (الإمبراطورية العثمانية) Multi-ethnic Muslim state ruled by members of the Turkish Osman dynasty. The empire existed between 1299 and 1923 with its capital in Istanbul from 1453 onwards, and extended across much of the Muslim world, including the Levant, Egypt, and coastal areas of the Arabian Peninsula.

Qur'an, the (القرآن) The central religious text in Islam, considered a revelation from God to His Prophet, Muhammad. The Qur'an is divided into 114 chapters (known as *surahs*) of varying length, which were revealed to Muhammad over a period of twenty-three years. The text is one of the foundations of the Islamic legal system.

Ramadan (شهر رمضان) The ninth month of the Islamic calendar, in which Muslims observe a period of fasting every day between sunrise and sunset. The festival of Eid al-Fitr (lit. *feast of breaking the fast*) occurs at the end of Ramadan.

Sacred Months, the (الأشهر الحرم) The four months of the Islamic calendar (Muharram, Rajab, Dhu al-Qid'ah, and Dhu al-Hijjah) during which fighting and warfare are traditionally not permitted.

Salafism (السلفية) A fundamentalist Islamic movement that uses the practices of the earliest Muslims and their community as the basis for their own practices.

Shahada, the (الشهادة, lit. *testimony*) In Islam, the fundamental declaration of faith shared by all Muslims; it asserts belief in the oneness of God and the acceptance of Muhammad as His Prophet. The typical wording of the Shahada is: 'There is no god but God, and Muhammad is His Prophet.'

Sharia, the (الشريعة, lit. *the pathway to water*) The religious law of Islam, which is based on the revelation made by God in the Qur'an and the acts and sayings of the Prophet Muhammad as defined in the *hadith*. The Sharia forms the basis of the Saudi Arabian legal system. In its strictest terms, the Sharia is believed to be the infallible law of God, unlike human legal judgements and rulings.

Sheesha (شيشة) A type of water pipe common across the Arab and Muslim world, and used to smoke tobacco, usually flavoured. Also known as a *hookah* or *narghile*.

Sheikh (شيخ, lit. *elder*) An honorific title used as a mark of respect across the Arabic-speaking world. The term is used when referring to anyone who is worthy of respect or veneration owing to their age or achievements, and is commonly used in the Arabian Peninsula as a designation of a renowned and capable religious scholar. Osama bin Laden was often referred to by his followers simply as 'the Sheikh'.

Shemagh (شماغ) Saudi name for the cotton headdress worn by Arabs. Also known as *keffiyeh*.

Shura Council (مجلس الشورى) A council of advisers, from the word meaning 'consultation'.

Subha (سبحة) A string of prayer beads used by Muslims. Similar in design to a Catholic rosary, the *subha* helps Muslims to keep count of the invocations made in their prayers. Also known as a *misbaha* or a *sibha*.

Sunni–Shia split (أهل السنة/الشيعة) The rift between the Sunni and the Shia, the two largest denominations within Islam. The majority of Muslims are Sunni, while the Shia account for the largest minority. Both share the fundamental beliefs and articles of faith in Islam, and the division between them can be traced to the issue of leadership in the early Islamic community. While Sunnis believe that the series of caliphs who followed the Prophet Muhammad were his legitimate successors, Shias trace the line of legitimate succession through the Prophet's cousin and son-in-law Ali and a series of imams who followed him. While the division between the two groups was, initially, political, the split has grown to encompass a number of social, cultural, and theological differences between Muslim groups. Antagonism between the two denominations has, historically, been widespread, and violence between the Sunni and the Shia continues to the present day. As part of its takfeeri ideology, Al Qaeda has denounced the Shia as heretics.

Takfeer (التكفير) In Islam, the act of accusing a fellow Muslim of unbelief. *Takfeer* is a feature of the ideology of AQAP and other Islamist extremist groups, who commonly not only refer to their foreign enemies – such as the Americans, the British, and the Israelis – as *kafir*s, or unbelievers, but also apply this label to the House of Saud.

Taraweeh (تــراويح) In Islam, prayers performed during the nights of Ramadan. These prayers are not compulsory.

Tawheed (الــتوحــيد) In Islam, the doctrine of monotheism that recognizes the oneness of God and rejects polytheism, or the belief in multiple deities, which is known as *shirk*. The centrality of the concept of *tawheed* is emphasized by the wording of the Shahada, or declaration of faith: 'There is no god but God, and Muhammad is His Prophet.'

Thobe (ثــوب, lit. *a garment*) An ankle-length robe with long sleeves worn by men across the Arabian Peninsula. Similar robes are worn across the Islamic world.

Two Holy Mosques, the (الحــرمــين الشــريــفين, pronounced *al-haramain al-sharifain*) Epithet of the two most important mosques in Islam, both located within Saudi Arabia: the Grand Mosque at Mecca and the Mosque of the Prophet in Medina. In 1986, King Fahd bin Abdulaziz adopted the title of Custodian of the Two Holy Mosques (*Khadim al-Haramain al-Sharifain*).

Umma (الأمّة, lit. *the community*) The Muslim community that is said to transcend geographical and political boundaries, uniting Muslims across the world. 'Umma' can be used to refer to a specific group of Muslims, but is more commonly used to describe Muslims as a whole.

Umra (عــمرة) In Islam, the 'minor pilgrimage', i.e. a pilgrimage to Mecca performed at any time of the year. It is not compulsory but highly recommended.

Voice of Jihad (صــوت الــجهاد, in Arabic *Sawt al-Jihad*) Propaganda magazine published fortnightly by AQAP between October 2003 and November 2004, featuring interviews with militants, accounts of operations and battles, and news from the jihadist community. Two isolated issues appeared in May 2005 and February 2007.

Wahhabism (الــوهــابــية) A puritanical, fundamentalist Islamic movement named after the eighteenth-century cleric

Muhammad ibn Abd al-Wahhab. Abd al-Wahhab made a pact with a member of the Saud dynasty that led to the formation of the first Saudi state (the Emirate of Diriyah). Descendants of Abd al-Wahhab have traditionally led the Saudi religious establishment.

Zakat (الزكاة, lit. *purification*) One of the Five Pillars of Islam, *zakat* is the practice of alms-giving or charitable giving by Muslims. It is a personal obligation incumbent on all Muslims who are able to do so.

Timeline

20 November 1979 A group of radical Islamists led by Juhayman al-Utaybi violently takes over the Grand Mosque in Mecca. The Saudi security services besiege the mosque for two weeks before retaking it. Hundreds of people are killed, including 127 soldiers, and most of the militants are executed. The episode leads the government to enforce the implementation of stricter Islamic practices throughout the Kingdom.

December 1979 Soviet forces arrive in Afghanistan. Afghan and foreign mujahideen fight against the Soviet forces and the communist government they support.

August 1988 Osama bin Laden founds Al Qaeda.

February 1989 Soviet forces withdraw from Afghanistan.

7 August 1990 In the run-up to the first Gulf War, American forces begin arriving in Saudi Arabia at the invitation of King Fahd.

17 January 1991 Operation Desert Storm marks the start of the Gulf War between Iraq and US-led coalition forces. A ceasefire comes into effect on 28 February.

March 1992–December 2005 The Bosnian War, part of the wider conflicts during the disintegration of Yugoslavia, begins. Arab mujahideen fight on the side of the Bosnian Muslims against the Serbs and, later, the Croats.

September 1994 The Saudi government begins a crackdown on the Awakening, a radical clerical reformist movement.

December 1994–August 1996 The first Chechen War. Foreign mujahideen participate in the conflict.

13 November 1995 A car bomb at the offices of the Vinnell Corporation off Olaya Street, Riyadh, kills seven, including five Americans. Five veterans of the anti-Soviet jihad in Afghanistan, believed to have been affiliates of Bin Laden, are charged with carrying out the bombing, and are executed.

25 June 1996 A truck bomb at the Khobar Towers housing complex near Dhahran kills nineteen American military personnel.

August 1996 Bin Laden issues his first fatwa, entitled 'A Declaration of War against the Americans Occupying the Land of the Two Holy Mosques'.

September 1996 The Taliban establish the Islamic Emirate of Afghanistan.

February 1998 A statement called 'Jihad Against Jews and Crusaders' is issued by the World Islamic Front, including Bin Laden.

7 August 1998 Al Qaeda attacks on American embassies in Nairobi (Kenya) and Dar es Salaam (Tanzania) kill over 200 people.

13 May 1999 Prince Muhammad bin Nayef is appointed assistant interior minister for security affairs.

August 1999–May 2000 The second Chechen War. Foreign mujahideen participate in the fighting. A guerrilla war continues until 2009.

July 2000 Yusuf al-Ayiri travels to Afghanistan and meets Bin Laden. He agrees to set up a branch of Al Qaeda inside Saudi Arabia.

12 October 2000 A suicide attack on the USS *Cole* in the port of Aden kills seventeen American military personnel. The attack was orchestrated by Abdul Rahim al-Nashiri.

20 January 2001 George W. Bush is inaugurated President of the United States.

11 September 2001 Al Qaeda launches coordinated suicide attacks that kill nearly 3000 people and injure over 6000 in New York and Washington, DC.

7 October 2001 US-led NATO forces launch Operation Enduring Freedom and invade Afghanistan.

October 2001 President Bush appoints Robert Jordan as ambassador to Saudi Arabia.

December 2001 After the battle of Tora Bora and the fall of Kandahar, Al Qaeda fighters begin fleeing Afghanistan.

February–March 2002 Al Qaeda leaders meet in Karachi, where Khalid Sheikh Muhammad is made responsible for operations outside Afghanistan and Pakistan. KSM appoints Abdul Rahim al-Nashiri to lead terrorist operations in the Arabian Peninsula.

March 2002 US-led NATO forces launch Operation Anaconda against remaining Al Qaeda and Taliban forces in Afghanistan.

12 June 2002 Nashiri arrives in Saudi Arabia along with his deputy Khalid al-Hajj and head of military operations Abdulaziz al-Muqrin.

6 October 2002 The *Limburg*, a French oil tanker, is bombed in the Gulf of Aden. The attack was orchestrated by Nashiri.

12 October 2002 Three coordinated bombs target the tourist resort of Kuta on the Indonesian island of Bali, killing over 200. Jemaah Islamiah, a terrorist group affiliated to Al Qaeda, is blamed.

2 November 2002 Radical cleric Abdullah al-Rashoud leads a confrontation between religious students and Saudi security forces at the General Presidency of Islamic Research and Fatwas in Riyadh.

8 November 2002 Nashiri is arrested in the UAE by members of the CIA.

18 March 2003 Fahd al-Saidi, a member of Al Qaeda who has recently returned from Afghanistan, accidentally sets off an explosive device, killing himself and alerting the authorities to the Organization's activities in Riyadh.

20 March 2003 Forces under a US-led coalition of over forty nations begin Operation Iraqi Freedom.

9 April 2003 Baghdad falls to American forces, inspiring Saudi mujahideen to travel to Iraq.

29 April 2003 American forces are withdrawn from their bases in Saudi Arabia, which they had used to launch attacks on Iraq, and relocated to Qatar.

8 May 2003 The MOI releases the List of Nineteen. Turki al-Dandani, leader of a nationwide network of cells, heads the list of most-wanted.

12 May 2003 Riyadh compound bombings. Al Qaeda launches three coordinated car bomb attacks on residential compounds in the capital, killing twenty-seven people and wounding over two hundred, mostly foreigners working in the Kingdom.

30 May 2003 Ayiri dies in a confrontation with police while fleeing from a security patrol.

26 June 2003 Ali al-Faqasi, leader of a network of cells in the Hijaz, turns himself in to the MOI. His surrender was mediated by the cleric Safar al-Hawali.

3 July 2003 A raid leads to the deaths of Dandani and four other militants. Hajj, the official leader of Al Qaeda in Saudi Arabia, goes into hiding, and Muqrin effectively takes over.

5 August 2003 Frances Townsend, deputy national security advisor for combating terrorism under President Bush, meets Prince Muhammad for the first time to discuss counterterrorism issues. Regular meetings lead to the establishment of a joint CIA–Mabahith intelligence-sharing task force.

September 2003 The first issue of *Voice of Jihad* is published.

23 September 2003 Jazan hospital siege. A confrontation between militants and the security forces in an apartment block attached to the hospital in Jazan leads to the death of Faqasi's deputy Sultan al-Qahtani.

1 November 2003 Reports emerge about the abuse of Iraqi prisoners at the Abu Ghraib prison near Baghdad.

8 November 2003 Muhaya bombing. A car bomb attack against the Muhaya compound in west Riyadh kills seventeen people and wounds over 100. An attack simultaneously targeting the Emergency Forces headquarters is called off.

4 December 2003 Saudi Major-General Abdulaziz al-Huwayrini is wounded in a gun attack by militants. The previously unknown Haramain Brigades claim responsibility. It soon becomes clear that the Brigades are a cover for Al Qaeda attacks that may be perceived negatively.

6 December 2003 The MOI releases its List of Twenty-Six. Muqrin tops the list.

11 December 2003 James Oberwetter replaces Robert Jordan as American ambassador to Saudi Arabia.

17 December 2003 The United States allows its non-essential diplomatic staff to leave Saudi Arabia, citing security concerns.

29 January 2004 The father of Riyadh cell member Khalid al-Farraj is killed in a confrontation between militants and security forces. This leads Farraj to recant. He becomes a valuable source of information for the MOI.

28 February 2004 A royal decree establishes the Saudi National Commission for Relief and Charity Work Abroad, which aims to ensure that charitable donations from Saudi citizens go towards humanitarian, not terrorist, causes.

March 2004 Muqrin begins planning Operation Volcano, a multiple truck bombing that will target Riyadh's Diplomatic Quarter and a residential compound.

11 March 2004 Ten explosions aboard four commuter trains in Madrid kill 191 people and injure 1800. Twenty-one militant Islamists are later convicted of the attack.

15 March 2004 Hajj is killed by security forces in an ambush in Riyadh. Muqrin formally becomes leader.

17 March 2004 Muqrin formally names the organization under his leadership Al Qaeda in the Arabian Peninsula (AQAP).

13 April 2004 Muqrin is forced to abandon Operation Volcano after a safe house belonging to his cell in Riyadh is raided and several of the car bombs prepared for the attack have to be abandoned as they are being moved to the capital. Arms smuggler Rakan al-Saikhan is mortally wounded in the raid.

15 April 2004 The United States evacuates most of its diplomats from Saudi Arabia and urges its citizens to leave the country, owing to 'credible and specific intelligence' of an imminent attack.

21 April 2004 Washm Street bombing. Five people are killed, including an 11-year-old girl, and nearly 150 are wounded in a car bomb attack on the General Directorate of Traffic on Washm Street in Riyadh.

22 April 2004 A raid on a Riyadh villa uncovers a large amount of video material prepared by militants. The villa was used by AQAP as their media centre.

1 May 2004 Yanbu massacre. Four militants attack the headquarters of a Swiss engineering multinational in the western city of Yanbu, killing seven people. Three of the attackers are killed and one arrested. Muqrin later claims responsibility for the attack, but investigations suggest that the cell operated independently of AQAP.

29–30 May 2004 Khobar massacre. Four members of a cell known as the Jerusalem Squadron, led by Muqrin's right-hand-man Turki al-Mutayri, attack multiple Western targets in the city of Khobar. They take a number of hostages and twenty-five people are killed. Three of the attackers manage to escape but one, Nimr al-Baqami, is captured by the security forces.

6 June 2004 BBC cameraman Simon Cumbers is shot dead and journalist Frank Gardner seriously injured in an attack by AQAP in the Suwaydi neighbourhood of Riyadh. Muqrin and his deputy Abu Ayub were present. Gardner was left partially paralysed by the attack.

12 June 2004 American engineer Paul Marshall Johnson is kidnapped by Muqrin's cell in Riyadh. A videotape demanding the release of imprisoned AQAP members appears the next day. On 18 June, a video showing the torture and decapitation of Johnson is posted online.

18 June 2004 Muqrin, leader of AQAP, is killed in a shootout with security forces. Abu Ayub and Mutayri also die in the confrontation.

22 June 2004 Prince Muhammad's position is elevated to ministerial rank by royal decree.

23 June 2004 The Saudi government begins a month-long amnesty for terror suspects. Only six men, mostly low-level operatives, hand themselves in to the authorities.

20 July 2004 Isa al-Awshen, head of AQAP propaganda and editor of *Voice of Jihad*, is killed in a raid in the King Fahd neighbourhood of Riyadh but AQAP leader Saleh al-Oufi escapes. Security personnel discover the head of American hostage Paul Marshall Johnson in a freezer.

September–November 2004 Raids and confrontations between militants and security forces lead to the arrests and deaths of a number of AQAP members.

21 September 2004 Saudi TV broadcasts the first episode of a series entitled *Inside the Cell*, featuring interviews with AQAP members who have recanted or been captured.

26 September 2004 French expatriate Laurent Barbot is shot dead in Jeddah. In the ensuing police chase, three suspects are wounded, and another is arrested.

October–November 2004 The last regular issue of *Voice of Jihad* is published.

6 December 2004 US consulate attack. Oufi's Jeddah-based cell raids the grounds of the US consulate in the city. The five terrorists kill a number of special consular guards but are unable to enter the main building. Security forces kill three of the attackers and detain two others.

29 December 2004 MOI headquarters attack. A dual suicide bombing targeting the MOI headquarters in Riyadh and the nearby Emergency Forces building fails. Both cars explode before they reach their targets, killing only the militants inside. On the same evening, a raid in Riyadh's Taawun neighbourhood kills a number of militants, including those responsible for the failed bombings.

20 January 2005 George W. Bush begins his second term as US president.

5–8 February 2005 The International Counterterrorism Conference is held in Riyadh. Prince Nayef delivers the opening address.

10 February 2005 Saudi Arabia holds its first ever municipal elections.

3–5 April 2005 Battle of Rass. An MOI raid on an AQAP safe house near the town of Rass leads to a three-day siege, in which fifteen militants are killed and five more are arrested. Among those killed is Saud al-Qatayni, who had taken over as leader of AQAP in the Najd after Muqrin's death.

18 May 2005 The American embassy in Riyadh revokes its advice to avoid all travel to the Kingdom.

19 June 2005 Lieutenant-Colonel Mubarak Al-Sawat, a senior police commander in Mecca, is shot dead. Sawat's suspected attackers are killed two days later in Mecca.

24 June 2005 Abdullah al-Rashoud is reported killed in an American air strike in Iraq.

3 July 2005 Yunus al-Hayari, who proclaimed himself AQAP leader after Qatayni's death, is killed in a shootout in Riyadh. Fahd al-Juwayr becomes leader of AQAP.

7 July 2005 Four suicide bombers target three underground train services and one bus in London, killing 52 people and injuring over 700.

20 July 2005 The American embassy in Riyadh warns its citizens to be alert following intelligence indicating that terrorist attacks are being prepared.

1 August 2005 King Fahd dies at the age of 84. He is succeeded by his half-brother Crown Prince Abdullah.

8 August 2005 The American, British, Australian, and New Zealand governments close their embassies and consulates across Saudi Arabia for two days, citing security concerns.

18 August 2005 Synchronized raids in Medina and Riyadh kill three terror suspects, including Oufi, leader of an AQAP network in the Hijaz.

4–6 September 2005 A siege of a villa in Dammam leads to the death of five militants and four security officers. Seventy people are wounded.

Early 2006 Nearly thirty AQ suspects escape from prisons in Saudi Arabia and Yemen.

24 February 2006 AQAP militants under the command of Juwayr launch a twin truck bomb attack against the Abqaiq oil refinery in the Eastern Province. Three security guards are killed, but no significant damage is done to the refinery.

27 February 2006 A raid kills the AQAP members responsible for the Abqaiq attack, including Juwayr.

23 June 2006 A raid in Riyadh kills Muhammad Rashid al-Julaydan and five others who are linked to an Iraqi AQ cell. A member of Julaydan's cell would later be implicated in the assassination attempt on Prince Muhammad.

3 November 2006 The Munasaha programme, aimed at rehabilitating former militants, is launched.

January–February 2007 The last issue of *Voice of Jihad* is published.

26 February 2007 Four French tourists are shot dead in the desert by men with links to Al Qaeda.

2009 AQAP is reorganized under the leadership of Nasir al-Wuhayshi, a Yemeni-born militant who had previously been Bin Laden's secretary. Rather than focusing exclusively on Saudi Arabia, the group plans attacks on international targets.

28 August 2009 Prince Muhammad survives an assassination attempt. Abdullah al-Asiri, who had insisted on surrendering to the prince personally, detonates an explosive device concealed in his rectum. Asiri dies in the attack but Prince Muhammad suffers only minor injuries.

25 December 2009 AQAP-trained Nigerian operative Umar Abdulmutallab tries to detonate plastic explosives hidden in his underwear while on board a flight between Amsterdam and Detroit. The attack fails.

29 October 2010 Two packages of plastic explosives are found on two cargo planes travelling between Yemen and the United States. One is defused in Britain and one in Dubai. AQAP later claims responsibility for the failed attack.

2 May 2011 Osama bin Laden is killed in a raid on his compound in Abbottabad, Pakistan.

June 2012 Prince Muhammad becomes interior minister.

Acknowledgements

A book like this one is never the work of the authors alone. We therefore have many people to thank: Abdulrahman Alrashed and Adel Alabdulkarim for putting their trust in us; the entire *Path of Blood* production team for capturing and elucidating the story: editors Peter Haddon, Kirsi Pyy, Peter Roemmele, and Bob Woodward, sound recordist Patrick Boland, and cinematographer Roger Chapman; the many translators who slaved away at an unholy amount of extremely difficult Arabic material: Simon Martin their irreplaceable leader, Paul Naylor, Francesco Lo Bello, Peter Dinshaw, Fergus Reoch, Dani Kabbani, Aran Byrne, Tom Casey, Saeed Meerkhan, Basel Abbas, Karl Eastham, and Simon Leese; our brilliant research assistant Jack Clift for dragging us over the finishing line; Khairi Al Amin, Abdulaziz al-Nafisa, and the entire team at OR Madarat in Riyadh for facilitating our research trips and for their irrepressible warmth and generosity; Christopher Mitchell and the OR Media team in London for housing us and for easing our way; Shareef Issa for, in record time, translating the manuscript for fact-checking; Scott Woolston for working so hard to get the artwork just right; Alex Christofi our agent and Mike Jones our editor for believing in the project; and Jennifer Speake our copy-editor for making us more eloquent than we are.

First and foremost, however, we wish to thank HRH Prince Muhammad bin Nayef for granting us such unprecedented access to the archives of the Ministry of Interior; Dr Tariq Alsheddi and his team at the Nayef Academy for National Security for working tirelessly on our behalf; the fighting men of the MOI who told us their stories; all our other interviewees who were so generous with their time; Abdulrahman al-Hammad and his team in the MOI's video archive; and the analysts and investigators of the MOI who offered us the fruits of their labours: Fahd al-Khorayef, Sultan Abu Melhas, Abdulaziz al-Tayyar, Nasser al-Subaei, Nasser al-Qahtani, Sami al-Arifi, and many others.

Notes

Prologue: The Head in the Freezer

1 Thomas Hegghammer, *Jihad in Saudi Arabia: Violence and Pan-Islamism since 1979* (Cambridge: Cambridge University Press, 2010), p. 210.

1 Blood Moon Rising

1 First adopted by the second Caliph Umar ibn al-Khattab, the title 'Commander of the Faithful' became one of the Caliphs' many imperial titles and was employed by them to back up their theoretical claims to the political allegiance of all Muslims.

2 Hegghammer and others put the figure at closer to 800, but the Mabahith say that is a gross exaggeration. Hegghammer, *Jihad in Saudi Arabia*, p. 74.

3 Michael Scheuer, *Osama bin Laden* (New York: Oxford University Press, 2011), Kindle edn, p. 106.

4 Ibid., p. 124.

5 Transcript of 1997 CNN interview with Osama bin Laden accessed on FindLaw's website in November 2013, news.findlaw.com/cnn/docs/binladen/binladenintvw-cnn.pdf.

6 'Text of the Global Islamic Front's Announcement of Jihad against Jews and Christians', *Al-Quds al-Arabi*, 23 February 1998, p. 3; accessed on Cornell University Library's website in November 2013, www.library.cornell.edu/colldev/mideast/fatw2.htm.

7 The United States also attacked Sudan, although in this case the CIA seriously miscalculated: they struck the country's largest pharmaceutical plant, in a stroke nearly wiping out the domestic supply of drugs.

8 Scheuer, *Osama bin Laden*, p. 108.

9 Bin Laden's location is based on what most news articles at the time reported. Some claimed Bin Laden was in Jowzjan to the far north or in the southern province of Helmand.

10 This is based on the results of Ayiri's trip. Once he was back in the Kingdom, he began working flat out in support of Al Qaeda and started laying the foundations of an Al Qaeda network inside Saudi Arabia. It is difficult to imagine him playing such a key role in Al Qaeda without having first met with Bin Laden in person to discuss it.

11 'Bin Laden Ordered Bamiyan Buddha Destruction', *Indo-Asian News Service*, 28 March 2006.

12 'Text of the Global Islamic Front's Announcement of Jihad against Jews and Christians', p. 3; translation ours.

13 This letter was captured by American forces in Afghanistan in 2001 and made public in 2006. Accessed on West Point's Combating Terrorism Center's website in November 2013, www.ctc.usma.edu/wp-content/uploads/2013/10/A-Memo-to-Sheikh-Abu-Abdullah-Translation.pdf.

14 Ali H. Soufan, *The Black Banners* (London: Penguin, 2013), p. 65.

15 According to Abu Jandal's statement; see Soufan, *Black Banners*, p. 265.

16 Ibid., p. 267.

17 Nidal al-Mughrabi, 'Militant Group Hamas and Egypt Group Back Taliban, Urge Muslim Unity', *Reuters*, 14 September 2001.

18 Elaine Sciolino, 'Don't Weaken Arafat, Saudi Warns Bush', *New York Times*, 27 January 2002.

19 Scheuer, *Osama bin Laden*, p. 180.

20 According to a radio transmission intercepted by the Americans; see Peter Bergen, *Manhunt: From 9/11 to Abbottabad – The Ten-Year Search for Osama bin Laden* (London:Vintage), p. 48.

21 *The 9/11 Commission Report* (New York: W.W. Norton, 2004), p. 251.

22 This is not known for certain, though it is a safe supposition. It is known that Bin Laden did appoint Adel military chief and that Adel was present at the meeting in Zurmat. See Nashiri's JTF-GTMO Detainee Assessment, p. 5, accessed on the *New York Times'*/NPR's 'The Guantánamo Docket' website in November 2013, projects.nytimes.com/guantánamo/detainees/10015-abd-al-rahim-al-nashiri/documents/11.

23 Saif al-Adel, 'My Experiences with Abu Musab al-Zarqawi', accessed on *Pulpit of Monotheism and Jihad* website in November 2013, www.tawhed.ws/r?i=ttofom6f; translation ours.

24 This is a supposition. Hegghammer believes Riyadh was Adel's

destination because his personal effects were discovered two years later in a Riyadh safe house. See Hegghammer, *Jihad in Saudi Arabia*, p. 165.

25 Saif al-Adel, 'My Experiences with Abu Musab al-Zarqawi'.

26 Clint Watts, Jacob Shapiro, and Vahid Brown, 'Al Qaeda's (Mis)adventures in the Horn of Africa', West Point's Combating Terrorism Center website, 2 July 2007, www.ctc.usma.edu/posts/al-qaidas-misadventures-in-the-horn-of-africa.

27 Hegghammer, *Jihad in Saudi Arabia*, pp. 125–6. Hegghammer writes that Ayiri was in prison for two months; however the Mabahith confirm his detention lasted three months and that the reason for his arrest was the extremist publications found in the wrecked car.

28 'Yusuf al-Ayiri: Glory in a Time of Humiliation', *Voice of Jihad*, no. 1 (2003), p. 17.

29 Ibid.

30 The cleric was Sheikh Sulayman al-Ulwan. He would be arrested in 2004 and sentenced to fifteen years for extremist preaching and providing financial support to Al Qaeda.

31 Hegghammer, *Jihad in Saudi Arabia*, pp. 125–6.

32 The interview was not broadcast until 31 January 2002, on CNN. Al Jazeera had buckled under US pressure and not aired it. See Bergen, *Manhunt*, p. 34.

33 Douglas Jehl, 'For Saudi Cleric, Battle Shapes Up as Infidel vs. Islam', *New York Times*, 5 December 2001.

34 Ibid.

35 In Arabic *jihad fi sabil Allah*.

36 This person may have been Walid bin Attash (aka Khallad), who was later arrested and sent to Guantánamo.

37 Spencer Ackerman, 'Qaeda Killer's Veins Implicate Him in Journo's Murder', *Wired Magazine* online, 20 January 2011, www.wired.com/dangerroom/2011/01/qaeda-killers-veins-implicate-him-in-journos-murder.

38 This man was Abdu Ali al-Haji al-Sharqawi (aka Riyadh the Facilitator), see his JTF-GTMO Detainee Assessment, p. 8, accessed on the *New York Times'*/NPR's 'The Guantánamo Docket' website in November 2013, projects.nytimes.com/guantánamo/detainees/1457-abdu-ali-al-haji-sharqawi.

39 They were Walid bin Attash (aka Khallad) and KSM's nephew Ammar al-Baluchi. See Attash's JTF-GTMO Detainee Assessment, p. 8, accessed on the *New York Times'*/NPR's 'The Guantánamo Docket' website in November 2013, projects.nytimes.com/guantánamo/detainees/10014-walid-bin-attash.

40 Nashiri's JTF-GTMO Assessment, p. 7.

41 Ibid., p. 5.

42 They were Muhammad al-Qahtani (aka Abu al-Maali) and Miflah al-Ghamdi, both in custody at the time of writing.
43 They were Muayd al-Qahtani and Ali al-Faqasi, also in custody. Ali al-Faqasi was in charge of the Syrian operation, and had in fact returned home to the Kingdom the previous December.
44 He was Badr al-Sudayri (aka Abu al-Zubayr al-Ha'ili), in custody at the time of writing.
45 Samir Abu Anaq and Muhammad al-Sahim were made fundraisers. Muhammad al-Ghamdi (aka Abu al-Tayyeb) was to find suicide bombers; he also established a business to act as a front for collecting money for the Organization.
46 Soufan, *Black Banners*, pp. 345–7.
47 Authors' interview with General Mansour al-Turki; see also Ron Suskind, *The One-Percent Doctrine: Deep Inside America's Pursuit of its Enemies since 9/11* (London: Simon & Schuster, 2006), p. 143.
48 The operative's name was Abdul Muhsen al-Yahya. He was in custody at the time of writing.
49 Nashiri's JTF-GTMO Assessment, p. 5.
50 Authors' interview with General Mansour al-Turki.
51 In Arabic *istiraha*, literally 'place of relaxation'.

2 Facing Facts

1 Authors' interview with Dr Tariq Alsheddi.
2 'Prince Ahmed bin Abdulaziz will preside over a graduation parade for new units from the students of the King Fahd Military College', *Asharq Al-Awsat*, 20 June 2002.
3 'Morocco investigates three Saudis suspected of being members of Al Qaeda on a plan to attack American and British ships in Gibraltar', *Asharq Al-Awsat*, 12 June 2002; Jean-Marie Pontaut 'L' "Opération Gibraltar" d'Al-Qaeda', *L'Express*, 10 June 2002; 'Prince Bandar: American intelligence has taken up from Saudi Arabia its war against Al Qaeda in Yemen', *Al-Quds al-Arabi*, 28 November 2002.
4 Patrick E. Tyler, 'Qaeda suspect was taking flight training last month', *New York Times*, 23 December 2002.
5 Douglas A. Frantz, 'Nuclear Secrets: Pakistan Frees Two Scientists Linked to Bin Laden Network', *New York Times*, 17 December 2001.
6 Ron Suskind, *One-Percent Doctrine* , pp. 146–8.
7 'Osama bin Laden: Prince Abdullah's Initiative is High Treason', *Al-Quds al-Arabi*, 28 March 2002.
8 Hegghammer, *Jihad in Saudi Arabia*, p. 227.
9 Authors' interview with Robert Jordan; Alaa Shahine, 'Saudi interior

minister says Jews were behind Sept. 11 Attacks', *Associated Press*, 5 December 2002.

10 'Saudi Arabia Moves to Arrest 750', press release from Saudi embassy in Washington, 18 June 2002, accessed on its website in November 2013, www.saudiembassy.net/archive/2002/press/page27.aspx.

11 'American officials: Sudanese national from Al Qaeda arrested on suspicion of planning to fire a missile at an American plane in the Gulf', *Asharq al-Awsat*, 14 June 2002. The Sudanese man was Hisham Makawi. The Sudanese government turned him over to the Saudis, who gave him a prison sentence for committing 'terrorist attacks against vital installations'. Ken Silverstein, 'Official Pariah Sudan Valuable to America's War on Terrorism; Despite once harboring Bin Laden, Khartoum regime has supplied key intelligence, officials say', *Los Angeles Times*, 29 April 2005. The Mabahith confirm the plane Makawi targeted was in fact an AWACS.

12 Authors' interview with General Mansour al-Turki.

13 Robert Lacey, *Inside the Kingdom: Kings, Clerics, Modernists, Terrorists and the Struggle for Saudi Arabia* (London: Hutchinson, Random House, 2009), p. 317.

14 Authors' telephone interview with Sir Sherard Cowper-Coles.

15 The figure of thirty-six sons is the official government figure. Some people claim the number is as high as forty-four.

16 John Roth, Douglas Greenburg, and Serena Wille, *Monograph on Terrorist Financing* (National Commission on Terrorist Attacks Upon the United States, 2004), ch. 7, 'Al Haramain Case Study'.

17 'Washington, Riyadh freeze assets of Bin Laden associate', *Agence France Presse*, 6 September 2002.

18 Authors' interview with General Mansour al-Turki.

19 Authors' telephone interview with Sir Sherard Cowper-Coles.

20 'Prince Bandar: American intelligence has taken up from Saudi Arabia its war against Al Qaeda in Yemen', *Al-Quds al-Arabi*, 28 November 2002. Prince Bandar says Nashiri was spotted in Sana'a in early February; this is not possible. It was likelier to have been in late March or early April.

21 'Prince Nayef Orders the Payment of 2.5 Million Riyals as a Reward to those who Participated in Uncovering Smuggled Contraband', *Asharq Al-Awsat*, 29 July 2002.

22 'The Yemeni President Discusses Saudi-Yemeni Links with Prince Muhammad bin Nayef', *Asharq Al-Awsat*, 21 July 2002.

23 'Senior Saudi official confirms Iran cooperating over Al Qaeda', *Agence France Presse*, 11 August 2002.

24 Authors' interviews with Robert Jordan, Frances Townsend, and James Oberwetter.

25 Ron Suskind, *One-Percent Doctrine*, p. 234.

26 'Yemen, UAE ship Al Qaeda suspects back home to Saudi', *Agence France Presse*, 12 August 2002.
27 This is according to official Mabahith records. According to Dandani's biography in *Voice of Jihad*, he was arrested for taking a gun to school and imprisoned for a year. See Abu Hajir al-Jawfi, 'Turki al-Dandani: Greatness and Courage', *Voice of Jihad*, no. 7 (2003), p. 33.
28 Ibid.
29 Hegghammer, *Jihad in Saudi Arabia*, p. 171.
30 Patrick Di Justo, 'How Al-Qaida Site was Hacked', *Wired Magazine*, 8 October 2002, accessed online in November 2013, www.wired.com/culture/lifestyle/news/2002/08/54455; Mike Boettcher, 'Pornographer Says He Hacked Al Qaeda', CNN.com, 9 August 2002, accessed online in November 2013, edition.cnn.com/2002/US/08/08/porn.patriot/.
31 Nashiri's JTF-GTMO Assessment, *op. cit.*, p. 8.
32 'U.S. concerned Al Qaeda targeting oil interests in Middle East', *Associated Press*, 16 October 2002; John McWerthy, 'Terror attempt on Saudi pipeline thwarted', *ABC News*, 14 October 2002, accessed online in November 2013, abcnews.go.com/WNT/story?id=130067.
33 Richard Norton-Taylor, 'Britain and U.S. Step up Bombing in Iraq', *Guardian*, 4 December 2002; 'Saudi FM holds talks with U.S. official', *Agence France Presse*, 1 October 2002.
34 Authors' interview with General Mansour al-Turki.
35 'Prince Nayef: Saudi anticipates that Saudi will be connected to the Kuwaiti investigation into Al-Qaeda – and says that the security of the GCC is one', *Asharq Al-Awsat*, 14 October 2002.
36 Bergen, *Manhunt*, p. 63.
37 'Prince Nayef: Khartoum has assured that the passenger who tried to hijack the plane will be extradited to us; we have men who are able to deal with situations like this', *Asharq Al-Awsat*, 17 October 2002; 'Saudis foil plane hijack', *BBC News*, 15 October 2002, accessed online in November 2013, news.bbc.co.uk/1/hi/world/middle_east/2330021.stm.
38 'Police investigate Saudi car blast', *BBC News*, 21 June 2002, accessed online in November 2013, news.bbc.co.uk/1/hi/world/middle_east/2055714.stm; Susan Taylor Martin, 'Target: Westerners', *St. Petersburg Times*, 22 July 2002.
39 'Riyadh blast was no terror attack – Prince Nawaf', *Arab News*, 1 October 2002.
40 'Naif rules out Arabs as bomb suspects', *Arab News*, 2 October 2002.
41 Sandra Laville, 'Saudi bomb points to jailed Britons' innocence', *Daily Telegraph*, 21 June 2002; Paul Kelso, David Pallister, and Richard Norton-Taylor, 'FO faces anger at Britons' ordeal in Saudi

jail', *Guardian*, 1 February 2002; David Pallister and Richard Norton-Taylor, 'Secret Report Detailed Violence', *Guardian*, 31 January 2002; *BBC News*, 21 June 2002; Taylor Martin, 'Target: Westerners'.

42 Authors' telephone interview with Sir Sherard Cowper-Coles, who confirmed that the swap took place; 'Sampson May Have Been Freed in Swap for Saudis', *Vancouver Sun*, 5 July 2004; 'Saudis deny Guantánamo Prisoner Swap', *ABC News* (Australia), 11 July 2004; Suzanne Malveaux, 'Questions Raised about Detainee Releases', *CNN.com*, 4 July 2004, accessed online in November 2013, www.cnn.com/2004/US/07/04/detainee.swap.report; David Pallister, 'Saudi Britons Freed in Swap', *Guardian*, 5 July 2004.

43 According to Investment International's website, accessed in January 2014, www.investmentinternational.com/news/latest/british-widow-thwarted-by-foreign-office-mendacity.html; '"I would have confessed to anything"', *Guardian*, 10 May 2005; 'Timeline: British "bombs" case', *BBC News*, 14 May 2003, accessed online in January 2014, news.bbc.co.uk/1/hi/world/middle_east/3028083.stm.

44 Gregory D. Johnsen, *The Last Refuge: Yemen, Al-Qaeda, and the Battle for Arabia* (London: Oneworld, 2012), p. 122.

45 Tyler, 'Qaeda suspect was taking flight training'.

46 See Nashiri's 'Petition for writ of Habeas Corpus', accessed on the *New York Times*'/NPR's 'The Guantánamo Docket' website in November 2013, projects.nytimes.com/guantánamo/detainees/10015-abd-al-rahim-al-nashiri/documents/13.

47 This is a supposition based on evidence from Muhammad ben Moujan's JTF-GTMO Assessment, p. 5, accessed on the *New York Times*'/NPR's 'The Guantánamo Docket' website in November 2013, projects.nytimes.com/guantánamo/detainees/160-muhammad-ben-moujan.

48 'Saudi says terror suspect caught after shootout in Riyadh', *Islamweb.net English*, 18 November 2002, accessed online in November 2013, www.islamweb.net/eramadan/index.php?page=articles&id=33118; Brian Whitaker, 'Saudis admit to al-Qaida threat as 100 are held', *Guardian*, 21 November 2002; 'Suspected terrorist arrested in Riyadh', *Agence France Presse*, 18 November 2002.

49 'Prince Bandar . . .', *Al-Quds al-Arabi*, 28 November 2002.

50 George Tenet, with Bill Harlow, *At the Center of the Storm: My Years at the CIA* (London: HarperCollins, 2007), pp. 272–3.

51 Suskind, *One-Percent Doctrine*, p. 143; authors' interviews with Robert Jordan and General Mansour al-Turki.

52 Robert Collier, 'Saudis take small step toward political reform: Conservative monarchy opens ears to criticism', *San Francisco Chronicle*, 28 January 2003.

53 'Saudi Arabia has jailed 90 with Al Qaeda links: security official', *Agence France Presse*, 6 February 2003.
54 Anwar Iqbal, 'Fear of violence overshadows Hajj', *United Press International*, 7 February 2003; 'Saudi authorities arrest eight suspects in January shooting', *Agence France Presse*, 7 February 2003; 'Some of those arrested in Saudi shooting may belong to Al Qaeda: minister', *Agence France Presse*, 8 February 2003.
55 'Fourteen killed in Hajj stampede', *BBC News*, 11 February 2003, accessed online in November 2013, news.bbc.co.uk/1/hi/world/middle_east/2749231.stm.
56 Suskind, *One-Percent Doctrine*, p. 207.
57 'Gunshots fired at Briton's car in Riyadh', *Agence France Presse*, 7 February 2003.
58 The shooter's name was Saud bin Ali bin Nasser. 'Briton killed in Saudi Arabia', *BBC News*, 21 February 2003, accessed online in November 2013, news.bbc.co.uk/1/hi/world/middle_east/2784977.stm; 'Briton defence worker shot dead in Riyadh by Yemeni-born Saudi', *Agence France Presse*, 20 February 2003.
59 Their names were Hamad al-Humaydi in Zulfi and Osama Uqayl al-Kawhaji in Riyadh.
60 Suskind, *One-Percent Doctrine*, pp. 204–6.
61 Soufan, *Black Banners*, p. 514.
62 P. K. Abdul Ghafour, 'Swiss Uncover Al-Qaeda Cells Planning Attacks in the Kingdom', *Arab News*, 13 December 2003.
63 Fawaz al-Nashimi, *Voice of Jihad*, no. 16 (2004), pp. 45–6.
64 Suskind, *One-Percent Doctrine*, pp. 217–18.

3 The Riyadh Compounds

1 A small network under the leadership of Ali al-Bariqi was set up on the east coast, but in time it would be absorbed into Muqrin's.
2 Brian Whitaker, *The Birth of Modern Yemen*, ch. 7, 'The International Dimension', accessed online at *Al-Bab* website, www.al-bab.com/yemen/birthofmodernyemen/bmy7.htm.
3 This was a common experience: new recruits would sign up to fight in a specific campaign, only to end up in an Al Qaeda camp near Kandahar.
4 Bin Laden's intermediary was Khalid al-Baatish, a Yemeni. At the time of writing, he was being held in prison in the United States.
5 This is according to Mabahith records. Twenty-two attacks in total were planned during Hajj's period as leader, but never carried out.
6 Osama bin Laden, Eid al-Adha sermon, 14 February 2003; translation adapted from Bruce Lawrence, ed., and James Howarth, trans.,

Messages to the World: The Statements of Osama bin Laden (New York: Verso, 2005), ch. 19, p. 188.

7 'Saudis warn U.S. over Iraq war', *BBC News*, 17 February 2003, accessed online in June 2013, news.bbc.co.uk/2/hi/middle_east/2773759.stm.

8 Qur'an 9:5.

9 Al-Bukhari, *Sahih*, no. 2932.

10 A copy of this letter was seized at the Al-Amana neighbourhood raid on 11 August 2003.

11 This letter was discovered when KSM was arrested, and was accessed on West Point's Combating Terrorism Center website in June 2013, www.ctc.usma.edu/wp-content/uploads/2013/10/Al-Adl-Letter-Translation1.pdf.

12 Though the compound bombing plot was Dandani's chief priority, he was developing other plans as well. One of his sub-cells was preparing two attacks outside Riyadh. One target was the King Khalid Air Base in Khamis Mushayt, in the far southwestern corner of the Kingdom, and the other was the Prince Sultan Air Base in Kharj, about 75 kilometres southeast of the capital. American soldiers and pilots were stationed at both bases; they used them to police the no-fly zone over Iraq.

13 One safe house was in the Granada district and the other one was in the Khaleej district.

14 Authors' interview with a teacher inside the university's media studies department at the time.

15 Donna Abu-Nasr, 'Residents relive a night of terrorism', *The Victoria Advocate*, 19 May 2003.

16 Al-Jawfi, 'Turki al-Dandani: Greatness and Courage', p. 34.

17 Authors' interviews with Major-General Saud al-Halal.

18 Authors' interview with Robert Jordan.

19 MOI announcement on Saudi TV, 8 May 2003.

20 'The 11 Rabi al-Awwal Operation' (Center for Islamic Research and Studies, 2003), pp. 38–43.

21 Hegghammer, *Jihad in Saudi Arabia*, p. 185.

22 Ibid.

23 Juhani was born in 1975 to a highly respected family mentioned in the hadith. In 1992, aged only eighteen, he travelled to Bosnia and for two years fought in the war against the Serbs before moving on to Afghanistan in 1996, where he joined Al Qaeda and became closely attached to Nashiri and Hajj. When the Americans invaded, he fled to Yemen along with several other mujahideen and crossed the border into Saudi Arabia. He was one of Nashiri's main contacts in the Kingdom (Hegghammer, *Jihad in Saudi Arabia*, p. 168) and after Nashiri's arrest he linked up with Hajj.

24 Ahmed al-Darbi's JTF-GTMO Detainee Assessment, p. 4, accessed on

the *New York Times*'/NPR's 'The Guantánamo Docket' website in June 2013.

25 It was the house of Muhammad Atef (aka Abu Hafs), who was Bin Laden's chief military officer before Saif al-Adel and KSM.

26 Juhani's parents corroborated her story; they said that the Afghan war had left their son mentally unstable, and even though parents of jihadists often invoked the excuse of mental illness to justify their sons' wayward activities, there is every reason to think that a young man such as Juhani, after everything he had experienced, would have been unbalanced.

27 *Wills of the Heroes: The Martyrs of the Two Holy Mosques*, Sahab Institute for Media Production (2003).

28 The safe houses were in the Granada and Khaleej districts.

29 Hegghammer, *Jihad in Saudi Arabia*, p. 185.

30 Based on an interrogation with a captured militant, as reported by Mabahith officers.

31 *Wills of the Heroes* included a live audio recording of the attack.

4 A Bloody Success

1 Neil MacFarquhar, 'Aftereffects: The Bombing; Saudis are Shaken as Jihad Erupts at their Front Door', *New York Times*, 16 May 2003.

2 John Qualls, 'A Night to Remember', blog post from 15 May 2003 on the website of the National Association for Business Economics, accessed online in June 2013, www.nabe-web.com/publib/qualls.html.

3 Michael Friscolanti, 'Butcher knife in hand, he waited for second wave: Canadian ready to fight', *National Post* (Canada), 14 May 2003.

4 David Kelly, 'Saudi Compound Grapples with Devastation', *Los Angeles Times*, 17 May 2003.

5 Authors' interview with Robert Jordan.

6 Kelly, 'Saudi Compound Grapples with Devastation'; Tacomaboywa, 26 August 2012 (9:32 a.m.), comment on *Dave's ESL Café*, accessed online in June 2013, forums.eslcafe.com/job/viewtopic.php?p=1043153.

7 Or perhaps it was more than just luck. A lawsuit raised against the royal family one year later alleged that the Saudi National Guard colluded in the attack. The night manoeuvres were scheduled at the last minute and were highly irregular, resulting in fewer guards on duty. Also, they claim that a detailed hand-drawn map found inside the assault car proves the terrorists received inside assistance; see Mark Hollingsworth, 'Saudi royal guards "aided al-Qa'ida" in Riyadh bombings that left 35 dead', *Independent*, 16 May 2004. These claims were later dismissed, but certainly the security failure was a tremendous

embarrassment to the National Guard. According to Robert Jordan, Crown Prince Abdullah later subjected his son Prince Mut'ab, then commander of the National Guard, to a public browbeating.

8 'One bombed compound owned by pro-Western Saudi', *CNN News*, 13 May 2003, accessed online in June 2013, www.cnn.com/2003/WORLD/meast/05/13/Saudi.jadawel.

9 Friscolanti, 'Butcher knife in hand, he waited for second wave'.

10 'FBI arrives amid predictions of more attacks', *St. Petersburg Times* online, 16 May 2003, accessed online in June 2013, www.sptimes.com/2003/05/16/news_pf/Worldandnation/FBI_arrives_amid_pred.shtml; 'Saudi Compound Bombings', IntelCenter, accessed online in June 2013, www.intelcenter.com/SCB-v1-4.pdf.

11 Authors' interview with Robert Jordan.

12 The gunman was Sami al-Luhaybi, who would kill himself on a mountainside on 4 November 2003.

13 NBC Universal Archives, accessed online in June 2013, www.nbcuniversalarchives.com/nbcuni/clip/51A3707_015.do.

14 NBC Universal Archives, accessed online in June 2013, www.nbcuniversalarchives.com/nbcuni/clip/51A3707_008.do.

15 'FBI arrives amid predictions of more attacks'.

16 Authors' interview with Robert Jordan.

17 Ibid.

18 Authors' interview with General Mansour al-Turki; see also Frank Gardner, *Blood and Sand: Life, Death and Survival in an Age of Global Terror* (London: Transworld, 2007), p. 270.

19 Jim Landers, 'Robert Jordan's Crucible', *Saudi-U.S. Relations (SUSRIS)* website, accessed online in June 2013, susris.sustg.org/2004/09/26/robert-jordans-crucible-by-jim-landers.

20 Brian Ross, 'U.S. Officials: Saudis ignored warnings', *ABC News*, 15 May 2003, accessed online in June 2013, abcnews.go.com/WNT/story?id=129701&page=1#.UcMG_vnVDoI.

21 'Prince Bandar's statement on the terrorist attacks in Riyadh', press release from Saudi embassy in Washington, 13 May 2003.

22 NBC Universal Archives, accessed online in June 2013, www.nbcuniversalarchives.com/nbcuni/clip/51A3707_007.do.

23 Muhammad al-Ghulaym and Ahmad Ghawi, '*Al-Riyadh* visits the wounded in King Fahd National Guard hospital', *Al-Riyadh*, 14 May 2003.

24 'Editorial: The Enemy Within', *Arab News*, 14 May 2003.

25 Abdullah Bajaber, 'The Explosions ... Trying to Understand', *Asharq Al-Awsat*, 15 May 2003.

26 Raid Qusti, 'Cleaning Up Our Own Backyard', *Arab News*, 28 May 2003.

27 In fact the title is *The 11 Rabi al-Awwal Operation*. 11 Rabi al-Awwal 1424 was 12 May 2003, and to avoid unnecessary exoticism, we have translated the book title to reflect that.

28 Tenet, *At the Center of the Storm*, p. 248.
29 'Saudi Arabia puts in place unprecedented security measures', *Deutsche Press-Agentur*, 20 May 2003; authors' interview with Major-General Saud al-Halal.
30 'Saudi Police Arrest Four More in Riyadh Bombing Probe', *Associated Press*, 22 May 2003.
31 Fareed Zakaria, 'The Saudi Trap: A Trip through the Kingdom Reveals What Really Needs to Be Done in the War on Terror', *Newsweek*, 28 June 2003.
32 Bootie Cosgrove-Mather, 'Shock and Fear in Riyadh', *CBS News* online, accessed June 2013, www.cbsnews.com/2100-500164_162-553938.html.
33 MacFarquhar, 'Aftereffects'.
34 Uthman al-Rawaf, 'Are the Islamist Masses Really Supporting Al Qaeda?', *Asharq Al-Awsat*, 2 June 2003.
35 Authors' interview with Sir Sherard Cowper-Coles.
36 Their ambition in this regard would be realized on 11 December 2005, when the Kingdom was admitted to the WTO.
37 An example of one such outburst was when national television broadcasts began in 1965. The clerics, who thought any artistic recreation of the human form was blasphemous, decried the introduction of television, and this inspired a large crowd led by one of the king's many nephews to attack a Riyadh television station. The police fired on the crowd, even killing the prince, and television was saved. Incidentally, the brother of the killed prince, in part seeking revenge, would go on to assassinate King Faisal in 1975.
38 Lacey, *Inside the Kingdom*, p. 189.
39 Susan Sevareid, 'Saudi Arabia's Rich and Poor Can Sleep Under Bridges', *Los Angeles Times*, 2 February 2003; John R. Bradley, 'Kingdom Enters a New Era', *Arab News*, 22 November 2002.
40 http://articles.latimes.com/2003/may/16/news/war-poverty16 Kim Murphy, 'Saudis' Quicksand of Poverty', *Los Angeles Times*, 16 May 2003.
41 When he became king in 2005, Abdullah curtailed royal allowances even further.
42 David Commins, *The Wahhabi Mission and Saudi Arabia* (London: I. B. Tauris, 2006), ch. 1.
43 Of course, the nub of the problem is, what is the definition of an unbeliever (*kafir* or *mushrik*)? In July 2002 Nasr al-Fahd, one of the Takfeeri Troika, gave a summary answer in his short pamphlet entitled 'On the Principle: Whoever does not do takfeer on a kafir is himself a kafir', which invoked Muhammad bin al-Wahhab's principle, see www.tawhed.ws/r?i=e7hqd4ju.
44 Lacey, *Inside the Kingdom*, p. 54.
45 Hegghammer, *Jihad in Saudi Arabia*, pp. 39–41.

46 Lacey, *Inside the Kingdom*, p. 52.
47 In Arabic *fasaad fi'l-ardh*.
48 Commins, *Wahhabi Mission and Saudi Arabia*, p. 184.
49 'Saudi Arabia fired 200 Muslim preachers for "incompetence": report', *Agence France Presse*, 28 May 2003.
50 'Can Saudi Arabia Reform Itself?' *ICG Middle East Report*, no. 28 (14 July 2004), p. 16.
51 Anthony H. Cordesman and Nawaf Obaid, *National Security in Saudi Arabia: Threats, Responses, and Challenges* (Westport: Praeger Security International, 2005), p. 287. The figure of over 150,000 is based on Cordesman's estimate from 2004.
52 Ibid., p. 292.
53 Maciej M. Latek, Seyed M. Mussavi Rizi, and Tariq A. Alsheddi, 'Optimal Blends of History and Intelligence for Robust Antiterrorism Policy', *Journal of Homeland Security and Emergency Management*, vol. 8, no. 1 (March 2011).
54 Cordesman and Obaid, *National Security in Saudi Arabia*, p. 294.

5 The Prince's Crackdown

1 Hegghammer, *Jihad in Saudi Arabia*, p. 152; Tenet, *At the Center of the Storm*, pp. 272–4.
2 'Saudi Arabia: Interior Ministry gives details of arrests in Medina', *BBC Summary of World Broadcasts*, 2 June 2003.
3 Authors' interview with Major-General Khalid al-Harbi.
4 'Yusuf al-Ayiri: Glory in a Time of Humiliation, part 2', *Voice of Jihad*, no. 2 (2003), pp. 17–18.
5 In fact, though five names from the List of Nineteen were killed in the Riyadh compound bombings, only four of them were confirmed by DNA samples. Interrogations revealed that a fifth, Hamad Fahd Al-Shamri, died in the attack on the Vinnell compound, though no evidence confirming this was discovered at the scene; no further news about him ever surfaced.
6 His real name was Muhammad Salim al-Ghamdi, see 'United States of America vs. Ahmed Omar Abu Ali', *United States Court of Appeals for the Fourth Circuit vol. 1 of 2* (2008), p. 7, accessed online in July 2013, www.ca4.uscourts.gov/opinions/Published/064334.P.pdf.
7 Ibid.
8 'Indictment, United States vs. Ahmed Omar Abu Ali' (February 2005), p. 8, accessed online in July 2013, www.washingtonpost.com/wp-srv/metro/daily/documents/AliIndictment.pdf.
9 'United States vs. Ahmed Omar Abu Ali', p. 46.
10 Suskind, *One-Percent Doctrine*, p. 201.

11 Abu Abdul Rahman al-Qaseemi, 'An Account of Heroism and Resistance', *Voice of Jihad*, no. 5 (2003), pp. 13–16.
12 'Al-Ghamdi turns himself in through the mediation of Sheikh Safar al-Hawali', *Islamtoday.net*, accessed online in July 2013, islamtoday.net/nawafeth/artshow-12-30449.htm.
13 Commins, *Wahhabi Mission and Saudi Arabia*, ch. 6.
14 Al-Jawfi,'*Turki al-Dandani: Greatness and Courage*'. He claims that Dandani's relative (who is unnamed) was tortured.
15 His name was Musaad al-Ruwayli.
16 Authors' interview with Lieutenant-Colonel Umar al-Adwan.
17 Abu Bakr al-Siddiq was the Prophet Muhammad's father-in-law and the first Muslim caliph.
18 Their names were Lieutenant Sattam bin Ghazay al-Mutairi and Sergeant Ali bin Ghazi al-Harbi.
19 According to footage obtained from Saudi TV.
20 '4 People Killed in Saudi Shootout', *Los Angeles Times*, 13 August 2003.

6 Salvaging a Friendship

1 Based on footage from Saudi TV.
2 'Terrorism: Growing Wahhabi Influence in the United States', Senate Hearing 108-267, (Washington: U.S. Government Printing Office, 2004), p. 12, accessed online in July 2013, www.gpo.gov/fdsys/pkg/CHRG-108shrg91326/pdf/CHRG-108shrg91326.pdf.
3 *The 9/11 Commission Report*, p. 171.
4 Simon Henderson, 'The September 11 Congressional Report: A Sea Change in U.S.-Saudi Relations?', *The Washington Institute for Near East Policy*, 30 July 2003, accessed online in July 2013, www.washingtoninstitute.org/policy-analysis/view/the-september-11-congressional-report-a-sea-change-in-u.s.-saudi-relations.
5 'Furious Saudis Reject U.S. 9/11 Claims', *Guardian*, 25 July 2003.
6 Helen Fessenden, 'Bipartisan Effort Under Way to Open Sept. 11 Report', *Congressional Quarterly Daily Monitor*, 30 July 2003.
7 Timothy O'Brien, 'Senators Push Saudi Arabia to Improve Antiterrorism Efforts', *New York Times*, 1 August 2003.
8 'NEWSWEEK: Classified Section of 9/11 Report Draws Connections Between High-Level Saudi Princes and Associates of the Hijackers; Al-Bayoumi May Have Visited Saudi Official Accused of Terrorist Ties Before Meeting 9/11 Plotters', *PR Newswire*, 27 July 2003.
9 'Bush Worked Behind-The-Scenes To Create New Anti-Terror Task Force With Saudis', *The White House Bulletin*, 25 August 2003.
10 Authors' interview with Captain Abdul Majid bin Muammar.
11 Authors' interview with Major-General Khalid al-Harbi.

12 Authors' interview with General Mansour al-Turki.
13 Ibid.
14 Ibid.
15 According to an MOI report, in the Amana safe house investigators also found copies of letters that had passed between Yusuf al-Ayiri and Saif al-Adel in Iran arguing about the best timing for the Riyadh compound bombings.
16 'The Battle of Suwaydi: The facts as they are', *Voice of Jihad*, no. 3 (2003), pp. 8–10.
17 'Saudi interior minister details clashes with extremists', *BBC Summary of World Broadcasts*, 14 August 2003.
18 Authors' interview with Captain Khalid al-Qahtani.

7 A Ruthless New Leader

1 Abdulaziz al-Muqrin, *Dawrat al-tanfidh wa harb al-'asabat* (Muaskar al-Shaheed al-Battar, 2004), p. 22, translation ours, pdf accessed online in July 2012, http://www.e-prism.org/images/battarbook_tanfeedh.pdf.
2 Norman Cigar, *Al-Qa'ida's Doctrine for Insurgency* (Dulles, Virginia: Potomac Books, 2009), p. 6.
3 'An interview with one of the most-wanted from the List of Nineteen, part 1', *Voice of Jihad*, no. 1 (2003), pp. 22–5; 'An interview with one of the most-wanted from the List of Nineteen, part 2', *Voice of Jihad*, no. 2 (2003), pp. 22–6; Cigar, *Al-Qa'ida's Doctrine for Insurgency*, pp. 6–13.
4 Shaykh Abdullah Azaam and A. B. al-Mehri, eds, *The Signs of Ar-Rahman in the Jihad of Afghanistan* (Birmingham: Maktabah), p. 36, accessed online in July 2013, www.scribd.com/doc/4572493/Miracles-in-the-Afghan-War.
5 The official reason given for his early release was that he memorized the Qur'an – a Saudi-specific version of 'good behaviour'. Khalid Antar, 'Abu Jandal, Osama bin Laden's Personal Bodyguard: Our Clerics and Our Sheikhs have Betrayed and Abandoned Us, part 1', *26September.net*, accessed online in July 2013, www.26sep.net/newsweekarticle.php?sid=17111.
6 Cigar, *Al-Qa'ida's Doctrine for Insurgency*, p. 7.
7 This figure is based on Hegghammer's analysis of 260 biographies of jihadists active in Saudi Arabia between 2003 and 2006, of which he estimates only 69 were 'core members' of the Organization; see Hegghammer, *Jihad in Saudi Arabia*, p. 181, fn. 46.
8 Muqrin, *Dawrat al-tanfidh wa harb al-'asabat*, p. 38, translation ours.
9 Hegghammer, *Jihad in Saudi Arabia*, pp. 223–4.

10 Zarqawi's Unity and Jihad movement did not formally merge with Al Qaeda until December 2004. Already in early 2003, before the invasion, there were reports of Saudi fighters going to Iraq. June saw the first arrests of Saudi militants, and later in the summer Iraqi websites sympathetic to Al Qaeda were eulogizing fallen Saudi 'martyrs'; see Hegghammer, 'Saudi militants in Iraq: Backgrounds and Recruitment Patterns' (Norwegian Defence Research Establishment (FFI), 2007), p. 10. At first the government had done little to keep jihadists from crossing the border. However, as their numbers increased sharply over the next sixteen months, the Saudi government began tightening border security and detaining would-be jihadists before they could cross northwards. Their shift in policy came about through a combination of American pressure and the realization that everyone they let through could return an experienced fighter, the last thing the government wanted.
11 Muqrin, *Dawrat al-tanfidh wa harb al-'asabat*, pp. 22, 34, translation ours.
12 Mohammad Alkhereiji, 'Charity Collection Boxes Banned', *Arab News*, 17 September 2003.
13 Muqrin, *Dawrat al-tanfidh wa harb al-'asabat*, p. 40, translation ours.
14 Ibid., p. 13, translation ours.
15 Ibid., p. 34, translation ours.
16 Following demographic breakdown based on Hegghammer, *Jihad in Saudi Arabia*, pp. 239–44.
17 Muqrin, *Dawrat al-tanfidh wa harb al-'asabat*, p. 40, translation ours.
18 Jarret M. Brachman, *Global Jihad: Theory and Practice* (Abingon, UK: Routledge, 2009), pp. 130–1.
19 Isa al-Awshen's obituary accessed on *Pulpit of Monotheism and Jihad* website in July 2013, www.tawhed.ws/a?a=pvecgndv.
20 Saad al-Matrafi, 'Saudi: The Compete Al Qaeda Most-Wanted File', *Al Arabiya* website, 1 November 2010, accessed in July 2013, www.alarabiya.net/articles/2004/07/22/5194.html.
21 Isa al-Awshen, *Thirty-nine Ways to Serve and Participate in Jihad*, accessed on *Pulpit of Monotheism and Jihad* website in July 2013, www.tawhed.ws/a?a=pvecgndv.
22 In Arabic *Sawt al-Jihad*.
23 Seymour M. Hersh, 'King's Ransom', *New Yorker*, 22 October 2001.
24 In Arabic *Muaskar al-Battar*.
25 Taken from an Arabic chatroom in July 2013, www.w6n.cc/vb/archive/index.php/t-8662.html.
26 *Wills of the Heroes* opens with 'Presented by Al Sahab Foundation for Media Production'. Al Sahab was Central Command's umbrella media wing. It is likely that Muqrin and Awshen wanted their video to have the legitimacy Al Sahab would give it; or

maybe Central Command vetted and approved the video before its release.

27 One of them was Sami al-Luhaybi, the gunman who had fired at an American in Jubail back in May.

28 Authors' interview with Major-General Saud al-Halal, 26 January 2013.

8 The List of Twenty-Six

1 Authors' interview with Major-General Abdulrahman al-Maqbal.

2 'Terrorism – Saudi Arabia', *Saudi-U.S. Relations Service (SUSRIS)* website, accessed in August 2013, susris.com/timelines/terrorism-saudi-arabia.

3 Specifically, Khalid al-Farraj in an interview with Saudi TV, broadcast in late 2004.

4 Javid Hassan, 'Five Security Men Killed in Shootout', *Arab News*, 30 January 2004.

5 The plumbers' merchant was in the Sulay district.

6 From an interview with Saudi TV, broadcast in late 2004.

7 Ibid.

8 Footage obtained from Saudi TV.

9 The safe house was in the Rawabi district.

10 'Terrorism – Saudi Arabia', *SUSRIS* website.

11 Authors' interview with Major-General Saud al-Halal.

12 Authors' interview with Major-General Abdulrahman al-Maqbal.

9 Operation Volcano

1 This communiqué was later republished in *Voice of Jihad*, no. 13 (2004). It is noteworthy that it makes no mention of Hajj's leadership role in AQAP.

2 Four of the vehicles belonged to the Mujahideen and two belonged to the Principality of Riyadh.

3 Qur'an 9:38

4 Qur'an Surah 93.

5 Mishaal al-Farraj was later arrested. It is from him that MOI investigators learnt what happened next.

6 His name was Abdullah al-Sahli.

7 Isa al-Awshen, 'Khalid al-Subayt: Redemption and Sacrifice', *Voice of Jihad*, no. 15 (2004).

8 One of the seven, Adel al-Dhubayti, was later arrested. It is from him that MOI investigators learnt the details of this story.

9 The trucks were driven by Mishaal al-Jasiri and Bandar al-Dukhayyel, Abu Ayub's brother.

10 Terror Strikes the Coasts

1 Early news reports described Wijdan as Syrian, but her nationality was soon changed to Saudi. Whether that means her father is Syrian and her mother Saudi is unknown. But it is an indication of the way the MOI was taking control of the narrative. A year later Wijdan would feature heavily in a TV programme dedicated to the Washm Street bombing called 'The Truth'.
2 Khalid al-Ahmad, Zayd bin Kami, Muneef al-Saqoufi, and Badr al-Matou, 'Washm Explosion: The terrorists have moved the war to the stage of attacking the state and Saudi society', *Asharq Al-Awsat*, 22 April 2004.
3 'Al Qaeda denies responsibility for the Washm explosion in Riyadh', *Islam Today* website, 28 April 2004, accessed in October 2013, islamtoday.net/nawafeth/artshow-12-43342.htm.
4 Turki al-Suhayl, 'Prince Salman greets those who have prayed over the body of the victims of the blast', *Al Riyadh*, 23 April 2004.
5 Much of what appears in this book is based on the tapes from Suwaydi.
6 Authors' telephone interview with Frances Townsend.
7 'Terrorism – Saudi Arabia', *SUSRIS* website.
8 These cell members were later arrested. At the time of writing their trials were ongoing, so they cannot be named here. But it is from the interrogation of them that much of this information is derived.
9 Authors' interview with Captain Sirhan Abdullah al-Ghamdi.
10 Lisa Meyers, 'Saudi prince: Zionism to blame for terror attack', *NBC News* website, accessed in October 2013, www.nbcnews.com/id/5218227/ns/nbcnightlynews/t/saudi-prince-zionism-blame-terror-attack.
11 'Interview with Saudi foreign minister', *Federal News Service*, 5 May 2004.
12 Mark Hosenball, 'Terror Watch: A New Rift?', *Newsweek*, 3 May 2004.
13 Fahda bin Saud, 'Anti-Saudi Campaign: Enough is Enough', *Abar News*, 6 May 2004.
14 'News and Views', *Muaskar al-Battar*, no. 10 (2004), p. 21.
15 Authors' interview with Major Nayef al-Tuwayr.
16 Authors' interview with Major Khalid al-Muhaya.
17 The Saudi embassy in Washington lists them as 20 Saudis, 41 Americans, and 88 Asians, including 8 Japanese, 34 Europeans, 8 Jordanians, and 10 Lebanese. See www.saudiembassy.net/archive/2004/news/page479.aspx.

18 The MOI's official press releases after the event list the nationalities of the hostages rescued from inside the hotel: 'ten Bengalis, a Filipino, 21 Indians, two Jordanians, a Lebanese, a Pakistani, and five Sri Lankans'. No mention is made of Westerners. See www.saudiembassy.net/archive/2004/news/page479.aspx.

11 The Khobar Massacre

1 They were Nimr al-Baqami and Adel al-Dhubayti.

2 'Turki bin Fuhayd al-Mutayri', *Voice of Jihad*, no. 20 (2004), pp. 31–4.

3 Mutayri himself, in the *Voice of Jihad* interview and in a video, makes this claim, and in 2006 other Al Qaeda publications confirmed it. The US government, however, dismisses this as propaganda. See 'Al Qaeda broadcasts a recording of the twentieth member of the 9/11 attacks', *Al Jazeera* website, 22 June 2006, accessed in October 2013, www.aljazeera.net/news/pages/4bda6c83-4ae9-4663-9c3a-b390bbf542d9; Christine Lagorio, 'Al Qaeda IDs a Would-Be 20th Hijacker', *CBS News* website, 21 June 2006, accessed in October 2013, www.cbsnews.com/stories/2006/06/21/terror/main1737160.shtml; '"Al-Qaeda video" of 20th hijacker', *BBC News* website, 21 June 2006, accessed in October 2013, news.bbc.co.uk/1/hi/world/middle_east/5101954.stm;

4 These included Ali al-Muabbadi (one of the Muhaya suicide bombers) and Talal al-Anbari (who died in the Safa raid).

5 Unlike the other three Khobar operatives, Baqami did not participate in Operation Volcano because he was already in the Eastern Province.

6 'Letter from the mujahid Turki al-Mutayri, may God have mercy on him, to Sheikh Osama bin Laden, may God preserve him', *Voice of Jihad*, no. 20 (2004), p. 25.

7 The guards were Turki Suhayl al-Naimi and Zayn Ali al-Abdali, and the Egyptian boy was Rami Samir al-Ghanimi; see Saeed Haider and Molouk Y. Ba-Isa, 'Bloodbath in Alkhobar', *Arab News*, 30 May 2004. AQAP denied causing Ghanimi's death. They wrote that 'Satan's soldiers killed him with their indiscriminate, random shooting' (*Voice of Jihad*, no. 18 (2004)).

8 Cowper-Coles describes Hamilton and his wife Penny as 'pillars of the classical music scene in the Eastern Province', and says they were due to leave the Kingdom shortly and to retire to Sussex. See Sherard Cowper-Coles, *Ever the Diplomat: Confessions of a Foreign Office Mandarin* (London: HarperPress, 2013), p. 267; Molouk Y. Ba-Isa, 'British Envoy Recalls Hamilton's Fondness for Saudi Arabia', *Arab News*, 31 May 2004.

9 He was Jimuel Tarrosa, an air-conditioning technician; see Dinan Arana and Romeo Navidad, 'Wife Remembers Slain Filipino's Love for His Kids', *Arab News*, 31 May 2004.

10 Cowper-Coles also says that Apicorp employees later scoured the intersection in search of Hamilton's signet ring. They managed to find it and handed it over to his widow. Cowper-Coles, *Ever the Diplomat*, p. 267.

11 Dave Montgomery, 'American was gunned down at his desk during siege', *Miami Herald*, 1 June 2004; 'Georgia man confirms his brother was American killed in terrorist attack', *Associated Press*, 1 June 2004; Barbara Ferguson, 'Dad Loved Saudi Arabia and Its People: Frank Floyd Jr.', *Arab News*, 3 June 2004.

12 Feliciano Dizon, aged forty-five, deputy finance officer at Resource Science Arabian Limited, and Joel Guiray, a driver; see Arana and Navidad, 'Wife Remembers . . .', and 'Why did they kill even Pinoys?', *Philippine Star*, 1 June 2004.

13 The guard's name was Hasan Muhammad Alil Asiri. Apparently a school bus full of children was caught in the crossfire, though that report has never been confirmed.

14 Incidentally, three Molotov cocktails were either placed underneath the front bumper or fell out of the car during unloading.

15 His body can be seen in the CCTV footage, but his identity is not known, nor whether he survived.

16 Molouk Y. Ba-Isa, 'Twelve hours of terror at Oasis compound', *Arab News*, 31 May 2004; Saeed Haider, '9-year-old recounts encounter with terrorist', *Arab News*, 1 June 2004.

17 Owen Bowcott, 'They killed two security guards then shot at the school van', *Guardian*, 31 May 2004.

18 Mutayri says the head was taken back to the main gate as a warning to others, but this is a lie. Johansson's throat was slit but he was not decapitated.

19 Neil MacFarquhar, 'Saudi Attacks Spurs More U.S. Workers to Pull Up Stakes', *New York Times Learning Network*, accessed in October 2013, www.nytimes.com/learning/students/pop/articles/03EXPA.html

20 The facilities manager was 45-year-old K. K. Pradeep Kumar; see 'Saudi Arabia: Eight Indians among 22 killed as Saudi hostage drama ends', *Deccan Herald*, 31 May 2004.

21 Rasheed Abou-Alsamh, 'How one OFW survived the Alkhobar attacks', *Arab News*, 4 June 2004.

22 Remarkably, though the bullet exploded inside his nose and ripped up much of his face, he survived; see Diana Arana, 'Victim of Alkhobar attack recovers after 4 surgeries', *Arab News*, 12 August 2004. His account of the event, including many pious embellishments, was posted online here: www.ncda.gov.ph/2009/07/employment-assistance.

23 http://www.philstar.com/headlines/252170/%C2%91why-did-they-kill-even-pinoys%C2%92 *Philippine Star*, 'Why did they kill even Pinoys?'.

24 This story is very hard to believe. It is absolutely illegal in Saudi Arabia to prevent Muslims from praying, and surely Cleopas would have stayed away. Nimr al-Baqami insists the call to Al Jazeera took place, although the channel has never confirmed it.

25 According to Cowper-Coles, among the soldiers was the owner of the compound, Maan al-Sanae. CCTV shows him wearing a flak jacket over his thobe and carrying a pistol. Accompanied by Emergency Forces officers, he sneaked into the hotel lobby before the direct assault and managed to rescue two American military personnel who were hiding in a ventilation shaft. Cowper-Coles, *Ever the Diplomat*, p. 268. The Mabahith doubt this happened.

26 Several hostages later confirm this, although they must have been moved somewhere else as during their search of the building the Special Forces did not come across them until they reached the lobby.

27 Much of his account is specious, that is certain. See Maher Abu Tayr, '22 Killed in Khobar hostage tragedy', *Al Dustour*, 31 May 2004.

28 Al Jazeera has never confirmed that this phone call was made either.

29 According to the forensic footage. The MOI's official number is twenty-two.

30 Ewen MacAskill, 'Saudis crack down on Islamic charities', *Guardian*, 3 June 2004; 'Saudi Arabia: A deal lies behind the escape of the hostage-takers', *Al Raya*, 2 June 2004; 'Saudi gunmen "tricked way to freedom deal"', *Reuters*, 3 June 2004; Jumana al-Rashed, 'Harvard University appoints Saudi analyst and researcher', *Al Riyadh*, 4 July 2012; 'Death of two men connected to the Khobar attacks', *BBC Arabic*, 2 June 2004.

31 'Saudi security forces "allowed kidnappers to go free"', *The Times*, 31 May 2004.

32 Transcript of *Anderson Cooper 360 Degrees*, 31 May 2004.

33 http://www.arabnews.com/node/250348 'Bloodbath in Alkhobar'.

34 http://www.arabnews.com/node/250462 Saeed Haider, 'Manhunt Continues for Three Escaped Terrorists', *Arab News*, 1 June 2004.

35 In fact, no soldiers were reported killed during their escape.

36 For several weeks, AQAP would continue to insist that Baqami had died. Although some news reports said that a terrorist had been arrested, TV footage of a terrorist being loaded into an ambulance covered in a sheet will have convinced AQAP that Baqami was dead. It is possible that the MOI wanted them to have that impression; any information Baqami gave up in interrogations would be more useful to the government if AQAP believed him to be dead. However, *The Times* would report on 8 June 2004 that three AQAP members dressed as women sneaked into the MOI's medical complex in Riyadh, where Baqami was

being held under armed guard, and attempted to rescue him. However, they failed to reach the prison wing and fled. So the Organization must have at least suspected by then that Baqami had survived.

37 Mutayri means by this awkward sentence that the government's claims that AQAP are just crazed bloodthirsty killers are no longer tenable, as so many of the people they encountered that day will know that they were not targeting Muslims and had specific goals, i.e. expelling non-Muslims from the Peninsula and so on.

12 The Assassination Cell

1 Authors' interview with James Oberwetter.

2 Authors' telephone interview with Sir Sherard Cowper-Coles.

3 One of the two militants was the husband of Wafa al-Shihri, whose teenage brother Yusuf al-Shihri was being held in Guantánamo Bay. She would go on to marry Yusuf's cellmate Saeed al-Shihri (no relation) once they were both repatriated back to Saudi Arabia. Saeed al-Shihri would eventually become deputy leader of AQAP in Yemen, where he was killed by a drone strike on 17 July 2013. Yusuf would be killed in a shootout with Saudi police on 18 October 2009.

4 *Voice of Jihad*, no. 18 (2004), p. 5.

5 Qur'an 5:33.

6 Prince Bandar bin Sultan, 'We will lose our war against terrorism, unless ...', *Al Watan*, 1 June 2004, translation provided by Saudi embassy in Washington, accessed on their website in October 2013, http://www.saudiembassy.net/archive/2004/statements/page12.aspx.

7 Abdulrahman Alrashed, 'The painful truth is, all terrorists are Muslims', *Asharq Al-Awsat*, 4 September 2004.

8 http://www.arabnews.com/node/250607 Abou-Alsamh, 'How one OFW survived the Alkhobar attacks'.

9 Neela Banerjee, 'Oil prices set another record, topping $42', *New York Times*, 2 June 2004.

10 Gardner, *Blood and Sand*, pp. 19–20.

11 The German was Jonathan Hermann Bengler. Bengler worked for a catering company which provided in-flight meals to Saudia Airlines. At around 6:15 p.m. on 22 May, he had just made a deposit at a branch of Arab National Bank and was getting into his car when two men in a Honda sped past and sprayed him with bullets; see Raid Qusti, 'German killed in drive-by shooting', *Arab News*, 23 May 2004. It was not clear at the time whether the attack was premeditated or if it had been carried out by members of AQAP. (AQAP never took responsibility for the killing, though they did briefly mention it in their news roundup in *Voice of Jihad*, no. 18.) However,

forensic analysis of bullet casings showed that the perpetrators' guns had been used in previous AQAP attacks. Also, eyewitnesses reported seeing the two gunmen eating at a fast-food restaurant inside the nearby shopping mall before carrying out the attack. According to authors' interview with Brigadier-General Zafir bin Hadi al-Shihri, the MOI's forensics experts sealed off the restaurant and gathered up everything that might have come into contact with the suspects – scraps of food, discarded rubbish, cutlery. They scoured this mass of evidence for DNA which they compared to blood samples taken from employees and other customers at the scene. They added their findings to the massive DNA database they were creating, which included readings not only from captured and killed suspects, but also from their extended families. This sort of rigorous forensic work was new to the Kingdom. If Bengler's killers had been apprehended, the database would have helped convict them. In fact the two were eventually spotted and killed in a shootout on 1 July 2004.

12 Their names have never been made public. *Voice of Jihad*, no. 18.

13 The MOI claims to have warned them away from Suwaydi. Gardner says he was given permission to go there. The presence of a government minder rather backs up his story.

14 Gardner was fully debriefed eighteen months later and describes the event in his book, *Blood and Sand*, ch. 10. The MOI corroborates his story.

15 Later arrested, Adel al-Dhubayti is the source of most of this information.

16 Authors' interview with Major-General Saud al-Halal.

17 Barbara Ferguson, 'Robert Jacobs loved going to camel races in Riyadh', *Arab News*, 10 June 2004.

18 AQAP filmed the attack and released the footage onto the Internet on 13 June 2004. On the identity of the killer, authors' interview with Brigadier-General Mudeef al-Talhi.

19 Later arrested, Mishaal al-Farraj is the source of most of this information.

20 Authors' interview with Colonel Dr Ahmad al-Janoubi.

21 'The search for him continues', *Al Arabiya* website, 16 June 2004.

22 Authors' interview with Major-General Saud al-Halal. The person who rented the car was later arrested during the battle of Rass.

23 'Riyadh won't negotiate with American hostage's abductors', *Agence France Presse*, 16 June 2004.

24 'The search for him continues'.

25 'U.S. to renew dire warning against travel to Saudi Arabia', *Agence France Presse*, 16 June 2004.

26 'American hostage's family make impassioned plea for his life', *Agence France Presse*, 16 June 2004.

27 'Bush watching fate of U.S. hostage in Saudi Arabia', *Agence France Presse*, 16 June 2004.
28 Rich McKay, '"Please teach me to pray for my dad"', *Daily Telegraph* (Australia), 15 June 2004.
29 'Crown prince says Saudis must protect expatriates', *Agence France Presse*, 16 June 2004.
30 Two of them, Mishaal al-Farraj and Adel al-Dhubayti, are, as of the time of writing, in prison. Their interrogations revealed the details of Johnson's death.
31 Abu Hassan was Abdul Majid al-Manie.
32 Authors' interview with Major-General Abdulrahman al-Maqbal.
33 Authors' interview with Brigadier-General Mudeef al-Talhi.
34 'Saudis Search for Slain Body', *Associated Press*, 20 June 2004.
35 'Saudis: Stop or Else', *Herald Sun* (Melbourne, Australia), 21 June 2004.
36 'Beheading evokes revulsion', *Arab News*, 20 June 2004.
37 http://vb.qloob.com/70079-%D8%A7%D9%84%D8%B3%D8%A4%D8%A7%D9%84-%D8%A7%D9%84%D8%AB%D8%A7%D9%85%D9%86-%D8%B9%D8%B4%D8%B1-%D9%85%D9%86-%D9%88%D8%AC%D9%88%D9%88%D9%88%D8%AF%D9%8A-%D9%85%D8%A7%D9%87%D9%88-%D8%B4%D8%B9%D9%88%D8%B1%D9%83-%D8%A8%D8%B9%D8%AF-%D9%85%D9%82%D8%AA%D9%84-%D8%B9%D8%A8%D8%AF%D8%A7%D9%84%D8%B9%D8%B2%D9%8A%D8%B2-%D8%A7%D9%84%D9%85%D9%82%D9%80%D9%80%D9%80%D8%B1%D9%86-%D8%9F%D8%9F%D8%9F.html.
38 Bruce Falconer, 'Al Qaeda, Online', *Mother Jones*, 16 February 2009.
39 Khalid bin Abdul Latif al-Maajil, 'Abdulaziz al-Muqrin, may God favour him', *Voice of Jihad*, no. 20, p. 24.
40 Hegghammer, *Jihad in Saudi Arabia*, p. 225, fn. 35.
41 'Their brother Paul Marshall Johnson', *Voice of Jihad*, no. 19, p. 21.
42 Qur'an 5:24.
43 Original Arabic found here: www.almajmaah.net/vb/archive/index.php/t-8409.html, translation ours.
44 Authors' interview with James Oberwetter.
45 William Branigin, 'Saudi Arabia announces limited amnesty offer', *Washington Post*, 23 June 2004.
46 Muneef al-Saqoufi, 'Amnesty for terrorists in Saudi Arabia ends, 6 have surrendered', *Asharq Al-Awsat*, 23 July 2004.
47 Along with the two already mentioned, the others were: Ibrahim al-Harbi and Fawzan al-Fawzan, who turned themselves in in Damascus; Khalid al-Harbi in Tehran; and Fa'iz al-Dosari in Ta'if.
48 Authors' interview with Brigadier-General Mudeef al-Talhi.
49 See www.sahab.net/forums/index.php?showtopic=55725.

13 The Network Splits

1 The Westerners were 63-year-old Irishman Anthony Higgins, who was shot at his desk in Riyadh on 3 August; a British expatriate called Edward Muirhead-Smith, who was shot in a Riyadh supermarket on 15 September; and a 41-year-old Frenchman called Laurent Barbot, who was killed in Jeddah on 26 September. On 11 August three security officers were wounded and one terrorist (Abdul Rahman al-Harbi) was killed in a shootout in Mecca. On 2 September in a shootout in Buraydah, three policemen were wounded and one was killed, along with two terrorists (Abdullah al-Harbi and Abdul Latif al-Khudayri). On 24 September in Tabouk four more security officers were wounded in a shootout and two terrorists arrested (Rida al-Najjar and Salah al-Najjar, who were behind the attempted bombing of two banks in Jeddah on 11 September 2004).

2 Number 25 on the list, a Moroccan called Hussein al-Haski, would be arrested in Belgium on 7 September, bringing the number down to nine.

3 One of them was Assam al-Otaybi, who had broken his parole. The other was Abdul Hameed al-Yahya, who had been in charge of the Wuroud safe house, where Paul Johnson was executed.

4 The killed man was Sami al-Subahi.

5 The killed man was Assam al-Mubaraki.

6 Authors' interview with James Oberwetter.

7 Authors' interview with Lieutenant-Colonel Bandar al-Baqami.

8 Ibid.

9 Michael Knights, 'JTIC Briefing: Jeddah Attack Underscores Fall in Capabilities of Saudi Militants', *Jane's Terrorism and Insurgency Center*, January 2005.

10 His name was Abdullah al-Anzi. He stood trial, received a death sentence, and, as of the time of writing, is on death row.

11 Knights, 'JTIC Briefing'.

12 Lawrence, *Messages to the World*, ch. 24.

13 Bandar al-Dukhayyel, 'The story of the siege of Al-Ammariya' (parts 1 and 2), *Voice of Jihad*, nos. 19 and 20.

14 Authors' interview with Dr. Tariq Alsheddi.

15 Ubayd's co-bomber was Nasser al-Mutayri.

16 Authors' interviews with Lieutenant-Colonel Bandar al-Duwaysh, Major Khalid al-Muhaya, and Major Nayef al-Tuwayr.

17 A transcript of Townsend's speech was accessed online in December 2014, www.saudiembassy.net/archive/2005/speeches/page22.aspx.

14 Stamped Out

1 'Probe seeks Saudi link to London bombers', *Reuters*, 7 August 2005.

2 Sabria S. Jawhar and Rob L. Wagner, 'The Battle of al-Ras: The Last Stand of the Who's Who of Al-Qaeda', *Saudi Gazette*, 12 April 2005.

3 As mentioned, Abdullah al-Rashoud, number twenty-two on the list, had disappeared and would be reported killed in Iraq in June 2005. Taleb al-Taleb, a mysterious figure and number fourteen on the list, has not been heard from to this day; investigators believe he may have been one of the Riyadh compound bombing suicide bombers, or maybe was among the dead at the King Fahd neighbourhood raid.

4 That is not exactly true. In January 2007, the thirtieth and final issue would see the light of day. However, by then the Organization as founded by Ayiri and nurtured by Muqrin was dead.

5 Authors' interview with Dr Tariq Alsheddi.

6 Basma al-Sati, 'Wife of slain security officer sends message to his killers', *Asharq Al-Awsat*, 20 June 2005.

7 Fawdah's accomplice was Masnour al-Thubayti.

8 'Saudi Arabia "failing to address human rights concerns"', *BBC News*, 21 October 2013; 'Saudi Arabia: Five beheaded and "crucified" amid "disturbing" rise in executions', *Amnesty International*, 21 May 2013, accessed online in December 2013, www.amnesty.org/en/news/saudi-arabia-five-beheaded-and-crucified-amid-disturbing-rise-executions-2013-05-21; British Foreign & Commonwealth Office, 'Saudi Arabia', *Human Rights and Democracy 2012*, accessed online in December 2013, www.hrdreport.fco.gov.uk/human-rights-in-countries-of-concern/saudi-arabia; Steve Robson, '"I have nine hours left until I die": Haunting last words of man executed in Saudi Arabia who confessed "because guards threatened to torture his mother"', *Daily Mail*, 13 March 2013.

9 Authors' interview with Major-General Khalid al-Harbi.

10 Authors' interview with documentary film producer Adel Alabdulkarim.http://www.muslm.org/vb/showthread.php?260384-%D8%A7%D8%B3%D8%AA%D8%B4%D9%87%D8%A7%D8%AF-%D8%A3%D8%B3%D8%A7%D9%85%D8%A9-%D8%A7%D9%84%D9%88%D9%87%D9%8A%D8%A8%D9%8A-%D8%A7%D9%84%D8%AA%D9%85%D9%8A%D9%85%D9%8A-%D9%81%D9%8A-%D8%A7%D9%84%D8%B9%D8%B1%D8%A7%D9%82-%D8%A3%D8%AD%D8%AF-%D8%A7%D9%84%D8%B0%D9%8A%D9%86-%D9%81%D8%B1%D9%88%D8%A7-%D9%85%D9%86-%D8%A7%D9%84%D8%B3%D8%AC%D9%86-%D8%B5%D9%88%D8%B1%D8%AA%D9%87-%D8%B4%D9%

8A%D8%A1-%D9%85%D9%86-%D8%B3%D9%8A%D8%B1%D8%AA%D9%87

11 Authors' interview with Sir Sherard Cowper-Coles.

12 Martin Bright, Antony Barnett, and Mohammed Alkhereiji, 'Saudis warned UK of London attacks', *Guardian*, 7 August 2005.

13 Antony Barnett, 'UK was warned of July suicide attacks', *Guardian*, 5 February 2006; Bob Woodward, *State of Denial: Bush at War, Part III* (New York: Simon & Schuster, 2006), Kindle edn.

14 John Simpson, 'Tricky task of interviewing Saudi king', *BBC News*, 30 October 2007.

15 The killed man was Muhammad al-Uwayda and the arrested man was Muhammad al-Samman.

16 One of the cell members, a young new recruit called Adel al-Yamani, was later arrested and provided the MOI with the details of the cell's plans.

17 Or perhaps eight. A year after the attack, a lone issue of *Voice of Jihad* appeared containing an account of the operation by a man the magazine calls Badr al-Humaydi. He is not included in the MOI's list of cell members.

18 Authors' interview with deputy minister of petroleum.

Epilogue: A New Kind of Assassin

1 They were killed while attempting to flee in an SUV which, perhaps as part of a plan to attack the royal family, had fake number plates identical to those of a car belonging to a Saudi princess.

2 One of those rounded up was Adel al-Yamani, the sole surviving member of the Abqaiq raid.

3 Some people would accuse the government that non-violent, liberal reformists were included in the round-up.

4 The Saudi exile was Salim Muqsif al-Nahdi. He delivered this tirade in *By the Lord of the Kaaba*, a propaganda video released by Ansar al-Mujahideen.

5 Policing inside the Kingdom also intensified. A cell in Mecca providing financial and media support to AQAP across the border was shut down in March 2009.

6 Chris McGreal and Vikram Dodd, 'Cargo Bombs Plot: U.S. Hunts Saudi extremist', *Guardian*, 31 October 2010.

7 http://carnegieendowment.org/files/cp97_boucek_saudi_final.pdf.

8 Authors' interviews with Frances Townsend and Robert Jordan.

9 Authors' interviews with Frances Townsend.

10 Authors' interview with General Mansour al-Turki.

Index

ABB Lummus, 239–40
Abdulaziz Al Saud, King, 48, 106, 173, 384
Abdullah bin Abdulaziz, Crown Prince, later King, xxviii–xxix, 30, 45, 48, 95–6, 99–109, 140–1, 142, 177–8, 189, 230, 240–2, 269, 273, 285, 289, 296–7, 299, 314, 315, 345–6, 349, 375, 377, 399
  and Prince Nayef, 48
Abdulmutallab, Umar Farouk, 372, 400
Abercrombie-Winstanley, Gina, 309
Abha, 298, 305
Abqaiq oil refinery, 351, 353, 356–8, 362, 399
Abu Ali, Ahmed Omar, 121–4
Abu Ayub, xxii, 53–4, 61, 161, 165–6, 180, 183, 192, 194, 195, 196, 207, 218–19, 224, 252, 253, 275–6, 277, 278, 281, 285, 288, 316, 397
  death of, 289–91, 397
Abu Ghraib prison, 272, 279, 293, 312, 379, 395
Abu Hajer, *see* Muqrin, Abdulaziz al-
Abu Hashim, 261
Abu Hassan, 169, 287–8, 308
Abu Hudhayfa, letter to Bin Laden, 18–19
Abu Jandal, 160
Abu Riha, *see* Sahim, Muhammad al-
Abu Sufyan, 366, 367, 368, 370, 372
Adel, Saif al-, xxi, 25–6, 29, 34, 36, 62, 74, 78, 171
  and Iran, 26, 34–5, 51
  and KSM, 78–9
Advice and Reform Committee, 240
Adwan, Lt-Col. Umar al-, 129–30
AEC, 278, 283
Afghanistan:
  as Al Qaeda base of operations, 20, 27, 50, 78, 116, 160, 359
  civil war in, 158, 172
  during Soviet period, 23, 156–9, 374, 391, 392
  and mujahideen, 13, 23, 25, 26, 28, 35, 42, 50, 52, 53, 176, 252
  and NATO invasion, 22–6, 40, 57, 121, 150, 168, 252, 295, 386, 393
  under Taliban, 11–12
Ahmed bin Abdulaziz, Prince, 43, 110

Ahsa, 128
Akur, Col Bandar al-, 310, 312, 338–9
Al Ashaikh, Saleh, 59
Al Jazeera (satellite television network), 29, 76, 230, 263, 264
Al Qaeda, 381
 and American invasion of Afghanistan, 23
 in the Arabian Peninsula, *see* AQAP
 beginnings of, 13, 391
 ethnic makeup of, 17, 74
 evolution of, xvi
 financing of, 13, 33, 48–9, 75, 135–9, 142, 231–2
 fleeing Afghanistan, 32–3, 34, 393
 franchises of, xvi, 78, 205, 344, 365, 377
 ideology of, 98–9, 101, 107, 127, 160, 366, 375, 382, 388
 in Iraq, 163–4, 205, 344, 363, 366, 377
 known as 'the Organization', 1
 in Kuwait, 55
 misconceptions about, xv–xvi
 in Morocco, 43, 205
 nuclear ambitions of, 44, 62
 propaganda videos by, 21
 rhetoric of, 54
 in Saudi Arabia, *see* AQAP
 and Taliban, xv–xvi
 as terrorist group, xv
 top leadership of, 17
 in United Kingdom, 100, 124, 240, 345
 in Yemen, *see* AQAP
 see also Advice and Reform Committee; AQAP; Central Command; Shura Council
Al-Nida website, 28, 52, 167, 381
Algeria, 35, 159
Alhambra Oasis Village compound, 87, 89–92, 93, 94, 101, 113, 120, 172, 177
Alrashed, Abdulrahman, 272–3
Amato, Antonio, 264–5
Ammariya mountains, 316
Amri, Uthman al-, 298
Anbari, Talal al-, 235–8, 243
And Incite the Believers, 171
Ansari, Mustafa al-, 240
Anzi, Abdulaziz al-, 169, 337–8
Apicorp, 253, 255–6
 see also Khobar massacre
AQAP, 124, 185, 198, 243, 254, 266, 273, 301, 322, 350, 373, 381–2, 392
 adopts name AQAP, 205, 396
 aims of, xiii–xiv, 18–19, 76, 88–9, 112, 161, 315, 373, 374
 armaments of, 38
 assassination cell of, 193, 194, 195–7, 252, 253, 275–80
 attack plans of, 73, 76, 79, 115, 125–6, 205–6
 attitude toward Saudi government of, 7, 147, 163, 177–8, 242, 257, 382
 attractions of, for recruits, 80, 82
 and clerics, 162, 301, 376
 escape tactics of, 4, 85–6, 306
 fatwas of, 118, 120, 190, 301
 fundraising for, 28–9, 36, 75, 78, 155, 163–4
 and House of Saud, 100, 120, 170, 173, 220, 222, 242, 257, 381, 388
 and Internet, 19, 28, 80, 86, 118, 163, 169, 194, 199, 205, 230, 240, 271, 279–80, 291, 294, 296
 and invasion of Iraq, xiii, 163
 leadership of, 25, 73, 76, 100, 109, 114–15, 118, 161, 200, 205, 304, 344, 351, 361, 366, 376
 legal committee of, 2, 301
 military wing of, 19, 35, 36
 nuclear ambitions of, xvi, 62, 73, 118, 128
 power struggles within, 36, 74–5, 79, 114, 161, 304–5
 propaganda of, xiv, 2, 18–19, 28, 80, 98–9, 118, 128, 144, 167–2,

191, 194, 205–6, 242, 251, 259, 286, 337, 371, 376, 383, 389
propaganda videos by, 171–2, 199–200, 210, 215, 219, 255, 280, 284, 291–2, 298, 313, 352, 366, 372, 397
and recruitment, 28, 36, 38–9, 65, 75, 78, 79, 122, 162–3, 168, 286, 303, 337, 377
recruits to, xvi, 32, 36, 39, 80, 82, 83, 115, 125, 152, 162, 165, 169, 172, 214–15, 303–4, 367, 375, 376, 379
shortcomings of, 113, 356, 376
and smuggling, 38, 80, 298, 309
strategy of, 18–19, 76, 164, 230, 277, 374–6
structure of, 73, 79, 112, 114–15, 143, 165
and suicide wills, 83, 84, 88, 172, 198, 200, 210–14, 231, 254, 369
surveillance operations of, 71–3, 115, 148, 165, 167, 193, 207–9, 253, 254, 305, 351, 354
and 'third-generation' fighters, xxvii, 314, 340
threat posed by, xvi, 76, 374
and training, training camps, 28, 38, 53, 65, 79, 172, 219
video footage shot by, xvi, 8, 9, 80, 172–8, 181–2, 183, 192, 193, 194, 197–8, 199–200, 207–9, 210–14, 215–16, 217–18, 219–22, 226–7, 231, 281–4, 286, 288, 352–8
views on security services, 125, 132, 190, 205, 216, 222, 226, 277, 298, 302
in Yemen, 122, 361, 364, 366, 367, 374, 382, 400
see also Abqaiq oil refinery; *Camp of the Sabre*; Emergency Forces HQ bombing; Emergency Forces recruitment office bombing; Haramain Brigades; Khobar massacre; List of Nineteen; List of Twenty-Six; MOI HQ bombing; Muhaya compound bombing; Operation Volcano; raids (MOI vs. AQAP); Riyadh compound bombings; safe houses; Shura Council; *Voice of Jihad*; Washm Street bombing
Arab Petroleum Investment Corporation, *see* Apicorp
Arab Spring, 375–6
Aramco, 53, 76, 244–5, 257, 274, 353, 355
armed forces (Saudi), 109, 110
Asfan training camp, 65
Asiri, Abdullah al-, 363–5, 368–72, 400
Asiri, Ibrahim al-, 361–5, 369, 370, 371, 372–3
Asir province, 309
Atef, Muhammad, xxi, 24
Attash, Walid bin, 74, 79
Aufhauser, David, 136–7, 141, 232
Awakening (clerical reform movement), 127, 382, 392
Awlaki, Anwar al-, 122, 373
Awshen, Isa al-, xxii–xxiii, 2, 8–9, 167–9, 170, 215–16, 226, 231, 287, 299, 301, 305, 315, 337, 381
death of, 4, 299, 397
recruited by Ayiri, 28
Ayiri, Yusuf al-, xxiii, 26–32, 33, 44, 52, 60, 66, 69–70, 73–4, 78–9, 86–7, 98, 121, 128, 155, 161, 163, 167–8, 169, 170, 175, 315, 337, 359, 362, 364, 365, 375, 376, 381, 392
agrees to set up AQAP, 19
in Bamyan, 16–19
book by, celebrating 9/11, 29
and Centre for Islamic Research and Study, 28
childhood of, 13
death of, 119–20, 394
lays foundations of AQAP, 28–9, 120

Ayiri, Yusuf al – *continued*
fundraising activities of, 14, 27, 28, 75, 78
and KSM, 36, 74, 79
and Osama bin Laden, 12–13, 17, 29
in prison, 27–8
recruitment activities of, 28–9, 32, 78
sets up *Al-Nida* website, 28
as 'the Sabre', 26
writings of, 26, 28, 29, 73
Azdi, Abu Bakr al-, *see* Faqasi, Ali al-
Azzam, Abdullah, 157

Badr of Riyadh, xxiii, 199–200, 210, 215
Bahrain, 65, 76, 199
see also New York subway plot
Bahri, Nasser al-, 160
Bali bombings (2002), 55, 393
Bali bombings (2005), 67
Bamyan, 16
Bandar bin Sultan, Prince, xxix, 44, 62, 97, 137, 138–9, 272
Baqami, Nimr al-, xxiii, 253–5, 258, 259, 261, 264, 265, 266, 267–8, 397
see also Jerusalem Squadron
Battle of Badr, 175, 178, 180, 382
Bayar, Abraham, 258
Beirut barracks bombing, 323
Berlusconi, Silvio, 265
Black, Cofer, 232
Blair, Tony, 76–7, 292
Blehed, Abdullah al-, 101
'booze bombers', 55–6
border guards (Saudi), 37, 109, 110, 364, 367–8, 374
Bosnia, 27, 35, 49, 88, 160, 172, 336, 392
British Airways, 200
Buraydah, 29, 51, 133, 217, 242, 308, 323, 327–8, 345, 365
Buraydah intifada, 27, 31
Bush, George H.W., xxix, xxx, 238
Bush, George W., xxix, xxx, 54, 76–7, 102, 122, 137–9, 141, 238, 285, 292, 323, 366, 378, 393, 394, 398
bin Laden, Osama, xiii, xxi–xxii, 22–5, 30, 35, 36, 50, 54, 57, 62, 75, 78–9, 127, 128, 160, 172, 240, 252, 254, 313, 314–15, 352, 359, 361, 375, 381, 382, 388, 391, 392, 400
aims of, for Saudi Arabia, 18–19, 62, 76–7, 100, 315
Al Jazeera interview (2001) with, 29
anti-American fatwa (1998) of, 15, 392
and Ayiri, 12–13, 17, 29, 119
and Bamyan Buddhas, 16
CNN interview (1997) with, 15
death of, 400
growing terrorist profile of, 13–14
and House of Saud, 45, 77, 102, 314
and Mullah Omar, 15–16
ordinary Saudis' view of, 14, 17, 22
nuclear ambitions of, 44
returns to Afghanistan, 15
and Saudi clerics, 17
sermon of, on Eid al-Adha, 76–7

Camp Farouq, 13, 16, 75, 252
Camp of the Sabre, 170–1, 206, 242, 295, 383
Cargo planes bomb plot, 372–3, 400
Casabag, Mariano, 262
Casablanca bombings (2003), 327
Central Command (Al Qaeda), 74, 75, 77, 79, 114, 161, 200
Centre for Islamic Studies and Research, xxiii, 28, 98
Centre for National Dialogue, 109, 230, 375
Chad, Chadians, 125, 133, 308
Chechnya, 8, 9, 27, 28, 53, 75, 99, 159, 168, 214, 392
CIA, 44, 51, 59, 62, 65, 86, 100, 110, 124, 138, 139, 168, 170, 394
black sites of, 60, 67
and Mabahith, 62–3, 65–6, 232–4

see also joint US–Saudi counterterrorism unit
Civil Defence (Saudi), 68, 143, 247, 321
Cleopas, E. Carlos, 263
clerics (Saudi), xvii, 29–30, 31, 44, 54, 56–9, 103–4, 108, 118, 127, 144, 156, 157, 168, 294, 298, 383, 390
and criticism of AQAP, 128, 162, 190, 375, 376
and criticism of Taliban, 13
and Grand Mosque siege, 107
and House of Saud, 103, 107
imprisoned by MOI, 27–8, 31
and Prince Nayef, 47–8
relationship with Bin Laden of, 17
Cole, USS, xxvi, xxviii, 20–1, 37, 44, 59, 60, 87, 393
as 'boats operation', 17
Committee for the Promotion of Virtue and the Prevention of Vice, *see* Mutaween
Cowper-Coles, Sir Sherard, xxx, 49, 270, 274–5, 276, 345
Crawford Ranch summit (2002), 102
Cumbers, Simon, 274–6, 318, 397

Dammam, 167, 244, 305, 350, 399
Dar es Salaam, *see* East Africa embassy bombings
Dent, Robert, 66
Dandani, Turki al-, xxiii, 51–2, 53, 66, 69, 71, 73, 75, 79, 80, 84–6, 87, 109, 113, 121, 126, 133, 155, 161, 164, 175, 394
death of, 128–32, 394
Dhaali, Ibrahim al-, 194
Dhahran, 238, 244, 351, 392
Dhubayti, Adel al-, 253, 255, 275
see also Jerusalem Squadron
Dosary, Mujab al-, 168–9
Dubai, 37, 59, 199
Dukhayyel, Ahmad al-, xxiii–xxiv, 61, 126, 133–4
Dukhayyel, Bandar al-, xxii, xxiii, 316, 321
Dukhayyel, Faisal al-, *see* Abu Ayub
Durayhim, Ibrahim al-, 166, 290
Duwaysh, Lt.-Col. Bandar al-, 318–20, 322

East Africa embassy bombings, 13–14, 392
and America's response, 16
Eastern Province, 133, 217, 243, 253, 254, 274, 305, 308, 351, 352, 375
Echo of the Brigades, 298
Egypt, 17, 47, 106
Eid al-Adha, 76
Emergency Forces (Saudi), 109–10, 116, 117, 129, 143, 145, 150–1, 166, 174, 179, 185, 223, 226, 229, 236–7, 243, 244, 249, 263–4, 266, 289, 299, 306, 308, 309, 317, 328, 329
see also Emergency Forces HQ bombing; Emergency Forces recruitment office bombing; Washm Street bombing
Emergency Forces HQ bombing:
first attempt (2003), 166–7, 172, 181–3, 186, 192, 200, 395
second attempt (2004), *see* Washm Street bombing
Emergency Forces recruitment office bombing, 317, 318–9, 398
Ethiopia, 160
expatriates in Saudi Arabia, 71–3, 76, 91–3, 94–5, 97, 188–9, 190, 191, 193, 225, 231–2, 238–9, 244–5, 249, 251, 259, 274, 277, 279, 285, 375, 396

Fahd bin Abdulaziz, King, xxix, 45, 48, 102, 105, 107, 345, 391, 399
Fahd, Munira, 84
Fahd, Nasr al-, xxviii, 31, 117–18, 190
see also Takfeeri Troika
Fahd, Rayan, 84
Fahda bin Saud, Princess, 241
Faisal bin Abdulaziz, King, 106, 293
The Fallujah Squadron: The Raid on the Crusader Consulate in Jeddah, 313

Faqasi, Ali al-, xxiv, 62, 73, 74–5, 115–16, 117–18, 121–4, 150, 155, 161, 395
surrender of, 126–8, 298, 394
Faqih, Mansour, 193
Farraj, Fahd al-, 210, 218, 224, 226–7
Farraj, Hamoud al-, 195–7
Farraj, Khalid al-, xxiv, 195–7, 210, 216, 253, 301–4, 316, 395
Farraj, Mishaal al-, xxiv, 215–16, 222, 278, 299
Farraj, Muhammad al-, 223
'Father of Perfume', *see* Sahim, Muhammad al-
Fawdah, Kemal, 339–40
Fawwaz, Khalid al-, 240
Fawzia, wife of Saleh al-Oufi, 5–6, 299
FBI, 21, 43, 59, 96, 110, 139, 170, 234
financing, of terrorism, 48–9, 95, 135–9, 140, 141–3, 231–2, 242, 285, 378
Floyd, Frank, 258
Foreign Office (UK), 193
French tourists attack, 365, 400

Gardner, Frank, 274–6, 397
General Directorate of Traffic (Riyadh), *see* traffic police
General Intelligence Presidency (GIP), 16, 110–11, 345
General Investigation Directorate, *see* Mabahith
General Presidency of Islamic Research and Fatwas, 57–9, 393
Ghaith, Muhammad al-, 215–16, 218, 220, 221–2, 352–6
Ghamdi, Capt. Sirhan al-, 236–7
Ghazali, Muhammad al-, 364–5, 368
Ghufayli, Nora al-, 331
Global War on Terrorism, xiii, 2, 34, 52, 77, 98, 135, 232, 279, 340, 345, 346, 373
'Golden Chain', 13
Graf, W. Maxmilian, 55
Grand Mosque siege (1979), *see* Utaybi, Juhayman al-
Grand Mufti (Saudi), 57, 144, 385
Guantánamo Bay detention camp, 33, 56, 57, 60, 168, 279, 293, 366, 367, 379
Gulf War (1991), 66, 102, 127, 150, 391

Habib, Kamal, 190
hadith, 77, 83
Ha'il Centre Compound, 257
Ha'il province, 118, 336
Ha'ir prison, 168
Hajj, 57, 63, 64–5, 115, 116, 336, 383–4
Hajj, Khalid al-, xxv, 35, 37, 38, 39, 73, 74–6, 78–80, 86, 87–8, 100, 114, 155, 161, 205, 315, 393, 394
death of, 200–3, 396
Halal, Maj.-Gen. Saud al-, 194–5, 276–7, 280, 285–6, 290
Halliburton, 255
Hamas, 19, 22
Hamilton, Michael, 256–7, 275
Hamza the Martyr, *see* Dandani, Turki al-
Haramain Brigades, 194, 230–1, 298, 395
Haramain Foundation, 48
Harbi, Col. Fahd al-, 328–9, 331, 333–4
Harbi, Maj.-Gen. Khalid al-, 116–17, 143, 319, 340–1, 349–50
Harithi, Abu Ali, 59
Hasiri, Majid al-, 347, 349
Hayari, Yunus al-, xxv, 336–8, 340, 342, 344, 345, 350, 398–9
Hawali, Safar al-, 127–8, 298, 382, 394
Heavenly Virgins, 160, 176, 215, 227, 384
Hijaz, 73, 115, 118, 121, 126, 150, 234–5, 243, 305, 308, 312, 336, 337, 347, 399
Holiday Inn, 239
houris, *see* Heavenly Virgins
House of Saud, xvii, 48, 76, 77, 100, 102–4, 138, 351, 374, 376, 384
anti-Zionism of, 240–2

AQAP's views on, 99, 170, 173, 220, 222, 388
and Arab nationalism, 106
and clerics, 103
and Muslim Brotherhood, 106, 386
and neo-Salafism, 106
and Osama bin Laden, 15, 45, 102, 314
wealth of, 105, 314
Human Rights Watch, 63
Humaydi, Hamad al-, 330
Hussein, Saddam, 50, 54, 76, 77, 102
Huwayrini, Abdulaziz al-, 193, 325, 395

Ikhwan, 272
Imam Turki bin Abdullah Grand Mosque, 231
Imam University (Riyadh), 52, 71, 168, 230
Inside the Cell, 301–4, 397
International Counterterrorism Conference, 323–6, 398
Interpol, 46
Iran, 26, 34–5, 36, 49–50, 53, 62, 171, 298, 323–4
Iraq, 26, 36, 49–50, 51, 54, 102, 106, 163, 164, 214, 255, 265, 305, 363–4, 373
no-fly zone over, 46
Iraq War (2003), 54, 62, 76–7, 79, 99, 150, 163, 271–2, 285, 295, 315, 363, 366, 376–7, 394, 398
Islam, 12, 15, 30, 31, 49, 50, 77, 81, 100, 115, 117, 126–7, 136, 140–1, 142, 144, 156–7, 175, 177, 178, 185, 190, 210, 230, 231, 232, 272, 285, 294, 314, 334, 352, 357, 382, 383, 384, 385, 387, 388, 389, 390
and *adab*, 83
Islamic University of Medina, 75, 121
Israel, 45, 99, 101, 293, 323

Jacobs, Robert, 277
Jadawel compound, 87, 92–3, 94
Jawf province, 52, 128
Jazan, 143, 149, 150, 152, 309, 395
Jeddah, 14, 65, 114, 115, 125, 127, 128, 139–40, 143, 177, 234–5, 239, 243, 288, 309, 310, 336, 338, 339, 340, 364, 365, 368, 369, 370, 397
Jerusalem Squadron, 253–68, 271, 275, 291, 306, 396
see also Baqami, Nimr al-; Dhubayti, Adel al-; Khobar massacre; Mutayri, Turki al-; Subaei, Abdullah al-
jihad, 32, 50, 57, 81, 99, 101, 107, 126–7, 160, 163, 293–4, 359, 376–7, 385
in Afghanistan, against Soviet Union, 12, 14, 16, 23, 50, 102, 106, 156–9, 167, 168, 210, 374, 386, 391, 392
in Afghanistan, against United States, 22, 122, 160, 303, 336
in Algeria, 35, 159–60
in Bosnia, 27, 28, 35, 88, 160, 172, 336, 386, 392
in Chechnya, 8, 9, 27, 28, 53, 75, 99, 159, 168, 210, 386, 392
in Iraq, 163, 164, 265, 303, 314, 344, 363–4, 376–7, 394
in Kashmir, 336
in Lebanon, 363
in the Philippines, 262
in Saudi Arabia, 2, 19, 40, 78, 88, 99, 101, 206, 314, 359
in Somalia, 13, 35, 160
in Syria, 374
in Tajikistan, 20
in Turkmenistan, 210
Jihad Wahl camp, 20, 158
Johansson, Magnus, 261
Johnson, Paul Marshall, xxx, 1–2, 10, 278–80, 281–8, 290, 291–2, 295–6, 299, 308, 316, 318, 397
Johnson, Thanom, 278, 295
joint US–Saudi counterterrorism unit, 62–3, 65–6, 233–4, 378, 394
Jordan, Robert, xxx, 93–7, 138, 140, 238, 393, 395
Jubail, 94

Jubeir, Adel al-, 140, 284
Juhani, Fayez, 312–13
Juhani, Khalid al-, 45, 87–8
Julaidan, Wa'el Hamza, 49
Julaydan, Muhammad Rashid al-, 399
July 7, 2005 terrorist attacks, 67, 124, 344–5, 399
Juwayr, Fahd al-, xxv, 215–16, 220, 221–2, 278, 337, 350–8, 359, 399

Kabul, 22, 23, 87, 158, 159
Kandahar, 11, 12, 16, 23–4, 252, 254, 393
Karachi, 19, 25, 32–3, 59, 79, 393
karamat, *see* miracles
Kashmiri, Hazim al-, 87–8
Kerry, John, 241
Khalidi, Ahmad al-, xxviii, 31, 117, 190
see also Takfeeri Troika
Khalidi, Turki al-, *see* Dandani, Turki al-
Khamis Mushayt, 66, 76, 113
Khan, Mohammed Sadique, 124
Kharj, 46, 150, 322, 337, 363
Khattab, Umar ibn al-, 254
Khobar, 143, 243–5, 251, 253, 254, 274, 306, 396
  see also Khobar massacre; Khobar Towers bombing
Khobar massacre, 243–8, 270, 271, 273, 275, 293, 305, 306, 311, 318, 334, 396–7
  and oil price, 273–4
Khobar Towers bombing, 27, 96, 392
Khost, 20, 158
Khudayr, Ali al-, xxviii, 31, 117, 190
  see also Takfeeri Troika
Khuzaim, Ismael, 281–4, 318
King Fahd Central Hospital (Jazan), 150
King Fahd football stadium, 288
King Fahd Security College, 41–3
King Khalid Air Base, 66, 76, 113
King Khalid International Airport (Riyadh), 279
King Saud University (Riyadh), 80, 198
Kingdom Tower, 39
King's Cup of Champions, 288–9
KSM, xxii, 23–4, 25, 32–7, 59, 60, 73, 75, 78–9, 100, 393
  arrest of, 67, 79
  and Ayiri, 36, 74, 79
  and Bali bombings, 55
  and 9/11, 24
  torture of, 100
  and World Trade Center bombing (1993), 24
Kunaydri, Wijdan al-, 229, 231
Kuwait, 55, 102
Kyl, John, 136

Lakshar-e-Taiba, 32
Lemieux, Monica, 310–11
Limburg (oil tanker), xxvi, 54–5, 393
List of Nineteen, 86–7, 115, 116, 121, 126, 132, 134, 152, 153, 169, 193, 394
List of Twenty-Six, 193, 198, 205, 224, 235, 238, 287, 298, 299, 305, 316, 322, 335, 336, 340, 350, 395
Lockheed Martin, 279
London, 100, 124, 200, 344–6, 399
Lukoil, 257

Mabahith, 42, 51, 53, 60, 61, 64, 85, 86, 88, 110–12, 122, 142–3, 145, 151, 168, 195, 198–200, 234–6, 289, 296, 299, 301, 305–6, 312, 316–19, 325–6, 328, 336, 337, 353, 363, 364, 367, 368, 374, 379, 385
  and CIA, 51, 62–3, 65–6, 232–4, 377
  and FBI, 96, 234, 377
  field agents of, 112
  headquarters of, 198
  intelligence gathering by, xiv, 50, 65, 109, 113–14, 120, 128, 155, 166, 178, 243, 277, 280, 285, 289, 304, 373
  and interrogations, 44, 64, 111, 120, 122, 124, 194, 197, 199, 235
  origins of, 46–7

reform of, 43, 47, 111–12, 296, 377
reputation of, 6, 46–7, 298, 303
surveillance operations of, 85, 234, 242, 306, 316
and terrorism hotlines, 191–2, 198, 333
and torture allegations, 47, 56, 124, 303, 338–40
and United Kingdom, 345, 377
and Yemen, 50, 366, 373
see also joint US–Saudi counterterrorism unit; List of Nineteen; List of Twenty-Six; raids (MOI vs. AQAP)
Madrid train bombings, 67, 327–8, 396
Malaysia, 52
Mali, Malians, 125
Maliki, Maj. Sultan al-, 125
Manie, Abdul Majid al-, *see* Abu Hassan
Maqbal, Maj.-Gen. Abdulrahman al-, 201–3
Martin, Michael, 55
martyrdom, 19, 69, 80, 120, 129, 147, 149, 157, 160, 168, 174–6, 182, 197, 198, 210, 214, 223, 226, 252, 254–5, 267, 271, 296, 351, 353, 359, 364, 385
Masri, Abu Hafs al-, *see* Atef, Muhammad
Massoud, Ahmed Shah, 12
Mazar-e-Sharif, 23
McDonald's, 239
Mecca, 32, 77, 106–7, 115, 118, 119, 124–6, 127, 143, 178, 179, 271, 309, 336, 338, 370, 382, 389, 398
media (Saudi), 97–8, 104, 132, 225, 229–30, 240, 272–3, 284–5, 292, 371
media (US), 96–7, 124, 135, 138, 150, 170, 177, 273–4, 323
Medina, 12, 75, 77, 115, 116–18, 121–2, 123, 127, 299, 305, 347, 349, 365, 382, 389
Mejjati, Adam al-, xxvi, 327, 328, 335
Mejjati, Karim al-, xxv, 88, 327, 334, 335, 337, 345
Mereno, Marvin, 262
Ministry of Defence (Saudi), *see* armed forces
Ministry of Interior (Saudi), *see* MOI
Ministry of Islamic Affairs (Saudi), 57–9, 66–7, 108, 144, 169
miracles, 156–7, 385
Mohawk, Hani, *see* Abu Ali, Ahmed Omar
MOI, xiv, 49, 86, 99, 115, 120, 126, 132, 134, 146, 169, 178, 181, 189, 197, 200, 222, 224, 225, 240, 251–2, 265–6, 269–71, 277, 301, 340, 350, 363, 364, 377, 378
and appeals to the public, 86, 108, 200
counter-propaganda campaign of, 108, 118, 144, 176, 188, 190–1, 230, 294, 301, 375
crackdowns on clerics, 27–8, 42, 47, 128, 190, 230, 330, 375, 392
forces of, 61, 109, 125, 143–4, 189, 243
forensics capabilities of, 96, 109–12
headquarters of, 46; *see also* MOI HQ bombing
obfuscates AQAP threat, 55, 61–2
pressure on, 194–5, 286
reform of, 43, 269–70, 296, 365, 373
reputation among Saudis of, 6, 237
and terrorist rehabilitation, *see* Munasaha programme
and training, 109, 112, 143–4, 178, 243, 269–70, 377
and treatment of women, 6, 118, 195–6, 299, 307
and United Kingdom, 345
and United States, 51, 101, 325
see also border guards; Emergency Forces; List of Nineteen; List of Twenty-Six; Mabahith; Mujahideen (tribal police force); raids (MOI vs. AQAP); Security Patrols; Special Forces; traffic police

MOI HQ bombing, 317, 318, 398
Monis, Lawrence, 257
Mont Blanc operation (Swiss), 60, 67
Morocco, 43, 46, 60, 105, 159, 205, 327, 336
Muabbadi, Ali al-, 172, 183
Muammar, Capt. Abdul Majid bin, 143
Mubarak, Hosni, 13
Mubraz, Muhammad al-, 126, 145
Mudayhish, Abdulaziz al-, 210–14, 215, 218, 223–4, 226–7
Muhammad, Prophet, 11, 12, 82, 83, 175, 178, 183, 198, 254, 272, 359, 382, 383, 386, 387, 388
Muhammad bin Fahd, Prince, 259
Muhammad bin Nayef, Prince, xviii, xxix, 43–51, 53, 54, 59, 63, 64, 65, 67, 69, 70, 73, 76, 99, 100, 109–12, 126, 128, 135, 141–3, 144, 149, 152, 153, 192, 223, 226, 231, 232–3, 269–71, 296, 301, 319, 323–6, 338, 345, 346, 350, 362–71, 373, 377–8, 392, 394, 397, 399, 400
  assassination attempts against, 76, 368–71, 400
  education of, 43
  and United States, 51, 54
Muhammad bin Nayef Centre for Counselling and Care, *see* Munasaha programme
Muhammad, Khalid Sheikh, *see* KSM
Muhaya compound, bombing, 166–7, 172, 189, 183, 185–8, 190, 191, 192, 193, 199, 200, 206, 207, 209, 231, 235, 253, 286, 309, 316, 395
Muhaya, Maj. Khalid al-, 243–4, 247, 249, 321–2, 334–5
mujahideen (Saudi), 13, 25, 28, 34, 36, 39, 42, 50, 75, 86, 88, 102, 111, 120, 156–8, 170, 284, 303, 315, 362–3, 378–9, 386
Mujahideen (tribal police force), 109, 110
Mullah Omar, 11, 14, 27
  and Bamyan Buddhas, 16
  capture of Jalalabad by, 15
  as 'Commander of the Faithful' 11, 13, 15
  and Osama bin Laden, 15–16, 22
Munasaha programme, 366–7, 373, 378, 399
Muqait, Muhammad al-, 81–4, 89
Muqrin, Abdulaziz al-, xxvi, 35, 37–9, 53–4, 60, 73, 74, 79, 126, 153, 155–67, 169–72, 175, 178–81, 194, 196, 197, 200, 205–6, 208–9, 214, 215, 216–22, 224–6, 230–1, 235, 240, 252–3, 254, 271, 276, 277, 279–81, 284, 285–6, 287, 292–3, 294–5, 296, 298, 299, 301, 304, 305, 315, 347, 350–1, 353, 361, 362, 364, 375, 393–8
  death of, 289–91, 397
  early years of, 156–60
  recruitment activities of, 38–9, 162–3
Muqrin, Abdullah al-, 305
Muslim Brotherhood, 22, 106–7, 127, 386
Mutaween, 47, 63, 108, 110, 312, 336
Mutayri, Turki al-, xxvi, 251, 252–70, 396
  death of, 291, 397
  see also Jerusalem Squadron
Muzayni, Ibrahim al-, 200–3

Nairobi, *see* East Africa embassy bombings
Najd, 74, 234, 305, 308, 336, 337, 350, 398
Namas training camp, 65
Nashimi, Fawaz al-, *see* Mutayri, Turki al-
Nashiri, Abdul Rahim al-, xxvi, 19–26, 32–40, 44, 50, 51, 59, 67, 73, 74, 79, 172, 393
  arrest of, 59–60, 394
  first meets Bin Laden, 20
  and KSM, 23–4

and *Limburg* attack, 55
and R'as Tanoura, 52–3
and Sagger anti-tank missile plot, 20, 44
and Strait of Hormuz plot, 21, 23, 24, 25, 34, 35, 52–3, 87
torture of, 60
and USS *Cole*, 20–1, 60
and USS *The Sullivans*, 20
National Dialogue conference, 108–9
see also Centre for National Dialogue
National Guard (Saudi), 72, 109, 110, 239, 275, 310, 311
National Security Agency, *see* NSA
Nayef bin Abdulaziz, Prince, xxix–xxx, 43, 45, 47–8, 55, 61, 63, 94, 110, 134, 138, 173, 189, 230, 242, 266, 338, 373, 398
and Crown Prince Abdullah, 48
neo-Salafism, 106, 273
New York subway plot, 65–6, 70, 79
New Yorker, 170
9/11, *see* September 11, 2001 terrorist attacks
Northern Alliance, 12, 15, 22–3, 386
NSA, 44, 59, 65, 170
nuclear weapons, xvi, 44, 62, 118, 128

Oasis Residential Resorts, 244, 251, 253, 258–9, 265; *see also* Khobar massacre
Obaid, Nawaf, 265
Obama, Barack, 373
Oberwetter, James, xxx, 238–40, 241, 270, 279, 292, 297, 298, 309–10, 395
Olaya Street bombing (1995), 13, 111, 392
Operation Infinite Reach, 16
The Operation of 12 May, 98–9
Operation Volcano, 205–6, 209, 215, 216, 218, 222, 225, 230, 231, 242, 253, 278, 337, 352, 395, 396
'the Organization', *see* Al Qaeda; AQAP
Organization of Arab Petroleum Exporting Countries, 255
Otaybi, Abdullilah al-, 180
Otaybi, Assam al-, 306
Otaybi, Sultan Bijad al-, xxvii, 172, 175, 176–8, 181, 286–7, 316, 317–18, 320
Othman, Nasser al-, 365–6
Ottoman Empire, 105, 386
Oufi, Muhammad al-, 366, 367
Oufi, Saleh al-, xxvii, 6, 7, 8, 161, 296, 299, 304–5, 312–13, 336, 337, 340, 347, 369, 397, 398
death of, 349–50, 399

Pakistan, 26, 32–3, 62, 70, 74, 116, 400
Palestine, 9, 214, 295
pan-Islamism, 106, 293
Pearl, Daniel, 33
Petroleum Centre, 253, 257–8
see also Khobar massacre
Powell, Colin, 76, 93, 95–6, 285
Prince Sultan Airbase, 46, 150

Qahtani, Capt. Khalid al-, 150
Qahtani, Sultan al-, xxvii, 116, 117–18, 121–4, 150
death of, 152, 395
Qaseem, 29, 80, 118, 120, 133, 143, 165, 167, 224–5, 226, 242, 243, 323, 327, 338, 350
Qatar, 36, 37, 76, 150, 394
Qatayni, Saud al-, xxvii, 161, 165–6, 167, 217, 223, 224–5, 305, 323, 327–8, 330, 332, 333, 335, 336, 337, 398, 399
Qur'an, 77, 83, 98, 125, 185, 211, 212, 220–1, 263, 276, 296, 382, 383, 386–7
see also Islam
Quwayz, Lt.-Col. Umar al-, 328–35

Radadi, Waleed al-, 365
raids (MOI vs. AQAP):
Amana district, 144–5, 149
Askan district (Medina), 116–17

raids – *continued*
Azhari district (Medina), 117, 121, 123, 126
Aziziya district, 178, 181
Bahar district (Medina), 349–50, 399
Dar al-Baida district, 192
Fayha district, 223–4, 396
Ghuday farm, 133–4
Jamia district (Jeddah), 309
Jazan hospital siege, 150–2, 395
Khalidiya district (Mecca), 124–6, 133, 134, 308
King Fahd neighbourhood, 1–10, 299, 337, 397
Marwa rest house (2002), 61, 75, 126, 133, 316
Maseef district (2003), 63–4
Maseef district (2005), 347–9, 399
Mubarikiya district (Dammam), 350, 399
Munisiya district, 192
Nahda district, 306–8
Nakheel district, 363
Nasiriya district, 226
Rawabi district, 149
Rawda district, 340–4, 399
Safa district (Jeddah), 235–8, 243
Seville district, 85, 94
Sharaye district, 178–9, 235
Shubra district, 145–9, 152
Sulay district, 192–3, 317, 318
Suwaydi district (2003), 179–80, 193, 197, 231
Suwaydi district (2004), 231, 396
Suwayr, 129–34, 394
Taawun district, 318–22, 327, 331, 334, 398
Wuroud district, 299
Yarmouk district, 359, 362, 399
Ramadan, 61, 175, 178, 185, 365, 383, 384, 387, 389
Rashoud, Abdullah al-, xxviii, 57–9, 169, 171, 175, 198, 301, 303, 305, 393, 398
Rashoud, Abdul Rahman al-, 303–4
Ra's Tanoura, 52–3
Rass, 327, 328, 336
battle of, 329–35, 336, 337, 398
Rawalpindi, 67
Rayyes, Ibrahim al-, 193
Reed, Dianne, 261
Rimi, Zubayr al-, *see* Qahtani, Sultan al-
Riyadh, 37, 38, 39, 80, 87, 111, 114, 118, 122, 129, 133, 138, 143, 165, 166, 167, 168, 172, 192, 193, 195, 200, 225–6, 234, 253, 275, 280, 288, 323, 336, 337, 344, 347, 361, 363, 365, 367
see also Riyadh districts and neighbourhoods
Riyadh compound bombings, 73, 78, 80, 84, 86, 87, 88–101, 109, 111, 120–1, 127, 128, 150, 155, 161, 171, 176–7, 189, 190, 231, 273, 302, 314, 327, 336, 346, 359, 374, 394
Riyadh districts and neighbourhoods:
Alhambra, 71
Amana, 144, 166
Aziziya, 178, 181
Cordoba, 71
Dar al-Baida, 166, 172, 178, 183, 192, 199
Diplomatic Quarter, 166, 206, 209, 218, 220, 223, 224, 303, 395
Duwayba, 317
Faisaliya, 351, 352
Fayha, 195, 206, 209, 218, 223
Granada, 71, 87
Izdihar, 85
Janadriya, 225
Jazeera, 68, 79, 86
King Fahd, 281, 299
Marwa, 61, 75, 126
Maseef, 63–4, 347
Melez, 289, 292, 344, 363
Munisiya, 166, 192
Nahda, 306
Nakheel, 363, 399
Naseem, 195
New Industrial Area, 38
New Manfuha, 317–18

Rawabi, 149, 337
Rawda, 316–17, 340
Sanaeiya, 336
Seville, 69, 71, 79, 84, 94
Shifa, 39, 87, 161, 166, 200–1, 316
Shubra, 145, 152, 166
Sulay, 192, 206
Suwaydi, 156, 166, 179, 197, 209, 218, 275, 277, 280, 397
Taawun, 316–18, 327, 398
Ulaysha, 198
Wadi Laban, 189
West Naseem, 202
Wuroud, 253, 281, 286, 299
Yarmouk, 359
see also raids (MOI vs. AQAP)
ROC compound, 206–9, 210, 218, 224, 352
Royal Dutch Shell, 257
Rumsfeld, Donald, 97
Ruways prison, 125, 338

'the Sabre', *see* Ayiri, Yusuf al-
Sadik, Jaufar, 311, 313
safe houses (AQAP), 39, 80, 84, 87, 115, 120, 122, 128, 148, 161, 166, 178, 179, 183, 186, 192, 197, 199, 200, 209, 223, 224, 231, 235, 253, 280, 286, 316, 319, 332, 358, 363, 385
life inside, 80, 210
see also raids (MOI vs. AQAP)
Sagger anti-tank missile plot, 14, 15, 20, 44
Sahim, Muhammad al-, 51, 60–1
Saidi, Fahd al-, 69, 394
Saikhan, Rakan al-, xxviii, 37–8, 74, 80, 87, 161, 172
death of, 224, 396
Sakeena campaign, 294, 378
Salaam Palace (Jeddah), 140
Saleh, Ali Abdullah, 50, 366
Salim, Muhammad al-, *see* Awshen, Isa al-
Sana'a, 38, 50
Saud al-Faisal, Prince, 61–2, 77, 136, 138–9, 241
Saudi Arabia, Kingdom of:
anthem of, 41, 81
charities of, 48, 135, 142, 285, 390, 395
and consensualism, 114
economy of, 53, 103, 104–5, 108
education in, 103, 104, 105, 106, 108, 314
fundraising in, for jihad, 14, 106
increased security in, 100–1, 192, 253, 289
inequality in, 105
and Internet, 31, 44, 163, 292–4
and Iraq, 77, 394
jihadists' views on, 7, 17–18, 163
misconceptions about, xvi–xviii
municipal elections in, 314, 336, 398
and 9/11, xvi, 42, 136
and oil, 18, 52–3, 96, 102, 104, 240, 351, 375
political system of, xvii, 114
and reform, xvi, xviii, 98, 108–9, 314, 340
religion in, *see* Wahhabism
Shi'ites in, 109, 375
structure of power in, 102–4, 114
and terrorist financing, 48–9, 135–9, 140, 141–3, 163, 231–2, 285, 378
unemployment in, 104
and United States, 54, 77, 96–7, 98, 102, 104, 135–9, 163, 193, 238, 325
and Yemen, 38
see also, Saudi Arabians; Saudi government
Saudi Arabian Oil Co., *see* Aramco
Saudi Arabians, 174, 348, 374, 378–9
anti-Americanism of, 271–2, 374
conservatism of, xvii–xviii, 29–30, 80, 98, 103–4, 108, 161, 196, 197
cooperate with the MOI, 108, 179, 191–2, 198–9, 327, 328, 375
and football, 288–9
and 9/11, 42, 45–6, 101, 102, 170

Saudi Arabians – *continued*
piety of, 42, 131, 144, 156
reactions of, to AQAP attacks, 97–8, 99–100, 101, 189–91, 205–6, 229–30, 231, 292, 375
sympathy of, for Al Qaeda, 101, 102, 105, 107, 206, 271, 292–3, 374
Saudi government, 123, 142, 239, 270, 274, 284, 292, 310, 323, 374, 391
and amnesty for terrorists, 297–8, 367–8, 397
campaign of, for religious moderation, 108, 190–1, 230, 273, 375
and clerics, 29, 55, 56–9, 96–7, 136
development of, 47
intelligence services of, 110–11
and Iran, 51
and Iraq, 54
and mujahideen, 14, 50, 61, 177–8
and 9/11, 45
and terrorist financing, 49, 95, 135–9, 140, 141–3, 163, 231–2, 285
and United States, 49, 54, 232, 285, 324–5, 377–8
Saudi National Commission for Relief and Charity Work Abroad, 232, 395
Saudi religious establishment, *see* clerics (Saudi)
Saudi royal family, *see* House of Saud
Saudi TV, 86, 134
Sawat, Misbah al-, 338–9
Sawat, Mubarak al-, 338–40, 398
Sayyari, Nasser al-, 172, 178, 183
Sayyed, Ashraf al-, 81–4, 89
Schumer, Chuck, 138
Scobey, Margaret, 93
Scroggs, Kenneth, 278
Security Patrols, 69, 85, 109, 143, 144–5, 179, 186, 192, 194, 202, 224–5, 243, 256, 261, 269, 289, 316–17, 337
Seder compound, 193
September 11, 2001 terrorist attacks, xvi, 22, 24, 25, 28, 29, 30, 35, 43, 62, 75, 96, 98, 101, 116, 122, 136, 167, 168, 170, 206, 220, 225, 241, 252, 254, 351, 377, 393
as 'planes operation', 17
Saudi reaction to, 42, 45
US congressional report into, 137–9, 141
7/7, *see* July 7, 2005 terrorist attacks
Shadhaf, Muhammad bin, 80–4, 87, 89–90
Sha'ir, Abu Hazim al-, *see* Hajj, Khalid Ali al-
Shakila, Musa, 308–9
Shamsan, Saleh al-, 333
Sheikh Omar, 33
Shibh, Ramzi bin al-, 59
Shihri, Amr al-, 180, 197–8, 224
Shihri, Saaban al-, 298
Shihri, Saeed al-, *see* Abu Sufyan
Shuaybi, Hamud al-, xxviii, 29–32, 67
see also Shuaybi School
Shuaybi School, xxviii, 30
Shura Council (AQ):
Bin Laden's, 25–6
Hajj's, 75–6, 86, 114
Muqrin's, 161, 162, 224, 296, 305
Sinan, Khalid al-, 316–17
Soha Tower Hotel, 244–50, 259, 262, 265, 269
see also Khobar massacre
Somalia, 13, 35, 49, 160
Souq al-Talh, 38
Special Forces (Saudi), 4, 42, 61, 109, 143, 243–7, 263, 266, 299, 310, 312, 318, 331, 338, 340, 343
Specter, Arlen, 138
State Department (US), 139, 193, 232
Strait of Gibraltar operation, 24, 44
Strait of Hormuz operation, 21, 23, 24, 25, 34, 35, 52–3, 87
Subaei, Abdullah al-, 253, 255, 258, 260, 266–7, 275–6, 318
see also Jerusalem Squadron
Subaei, Musaed al-, 172, 173, 181
Subayt, Khalid al-, 209–10, 223

Sudan, 15, 17, 46, 55
Sudayri Seven, xxix, 48, 314
suicide bombers, bombing, 36, 43, 54, 69, 91, 92, 167, 172, 176, 180, 210, 214–15, 217, 236–7, 252, 344, 350, 352, 362
The Sullivans, USS, 20
Suwayr, 129
Syria, 26, 36, 75, 106, 168, 298, 323, 346, 374
Sykes-Picot Agreement, 76–7

Ta'if, 179
Tajikistan, 20
takfeer, takfeerism, 31, 105–8, 190, 226, 272, 288, 302, 315, 347, 366, 375, 376, 388
  see also neo-Salafism
Takfeeri Troika, xxviii, 31, 67, 117–18, 162, 163, 189
  see also Fahd, Nasr al-; Khudayri, Ali al-; Khalidi, Ahmad al-
Talhi, Abdulmajid al-, 235, 243
Talhi, Brig.-Gen. Mudeef al-, 290, 299, 306–8, 322, 347–9
Taliban, 11, 22, 167, 254, 386, 392, 393
  and American invasion of Afghanistan, 23, 393
  Arab recruitment to, 12, 22
  and Pakistan, 12, 16
  Saudi criticism of, 13
  Saudi fundraising for, 13
Tenet, George, xxx, 44–6, 51, 62, 73, 100, 118
Thirty-Nine Ways to Serve and Participate in Jihad, 168
Tinaco, Camilo, 262, 264
Tora Bora, 23, 24, 75, 116, 393
Townsend, Frances, xxx, 139–43, 232–4, 323–6, 378, 394
traffic police (Riyadh), 186, 201, 229, 277
Treasury Department (US), 136, 138, 142, 232, 234
Treatise on the Use of Weapons of Mass Destruction against the Infidels, 118
The Truth of the New Crusade, 29
Turkey, 26, 53
Turki al-Faisal, Prince, 345
Turki, Gen. Mansour al-, 144
Turkmenistan, 210
Tuwayjiri, Abdullah al-, 352–7
Tuwayr, Maj. Nayef al-, 243, 245–6, 319–22

UAE, 36, 37, 59–60, 115, 394
Ubayd, Dakheel al-, 215–16, 220, 221–2, 318
Unayzah, 308
United Kingdom, 33, 43, 45, 56, 67, 76, 100, 124, 200, 240, 270, 325, 328, 344–7, 399
United States, 22, 33, 34, 45, 48–9, 51, 53, 56, 77, 96–7, 101, 104, 111, 122–3, 193, 271–2, 293, 338, 346, 373, 377–8, 395, 396
  and Afghan War, 22–3, 40, 57, 121, 252
  and Ayiri, 52
  bombs Tora Bora, 24–5
  citizens' views on Saudi Arabia, 96, 280, 297
  consulate of, in Jeddah, 14, 239, 309–14, 315, 398
  and drone strikes, 59, 373
  embassy of, in Riyadh, 76, 93, 94, 142, 225, 238, 284, 338, 398, 399
  as enemy of Al Qaeda, 15, 86, 88, 98–9, 131, 173
  and Iraq, 54, 77, 79, 102, 150, 373, 391, 394, 398
  military presence of, in Saudi Arabia, 42, 46, 66, 97, 99, 102, 150, 163, 206, 275, 310–12, 374–5, 394
  and neo-imperialism, 99
  and terrorist financing, 48–50, 95, 135–9, 140, 141–3, 231–2, 285, 378
Utaybi, Juhayman al-, 106–7, 391

Veness, Simon, 55

Vinnell compound, 84, 87, 92, 93, 95, 177, 206, 336
see also ROC compound
Vinnell Corporation, 84, 111, 176–7, 206, 207, 208, 277
see also Olaya Street bombing; Vinnell compound
Voice of Jihad, xxiii, 85, 169–71, 191, 210, 223, 251, 252, 254, 295, 298, 316, 337–8, 359, 389, 395, 397, 398, 399

Wahaybi, Osama al-, 341–4
Wahhabism, xvii, 30, 48, 103, 105–7, 136, 144, 214, 375, 389–90
and *fitna*, 107
see also Islam
war on terror, *see* Global War on Terrorism
Washington, DC, 44, 49, 62, 122
Washm Street bombing, 226, 229–30, 231, 234, 242, 253, 293, 298, 396
Wills of the Heroes, 171–2, 199
World Trade Center bombing (1993), 24
World Trade Organization, 103
Wuhayshi, Nasser al-, 361, 366, 400

Yanbu, 239–40, 242, 244, 253, 293, 396
Yaziji, Abdul Kareem al-, 336
Yaziji, Abdul Rahman al-, 336
Yemen, Yemenis, 17, 20, 21, 37, 38, 49–50, 54–5, 59, 74, 80, 111, 122, 160, 172, 239, 240, 309, 361, 363–4, 370, 373
drone attacks in, 59, 373
Zahrani, Faris al-, 169, 301, 305
Zarate, Juan C., 232
Zarqawi, Abu Musab al-, 314, 344, 377
Zawahiri, Ayman al-, 23
Zulfi, 323, 327, 330
Zurmat, 24–6